NORMAN BETHUNE
his times and his legacy
son époque et son message

Canadian Public Health Association
L'Association canadienne d'Hygiène publique
1982

NORMAN BETHUNE
Photograph by Charles Comfort O.C., R.C.A., 1936
Photographie de Charles Comfort O.C., A.R.C., 1936

NORMAN BETHUNE
his times and his legacy
son époque et son message

Edited by/Édité par
David A.E. Shephard
and/et
Andrée Lévesque
for/pour
The Bethune Foundation/La Fondation Bethune

Published by/Publié par
The Canadian Public Health Association/
L'Association canadienne d'Hygiène publique
1982

Price: $11.50
Coût: $11.50

First Edition 1982
Première édition 1982

Copyright 1982 Canadian Public Health Association
1335 Carling Avenue, Suite 210, Ottawa, Ontario, Canada K1Z 8N8
Tous droits réservés, 1982. Association canadienne d'Hygiène publique
1335 avenue Carling, pièce 210, Ottawa, Ontario, Canada K1Z 8N8

All rights reserved including the right to
reproduce in whole or in part in any form.
Tous droits réservés, y compris celui de reproduire
en tout ou en partie, sous quelque forme que ce soit.

Cover/Couverture: Ted Beament

Printed in Canada by/Imprimé au Canada par
M.O.M. Printing, 300 Parkdale, Ottawa, Ontario K1Y 1G2

ISBN 0-919245-11-0

Canadian Cataloguing in Publication Data
Données de catalogue avant publication (Canada)

1. Bethune, Norman, 1890-1939 — Addresses, essays, lectures. 2. Surgeons — Canada — Biography — Addresses, essays, lectures. 3. Medicine — Canada — History — Addresses, essays, lectures. I. Shephard, David A. E. II. Lévesque, Andrée. III. Bethune Foundation. IV. Canadian Public Health Association.
R464.B4N67   617'.092'4   C82-090058-3E

1. Bethune, Norman, 1890-1939 — Discours, essais, conférences. 2. Chirurgiens — Canada — Biographies — Discours, essais, conférences. 3. Médecine — Canada — Histoire — Discours, essais, conférences. I. Shephard, David A. E. II. Lévesque, Andrée. III. Fondation Bethune. IV. Association canadienne d'Hygiène publique.
R464.B4N67   617'.092'4   C82-090058-3F

Contents — Table

Preface: David A.E. Shephard	vii
Préface: Andrée Lévesque	x
Acknowledgments — Remerciements	xii

His Life and His Forbears / Sa vie et ses ancêtres

Norman Bethune: A Biographical Outline Wendell MacLeod and Hilary Russell	2
Chronology of Norman Bethune's Life	7
La vie de Bethune: Chronologie	8
"I Come of a Race of Men" Hilary Russell	10

Canada 1890-1936

The Religious Setting of Norman Bethune's Early Years Richard Allen	22
Norman Bethune and Frontier College, 1911-1912 Marjorie Zavitz Robinson	32
Frontier College Today: From Norman Bethune's Times to the Present Jack Pearpoint	40
Battlefield Surgery and the Stretcher-bearers' Experience Charles G. Roland	44
From "A Social Disease with a Medical Aspect" to "A Medical Disease with a Social Aspect": Fighting the White Plague in Canada, 1900-1940 Katherine McCuaig	54
Norman Bethune and Tuberculosis G.J. Wherrett	65
Edward Archibald, The "New Medical Science" and Norman Bethune H. Rocke Robertson	71
The Royal Victoria Hospital, Montreal: Common Diseases in the 1920s and 1930s Jessie Boyd Scriver	79
Norman Bethune: l'influence de l'hôpital du Sacré-Coeur Pierre Delva	85
Creativity in Norman Bethune: His Medical Writings and Innovations David A.E. Shephard	92
Norman Bethune and His Brethren: Poetry in Depression Montreal Lee Briscoe Thompson	104
"They could split rock . . .": Painting in Montreal in the 1930s, and the Children's Creative Art Centre — A Conversation Piece Charles Hill, Louis Muhlstock, Marian Scott, Leo Kennedy	114

The Health of the People: Montreal in the Depression Years Terry Copp	129
The Bethune Health Group Libbie Park	138
Political Commitment in the 1930s Stanley B. Ryerson	145

L'engagement politique après les années trente:
   l'organisation des travailleurs
   Madeleine Parent
	150

Spain / Espagne 1936-1937

Henning Sorensen to Graham Spry: a Letter	156
With Norman Bethune in Spain Ted Allan	157

The Vivid Air Signed With His Honour:
   In Memory of Norman Bethune
   Hazen Sise
	162

The Spanish Civil War: Reminiscences of a Veteran of the
   Mackenzie-Papineau Battalion
   Ross Russell
	170

Norman Bethune and the Development of
   Blood Transfusion Services
   Paul Weil
	177

China / Chine 1938-1939

Norman Bethune in China Ma Haide (George Hatem)	182
The Living Bethune Paul Lin	193
Contributions of Norman Bethune to Developing China Lü Wanru	195

The Legacy / Le message

The Bethune Legend: Norman Bethune as Hero Maurice McGregor	201

Après Bethune: l'expérience des soins médicaux au Québec
   Table ronde — Rob Robson, Pierre Delva, Suzanne Dubreuil,
   Claire Dutrisac, Marc Lavallée, Marc Renaud, Denis Lazure
	206

Reflections — Réflexions: Wendell MacLeod	229
Appendix — Annexe A	223
Appendix — Annexe B	236
Appendix — Annexe C	238
Appendix — Annexe D	243
Contributors' Biographies — Biographies des collaborateurs	247

Preface

Reference to Norman Bethune elicits various responses. In Canada, the land of his birth, mention of his name— if it is known at all — either commands admiration and respect or provokes discomfort and irritation. Outside Canada, the situation is different. In Spain, Bethune is renowned for introducing a mobile blood transfusion service during the civil war; in China, Bethune is honoured by millions as a dedicated military surgeon who served with the Chinese in their war against the Japanese.

In China today, Bethune the foreigner is accorded the status of hero, in part, of course, because he died in 1939 for the Chinese. So, paradoxically, Bethune the Canadian is known and respected by many more people outside Canada than in his native country, where his work is still relatively little known — and understood even less. This is not entirely surprising, for Bethune's career in Canada spanned only 8 years (from 1928 to 1936) and the final 3 years of his relatively short life were spent outside Canada, in Spain and China. On the other hand, during his career in Montreal, he did contribute significantly to medicine and health care — he was a leading thoracic surgeon, he invented several useful surgical instruments, he wrote more than a dozen articles in medical journals and he produced constructive proposals for health care in the province of Quebec. Similarly, in Spain, his blood transfusion work was original and, in China, his practical work as a surgeon was the very stuff of military medical history. Yet most of his compatriots find it difficult to know what to make of Bethune — perhaps because reactions to him vary and are often extreme.

Of compelling interest to historians and biographers must be the basis of this controversy that Bethune's name generates; it should be, too, for Canadians in general. So bipolar a response is the key not only to our understanding of Bethune as a Canadian but also to his place in history. Whatever one's opinion of Bethune, he was a Canadian and his life, as Stanley Ryerson emphasizes elsewhere in this book, still has a meaning for Canadians today, some 50 years after his death. And since for a great many Chinese the name of Canada has become synonymous with that of Bethune, it is certainly of interest to ask what this Canadian did to have him become a Chinese hero. But, more than all this, the controversy should make us consider, as objectively as we can, exactly what Bethune *created*, for the good of his fellows, in his brief span on earth of 49 years.

But an objective look at a controversial figure is a difficult task. With Bethune, while it is a relatively straightforward matter to accept him for his tangible creations — like his rib shears or his pneumothorax apparatus — it is much more difficult to accept him for his more abstract creations, those relating to ideas concerning good and evil, right and wrong, just and unjust, in society. It is difficult because Bethune seldom was satisfied with anything less than what seemed to others so often an extreme and often a minority, point of view.

We can, nevertheless, start by asking some pertinent questions. If, for example, one scorns Bethune because he did not conform to orthodox professional behaviour as exemplified by the Montreal establishment of the 1930s, one might do well to ask whether orthodox behaviour, especially if this determined so trivial an issue as one's form of dress, was any more conducive to good medicine than Bethune's individual behaviour. If one despises Bethune for his socioeconomic views concerning the health of the people of Montreal, one might do equally well to enquire bluntly why Montreal of the 1930s, as Terry Copp shows in this book, had such a dismal record of public health, despite its adequacy of physicians and nurses and hospitals. If one dismisses Bethune from further consideration because he was a communist, one might do well to speculate what it was in the Canadian society of the 1930s that induced him to become a communist and to wonder why no other avenue seemed to lead to even the possibilities of the kind of social change he felt necessary. And if one rejects Bethune because he left Montreal for Spain, and later for China, one surely does well to wonder why Bethune felt he had to leave, to commit himself to action, in order to warn his fellow Canadians of the advancing tide of fascism and its threat to world peace — the reality of which, in due course, confirmed his perceptiveness and the validity of his urge to act on what he, but few others, could see were truly the realities of the world around him.

This book will, we hope, stimulate readers to ask such questions. Its purpose is to present material that will enable readers to examine what Bethune did in the light of his times and to permit readers to make this examination as objectively, and from as broad a standpoint, as possible. The book differs from other books about Bethune in comprising material that is multidisciplinary and that has been written by many different authors. Many of the contributions have been prepared by researchers with an academic interest in Bethune's work; others give unrivalled first-hand accounts of Bethune the man; and the book concludes with a section that considers the legacy of Bethune in the light of health care issues in one province of modern Canada. Its origin lies in a conference that was sponsored by the Bethune Foundation and was held at McGill University, Montreal in November 16-18, 1979, to recognize the 40th anniversary of Bethune's death, and most of the chapters are based on papers that were prepared for that conference. (The program is reproduced in Appendix A.) After the decision had been made to publish the conference proceedings, the publication committee agreed to include other material that would not only help create a *book* rather than simply the text of one more conference's proceedings but also both attract readers with a general interest in Bethune and provide others of a more academic bent with source material concerning Bethune, his work, his times and his legacy. The book, then, is a multifaceted one — but one with no more varied faces to it than had Bethune's own career.

Editing this book has been a rare privilege. On a historical level, the reading in close detail of the manuscripts that the many contributors to the conference so graciously released for publication has enabled me to come to better understand Bethune and his times — and, in the process, Canada, Spain and China. On a personal level, I have had the good fortune to share in the creation of this book with my colleagues of the publication committee, whose views, too, have given me deeper insight into Bethune: Wendell MacLeod, who knew Bethune and whose friendship with him has both facilitated the editing and has taken me, as it were, on a time machine back to the 1930s and to a reinforcement of the historical link I sensed in reading the manuscripts; Hilary Russell (a historian with Parks Canada and an authority on Bethune's forbears) who, with Wendell MacLeod, was largely responsible for the 1979 conference and thus deserves an especial vote of thanks; Pierre Delva, president of the Bethune Foundation, and a medical colleague from my own Montreal days; Charles Roland, a medical historian with a specific interest in Canadian military history, who is a valued friend and colleague in editorial work; H. Rocke Robertson, whose knowledge of medicine and surgery in Canada, particularly in Montreal, has given the publication committee advice that might have otherwise been lacking; Gerald Dafoe, whose job as executive director of the Canadian Public Health Association has been to steer the book towards publication and has given encouragement throughout; and Andrée Lévesque, my co-editor, who has taken the responsibility for editing the French manuscripts and with whom I have shared editorial decisions. In referring to my pleasure in working with them, I acknowledge my debt and gratitude to them.

A few further acknowledgements are in order. The 1979 Conference was held at McGill University, to which thanks are due for the physical facilities and other assistance that were made available. The 1979 conference eventually led to the publication of this book, but not without the generous financial assistance of the Bethune Foundation, the Hannah Institute for the History of Medicine, Associated Medical Services, Inc., and the Samuel and Saidye Bronfman Foundation; nor would the book have become possible without the persistent support of the publisher, the Canadian Public Health Association. Thanks are due to other large groups, though the individuals in them are too numerous to mention by name, but especially those who presented the papers at the conference (and whose statements we recognize and accept in publishing this book, as theirs rather than necessarily ours) and those who attended the conference, primarily to listen and to participate in discussion — some of whom honoured us by coming from across the sea, from China. For these two latter groups, publication of this book will, we hope, be welcome as a crystallisation of the proceedings of the conference, but all who have worked on this book hope that it will bring Bethune to a much wider group and that it will serve as a stimulus to broadening the base of a growing interest in a man who was, by any reckoning, an unusual and remarkable human being.

David A.E. Shephard
Regina, Saskatchewan, Canada

Préface

Presqu'entièrement méconnu au Canada il a quelques années, Norman Bethune fait maintenant partie de la légende. La Fondation Bethune, ce groupe d'amis et d'admirateurs de Bethune, a joué un rôle important pour faire connaître l'illustre médecin. Les textes présentés ici firent d'abord l'objet de communications à une conférence organisée par la Fondation Bethune à l'Université McGill, en novembre 1979, pour célébrer le quarantième anniversaire de la mort de Bethune. Il ne faut pas y voir une hagiographie. Certe des contemporains, des amis et collègues ont apporté leurs témoignages sur le Bethune qu'ils ont connu, mais des spécialistes, médecins et historiens, ont traité de ses contributions, de son implication dans les grands conflits de son époque, et les ont placées dans leur contexte politique et social. De plus, des "héritiers" du message de Bethune, des professionnels de la santé, par exemple, qui ont pris la relève, ont aussi collaboré pour établir le bilan de l'état de santé au Québec aujourd'hui.

La présente publication a donc pour but de faire part au lecteur des travaux présentés en 1979, travaux dont le fil conducteur est fourni par la carrière même de Bethune. La diversité de ses talents, de ses expériences et de ses contributions explique l'éventail des textes. Après une esquisse biographique de Wendell MacLeod et Hilary Russell, Richard Allen et Marjorie Zavitz Robinson situent sa jeunesse dans son atmosphère évangélique puis au service des travailleurs de chantier de *Frontier College* que décrit Jack Pearpoint. La première guerre mondiale retrouve Bethune comme brancardier et Charles G. Roland nous présente la pratique médicale dans les tranchées et auprès des blessés de guerre.

De retour au pays, Bethune opte pour une carrière médicale dans un milieu que nous décrivent G.J. Wherrett, H. Rocke Robertson, Jessie Boyd Scriver et Pierre Delva. Il connaitra lui-même l'expérience de la maladie lorsqu'il sera atteint de tuberculose, maladie que Katherine McCuaig et Terry Copp placent dans son contexte québécois. Il n'en fera pas l'expérience passive et David Shephard montre comment Bethune, spécialiste en médecine thoracique, puisera dans son baggage de patient et de praticien l'inspiration pour inventer des instruments chirurgicaux qui faciliteront le travail du médecin et contribueront au confort du patient.

Son élan créateur devait aussi se manifester dans la vie artistique en tant que peintre et poète dans un climat que font revivre Lee Briscoe Thompson, Charles Hill, Louis Muhlstock et Marian Scott. Pendant la crise économique, l'artiste et le médecin prend un engagement politique que tente d'expliciter Stanley Bréhaut Ryerson, et qui vit son application concrète, à Montréal, dans sa participation au groupe de recherche pour la santé communautaire, le *Montreal Group for the Security of the People's Health*, dont l'action politique est décrite par Libbie Park. Cet engagement politique a conduit Bethune à combattre le fascisme en Espagne pendant la guerre civile et à y mettre ses connaissances médicales au service des combattants républicains et des civils. Hazen Sise nous explique la motivation idéologique de cette prise de position alors que Paul Weil situe son rôle dans le développement des techniques de transfusion sanguine, Ross Russell témoigne de la situation des volontaires canadiens dans les Brigades internationales et Ted Allan partage ses souvenirs de cette époque de la carrière de Bethune.

En 1938, le même idéal humanitaire et politique a poussé Bethune a accompagner la 8e armée de Mao Zedong dans sa lutte contre l'invasion japonaise. Maurice McGregor rappelle la portée du dévouement du médecin canadien en Chine, Ma Haide décrit la situation difficile et héroïque à Yenan et Paul Lin traite de son apport scientifique à l'évolution de la Chine moderne. Lü Wanru fait le bilan des réalisations de la Chine révolutionnaire et de sa dette de gratitude envers Bethune.

Au Québec, l'esprit combatif, humanitaire et révolutionnaire de Bethune n'est pas éteint. La syndicaliste Madeleine Parent relate les luttes de la classe ouvrière depuis la dépression économique. Enfin, une table ronde discute de la médecine communautaire et populaire au Québec quarante ans après le départ de Bethune. Pour mieux permettre de situer les différentes étapes de la vie de Bethune, et de retracer son oeuvre écrite, Hilary Russell a préparé une courte bibliographie.

C'est animés de "l'esprit de Bethune" que les participants ont voulu communiquer le fruit de leur recherche, leurs souvenirs personnels, leur application du message qu'a légué Bethune. Ils ont ainsi apporté leur contribution non seulement à la reconstitution de la vie d'un médecin engagé, mais aussi à l'écriture de l'histoire de la médecine sociale de la classe ouvrière et des mouvements révolutionnaires. Historiens, médecins et profanes leur en sont reconnaissants.

Andrée Lévesque
Ottawa, Ontario, Canada

Acknowledgments

☐ In addition to grants from The Bethune Foundation, The Samuel and Saidye Bronfman Family Foundation, The Hannah Institute for the History of Medicine and Associated Medical Services, Inc., generous donations by individuals, invaluable aid was given by officers of The Bethune Foundation, especially Pierre and Joan Delva and Francis McNaughton for their careful transcription of a number of conference tapes, as well as by members of staff of the National Library of Canada; the Osler Library, McGill University, Montreal; and The Public Archives of Canada.

☐ Special gratitude is expressed to Tib Beament, who contributed the design of the cover and frontispiece, aided by Irene Kon; also to Marcel Knecht and staff who have aided in promotion of the book, all of Montreal. Two others require special mention, Rolande O'Brien of the Canadian Public Health Association and her colleague, Edward Finnigan of M.O.M. Printing, Ottawa, for their patient and generous attention to the task of converting edited page proofs to the finished volume.

☐ Acknowledgement is accorded also to the artists, owners or others concerned for permission to produce the photographs appearing on the pages within parentheses listed at the foot of this page.

Remerciements

☐ Outre les subventions accordées par la Fondation Bethune, la Fondation de la Famille Samuel and Saidye Bronfman, le Hannah Institute for the History of Medicine l'Associated Medical Services, Inc., et par les dons généreux de plusieurs particuliers, cette publication a été rendue possible grâce à l'aide inestimable apportée par les directeurs de la Fondation Bethune, notamment Joan Delva, Pierre Delva et Francis McNaughton qui ont transcrit sur ruban plusieurs communications, et par les bibliothécaires et archivistes de la Bibliothèque nationale du Canada, de la Bibliothèque Osler de l'Université McGill à Montréal et des Archives publiques du Canada.

☐ Nous tenons à exprimer nos profonds sentiments de gratitude à Tib Beament, aidé de Irene Kon, à qui nous devons la page couverture et le frontispice, ainsi qu'à Marcel Knecht et les membres de son personnel pour leur rôle dans la promotion de cet ouvrage. Deux autres personnes méritent une mention spéciale: Rolande O'Brien de l'Association canadienne d'Hygiène publique et Edward Finnigan de M.O.M. Printing, Ottawa. Grâce à leur patience illimitée, la fouillis des épreuves céda la place au présent volume.

☐ Nous remercions les artistes, les collectionneurs, ainsi que toutes les autres personnes qui nous ont accordé la permission de reproduire certaines oeuvres aux pages indiquées ci-dessous.

Paraskeva Clark (176); Charles Comfort, O.C., RAC/ARC (ii); Frontier College/ Collège Frontière (33); Sylvia DuVernet (122); l'Hôpital du Sacré-Coeur/l'hôpital du Sacré-Coeur (86); Hugh McLennan (123); Francis L. McNaughton (115); Louis Muhlstock (115, 116, 117); M. Dobie Munroe (80); National Gallery of Canada/Galerie nationale du Canada (117, 122, 123); Public Archives of Canada/Archives publiques du Canada (124, 125, 126, 176, 194, 205); Royal Victoria Hospital/L'hôpital Royal Victoria (80, 124); Marian Scott (121, 122, 123); Dr. and/et Mrs. Max Stern (121); The People's Press, Beijing, 1979 (cover).

His Life and His Forbears/
Sa Vie et ses Ancêtres

A young tree in the wind.
A white flower in the grass,
A quick bird in flight,
A breath of sun-named air
And the whole world is emptied of delight
Like a cup turned upside down . . .

— Norman Bethune
From "Remembrance"

Source: Stewart, The Mind of Norman Bethune,
Fitzhenny and Whiteside, Toronto, 1977, p. 31

Norman Bethune:
A Biographical Outline

Wendell MacLeod and Hilary Russell

Henry Norman Bethune was born in the manse in Gravenhurst, a small Ontario town, in 1890. He died a hero 49 years later in a peasant's one-room house in a tiny village in North China. In between, he served the wounded in three wars and made his mark on three continents.

He had worked as a labourer and lumberjack, battled tuberculosis as a patient and a doctor, gained international recognition as an inventive thoracic surgeon, had his poetry published and painting exhibited, organized art classes for poor children, married the same woman twice, joined the Communist Party, became a skilled propagandist, and aroused in many people either abiding love and admiration or profound dislike or disapproval.

What are the sources of this extraordinary personal mosaic? How was he influenced by his family background, home life, special experiences and crises, and by the social, economic and political features of his times? In this brief biographical outline, we touch on these questions and highlight the main events in Bethune's career, as an introduction especially for the benefit of readers whose acquaintance with Bethune's story is slight. This outline, however, does little to reveal the essence or the spirit of the man — his formidable energy and enthusiasm, and his profound impact on so many people who knew him, for these aspects of Bethune are discussed in detail elsewhere. Further study of Bethune's life and work may be pursued with the aid of the Bibliography of writings by Bethune himself and about him; this bibliography is contained in Appendix B. In addition, we have prepared a chronology of Bethune's life, which appears at the end of the chapter.

* * *

Bethune came from a family line of physicians, clergymen, fur traders and businessmen. His father was an evangelistic Presbyterian minister who moved frequently from one small Ontario town to another. The effects of these moves, mostly in northern Ontario, and of being a son of the manse and of an evangelist may have been considerable.

Two attachments appeared in Norman's youth: to the north country, and to becoming a surgeon, like his grandfather, the first Dr. Norman Bethune. His formal education towards the second goal was deferred twice while worked in northern lumber camps. His first stint followed secondary school; the second, two premedical years at the University of Toronto. Through the winter of 1911-12 as a labourer-teacher with Frontier College, he swung an axe by day and taught the "three Rs" to fellow workers by night.

He interrupted his studies again in 1914 to enlist at the onset of World War I in a field ambulance unit of the Canadian Army and faced the horrors of the front for 2 months as a stretcher bearer before being wounded during the second battle of Ypres. He was invalided home to complete his medical studies. After graduating, he joined the Royal Navy and tasted something of the life of an officer and gentleman as a surgeon-lieutenant. The war over, he continued to experience the perquisites of British society while in London and Edinburgh undertaking postgraduate training. It was of a type suitable for practice anywhere but in an academic centre such as he encountered later at the Royal Victoria Hospital in Montreal.

Bethune may have had the training and the inclination to work in a frontier setting, but this would have been impossible for the upper-middle-class Edinburgh woman he married in 1923 — Frances Campbell Penney. Their temperaments clashed in many respects, and, as she recalled, he announced on their wedding day, " 'Now I can make your life a misery, but I'll never bore you — it's a promise.' A promise kept"[1].

At age 34, Bethune began a reasonably successful private practice in the booming automobile city of Detroit. But his life was clouded by two personal catastrophes — the departure of Frances and the discovery of tuberculosis in both of his lungs. The eventual divorce and his sanatorium experience brought on intense introspection and, following his recovery, a revision of his professional goals. He would now devote himself to bringing the new techniques in thoracic surgery to other victims of tuberculosis. In 1928 he joined the surgical team of Dr. Edward Archibald, a pioneer in this field, at Montreal's Royal Victoria Hospital.

Bethune's eight Montreal years were crucial and dynamic, professionally, personally and politically. They were marked by progress in his surgical specialization, and by creative outbursts that produced over a dozen medical instruments and 14 articles in professional journals. On the other hand, he provoked criticism from less impetuous and less flamboyant surgeons, including his chief, Archibald. His subsequent appointment at l'Hôpital du Sacré-Coeur, to found a division of thoracic surgery and to train his successor, was less frustrating and more fulfilling. His reputation, and that of Sacré-Coeur, grew.

In his personal life, his obsessive and complicated relationship with Frances resulted in an Armistice-Day remarriage and a redivorce, though he retained a tender regard for her all his life. They had no children.

His creativity also found expression in painting, poetry and prose, old interests that steadily matured. Bethune's love of children and his interest in art came together in the art classes in his apartment he helped to organize. Primarily for the children of the unemployed, these classes also reflected his political transformation.

This began with his growing disillusionment with surgical treatment of the tuberculous. Patients whose disease had been arrested by operation too often became ill again and died after returning to the squalid and impoverished surroundings in which they became re-infected. Bethune perceived a sick society whose experts could neither preserve health nor avoid devastating economic depression. After a visit to the Soviet Union and much soul-searching, he secretly joined the Communist Party in late 1935. His political awareness and commitments, during his Montreal period, led him to introduce a clinic for the unemployed, to challenge his profession in two memorable lectures at the Montreal Medico-Chirurgical Society, and to form a study and action group to promote reform in medical care and health services. He was coming to terms with himself and his future.

* * *

His work in Montreal was interrupted by the outbreak of the Spanish Civil War in July 1936. Within months, he was in Spain to aid the beleaguered Republic in its struggle with the forces of Franco, Mussolini and Hitler. There, he quickly organized a mobile blood transfusion service, the first of its kind, which was extended to a 1,000-km front. The improvising genius he demonstrated in Spain, and his insistence that doctors must go to the wounded and not vice versa, forecast some of his great successes in China. Yet his record in Spain is mixed. He had serious difficulties adapting to the muddled authority and disunity on the left. Bethune's long-standing impatience with inefficiency and disorder, his explosive temper and his resort to alcoholic excess led to strains and to his recall in 1937.

That summer he campaigned across Canada to raise money for medical aid and for Spanish refugee children. Even while on tour, his attention was turning to China, where Japanese occupation forces had mounted a savage new offensive. "Spain and China are part of the same battle," he wrote[2]. So he left to join it because of the principle at stake — again a military dictatorship was on the march — and because he was needed. He went specifically to assist the Eighth Route Army in its effort to repel the invader and to build a new society. His achievements during his 18 months in the guerilla war area were of immense proportions. Where there were no hospitals or operating rooms, he improvised or planned and helped to build them. Where there were not enough medical personnel, he trained them or helped them train themselves. No medical texts or manuals on public sanitation? — he wrote them. When instruments and special devices appropriate to harrowing war conditions were needed, he designed and constructed them. He insisted on no more than the rations and clothing of an Eighth Route Army soldier, and usually gave these, and even his own blood, to the wounded. Not only did he work tirelessly, willingly engage in manual labour and treat compassionately hundreds of soldiers and civilians, but he truly adopted the Chinese cause and the Chinese people as his own. From them, he wanted nothing, especially not their souls.

Of course, he continued on occasion to revert to angry, peremptory, and even arrogant behaviour. But the dedication, unselfishness, and self-reliance of his comrades in the Eighth Route Army brought out the best in Bethune. In turn, he set his own example, especially as a foreigner, and he inspired thousands long before his accidental death from septicemia on November 12, 1939.

Mao Zedong's essay 1 month later, "In Memory of Norman Bethune", listed the qualities he exemplified and from which all communists must learn: his spirit of internationalism, his great sense of responsibility towards his work and constant attention to improving technique, and his "utter devotion to others without thought of self"[3].

* * *

It is clear, 40 years after his death, that the force of Bethune's example has not diminished. The Chinese continue to learn from him. In his own country, too, his life is an inspiration and a challenge.

* * *

REFERENCES AND NOTES
1. Quoted in Roderick Stewart, *Bethune*, Toronto, 1973, p. 12.
2. Cited by Ted Allan and Sydney Gordon in *The Scalpel, The Sword: The Story of Dr. Norman Bethune*, Toronto, 1971, p. 167.
3. The full text of Mao Zedong's essay is reproduced, in English, in Stewart, p. 196. See also *Selected Works of Mao Tse-tung, Vol. 2,* Foreign Language Press, Peking, 1967, p. 337.

* * *

Abstract

Bethune was born in Gravenhurst, Ontario in 1890 and died 49 years later in North China. A prominent Canadian thoracic surgeon and a talented poet and artist, he was led by world political circumstances to serve the wounded in three wars and to make his mark on three continents. He early felt the urge to serve others, and at age 21 he worked in an Ontario lumber camp as a labourer-teacher; then he enrolled as a medical student. In 1915, he interrupted his medical studies to become a stretcher bearer with the Canadian army in France; a wound enforced his being invalided home, where he completed his medical studies in time to serve again in the Great War, as a Surgeon-lieutenant in the Royal Navy. He took post-graduate medical and surgical training in Britain, married Frances Campbell Penney and, in 1924, set up private practice as a surgeon in Detroit. But two catastrophes clouded his life: his wife left him and he contracted pulmonary tuberculosis. He revised his goals and decided to serve the tuberculous — of whom he had been one — by becoming a thoracic surgeon. He joined Dr. Edward Archibald in Montreal in 1928 to achieve this goal, and soon became an accomplished and innovative thoracic surgeon. Development of other interests in poetry, art and health care led to a period of creativity and of coming to terms with himself and his future. But then came the Spanish Civil War in July, 1936, and with it, his awareness, with very few others, of the dangers of fascism. He went to Spain to assist the beleagured Republicans, aiding them by means of an original mobile blood transfusion service. Almost immediately, the Japanese onslaught in China convinced him of the need to aid the Chinese in their fight against fascism, and he left for China in 1938. His achievements as a military surgeon were of immense proportions in China: his skill as a surgeon, his improvisational genius, his teaching ability and above all his dedication to the Chinese inspired them. When he died for them he had become a hero. Since his death he has continued to inspire thousands, mostly in China but more and more in Canada also.

Résumé

Bethune naquit à Gravenhurst, Ontario, en 1890, et mourut en Chine du Nord quarante ans plus tard. Chirurgien thoracique canadien de réputation, poète et artiste de talent, il fut conduit, par des circonstances politiques mondiales, à servir les blessés dans trois guerres et à laisser sa marque sur trois continents. Il ressentit très tôt le besoin de servir et à l'âge de 21 ans, travailla dans un camp de bûcherons comme travailleur-enseignant puis s'inscrivit ensuite comme étudiant en médecine. En 1915, il interrompit ses études médicales pour devenir brancardier dans l'armée canadienne en France. Une blessure le mit hors de combat et il dut revenir au pays où il termina ses études médicales à temps pour reprendre son service pendant la Grande Guerre en tant que chirurgien-lieutenant dans la Marine Royale. Il poursuivit des études médicales avancées et fit son stage de chirurgien en Grande-Bretagne. En 1942, il épousa Frances Campbell Penney et ouvrit une pratique privée à Détroit. Mais deux épreuves vinrent l'affliger: son mariage sombra et il contracta la tuberculose pulmonaire. Guéri, il revisa alors ses objectifs et entreprit de se mettre au service des tuberculeux en devenant chirurgien thoracique. C'est dans ce but qu'il vint travailler avec le docteur Edward Archibald à Montréal en 1928, où il devint un chirurgien thoracique accompli et innovateur. L'évolution de ses intérêts dans la poésie, l'art et les soins médicaux menèrent à une période de créativité et à une révélation de sa vie et de son devoir. Quand vint la guerre civile espagnole, en juillet 1936, Bethune et très peu d'autres, prirent conscience des dangers du fascisme. Il partit pour l'Espagne pour assister les républicains assiégés et leur venir en aide en établissant un service mobile original de transfusion sanguine. Presqu'immédiatement, l'attaque japonaise sur la Chine le convainquit de la nécessité d'aider les Chinois dans leur lutte contre le fascisme et il partit pour la Chine en 1938. En Chine, ses réalisations comme chirurgien militaire furent considérables: son adresse en tant que chirurgien, son génie improvisateur, sa compétence dans l'enseignement et surtout son dévouement pour les Chinois leur fut une source d'inspiration. Quand il mourut, il devint pour eux un héros et, depuis sa mort, il a continué à inspirer des milliers d'individus en Chine surtout et de plus en plus au Canada.

Chronology of Norman Bethune's Life

1890	March 3: born at Gravenhurst, Ontario; son of the Reverend Malcolm Nicolson and Elizabeth Ann (Goodwin) Bethune.
1893-1907	Moved with family to Beaverton, Ont. for 4 years and thence within Ontario to Toronto (twice), Aylmer and Blind River.
1903-07	Secondary school at Sault Ste. Marie and Owen Sound, Ont.
1907-08	Worked as lumberjack in northern woods of Ontario.
1909	January to June, rural school teacher at Edgley, Ont.
1909-11	Student at University of Toronto, registered in Physiology-Biochemistry option to prepare for medical studies.
1911-12	Labourer-teacher, under auspices of Frontier College, at lumber camp at Whitefish, Ont., for 5 months; then worked as reporter on the *Winnipeg Telegram*.
1912-14	Medical student, University of Toronto.
1914	September, enlisted as private soldier in a medical unit, Canadian Expeditionary Force.
1915	Served in France and Belgium as stretcher bearer. Wounded on April 29 at Second Battle of Ypres; in military hospital in England for nearly 3 months.
1915-16	Resumed medical studies in accelerated course at the University of Toronto, receiving M.D. degree in December, 1916.
1917	Gained clinical experience relieving two physicians in private practice in Stratford, Ont.
1917-18	Overseas service as junior medical officer in the Royal Navy; served 14 months in the aircraft carrier, HMS Pegasus.
1919	After demobilization in February, 6 months of surgical internship at Great Ormond Street Hospital for Sick Children London, England, and further medical practice in Ontario, in Stratford and Ingersol.
1920	After 7 months as medical officer in the Canadian Air Force, returned to England to continue surgical training.
1920-21	Worked in surgery at the West London Hospital (12 months), then to Edinburgh to study at the Royal Infirmary.
1922	February, admitted to Fellowship in the Royal College of Surgeons of Edinburgh; then returned to the West London Hospital for 18 months as Resident Surgical Officer.
1923	Marriage to Frances Campbell Penney of Edinburgh, followed by 6 months of travel in Europe.
1924	Settled in Detroit, Michigan, after search for openings in practice in Ontario and at Rouyn, Quebec; also 2 months' observation in surgical specialties at Mayo Clinic, Rochester, Minnesota.
1926	Rest cure for tuberculosis, begun at Calydor Sanatorium, Gravenhurst, was continued in December at Trudeau Sanatorium at Saranac Lake, New York.
1927	October 24, received news of divorce; October 27, pneumothorax treatment begun; and December 10, discharged from the sanatorium.
1928	April, after 3 months in laboratory research at Ray Brook, N.Y., moved to Montreal to work under Dr. Edward Archibald in thoracic surgery at the Royal Victoria Hospital.
1929	November 11, remarriage to Frances.
1931	Manufacture and distribution of his new surgical instruments undertaken by Pilling and Company, Philadelphia; and in fall, visited sanatoria and lectured in American Southwest.
1932	January, pneumothorax treatment discontinued after phrenicectomy (cutting left nerve to diaphragm) at University of Michigan Hospital, Ann Arbor; March, for 6 months, was acting head, thoracic surgery at the Herman Kieffer Hospital, Detroit; and in fall, appointment at Royal Victoria Hospital ended; second divorce proceedings pending.
1933	January, appointed Chief of Pulmonary Surgery and Bronchoscopy, at l'Hôpital du Sacré-Coeur in Cartierville, near Montreal.
1935	June, elected to Council of American Association for Thoracic Surgery; August, attended International Physiological Congress, Leningrad and Moscow, and visited sanatoria and child and maternal health centres; November, joined Communist Party

	in Montreal; December 20, member of panel reporting to the Medico-Chirurgical Society of Montreal on the Congress and the Soviet health system.
1936	January to August, Montreal Group for the Security of the People's Health reviewed various health systems and forwarded proposals to health professional organizations and to candidates for the Quebec election (August 17, Maurice Duplessis elected.); April 17, participated in a symposium on medical economics at Medico-Chirurgical Society of Montreal; October 24, left for Spain, arriving Madrid November 3; and mid-December, the Canadian Blood Transfusion Service formed, with colleagues Henning Sorensen and Hazen Sise from Montreal, Celia Greenspan from U.S.A. and Spanish personnel.
1937	April 12, transfusion unit taken over by the Spanish Ministry of War; May 18, left Madrid and was welcomed in mid-June in Toronto and Montreal; July to September, cross-Canada lecture campaign, sponsored by Committee to Aid Spanish Democracy; late summer, decided to go to China to join Mao Zedong and Red Army in Yanan.
1938	January 8, sailed from Vancouver with Dr. C.H. Parsons and Canadian nurse, Jean Ewen, arriving at Hong Kong January 27, and then on to Hankow (meeting with Zhou Enlai, Agnes Smedley and others); March 31, arrived at Yanan, with welcome by Ma Haide (Dr. George Hatem) and meeting with Chairman Mao Zedong; May 2, left Yanan, stopping for 16 days of surgery at army's base hospital at Zhoujiajion, then on to Chin-kang K'u, headquarters of the Chin-Cha-Chi Military Border Region, arriving June 17; and September 15, opening of Model Hospital at Songyankou, soon to be destroyed by Japanese soldiers.
1939	August, planned to leave in November for Canada to get rested, to raise funds to return with drugs and equipment; September 18, opening of medical school and model hospital at Niu-Yen K'ou (later named the Norman Bethune International Peace Hospital and relocated to Shijiazhuang in 1952).
1939	November 12: died of septicaemia from infected finger at Huangshikou, "Yellow Stone Pass".

La vie de Bethune: Chronologie

1890	3 mars: naissance de Bethune à Gravenhurst, Ontario, fils de Révérend Malcolm Nicholson et d'Elizabeth Ann (Goodwin) Bethune.
1893-1907	Avec sa famille, vit à Beaverton, Ontario, pendant 4 ans puis à Toronto, Aylmer et Blind River, Ontario.
1903-07	Études secondaires à Sault-Ste-Marie et à Owen Sound, Ontario.
1907-08	Bûcheron dans le nord de l'Ontario.
1909	Janvier à juin: instituteur à l'école rurale de Edgley, Ontario.
1910-11	Étudiant à l'Université de Toronto, inscrit en physiologie-biochimie en préparation à la médecine.
1911-12	Travailleur-étudiant sous les auspices de Frontier College, au camp de bûcherons de Whitefish, Ontario, pendant cinq mois, puis reporter pour le *Winnipeg Telegram*.
1912-14	Étudiant en médecine, Université de Toronto.
1914	Septembre: enrôlement comme soldat dans une unité médicale du Corps expéditionnaire canadien.
1915	Brancardier en France et en Belgique. Blessé le 29 avril à la deuxième bataille d'Ypres; confiné à l'hôpital militaire en Angleterre pendant 3 mois.
1915-16	Poursuite de ses études en médecine dans un programme accéléré à l'Université de Toronto où il reçoit son diplôme en décembre 1916.
1917	Expérience clinique lors du remplacement de deux médecins en pratique privée à Stratford, Ontario.
1917-18	Service outremer en tant qu'officier médical junior dans la Marine royale, dont 14 mois sur le porte-avions HMS Pegasus.
1919	Démobilisation en février suivie de 6 mois d'internat en chirurgie à l'hôpital pour enfants Great Ormond Street à Londres et de pratique médicale en Ontario à Stratford et Ingersol.
1920	Après 7 mois dans l'aviation canadienne en tant qu'officier médical, retour en Angleterre pour la poursuite d'études en chirurgie.

1920-21	Chirurgie au West London Hospital pendant 12 mois et poursuite de ses études à la Royal Infirmary d'Edimbourg.
1922	Admission, en février, au Fellowship du Royal College of Surgeons d'Edimbourg, puis retour au West London Hospital pour 18 mois comme officier chirurgien résident.
1923	Mariage de Frances Campbell Penney et Norman Bethune à Edimbourg et voyage en Europe pendant 6 mois.
1924	Il s'établit à Détroit, Michigan, après avoir cherché un poste en Ontario et à Rouyn, Québec; il passe 2 mois d'observation des spécialités chirurgicales à la clinique Mayo à Rochester, Minnesota.
1926	Atteint de tuberculose, il suit une cure de repos au sanatorium Calydor de Gravenhurst et au sanatorium Trudeau à Saranac Lake, New York.
1927	24 octobre, divorce; 27 octobre, début des traitements au pneumothorax; il est renvoyé du sanatorium le 10 décembre.
1928	Avril: après 3 mois de travail en laboratoire à Ray Brook, N.Y., il s'établit à Montréal pour travailler avec le docteur Edward Archibald en chirurgie thoracique à l'hôpital Royal Victoria.
1929	11 novembre, il se remarie avec Frances Campbell Penney.
1931	Pilling & Co. de Philadelphie fabrique et distribue ses nouveaux instruments chirurgicaux; à l'automne, visite des sanatoriums et tournée de conférences dans le sud-ouest américain.
1932	Janvier: fin des pneumothorax suite à une phrénicectomie (coupure du nerf gauche du diaphragme) à l'hôpital de l'Université du Michigan; mars: pendant 6 mois, chef de section par intérim en chirurgie thoracique à l'hôpital Herman Kieffer de Détroit; à l'automne, il termine son poste à l'hôpital Royal Victoria.
1933	Janvier: il est nommé chef de service de chirurgie pulmonaire et de broncoscopie à l'hôpital du Sacré-Coeur de Cartierville en banlieu de Montréal.
1935	Juin: il est élu au conseil de l'Association américaine pour la chirurgie thoracique; août: il assiste au Congrès international de physiologie à Leningrad et Moscou et visite des sanatoriums et des centres pour la santé de la mère et de l'enfant; 20 décembre: il participe à une table ronde de la Société médico-chirurgicale de Montréal sur le Congrès et sur le système de santé soviétique.
1936	Janvier à août: le *Montreal Group for the Security of the People's Health* étudie plusieurs systèmes de sécurité sociale et envoie des propositions aux organisations de professionnels de la santé et aux candidats aux élections provinciales au Québec (le 17 août, Maurice Duplessis est élu Premier ministre); le 17 avril, il participe à un symposium sur l'économie médicale à la Société médico-chirurgicale de Montréal; 24 octobre, il part pour l'Espagne et arrive à Madrid le 3 novembre; à mi-décembre, il met sur pied avec ses collègues Henning Sorensen et Hazen Sise de Montréal, Celia Greenspan des États-Unis et un personnel espagnol, le Service canadien de transfusion de sang.
1937	12 avril: l'unité de transfusion de sang passe sous le contrôle du Ministère de la guerre espagnol; 18 mai: départ de Madrid, accueil chaleureux à Toronto et Montréal; juillet à septembre; tournée de conférences au Canada sous les auspices du Comité d'aide à la démocratie espagnole. A la fin de l'été, il décide d'aller en Chine rejoindre Mao Zedong et l'Armée rouge au Yanan.
1938	8 janvier: il s'embarque à Vancouver avec le docteur C.H. Parsons et une infirmière canadienne, Jean Ewen, et arrive à Hong Kong le 27 janvier, d'où il se dirige vers Hankao où il rencontre, entre autres, Agnes Smedley; 31 mars: il arrive au Yanan où l'accueille Ma Haide (docteur Georges Hatem) et rencontre Mao Zedong; 2 mai: il laisse Yanan, s'arrête 16 jours pour pratiquer des interventions chirurgicales à l'hôpital militaire de Zhoujiajion, se rend à Chinkang K'u, le quartier-général de la région frontalière militaire de Chin-Cha-Chi où il arrive le 7 juin; 15 septembre: inauguration de l'hôpital modèle de Songyenkou bientôt détruite par les Japonais.
1939	Août: il se propose de partir en novembre pour se reposer au Canada, y recueillir des fonds et retourner avec des médicaments et de l'équippement; 18 septembre: inauguration de l'école de médecine et de l'hôpital modèle de Niu-Yen K'ou (qui deviendra, plus tard, l'hôpital International de la Paix Norman Bethune, transféré à Shijiazhuang en 1952).
1939	12 novembre, Bethune meurt d'une infection au doigt, à Huangshikou, "Le col de la pierre jaune".

"I Come of a Race of Men...":

Hilary Russell

> You must remember my father was an evangelist, and I come of a race of men, violent, unstable, of passionate convictions and wrong headedness, intolerant yet with it all a vision of truth and a drive to carry them on to it even though it leads, as it has done in my family, to their own destruction...
>
> — Norman Bethune to Marian Scott, October 1935.

This judgement on the ancestors of Henry Norman Bethune and their determining influence on his life has been taken seriously. It introduces the retrospective portion of the National Film Board's *Bethune*, opens Roderick Stewart's biography of Bethune, and is the first quotation on Bethune used in the modern display in the Bethune Memorial House, Gravenhurst. The quotation is used to provide an easy and logical explanation for his rebelliousness, passion and disregard for personal consequences, especially during the last 4 years of his life. But, while the quotation is marvellously romantic, and may reveal the attributes Bethune considered should be ascribed to his forbears and to himself at that critical period of his life[1], its primacy as a source of motivation is at least open to question.

To whom was Bethune referring? It is usually assumed that he was thinking not of racial or cultural stereotypes, but of his father's ancestors, and, literally, of the males from whom he was descended. He could have had some remote French and Scottish relatives in mind. According to his friend, Aubrey Geddes, "he was proud of his aristocratic lineage, fond of talking about the Bethunes of France who date back to William the Conqueror and before"[2].

The line has been painstakingly traced by various Bethunes from 11th-century France to Scotland[3]. Among the notables supposedly in it (whom Bethune may have included in his "race of men") were Canon de Béthune, 12th-century poet at the Court of France and crusading Regent of Constantinople, Maximilien, Duke of Sully and minister to Henry IV, and, in Scotland, James and David Beaton or Bethune, primates of the Holy See, Chancellors of Scotland and persecutors of protestants. But, even if the Bethune genealogies are correct, Bethune was descended neither from these men, nor (as he claimed to Aubrey Geddes) from Mary Bethune, who accompanied Mary Queen of Scots to France[4]. Instead, these elaborate family trees indicate that he was descended from a much less dramatic branch, and one not particularly noted for its "courage and independence"[5].

This branch settled in the island of Skye, produced four consecutive generations of surgeons, little or no violence, instability or intolerance, and was not even much involved with the cause of Mary Stuart. "Prudent," "kind and friendly," and "wise and judicious" are among the adjectives applied to these Bethunes, a scholarly, settled and respectable lot from whom John Bethune, Bethune's great-great-grandfather, is said to have been descended[6].

* * *

With John Bethune's appearance, Bethune genealogies are on firmer (and more accessible) ground. He is said to have been born in Skye in 1751. No evidence was discovered that he opposed "English domination" while in Scotland[7], though a family story claims that his father was wounded at Culloden[8]. Most accounts of John Bethune also state that he was educated at King's College, Aberdeen, and was ordained as a Presbyterian minister in Scotland. No record of this ordination has been found. He appears to have been a licentiate of the Church when he left Skye in 1772 or 1773 for North Carolina[9].

Along with the great majority of his countrymen there, John Bethune espoused the Loyalist cause with the outbreak of the Revolutionary War. A vision of truth, perhaps? Certainly it was a conventional one in that area of settlement. He became a chaplain in the Royal Highland Emigrants and, in this capacity, was made a prisoner of war in February 1776 with 800 others following a disastrous encounter with rebel militia forces. It was asserted later on his behalf that he had ". . . suffered a tedious imprisonment of two years and a half, with every hardship and indignity which a vindictive enemy could inflict on a man of his principles." On top of this, he is said to have lost "all" of his property in America[10].

But John Bethune was hardly "destroyed." He made his way to Canada following his release, and, among other achievements, organized the first Presbyterian congregation in Montreal[11] and became the first settled minister of that faith in what is now Ontario. His ministry was active and presumably rewarding, John living on his half-pay as a retired chaplain, 50 pounds per annum from the Society for the Propagation of the Gospel in Foreign Parts, and the contributions of congregational members. (The latter included, by Bethune's own account, a number of prosperous people, though he implied that they were a parsimonious group[12].) He also benefited from his allotment of about 2,000 acres of land in Charlottenburg (now Williamstown, near Cornwall) and a commodious residence he owned personally[13].

It is hard to recognize a reckless, violent, rebellious, intolerant and self-destructive man in John Bethune. Comments on his character and personality by some important persons who knew him indicate that he was "one of the best of men"[14], "worthy . . . by all accounts"[15], and "very respectable"[16]. The only chink in this armour was Governor Simcoe's remark on a petition complaining of the Church of England's monopoly he thought Bethune had authored as being "the product of a wicked head and a most disloyal heart"[17].

John Bethune also seems to have had a fulfilling personal life. He married Véronique, the daughter of Jean Etienne Wadden, a prominent fur trader and "a Swiss gentleman of strict probity and known sobriety"[18]. The Bethunes had nine children, nearly all of whom married well and became, at one time or another, pillars of the community. Two of them, Alexander Neil and John, became prominent Anglicans, the former the second Bishop of Toronto and the latter the Dean of Montreal Cathedral and a Principal of McGill University. Four of the sons were renowned in the business world[19].

* * *

One of John Bethune's sons was Bethune's great-grandfather, Angus Bethune. Like his grandfather Wadden, Angus entered the fur trade and he rose to become a partner in the North West Company by the time he was 30 years old. Notwithstanding, compared to his brothers and sisters, Angus Bethune was something of a black sheep, as he spent nearly all his life in "Indian country" and never married a white woman.

Until Henry Norman, likely no Bethune had travelled, or roughed it, more than Angus. He lived at campsites and remote fur trade posts, and, at least until the early 1820s, was threatened quite frequently by men and by nature[20]. He crossed the continent several times, as well as the Atlantic and Pacific oceans. From the north-west coast of America, Angus Bethune embarked as supercargo on two trading voyages to China in 1814 and 1815, spending about 6 months in Canton and stopping in the Hawaiian islands, Russian Alaska, and Spanish California[21]. He crossed the Atlantic Ocean in 1820, when he assumed an important role in the negotiations that led to the coalition of the two great rivals in the fur trade — the North West Company and the Hudson's Bay Company. With Dr. John McLoughlin, he went to London to negotiate with the English concern on behalf of the "wintering partners" of the North West Company (those who wintered in Indian country) and in opposition to the Company's Montreal agents.

Was Angus Bethune's role the result of some passionate conviction or vision of truth? Since none of his papers during this period are available, it is difficult to say. He detested the Montreal agents of the North West Company and the agents heartily reciprocated this dislike[22]. (The enmity was not new: the agents had opposed his selection as supercargo to China and blamed him for some of the mission's failures.) The "vision" the wintering partners sought in the negotiations was a more profitable trade, free of the Montreal agents and of the prolonged and costly conflict with the Hudson's Bay Company[23].

The impact Bethune and McLoughlin had on the coalition agreement is not clear[24]. In any event, it ended the conflict and the name of the North West Company. Angus Bethune and other ex-Norwesters assumed a majority of shareholding positions as officers of the Hudson's Bay Company, though the elimination of the Montreal agents was not achieved. Angus Bethune became a Chief Factor in the new company. Soon, however, he clashed with his superior, Governor William Williams. Again, the feud was based on no vision of truth, but on personal animosity and ambition, and it provides some good examples of Angus' truculent and abrasive personality[25]. Williams' successor, Governor George Simpson, was more adept at stifling him, but found him as tiresome and incompetent as Williams had, referring to him in a confidential journal as "a very poor creature, vain, self sufficient and trifling, who makes his own comfort his principal study, possessing little nerve and no decision in anything..."[26]. The Governor's assessment that Bethune was "neither liked nor respected by his associates, servants or Indians" is hard to contradict. Evidence is quite abundant of his recriminations and squabbles with members of all these groups, and with one missionary.

More of the same followed his retirement to Toronto while he served as alderman for St. David's Ward. Though, certainly, controversy was commonplace on City Council, Angus may have inspired more than his share — hence a quotation from the minutes directed to him: "What does the venerable chief want? . . . Are he and his colleagues always to be at war? Are we never to be at peace? It seems to me that he intends to fan the embers of discord all year"[27].

His personal life was similarly turbulent. He quarreled with nearly all of his children, especially with Angus, his son by an unknown Indian woman[28], and with Donald, his first son by Louisa McKenzie, the mother of six of his children and the daughter of an unknown Indian woman and the Honourable Roderick McKenzie of Terrebonne, fur trader and politician[29].

In his will, Angus ruthlessly excluded Donald from any inheritance, and allowed two other sons, John Wadden and Alexander Norman, only 50 pounds per annum for life. Since the estate was later valued at $56,498[30], the will wreaked havoc among Angus's children[31]. His favorite child, Norman, his second son by Louisa, was left the use of the estate's assets and its earnings during his life and only Norman's children were empowered to dispose of his legacy.

Angus Bethune's complicated and vindictive will exemplifies aspects of his personality. He may have possessed some of the qualities of the opening quotation — certainly, he was not a stranger to violence, intolerance and wrongheadedness — but the most important aspect, a vision of truth, even to self-destruction, is not apparent.

In many other respects, Angus was very much unlike his great grandson, Norman. His surviving papers show him to be selfish, egotistical, even unprincipled, and his career reveals little of a creative, constructive, or inspiring nature. But this was not his great-grandson's fault, and should not affect one's assessment of him — though some telling similarities (or perhaps coincidences) can be found between the two. Both were world travellers, imbued with spirits of adventure; both became deeply implicated in significant and controversial events; and neither could be accused of being shy and retiring, or of avoiding strife and antagonisms.

* * *

The same could be said of Angus's favoured son, Norman, grandfather of Henry Norman, and, evidently, a telling influence on his grandson. This Norman was the first of the Canadian descendants of the surgeons of Skye to enter that profession. As well as matching his strong views, his unorthodoxy, and his scientific inclinations, Norman Bethune's grandson is supposed to have taken after him in his reforming zeal and in battling an establishment[32]. The example cited for the latter is the senior Dr. Bethune's role in the formation and dissolution of Trinity College Medical School, a consequence of a vision of truth, pursued at any cost.

This conclusion is open to question, as a close examination on Trinity College records reveals that the sequence of events and the issues at stake have been misrepresented. It is not the case that the school was closed in its sixth year ". . . when Dean Bethune and his entire faculty resigned in protest against a new university regulation that barred non-Anglicans"[33].

Far from having no religious requirement for entry at its founding in 1850, Trinity College Medical School was established unequivocally by Bishop Strachan as a Church of England institution, and all candidates for degrees were required to be members of that Church. The Bishop had been offered the services as a medical faculty of a group of six young doctors formed by Doctors Hodder and Bovell[34]. Norman Bethune was one of the group — not, apparently, its prime mover — and was a professed Anglican at the time[35].

The religious requirements might not have posed a problem had the medical faculty been on salary. Until the College could afford "permanent remuneration," the medical professors were allowed to keep the medical students' fees[36].

The six professors were not independently wealthy; Norman Bethune had £300 a year "by his wife," but three had no outside income[37]. It was in the interests of the faculty to sidestep the regulations, which were increasingly affecting their livelihood. They did this in 1853 and 1854 by printing circulars publicizing that occasional students were not required to be Anglicans. These students paid regular fees, and, with Trinity certificates, could obtain their degrees at other institutions, including the "Godless" University of Toronto.

Trinity Council objected to the circulars and to these subversions of the founding principle of the College. The Council's relationship with the medical faculty was further chilled in 1855 by the latter's plan, submitted to provincial authorities without Council's approval, to affiliate with the University of Toronto. This move would have meant salaries for the faculty. Dr. Norman Bethune was its Dean that year. The Council's condemnation led to the accusation that it was ungrateful and indifferent to the welfare of the medical professors[38].

The last straw was a newspaper advertisement in June 1856 (signed by "N. Bethune") repeating the notion of non-Anglican occasional students. The Council's demand for the immediate withdrawal of this "objectionable advertisement" led to the response from the faculty that they were "utterly at a loss" to discern what the Council found objectionable. To "avoid all difficulties in future," and being convinced that their attempts to advance Trinity's interests met with "repeated rebuffs," they offered their resignations. These were accepted without a murmur, and had practically been encouraged by Council the previous year[39].

Whether Norman Bethune, as Dean of the faculty, was responsible for the course taken is not clear. (He may well have been as quarrelsome and headstrong as his father had been, and as prone to clash with authority figures.) Even less clear is whether the dissolution of the faculty was prompted exclusively by clear-sighted and liberal ideals, rather than by a mixture of financial considerations, pique and wounded pride.

Was Norman Bethune "destroyed" by the dispute? Perhaps, to some extent, though he became a member of the faculty of the Toronto School of Medicine in 1857-1858, went to Edinburgh for 9 years to practice and to obtain his Fellowship of the Royal College of Surgeons, and returned to teach at Victoria University, Toronto, in 1869[40]. There, evidence of trouble surfaced in a note to the Dean of the medical faculty:

> Dr. Bethune to receive $50 for his partial course. The students refused to take out Medicine or to pay for it and several... on account of the broken imperfect course also decided... not to take out any of the final branches. This has been the cause of much loss to the college[41].

Still, he continued teaching until 1881, in 1871 being appointed to the revived Medical Department of Trinity College. Now the medical professors were paid a salary of about $1,300 a year, and were no longer required to be Anglicans[42].

Whatever fulfilment this brought was clouded by personal tragedy — the death in about 1872 of his wife, Janet Ann Nicolson (of Edinburgh). Norman was left with six children, four of whom were under 10 years of age[43]. He sent some of them to Scotland to be brought up by his wife's sister, and in 1877 was sued for recovery of the costs of their maintenance. The writ secured and the train of litigation set in motion revealed that Dr. Norman Bethune was insolvent, and that he had frittered away a large portion of his father's estate, contrary to the terms of the will[44]. Apparently, in this period Norman was drinking heavily[45]. His financial position was about to become even more precarious, as after 1881 he was no longer on staff at Trinity College and was receiving no income from his father's estate, now in the hands of a receiver.

Norman spent most of the last 3 or 4 years of his life living with his son, Malcolm, and his family in Toronto and Gravenhurst. Following a series of paralytic strokes, he died in October 1892 in a Toronto home for "incurables," intestate, his estate valued at "nil"[46]. Trinity College *Magazine* and Toronto medical journals seem to have taken no note whatsoever of his passing.

It is likely that he had ruffled some important feathers at Trinity College and elsewhere. He may even have been destroyed, though not necessarily, by a vision of truth or passionate convictions. Like his father and his grandson, the first Dr. Norman Bethune was a controversial figure. Like his grandson, he was a talented amateur artist and writer, enjoyed renown in his surgical specialty, travelled widely[47], and had trouble hanging onto money. His influence on his grandson was considerable, though this does not mean it was genetic.

Though Dr. Norman Bethune died when Henry Norman was only 2½ years old, the child is said to have retained a memory of his grandfather, and was known to emulate his limp. When the lad announced he wanted to be called "Norman" and hung his grandfather's shingle on his door, perhaps no one suspected that this would be one of the crucial decisions of his life.

* * *

The last link in the chain of "passionate men" is Malcolm Nicolson Bethune, the second son of Norman and Janet Ann. What is known of his early life reveals some family patterns. Like his father, he attended Upper Canada College, and, like Angus Bethune, Roderick McKenzie and Jean Etienne Wadden, he became involved in trading furs, being employed in Toronto as a wholesale furrier. He also sought adventure across the ocean and, at the age of about 23, he "... left the Country intending to take a voyage around the world ... but when he arrived in Australia he left his ship as he did not like the captain ... and falling in with a connection he went into sheep farming"[48]. He failed utterly in this endeavour, and in 1880, in "extreme want of money," he desperately wanted to come home. The receiver of his grandfather's estate provided $250 for his passage in steerage from Brisbane to San Francisco.

How did he, broke and discouraged, end up in Hawaii seeking investments in orange groves, as Allan and Gordon maintain? In Honolulu he is said to have met Elizabeth Goodwin, an English Presbyterian missionary, and to have become converted to the church of his fathers, after which he returned to Toronto and Knox College "with her blinding vision"[49]. I cannot account for the orange grove story, nor for the apparent absence of any record of Elizabeth Goodwin as a missionary in relevant archives. Still, Malcolm's obituary references to his early life are somewhat consistent with this tale:

> As a young man his life was one of adventure. He often gave, in his own dramatic way, his experiences at sea. During those years he visited many countries, enlarging his knowledge and outlook on life. After experiencing a change of heart, he felt called to the Ministry. Through the originality of personal circumstances, the call was mediated to his soul[50].

Since no family papers have survived relating to Malcolm Bethune's ministerial career, it is difficult to assess it with any degree of assurance. His wife conveyed a "stormy picture" of it to Ted Allan, though George Mooney had the impression that there was "no record of tempest" in the "well-ordered" home in which his friend, Norman, grew up[51]. No Presbytery records were found to sustain the claim that Malcolm Bethune was forced to leave any of his charges[52]. Perhaps he was encouraged to resign on one or more occasions, as there is some testimony that he was not averse to rebuking elders and other weighty Presbyterians and that some found his zeal excessive. And one reference to his Gravenhurst ministry conveys his evangelism and reported dogmatism: "Mr. M.N. Bethune ... spoke forcibly on the Gospel as the only power for the salvation of men, and uttered emphatic dissent from the opinions of Canon Taylor and others of unsound views"[53].

Malcolm Bethune did not rise in the hierarchy of the church. The sizes of his congregations and stipends tended to decrease over the years, especially after he entered the mission field in 1903 and when he served in some areas of northern Ontario where his grandfather had served the Hudson's Bay Company[54]. Malcolm may not have wanted anything else, and, according to his wife, he refused calls from wealthy congregations[55].

Perhaps this was not the way his son, Norman, saw it. The opening quotation does not end there, where it is usually ended — it continues, "... as it did my father" — and he may have been thinking mostly of his father when he wrote the paragraph in 1935, even though available documents do not exactly sustain that image of Malcolm Bethune, either. Of course, he may not have meant them as seriously and as literally as they have been taken, by me as well as by others.

* * *

I have tried to demonstrate that the opening quotation should not be held up uncritically as an accurate portrait of the ancestors of Norman Bethune. In spite of some important points of similarity (and coincidence), there are even more significant differences between Norman Bethune and the "race of men" from whom he descended. In my view, they did not make him what he was, and their strengths and shortcomings need not be ascribed to him. They did not "program" him or themselves for self-destruction. And one would not need all the right ancestors to do what Bethune did in China, or to follow his example.

* * *

REFERENCES AND NOTES

1. Bethune was considering taking a plunge and accepting the chairmanship of Friends of the Soviet Union.
2. Quoted in Roderick Stewart, *Bethune*, Toronto, 1973, p. 53.
3. Ontário, Public Archives, unpublished book manuscript of Bethune compiled by Louisa Blanchard Bethune, Buffalo, New York (hereafter cited as Bethune manuscript); private collection, Bethune genealogies and family papers (hereafter cited as Bethune family papers).
4. Quoted in Stewart, p. 53.
5. Ibid., p. 193.
6. See *An Historical and Genealogical Account of the Bethunes of the Island of Sky*, attributed to the Rev. Thomas Whyte, Edinburgh, 1778. Reprinted in London for Alfred Bethune-Baker, 1893, pp. 7-31.
7. Stewart, p. 193.
8. Mary Larratt Smith, *Prologue to Norman: The Canadian Bethunes*, Oakville, 1976, p. 17.
9. James MacKenzie, "John Bethune: The founder of Presbyterianism in Upper Canada," in *Called to Witness: Profiles of Canadian Presbyterians*, ed. W. Stanford Reid, N.p., 1975, p. 106. See also Reverend Robert Campbell, *A History of the Scotch Presbyterian Church, St. Gabriel Street, Montreal*, Montreal, 1887, p. 25; A.H. Young, "The Bethunes," *Ontario Historical Society, Papers and Records*, Vol. 27, 1931, p. 553.
10. John Graves Simcoe, *The Correspondence of Lt. Gov. John Graves Simcoe*, ed. E.A. Cruikshank, Toronto, 1925, Vol. 3, p. 263; William Canniff, *The Settlement of Upper Canada*, Belleville, 1971, facsimile of 1869 ed., p. 269. It was alleged in his obituary notice that his imprisonment during the war, 37 years before, had ". . . probably laid the foundation of the disease which has ultimately caused his death": Canada, Public Archives (hereafter cited as PAC), RG4, D1, *Quebec Gazette*, 28 Sept. 1815, no. 2643.
11. He did not build St. Gabriel's Street Church, which was not the first Presbyterian church in Canada; see Stewart, p. 193. The 1792 Church was built for the congregation Bethune had organized; see Robert Campbell, pp. 27, 41, 46.
12. Bethune family papers, letter from John Bethune to congregations in Glengarry and Williamstown, Sept. 16, 1815. For the Society for the Propagation of the Gospel allowance see PAC, MG17, B1, Vol. 25, reel A157, p. 53, Journal, 15 February 1788. Bethune established four congregations (in Williamstown, Lancaster, Martintown and Cornwall, respectively), baptized 2,379 persons in Glengarry, and travelled regularly to Grenville County to perform services.
13. The manse (or White House) was sold by his widow to explorer David Thompson and still stands; see Marion Macrae and Anthony Adamson, *The Ancestral Roof: Domestic Architecture in Upper Canada*, Toronto, 1963, pp. 2, 19, 20, 23, 24, 30-1. 84.
14. PAC,RG5, A1, Vol. 106, #6024, John Strachan to Z. Mudge, March 26, 1831.
15. Thomas Douglas, 5th Earl of Selkirk, *Lord Selkirk's Diary, 1803-1804*, ed. Patrick C.T. White, Toronto, 1958, p. 197.
16. Comment by Bishop Mountain, 1794, quoted in Richard A. Preston (ed.), *Kingston Before the War of 1812: A Collection of Documents*, Toronto, 1951. p. 293.
17. John Graves Simcoe, p. 235. For the text of the petition see pp. 242-4.
18. Alexander Mackenzie, *Voyages from Montreal on the St. Lawrence Through the Continent of North America*, London, 1801, p. xvi. Wadden (or Wadin, Waddens, etc.) was shot to death at

Lac La Ronge in 1782; he was erroneously identified by a descendant as "Professor Wadden of the University of Geneva"; A.H. Young, p. 559.
19. See A.H. Young, *Dictionary of Canadian Biography,* Toronto, 1972, Vol. 10, s.v. "Alexander Neil Bethune," "John Bethune;" Peter Baskerville, "Donald Bethune's Steamboat Business: a Study of Upper Canadian Commercial and Financial Practice," *Ontario History*, Vol. 67, No. 3 (September 1975), pp. 135-49; "The Entrepreneur and the Metropolitan Impulse: James Grey Bethune and Coburg, 1825-1836," in *Victorian Cobourg*, ed. J. Petryshyn et al., Belleville, 1976.
20. Among his adventures were encounters with hostile Indians, a terrible journey to Fort William in 1817 visited with perils, violence and cannibalism, and two challenges to duel. See Hilary Russell. "Angus Bethune," in *Old Trails and New Directions: Papers of the 3rd North American Fur Trade Conference*, Toronto, 1979.
21. See Hilary Russell, "The Chinese Voyages of Angus Bethune," *The Beaver*, Outfit 307, No. 4 (Spring 1977), pp. 22-31.
22. See Colin Robertson, *Colin Robertson's Correspondence Book, September 1817 to September 1822*, ed. E.E. Rich, Toronto, 1939, p. 162; PAC, MG19, E1, Vol. 18, fos. 6994-7, Gale to Colville, 28 October 1820.
23. See John McLoughlin, *John McLoughlin's Business Correspondence,* ed. William R. Sampson, Seattle, 1973, p. xxii; John M'Lean, *Notes of a Twenty-five Years' Service in the Hudson Bay Territory*, London, 1849, Vol. 2, p. 219.
24. In some accounts of the negotiations, their presence was of no real consequence. In others, it gave the Hudson's Bay Company the whip hand. See Burt Brown Barker, *The McLoughlin Empire and its Rulers*, Glendale, Ca., 1959, p. 43; M'Lean, p. 219; W. Stewart Wallace, ed., *Documents Relating to the North West Company*, Toronto, 1934, p. 30; E.E. Rich, *The History of the Hudson's Bay Company 1670-1870*, London, 1959, Vol. 2, p. 396.
25. See Russell, "Angus Bethune," pp. 182-4.
26. Glyndwr Williams, ed., *Hudson's Bay Miscellany 1670-1870*, Winnipeg, p. 178.
27. *British Colonist* (Toronto), 6 March 1846, p. 3. No "vision of truth" was at stake here, either. Angus was accused of pocketing some of the ward's money.
28. Bethune family papers. Angus, Jr. was born in Indian country in about 1810 and baptised at St. Gabriel's Church, Montreal, in 1815; he became a barrister in Brantford, Ontario, and died in his 38th year: Registers of St. Gabriel's Presbyterian Church, October 1815; William D. Reid, comp., *Death Notices of Ontario*, Lambertville, N.J., 1980, pp. 252, 299.
29. Bethune manuscript; Anges W. Turcott, *Land of the Big Goose: a History of Wawa and the Michipicoten Area*, Dryden, Ont., 1962, p. 127. Louisa died from the effects of a miscarriage in 1833, leaving six children, four of whom were under 10 years old. See PAC MG19, A21, Ser. 1, Vol. 3, fol. 577, T. McMurray to J. Hargrave, May 10 1833.
30. Ontario, Public Archives (hereafter cited as PAO), York County Surrogate Court Register, Book 11, pp. 393-9, Will of Angus Bethune; see also PAO, High Court of Justice, Chancery Division, Nicolson v. Bethune, report filed 26 September 1878.
31. The disappointment is said to have "formed a crisis" in Donald's life, and this ". . . clever man, well educated, with marked ability in his profession [law], and a great talent for drawing" never regained ambition. John Wadden left home immediately and was spotted later as "the captain of an East Indian clipper ship." The reaction of Alexander Norman, a medical doctor, was not recorded — see Bethune manuscript.
32. Ted Allan and Sydney Gordon, *The Scalpel, the Sword: the Story of Dr. Norman Bethune*, Toronto, 1952, p. 10; Stewart, p. 1.
33. Stewart, p. 194.
34. Toronto University, Trinity College Archives (hereafter cited as TCA), Corporation Minutes, Trinity College, Vol. 1, 4 December 1851, p. 70, "Act to Incorporate Trinity College," TCA, *Trinity College Calendar, 1853*; Henry Melville, *The Rise and Progress of Trinity College, Toronto*, Toronto, 1852, p. 161; J. George Hodgins, *The Establishment of Schools and Colleges in Ontario, 1792-1910*, Toronto, 1910, Vol. 3, pp. 132-3; J.L.H. Henderson, "The Founding of Trinity College, Toronto," *Ontario History*, Vol. 44, No. 4 (October 1952), p. 11; T.A. Reed, ed., *A History of the University of Trinity College, Toronto*, Toronto, 1952, p. 57; George W. Spragge, "The Trinity Medical College," *Ontario History*, Vol. 58, No. 2 (June 1966), p. 65.
35. In writing about John Bethune, the Reverend Robert Campbell rejoiced, "Mr. Bethune's grandson, . . . Dr. Norman Bethune of Toronto, has lately connected himself with the communion to which he by descent belongs, after worshipping for many years in the Anglican Church. This is what Darwin would have called a return to the original type." Campbell, p. 38.
36. TCA, Corporation Minutes, Trinity College, Vol. 1, 8 January 1852, p. 77.
37. G.W. Spragge, p. 72.
38. TCA, *Circular of the Medical Faculty of Trinity College, Toronto,* Toronto, 1853, 1854; Corporation Minutes, Trinity College, Vol. 1, 22 February 1855, pp. 175-8; 24 March— 14 April 1855, pp. 179-87. G.W. Spragge, pp. 71-4.
39. *Leader* (Toronto), 19-28 June 1856, p. 3; TCA, Corporation Minutes, 24 June — 2 July 1856; G.W. Spragge, p. 76.

40. George P. Ure, *The Handbook of Toronto*, Toronto, 1858, p. 111; C.M. Godfrey, "The Evolution of Medical Education in Ontario," M.A. Thesis, University of Toronto, 1974, p. 95; William Canniff, *The Medical Profession in Upper Canada 1783-1850*, Toronto, 1894, p. 251.
41. PAO, William Canniff papers, undated memo, S.A.S. Sangster to William Canniff.
42. TCA, Corporation Minutes, Vol. 2, May 10, 1871, p. 35, January 15, 1873, p. 52; Walter B. Geikie, "An Historical Sketch of Canadian medical education," *Canada Lancet*, Vol. 34, No. 5 (January 1901), p. 233; G.W. Spragge, p. 81.
43. PAO, High Court of Justice, Nicolson v. Bethune, PAC, RG31, Dominion Census, 1871, Province of Ontario, District 47, Toronto E, Sub-District B, St. James' Ward, Nominal return of the living, p. 3. Norman was left in the same predicament as his father — see footnote 29.
44. PAO, High Court of Justice, Nicolson v. Bethune, op. cit.
45. See Mary Larratt Smith, op. cit., number 8, p. 76.
46. Ontario, Surrogate Court, County of York, Petition for administration, Norman Bethune, 1908.
47. Apparently, at the Toronto General, ". . . most of the important eye cases were handed over to Dr. Norman Bethune," who was "esteemed" for his surgical ability, C.K. Clarke, *A History of the Toronto General Hospital*, Toronto, 1913, p. 87. On one of his many crossings of the Atlantic, a trip from Sheerness, England, to Moose Fort in 1849, Norman Bethune kept a diary that ". . . exhibits fine descriptive ability and no little talent in sketching the icebergs he saw in the way, and some ship scenes," Canniff, p. 251. No diary or any other personal papers of Dr. Norman Bethune (Sr.) were located.
48. Nicolson v. Bethune, op. cit., affidavit by Walter Read, December 1880.
49. Allan and Gordon, p. 10.
50. United Church of Canada, Central Archives, obituary notice, Rev. M.N. Bethune.
51. Ted Allan, personal communication; PAC, MG30, D187, vol. 31, p. 3. George Mooney thought that Malcolm Bethune had, at the age of 14, run away to sea and had spent some time in the South Sea Islands before becoming a Presbyterian minister.
52. Cf. Roderick Stewart, p. 2.
53. *Canada Presbyterian*, Feb. 12, 1890, p. 108.
54. After he entered the mission field he was appointed to, respectively, Massey, Blind River, Daywood, Owen Sound and Desboro, Blackheath, Collingwood and Sundridge. United Church of Canada. Central Archives, Register of United Church ministers; *The Acts and Proceedings of the General Assembly of the Presbyterian Church in Canada*, Toronto, 1889-1922.
55. Allan and Gordon, pp. 10-11.

* * *

Abstract

Bethune wrote that he came from "a race of men . . . of passionate convictions and wrong headedness, intolerant yet with it all a vision of truth and a drive to carry them on to it even though it leads . . . to their own destruction." This quotation has been widely accepted as a determining influence in Bethune's life, but it is open to question as to whether it should be accepted uncritically as an explanation of Bethune's personality, motivations and career. A review of the lives and personalities of some of Bethune's forbears — John Bethune, Angus Bethune, Norman Bethune and Malcolm Bethune in particular — suggests rather that, in spite of points of similarity (and coincidence), there are significant differences between Bethune and those from whom he was descended.

Résumé

Bethune a écrit qu'il était issu d'un "race d'hommes aux convictions passionnées, obstinés, tolérants et, cependant, avec une vision de la vérité et un élan pour les emporter même s'il devait mener à leur propre destruction". Cette citation a été largement acceptée comme ayant eu une influence déterminante sur la vie de Bethune, mais on peut se demander si elle peut être acceptée telle quelle comme une explication de sa personalité, de ses motivations et de sa carrière. Un examen de la vie et de la personnalité de quelques-uns des ancêtres de Bethune — en particulier de John Bethune, Angus Bethune, Norman Bethune et Malcolm Bethune — suggère que, malgré certaines similarités ou coïncidences entre Bethune et ceux qui l'ont précédé, il existe des différences profondes, et qu'ils ne l'ont pas "programmé" pour sa destruction ou pour tout autre trait de son caractère. Bethune n'avait besoin d'aucun antécédent pour parvenir à ce qu'il a accompli.

Canada
1890-1936

The mirror of our pale and troubled gaze,
Raised to a cool Canadian sky . . .

   — Norman Bethune
     From "Red Moon"

Source: Canadian Forum, 17 July 1937, 118

The Religious Setting of Norman Bethune's Early Years
Richard Allen

"You must remember, my father was an evangelist," wrote Norman Bethune[1]. Obviously he was conscious of the effects of being brought up a son of a zealous Presbyterian minister. However, there appears to be little evidence on which to develop any close correlation between Bethune's youthful development and either the more immediate or the distant religious setting of his upbringing as a son of the manse. This paper is therefore only incidentally biographical, although it suggests that certain of the tensions and conflicts of Bethune's complex personality, such as the contrary pulls of urbane sophistication and the austerity of earnest religious commitment, a certain desire for social success and a deep awareness of basic injustice in society, can in part be seen as intensified reflections of issues endemic in the religious setting of his youth.

* * *

Yes, Bethune was aware of the consequence of being his father's son. Indeed, can any child of the ministry forget the intensity of that experience? Which other children in the community have been so publicly committed, especially in Bethune's age, to a clearly conceived style and quality of life? Which other young people listened week in, week out, for years on end to their fathers' declamations on the central issues of life and faith? In some measure, perhaps, they were saved by grace of also sitting around the breakfast table with him! And there was, thankfully, also a certain common sense in ministers that sometimes escaped the more pious laity. As the most popular Canadian evangelists of Bethune's younger years, Crossley and Hunter, would say, "Many think they need more grace, when it is rest of body or mind, fresh air, sleep or medicine they need."[2] But, tempered as it might be, the effects of a ministerial upbringing were indelible. Particularly was that so for ministerial families that moved often, as the Bethunes did. One could easily learn to be sociable without learning the riches and discipline of enduring relationships among one's peers. The sense that the ministerial family belonged to the congregation — even to the community — could equally forge a never-to-be forgotten closeness and security or a claustrophobic resentment and bitterness. For the son of the manse at the turn of the century, the heroism that was enjoined in the secular education of young imperialists was compounded by moral earnestness of the Sunday School's singing "Dare to be a Daniel" and marching in a prohibition parade, and was further reinforced by a home in which seriousness and commitment lay all around.

Not surprisingly, many rebelled. Indeed, one was almost expected to do so — that was part of the mythology about preachers' families with which one grew up. However, it was not so much simple rebellion as a complex pattern of creative absorption, adaptation, and rejection of the inheritance that marked the careers of such prominent sons of the manse in Bethune's period as, for example,

J.S. Woodsworth and L.B. Pearson. But there was also Hartley Dewart, son of the editor of the *Christian Guardian*, who threw over his father's prohibitionism to become the hard drinking leader of the Ontario Liberal party in 1917; also A.R. Carman, son of the redoubtable General Superintendent of the Methodist Church, who abandoned his father's biblicism to become the cultivated editor-in-chief of the *Montreal Daily Star*[3]. Ministerial parents and sons, though, were not usually so prominent, indeed were often quite undistinguished. Two Canadian novels of Bethune's younger years, however, do tell a common story and present an ideal solution. In *Roland Graeme, Knight* (1892) and *The Preparation of Ryerson Embury* (1900), Agnes Maule Machar and A.R. Carman, themselves children of the manse, depict the struggle of their counterparts with the rigid doctrinal and biblical attitudes, and the self-righteousness and irrelevance they perceived in the church. On the brink of putting it all behind them, the heroes are brought face to face, on the one hand with industrial crisis and the working class, and, on the other, with the "Christ-like" figures of rather solitary, practical clergy, who have given their lives to the urban poor and think of Jesus as a social reformer as well as a personal transformer of men. Somewhere in the story of Henry George's influential work, *Progress and Poverty* makes its mark, and the heroes set off respectively to establish a cooperative factory and to become a labour lawyer[4].

The Protestantism with which the children of the manse, and perhaps sensitive young people more generally, struggled was hardly itself a static entity. Presbyterians and Methodists were, of recent date (1875 and 1884), nationally united denominations with large corps of clergy deployed to realize a long-standing vision of a righteous Canada[5]. The imposing Gothic edifices that dominated church architecture from the Confederation decade onward symbolized not only the openness of a people to divine impression but also the triumph of Protestantism in the mid-century commercial and early industrial city[6]. Between 1841 and 1881, for instance, Methodism in Ontario had increased by more than seven times, and Presbyterianism by more than five — increases above that of the general population, which had multiplied four times.

* * *

The growth of that period had not come about without strain and stress as the evangelical churches at once accommodated themselves and contributed to an increasingly complex society. An emerging cradle-to-grave Protestantism did much to shape the rhythm of life and the inner discipline of the broad spectrum of new classes from the artisan upwards that was created by the burgeoning commercial and early industrial urban order[7]. It was in this period that what came to be known as the Canadian Sunday was established[8]. Camp meetings, revivals and protracted meetings either declined or took on a more subdued, even sophisticated, tone. Sunday Schools underwent a notable transformation and rapid growth as more optimistic views of childhood prevailed. The machinery of an international Sunday School movement, with standardized lessons and joint denominational efforts in the weekly preparation of Sunday School teachers, spread widely through urban Canada, catering to adults as well as to children[9]. Protestant women's movements, originating in the early 1880s, spread through the churches. Emphasizing the missionary role of the church, women's missionary societies became a way station in the march of the mid-Victorian ideal of true womanhood from the family to the reform movements of the next generation. Even more clearly, the Women's Christian Temperance Union performed that function, though there were many men, apparently, who forbade their wives and daughters to join so activist a body. Constricted in their domestic roles in a double sense — in family and nation — the more adventurous young women began to find in foreign missionary careers a means of bringing feminine ideals to bear on the world of their time[10].

Men, of course, and especially the more "successful" among the membership, had dominated the general oversight of congregational life, and, as the local, regional and national church structures expanded, their skills became ever more important in refining methods of ecclesiastical administration. They were not to be left out of the march toward more specialized organizations for themselves. Men's brotherhoods reaching out to men on the fringe of the church were imported from overseas in the 1890s, to be followed a decade later by the formidable American-based Laymen's Missionary Movement. As the brilliant biographies of N.W. Rowell and J.W. Flavelle show so well, the men's movements in the church represented the impulses dominating late 19th century Canadian Protestantism — a merger of a deeply embedded evangelical ethic, Victorian philanthropy and metropolitan expansiveness[3,11]. For men as for women and children, foreign missions were not only an evangelical enterprise, but a projection of their own progressive march toward civilization and a major, if exotic, form of philanthropy.

In short, the Protestantism that Bethune's generation inherited, and against which some choice spirits would rebel, was far from a fossilized institution. Reverberations of old and the sound of new issues still accompanied its advance. Presbyterians had had their organ controversies and Methodists were upset about gowns in the pulpit. The more potent controversies over science and religion, which in fact had existed most of the century, were now keenly debated by a more educated clergy and laity. From early in the century, and through the debate over "Darwin," the essence of their position was that true science and true religion could not conflict, but only pseudo-science and pseudo-religion[12]. Even the most notable Canadian scientist of the 19th century, and prominent Presbyterian, John William Dawson, despite his concern to hew as closely to scripture as possible, extended creation days into ages and allowed so much variation by natural selection into species that it has been asked why he did not go all the way with Darwin[13]. George Munro Grant, the Principal of Queen's University declared that one only needed now to believe that what had happened at a single stroke occurred rather in succession over a long period of time. And the well-known Presbyterian divine, C.W. Gordon (alias the novelist Ralph Connor), recalled his mother reading to him from Henry Drummond's *Natural*

Law in The Spiritual World[14], the thesis of which was that evolution had been presented to the world out of focus. In a revision of Darwin that was to become increasingly popular, Drummond declared that the mechanism of evolution was not the struggle for the survival of self but the struggle for others in the survival of species. That is not to say that young Bethune grew up in a church where the matter was settled. There was indeed intense debate, often between generations and between metropolis and hinterland, as young people went off to college and imbibed the new theories, the better minds among them aware that finally natural selection could not be accommodated to a purposeful universe. Bethune would appear to have been one of them.

The "Old Faith and the New Philosophy" also met on the ground of Biblical "higher criticism." George Munro Grant might take a large view of the matter and publicly support the much maligned American Presbyterian higher critic, Professor Briggs, and Nathaniel Burwash, the leading Methodist theologian, might push aside his old notes and say "Gentlemen . . . we now have a new and better method of understanding this material."[15] Nonetheless, though often skilfully contained, controversy raged. In the course of Bethune's youth several Biblical scholars lost their postings in Canadian colleges. In a related doctrinal issue, D.J. Macdonnell, prominent Presbyterian cleric, was harried to an early death in 1896 for questioning the church's doctrine of eternal punishment for unrepentant sinners[16].

What one might call hinterland revivalism of the Ralph Horner type in the Ottawa valley attempted to hold the line against the new trends in the churches[17], but revivalism, too, was becoming more urbane, sophisticated — and more sentimental[18] — in the hands of persons like Crossley and Hunter, the famous Canadian revivalists. Crossley, for example, was prepared to revise parts of St. Paul in the light of contemporary ideas and advocate women's suffrage[19]. It was not just metropolitan centres but also western towns that desired their services. The "goods" of the city (if not its vices) were wanted on the frontier. As a plaintiff clergyman at an isolated charge wrote in 1907 to Salem Bland, the urbane Wesley College Professor in Winnipeg, "Come, if you can, Doctor, we do not often have college men come out to the frontier points."[20] So undoubtedly it was in the "outback" Ontario of Bethune's youth.

* * *

By the 1890s then, the Protestant churches, with their now elaborate "social means of grace", had made a remarkably creative response to the mid-century challenge of the city, and through their urban leadership sat astride the metropolitan network that dominated the Canadian hinterland. But if the sirens of a more cultured Protestantism were calling, the terms in which the quest for a Christian Canada had been established were now put in question by a remarkably rapid process of industrial consolidation. No doubt partly initiated by the severe depression of the early 1890s, in city after city in central Ontario the number of industrial firms decreased sharply, while the work force remained roughly constant[21]. With the creation of larger more impersonal units of production came a challenge to the heavily personal form in which the Protestant ethic had been cast, and upon which artisans, the middle class and entrepreneurs alike relied. Industriousness, sobriety, thrift and a faithful acceptance of one's lot as divine providence were not enough. Labour spokesmen and local social critics in Toronto and elsewhere petitioned annual meetings of the major Protestant churches in the early 1890s, asking them to raise their voices against a "system of monopoly of land and capital and competition among workers", which was nothing less than "organized robbery." The responses were ambivalent. Replies were warily drafted, suggesting that the influence of 'advanced' social critics was already at work among church members[22].

The problem for those of sensitive social conscience, or who themselves were on the lower rungs of the economic ladder, was not simply the newly aggregated impersonal labour relations. Sheer subsistence, as recent studies have shown, was the lot of the average working man's family, and working conditions, if not as bad as the most lurid accounts would have it, were a standing affront to a Christian community[23]. It would be pleasing to be able to say that the Protestant churches reacted massively and effectively in response to the twin challenges of the new industrial order: the need for a new social ethic and substantially improved conditions of life and labour for the mass of the population. That was not to be, and perhaps it is too much to expect; but at least it was the direction in which the churches moved.

Principal George Grant, of Queen's University, might reject Henry George, while Albert Carman, Superintendent of the Methodist Church, was attracted to Georgite solutions[24], but at mid-decade Grant was promoting annual Alumni Conferences on social problems and related issues, and Toronto Methodists followed suit. Ministerial associations, in Hamilton, for instance, picked up the refrain, and social questions became topical fare in the Protestant press and pulpit. Herbert Casson gave up his Methodist circuit in Ontario to found a Labor Church in Lynn, Massachusetts, and, shortly after, S.S. Craig left his Presbyterian congregation at Oakville to set up a "social reform pulpit" in Toronto. The Toronto Methodist Conference found its way to support a general railwaymen's strike against the Grand Trunk in mid-1899, a year after the General Conference of that church, undoubtedly reflecting the anxiety of small businessmen as much as working class conditions, struck out against "heartless combinations." In the same breath, however, it counselled Methodists not to be too hasty in subscribing to "untried solutions" to the ills of the age[25].

Canadian Protestantism, however, in the first decade of Bethune's life, was above all preoccupied with ringing up huge majorities in futile efforts to usher in provincial prohibition or with getting a more recently initiated sabbatarian crusade off the ground. Each in its own way was a response to the issues of the new industrialism — problems of urban poverty and social discipline — as broadly middle-class Protestants saw them. For working class Protestants, arguments of social justice were more to the fore. In short, the 1890s saw the beginning in an organized and systematic way of the Protestant social gospel, a movement reaching into virtually all the agrarian, urban, labour and social welfare movements of the next generation in English Canada. Hence, it was largely under Protestant church sponsorship that the first major national congress on the social ills of the nation was held on the eve of the Great War[26]. An analogous movement of social Catholicism was likewise in its beginnings in English and French Canada at the same time, but has little significance for the background to Bethune's life.

* * *

By the turn of the century, for Presbyterians as for Methodists, the impact on their traditions of a tumultuous period of development was severe. All the developments sketched above ground the edges off distinctive positions. Furthermore, the encounter of evangelicalism and Calvinistic predestinarian theology heavily modified the latter's emphasis on the distance of a sovereign God in favour of the nearness of His Love. Methodism, in turn, was pressed further toward Arminian free will[27]. The need of such a time was for an integrating philosophy. In Canada, as elsewhere in the English-speaking world, that was found in a form of the idealism fostered by T.H. Green, of Oxford, and Edward Caird, of Glasgow.

In Canada, John Watson, of Queen's University, became the leading spokesman of this movement, ably seconded by George Paxton Young, of Toronto, and T.B. Kilpatrick, who taught at Knox College when Malcolm Bethune was studying there. All were Scottish Presbyterians. Stressing an essential Christianity and the final unity of all things in the divine mind, idealism appeared for a time to charm away the niggling difference between denominations, the tension between urbane culture and religious commitment, and the contentions of religion and science, even while it offered a resolution of the claims of personal and social salvation[28]. Watson and his colleagues considered that art, science and religion were integrally linked as expressions of man's participation in the divine mind and together were mutually working for the realization of a "community of free beings by which the ideal of an organic unity of humanity is in process of realization." By no means did Watson and company carry all of Canadian Protestantism with them, but they provided the reigning philosophy as the churches moved into the era of liberal theology and the social gospel[29].

On the fringe of all this moved the spokesmen of the nascent labour movement. They, too (and how many of their followers?), constituted an important part of the religious background of the age. T. Phillips Thompson, editor of the *Labour Advocate*, attacked the church for submitting to the insidious influence of wealth. With notable exceptions, he thought, the ministry had become "the servile tools" of "rich men's social clubs and Sunday opera companies."[30] But Thompson was a Quaker turned Theosophist, and, with most of the labour newspaper editors of the generation from 1880 to 1910, he saw his task in a religious light[31]. That was not surprising for, quite apart from whether they had been subject to formal church influence (most had), they were spokesmen for an artisanal class whose lodges depicted work as a meaningful activity in a world made by a divine artificer and moving toward his ends through the agency of willing human collaborators[32]. The labour movement was the contemporary vehicle of God's spirit, realising a world of human brotherhood and social justice. This conviction was not just a subscription to the "undying ethics of Jesus," but entailed a potent millennial and immanent theological conception. In its own way, it too, could — and did — claim to be essential Christianity. There was, after all, a common intellectual base for Thompson and Watson, and it was on that base that G.W. Wrigley at the turn of the century attempted to woo clergy into his Christian Socialist Leagues[33]. Such ventures were just successful enough to be small straws in the wind.

It was in the Protestant youth movements, however, arising in the mid-1880s, that these notions of an essential Christianity with a contemporary social and intellectual bias came most readily to the fore. The Ontario Christian Endeavour Convention of 1899 listened intently as the young reformist preacher, Salem Bland, urged members to abandon the pessimistic world view of their elders and sound the note of Christian triumphalism by working wholeheartedly at municipal reform[34]. In the same year the student YMCA at Wesley College, Winnipeg, urged students into international action on the ground of social solidarity because, "strictly speaking, there is no longer any such thing as individual salvation."[35] There was clearly a certain caricature of the old as young people of Bethune's youth reached out for a new world. It was, after all, Matthew Arnold of their fathers' generation whom their English professors thrust at them: culture, Arnold had said, was not realized in any until it was realized in all. Imperialism or prohibition might still be a means of rising above self, but when members of the Methodist Epworth League rallied around James Simpson, the perennial and successful Toronto labour-socialist candidate for civic office, something new was brewing. Just how far their new social impulses and intellectual conceptions would carry these pre-war youth and students was not yet clear at the time of Bethune's career as an undergraduate at the University of Toronto. Eager to do more than read Jenk's *Jesus and the Social Question*, they followed the example of British students and founded university settlement houses[36], or followed a Canadian innovation and became, like Bethune, the labourer-teachers of Frontier College[37].

Then came the war, a heightening of social-religious idealism, and the radical aftermath — the 1920s, and the crisis at once of the older moral reform movement (prohibition) and the newer social gospel. Reform was in crisis, smitten by disillusionment and outright skepticism[38]. But a more realistic and radical Christian social ethic was being fashioned by young Canadians of Bethune's age or slightly younger, often veterans of the war, studying now in Oxford, or at New York with Reinhold Niebuhr and Harry F. Ward. Early in the Depression these young intellectual Protestants formed the Fellowship for a Christian Social Order, and in 1936 published a volume entitled *Towards the Christian Revolution*[39], which John Strachey, the British Marxist, praised[40]. Perhaps its most provocative statement was from the pen of Eugene Forsey: "This generation seeketh after a sign, and there shall be no sign given it but the sign of the prophet Marx. Until Christians learn to understand and apply the lessons of marxism they cannot enter into the Kingdom of Heaven — nor, probably, can anyone else[41]." Agnes Machar's Roland Graeme, Knight, had taken a large step since 1892. New sons of the manse and their colleagues were finding a Christian frame of reference that would comprehend a Norman Bethune, whether he accepted it or not. They were hardly a majority among Protestants of the 1930s, but they were among the more notable voices of that decade. Like Bethune they were alarmed at the spread of the fascist menace. They picketed scrap-iron shipments to Japan, joined hands in support of the Committee for the Defence of Spanish Democracy, and, whether they liked him or not, they were ready to second his efforts as he went about his historic task in those momentous years.

* * *

REFERENCES AND NOTES

1. Cited in Roderick Stewart, *Bethune*, Toronto, 1973, p. XIV.
2. H.T. Crossley, *Practical Talks on Important Themes*, Toronto, 1895, p. 33.
3. See Margaret Prang, *N.W. Rowell, Ontario Nationalist*, Toronto, 1975, pp. 74, 180.
4. For a discussion of these themes in the books see Mary Vipond, "Blessed Are the Peacemakers; the Labour Question in Canadian Social Gospel Fiction, "*Journal of Canadian Studies*, X, 3 (1975).
5. John S. Moir, *Enduring Witness*, Toronto, 1975, ch. VII, "An Age of Unions"; J. Warren Caldwell, "The Unification of Methodism, 1865-1884," *The Bulletin of the United Church Archives*, XIX (1967).
6. William de Villiers Westfall, "The Dominion of the Lord: Victorian Protestant Ontario," *Queens Quarterly*, LXXXIII (Spring, 1976).
7. William Magney, "The Methodist Church and the National Gospel, 1884-1914." *The Bulletin*, XX (1968).
8. For the emergence of the Canadian Sunday and the struggle for its defence see Sharon Meen, "The Battle for the Sabbath: The Sabbatarian Lobby in Canada, 1890-1912," chs. I, II (unpublished doctoral dissertation, University of British Columbia, 1979).
9. An extended account of the transformation of urban Methodism is contained in Neil Semple, "The Impact of Urbanization on the Methodist Church in Central Canada, 1854-1884" (unpublished doctoral dissertation, University of Toronto, 1979).
10. Christopher Headon, "Women and Organized Religion in mid and late Nineteenth Century Canada," *Journal of the Canadian Church Historical Society*, XX, 1-2 (1978); Susan Walma, "Alma College and the 'Women Question': 1877-1899" (unpublished Master's research paper, McMaster University, 1978).
11. See Magney, pp. 48-50; Richard Allen, *The Social Passion: Religion and Social Reform in Canada*, 1914-1928, Toronto, 1971, pp. 7. 11, 231; Prang, pp. 64-7; Michael Bliss, *A Canadian Millionaire, The Life and Times of Sir Joseph Flavelle, Bart., 1858-1939*, Toronto, 1978, especially chapters IV-VIII.
12. Charles F. O'Brien, *Sir William Dawson, A life in Science and Religion*, Philadelphia, 1971, ch. II; D.C. Masters, *Protestant Church Colleges in Canada*, Toronto, e.g. pp. 34, 89-90; Robert J. Taylor, "The Darwinian Revolution: The Responses of Four Canadian Scholars" (unpublished doctoral dissertation, McMaster University, 1976).
13. O'Brien, ch. V., esp. p. 123.
14. From original draft of Gordon's Autobiography, *Postscript to Adventure*, New York, 1938, C.W. Gordon Papers.
15. Masters, pp. 90-91; Prang, p. 74.
16. Masters, pp. 133-135; J.C. McLelland, "The Macdonnell Heresy Trial," *Canadian Journal of Theology*, IV (1958); W.L. Grant and C.F. Hamilton, *Principal Grant*, Toronto, 1905, pp. 151-61.
17. Brian R. Ross, "Ralph Cecil Horner: A Methodist Sectarian Deposed, 1887-1895," joint issue of *The Bulletin* and *Journal of the Canadian Church Historical Society*, XIX, XXVI (1977), 1-2 (1977).
18. Semple, ch. V.
19. Crossley, pp. 83-85.
20. John E. Lane to Salem Bland, May 3, 1907, Salem Goldworth Bland Papers, #885, Miscellaneous Correspondence, United Church Archives.

21. Jacob Spelt, *Urban Development in South Central Ontario*, Toronto Carleton Library reprint), 1972, pp. 176-186.
22. Ramsay Cook, "Henry George and the Poverty of Progress in Canada," *Historical Communications/Communications Historiques*, Canadian Historical Association, 1977, p. 150.
23. See Terry Copp, *Anatomy of Poverty, The Condition of the Working Class in Montreal*, Toronto, 1974, esp. ch. II; Greg Kealey, *Working Class Toronto at the Turn of the Century*, Toronto, 1973, esp. pp. 14-23.
24. Cook, op. cit.
25. Allen, ch. I.
26. *Ibid.,* ch. II.
27. Those were the tendencies of Anglo-American theology, and the signs were not lacking in Canada (Robert E. Chiles, *Theological Transition in American Methodism: 1790-1935*, New York, 1965).
28. Masters, pp. 91-2; Brian Fraser, "Theology and the Social Gospel among Canadian Presbyterians: A Case Study, *"Studies in Religion/Sciences Religieuses* VIII, 1 (1979). On the role idealism played for cultured evangelicals in a time of turmoil, see Melvin Richter, The *Politics of Conscience: T.H. Green and His Age.* London, 1964.
29. Taylor, pp. 202-208; but see especially Brian McKillop's masterful recent work, *The Disciplined Intelligence,* Toronto, 1979.
30. T. Phillips Thompson, *The Politics of Labor,* Toronto, 1975 (reprint of 1887 edition), p. 172.
31. Jim Stein, "Labour and Religion in the Canadian Labour Press, 1872-1891" (unpublished Master's paper, MacMaster University, 1975); Joan Sangster, "Religion and the Prairie Labour Press, 1900-1910" (unpublished Master's research paper, McMaster University, 1976).
32. This note keeps cropping up in the new studies of Canadian working class culture by Gregory Kealey, Wayne Roberts, Russell Hann, Bryan Palmer and others.
33. See especially the early issues of Wrigley's reform journal, *Citizen and Country.*
34. Salem Goldworth Bland Papers, #20, "The New Christianity," Nov. 8, 1899.
35. *Vox Wesleyana*, II, 6 (1898), p. 178.
36. Allen, pp. 11-12.
37. See the following paper by Marjorie Robinson in this collection on the subject of Frontier College (pp. 32-39).
38. This general trend of development is recounted in Allen, *The Social Passion*, but for a briefer treatment see Richard Allen, "The Social Gospel and the Reform Tradition in Canada, 1890-1928," *Canadian Historical Review* XLIX, 4 (1968).
39. Wendell MacLeod has provided an interesting brief account of the background to these developments as part of the setting of Bethune's Montreal years (Wendell MacLeod, Libbie Park, and Stanley Ryerson, *Bethune: The Montreal Years,* Toronto, 1978, pp. 25-29, 65-66). The larger story of this new wave of radical Protestantism is told in Roger Hutchinson, "The Fellowship for a Christian Social Order" (unpublished doctoral dissertation, University of Toronto, 1975).
40. See his review, *The Left News*, May, 1937, pp. 369-371.
41. R.B.Y. Scott and Gregory Vlastos (eds.), *Towards the Christian Revolution*, Chicago, 1936, p. 139.

* * *

Abstract

Bethune, whose father was an Evangelical Presbyterian Minister, grew up in a milieu of seriousness and commitment, aware of a sense of the minister's family belonging to the congregation. His early years coincided with a period of development of the Protestant churches towards a righteous Canada in which men's and women's church movements and missionary zeal were growing and in which issues such as science versus religion, revivalism and Biblical higher criticism were much to the fore. At the same time, the rapidity of industrial consolidation demanded a realistic response from the Churches, and the 1890s saw the beginning of a Protestant social gospel that would reach into agrarian, urban, labour and social welfare movements of the 20th century. While some of religious conviction concerned themselves with a need to develop an integrating philosophy to explain the importance of art, science and religion in man's life, those with a more sensitive social conscience concerned themselves rather with the need for a new social ethic and for improved conditions of life and labour. For these latter Canadians, the influence of wealth that was accumulating in the industrial era was insidious, and they attacked the Churches for submitting to this influence. On the fringes of Protestantism arose Christian socialist movements and Protestant youth movements, the latter attracting young people of Bethune's youth as they reached out for a new world. Many followed the example of British students in founding university settlement houses; others followed a Canadian example and, like Bethune himself, became labourer-teachers with Frontier College. By the time Bethune was of university age, a more realistic and radical social ethic was thus being fashioned, an ethic that would lead many, Bethune included, to become alarmed at the fascist menace that eventually shaped the 20th century international world.

Résumé

Bethune, dont le père était un pasteur évangélique presbytérien, grandit dans un milieu sérieux et engagé, conscient du fait que sa famille appartenait à une congrégation. Ses premières années s'écoulèrent à une époque où les églises protestantes orientaient leurs efforts vers l'édification d'un Canada juste dans lequel les mouvements d'hommes et de femmes et le zèle missionnaire étaient en expansion et dans lequel des questions telles que les relations entre la science et la religion, le revivalisme et la critique de la Bible étaient à l'honneur. En même temps, la rapidité de la consolidation industrielle demandait une réponse réaliste de la part des églises et les années 1890 virent les débuts d'un évangile social protestant qui allait s'étendre aux mouvements de réformes agraires, urbaines, ouvrières et sociales du XXe siècle. Alors que certains individus imbus de convictions religieuses s'attachèrent au besoin de développer une philosophie intégrale pour expliquer l'importance de l'art, de la science et de la religion dans la vie, d'autres, doués d'une conscience sociale plus aiguisée, étudièrent plutôt la nécessité d'une nouvelle éthique sociale et de meilleures conditions d'existence et de travail. Ces derniers considéraient comme pernicieuse l'influence des richesses accumulées dans cette ère industrielle et dirigèrent leurs attaques contre les églises pour s'être soumises à cette influence. Aux limites du protestantisme s'élevèrent les mouvements socialistes protestants et les mouvements de jeunesse protestante qui attirèrent de jeunes contemporains de Bethune à la recherche d'un monde nouveau. Plusieurs suivirent l'exemple des étudiants britanniques et fondèrent des centres communautaires sur le modèle des university settlements; *d'autres adoptèrent un exemple canadien et, comme Bethune lui-même, devinrent travailleurs-enseignants pour* Frontier College. *Quand Bethune atteignit l'âge des études universitaires, une éthique sociale plus radicale et plus réaliste était en voie de développement, une éthique qui susciterait chez plusieurs personnes, dont Bethune, une inquiétude devant la menace fasciste qui éventuellement dominerait la situation internationale.*

Norman Bethune and Frontier College, 1911-1912

Marjorie Zavitz Robinson

About the middle of September, 1911, a young man of of 21 years, H.N. Bethune, arrived for an interview at the cluttered, disorganized and crowded offices of the Reading Camp Association in Toronto. There he considered accepting the challenge of working as a Reading Camp instructor. He was informed that, in addition to labouring for the Victoria Harbour Lumber Company at one of their camps at Pinage Lake, near Whitefish, Ontario — a 10-hour a day, 6-day a week position — he would have to conduct elementary classes for 1 to 2 hours each night and to hold a Christian service each Sunday. Once accepted, he was expected to stay at the camp until it broke up in the Spring. He would draw the same wages as the other labourers, and would eat, sleep, and live with the men, thus winning their confidence and respect, following the exhortation of Froebel, "Come, let us live with our students." No training session was provided, but Alfred Fitzpatrick, founder and guiding force of the Reading Camp, usually performed the task of telling an applicant a little of its philosophy, something about the camp he might work for, and a little about the type of teaching expected. At this time, however, as Fitzpatrick was travelling in Vancouver and California, attempting to complete a novel he had been working on for a few years, Bethune instead talked with a part-time helper, Joseph Wearing[1].

It is fair to assume that Bethune, who had just completed his second year at the University of Toronto, knew something about the Reading Camp and its work, as quite a few university students had served as instructors. In fact, the previous year, four were sent out, and one of them worked at Harley's Camp at the Victoria Harbour Lumber Company at Pinage Lake[2]. Just what Bethune knew of the Reading Camp we cannot definitely say, but we can surmise that something of its challenge and ideal of service to others appealed to him.

* * *

The Reading Camp Association (now known as the Frontier College) had been born in 1899. It was then, and is now, dedicated to taking educational opportunities where none currently existed.

The idea behind Frontier College was conceived by Alfred Fitzpatrick, born in Pictou County, Nova Scotia, of United Empire Loyalist stock. A student and friend of George Munro Grant, of Queen's University, he was trained as a Presbyterian minister. Fitzpatrick was described years later by people who had known him as eccentric, with piercing blue eyes, a shy man so dedicated to his endeavours that he would not allow that aspect of his personality to interfere with his plans. Many spoke or wrote of his intelligence, and of his quick, innovative mind. Frontier College remains a testimonial to the fact that he was a visionary — a man years ahead of his time. While preaching in the lumber camps of Northern Ontario in the 1890s, and observing the filthy living conditions and

Pinage Lake, Ontario, 1911-12. Alfred Fitzpatrick is third from right.

Lac Pinage, Ontario, 1911-12. Alfred Fitzpatrick est le troisième à partir de la droite.

the working slavery the men were subjected to, Fitzpatrick realized the ineffectiveness of a missionary's occasional sermon[3]. A couple of years later he wrote, "The mere oracular expression of God's love is not the whole Gospel. To teach men that it is criminal to be filthy . . . this is part of preaching the Gospel"[4].

So Fitzpatrick left the church and began the Reading Camp Association to attempt to take education to these men living on the periphery of civilization. In 1901, he wrote, "Life in the lumbering and the mining camps of Canada is dull and deadly. Gambling, whiskey and disease relieve the monotony, but bring their own reward. The camps need reading rooms and libraries"[5]. His solution was a simple ideal: "Access to the best literature, entertainment and social intercourse with his neighbours, will uplift the soul and inspire the solitary to newness and cleanness of life"[6]. "The problem", he insisted, "is in the main educational"[7]. And he fervently believed that "education is the God-given right of every man . . ."[8], revealing perhaps the influence of Thomas Carlyle, one of the thinkers he often quoted. Fitzpatrick believed, too, that "the scene of men's labour is the proper place for their education"[9]. But, interestingly, to anyone who dared question the religiosity of his work, he argued that "all educational work is more or less religious. . . Many of our students preach the Gospel in the regular way. All live it before the men. In rain and sunshine, in mud and muskeg, it is the aim of the instructor to help the men to a better life"[10]. The Reading Camp Association became his lifelong crusade. As he wrote, "the object of life and the path to the attainment of the highest good is service"[11].

Fitzpatrick established many enduring lines of attack for the Reading Camp Association in its first couple of years. To accomplish his goals, he carried newspapers, magazines and books (on his back) to lumber camps; he approached the Ontario Government to extend the scope of the Public Libraries Act so as to embrace the needs of lumber and mining camps; and he persuaded camp owners to erect reading rooms on their property for the men's use and relaxation, an unheard of luxury. This reserved and nervous man energetically campaigned through newspapers, magazines, and speeches to arouse government leaders, businessmen, and the public to the desperate plight of the camp men, and to enlist their support in agitating for reforms. He approached businessmen-philanthropists, churchmen, and influential, social-minded citizens to serve on a Board of Governors of the Association and to help in soliciting financial support.

Feeling that young, educated men and women would provide a good influence supervising and teaching in the reading rooms, Fitzpatrick approached a few. Their response was an eager Yes. An interesting thing happened: one of these first instructors — a university-educated, middle-class fellow — became bored with idly waiting for the camp men to finish work so he could begin teaching them. He found a pair of overalls and joined them at their labours. So, in 1902, a new concept in education, the labourer-teacher, was born.

One of the first labourer-teachers was Edmund W. Bradwin, a robust giant of a man, who from his first contact with the Reading Camp Association in 1903 to his death in 1954, then Principal of Frontier College, devoted all of his considerable energies to the furtherance of its goals. He became, in fact, the ideal instructor and worker, the labourer-teacher personified. From 1903 to 1914, he moved from camp to camp, working and teaching, making a great contribution in drawing up lessons for instructors to follow with their classes of both English and non-English-speaking camp men — and in his spare time, completing the necessary courses for an M.A. degree from Queen's University without ever attending a lecture. He was a philosophical and practical man; a man of eloquent prose; a man who loved and understood the North, Canada and her workers[12].

Under the direction of these two men — Alfred Fitzpatrick and Edmund Bradwin — the Reading Camp Association grew from its modest beginnings (total receipts the first year were $49)[13]. By 1913, eight provincial governments contributed grants to help support the work. That year a total of 79 labourer-teachers were established in eight provinces in mining, lumbering, hydroelectric construction camps, and on the three transcontinental railways on a budget of $17,807[14]. To summarize, not only were the labourer-teachers pioneering adult education, they were establishing libraries in frontier areas, attempting to "Canadianize" the thousands of immigrants swelling the ranks of camp men, and acting as guide and friend to unskilled workers across the country.

* * *

This, then, was the organization Bethune became part of in 1911. At the time he applied, the Reading Camp was looking for men to send to the lumber camps for the winter. Joseph Wearing wrote Fitzpatrick, "As usual it seems to be a little difficult to get men for the lumber camps. We have lots of applications but neither Miss McMechan [Fitzpatrick's secretary] nor I have any notion of sending out a man unless we think he is A 1"[15]. Bethune, however, filled the Reading Camp requirements — he was a university student, had experience of teaching, was "used to roughing it"[16] and presumably could sing well enough to lead the men in "sing-songs" or in a Sunday service. He was also recommended by Mr. Dougal McLeod, a scaler[17].

On October 12, 1911, Miss McMechan wrote Fitzpatrick an account of Bethune's beginning:

> Mr. Bethune ... decided he would go out for us and he left for Robinson's camp this morning. I got him a CNR pass and told him to pay his fare from Sudbury to Whitefish. I gave him two boxes of books and magazines ... [and] letters of introduction to Robinson and McDermott [the foremen]. Bradwin wrote me from Sudbury yesterday and I told him to meet Bethune if he was there tonight[18].

It looked as if Bradwin did not make it to help as Bethune wrote a month later:

> I formally took possession on the 19th day of October and declared the building open that night. The next seven days were spent in laying in a supply of wood, plastering and arranging the comforts of an effete civilization in conformity with the strict mission-style furnishings of my bungalow.

In this, his first letter, Bethune revealed something of himself as he playfully admonished Fitzpatrick's secretary:

> "Where, oh where, did you collect that exhibit of the old masters? They make a truly wondrous and stilling effect on the walls of the drawing-room. I wake up every morning with a start, to find the glassy menacing eye of that bull fixed intently on my helpless form. It's as good, believe me, as an alarm clock. Forgive my seeming levity. The boys appreciate them immensely and they brighten the place up in a surprising fashion."

His work on the road he found "a little hard, with the resultant effects — blisters and fully developed symptoms of a kink in [the] vertebral column." (He also, in apologizing for not writing until a month after being sent out, blamed it on "a combination of work, lack of time and sore hands — the latter possibly being the greatest.") However, he continued, "I enjoy it, and am sure I shall like it immensely later on"[19]. He apparently worked as an axeman and at tending the cable in connection with the engine used in assisting big loads of logs up the steep hill. Neither of these were easy jobs[20].

Bethune asked for teaching supplies in the form of a dictionary, paper and envelopes, Bibles, magazines and a hymn book, and indicated that his mother would forward some of his school text books. Also, he requested a subscription for the *Saturday Evening Post* as it was read "with a great deal of interest."

Indicating his willingness to put his money where his concerns were, he wrote, "I will gladly pay ... to have it in the camp." One of his most indispensable teaching tools was the phonograph. He was quick to note this and request a "couple of dozen" more records, as "some of the records here are practically useless from rough usage, resulting in cracks, etc. producing a combination of shrills and shrieks not included in the original definition of harmony by the great Wagner"[21]. At the end of November, Bradwin wrote his boss, "You have by long odds the best lot of winter instructors ..."[22].

In December 1911, Bradwin sent each instructor a typed outline for classes that would have covered about 15 weeks of work. Bethune, like the other instructors, presumably would have tried to follow the suggestions. Bradwin stressed that the Reading Camp wished to "uplift the men in every way." He challenged the instructor to "let them feel each night that they have learned something, some advancement made which would have been lost by remaining in the bunkhouse." He noted the importance of involving the men in the lessons by asking them to share some of their expertise such as tying knots in ropes. His outlines for classes in arithmetic, history, hygiene, spelling, geography, letter writing and penmanship were dotted with little gems of advice: "Do not attempt too much;" "Get plenty of sleep;" and "Speak plain truths on sex"[23]. By the end of December, Bethune wrote that he was "glad to be able to report that the work is proceeding very well and the men, especially the English-Scotch, appreciate the Reading Camp a great deal." However, he noted, "At Christmas the usual 'jumping' (leaving the camp) took place, reducing to a great extent the classes"[24].

From 1906 the Reading Camp instructors noticed the large influx of recent immigrants into the camps. Fitzpatrick wrote that there was "no greater service that a young Canadian University man can render our country than that of working in our frontier camps side by side with the foreign workman for the purpose of convincing him that we are deeply interested in him, teaching him our ideas of citizenship and our ideals of life"[25]. Bethune seemed to try to do all he could for the dozen men in his camp who could not speak English. He had asked in November and again in December for instruction books in Polish and French, for "it is extremely desirable that they know something ... about the language, when they leave in the spring ..." His duty to them, he showed, was not only in teaching English. "I am leaving this afternoon with a Pollack who had his leg broken yesterday," he wrote on New Year's Eve, [and] "administered first aid ... Will have him to Whitefish and telegraph for ambulance to meet the train at Sudbury"[26].

Bethune did ask for letters but never complained of feeling alone without the contact of his social peers. Fitzpatrick visited him on February 16, 1912, and took a photographer — hence the very good shot of Bethune and the lumberjacks (Figure p. 33) — and he wrote, "Bethune is getting on OK"[27]. On March 15, Bethune telegrammed that the camp was breaking up and that he required his railway pass to get back to Toronto. There, he dropped into the office to pick up his pay for teaching — $20 a month[28].

There is no record of what the experience meant to Bethune except a letter dated July 10, 1912, wherein he stated that he would "be very glad to go into the work again for the next two and a half or three months"[29]. There were, unfortunately, no openings, and Bethune went on to other endeavours. Yet it is characteristic of him that, early in his career, he should have followed the path of service to others, service that was here summarized by Fitzpatrick in the following words: "Since the beginning of our work over 250 Christian college men have gone down to the ditch, the mine and forest and engaged in every conceivable kind of frontier labour side by side with the woodsman, miner, navy and fisherman"[30]. Norman Bethune served his time as one of them.

* * *

Acknowledgement

This chapter is based on the research material of Dr. G.L. Cook and Marjorie Zavitz Robinson, compiled during preparation of a history of Frontier College.

* * *

REFERENCES AND NOTES

1. Public Archives of Canada, Frontier College Papers, 11.
2. Public Archives of Canada, Frontier College Papers, 132, Annual Report, 1910.
3. Public Archives of Canada, Frontier College Papers, and Jessie Lucas, interviewed by Ian Morrison, former President, Frontier College. (Taped from Jan., 1973 to July 19, 1973).
4. Alfred Fitzpatrick, "The Neglected Citizen in the Camps", *The Canadian Magazine,* 25 (May, 1905), p. 45.
5. Fitzpatrick, "Life in Lumbering and Mining Camps", *The Canadian Magazine,* 27 (May, 1901), p. 49.
6. *Ibid.*, p. 51.
7. Fitzpatrick, "The Neglected Citizen in the Camps".
8. *Ibid.*
9. Fitzpatrick, "Education on the Frontier", *Queen's Quarterly,* 21 (1913-14), p. 66.
10. *The Mail and Empire,* Toronto, June 17, 1912.
11. Fitzpatrick, "The Education of the Frontier Laborer", Public Archives of Canada, Frontier College Papers, 132, Annual Report, 1904-05.
12. Public Archives of Canada, Frontier College Papers and Lucas.
13. Fitzpatrick, "Library Extension in Ontario Travelling Libraries and Reading Camps", Public Archives of Canada, Frontier College Papers, 132, Annual Report, 1899-1901.
14. Public Archives of Canada, Frontier College Papers,132, Annual Report, 1913.
15. Public Archives of Canada, Frontier College Papers, 186, Joe Wearing to Alfred Fitzpatrick, Oct. 6, 1911.
16. Public Archives of Canada, Frontier College Papers, 11, Miss McMechan to Foreman Robinson, Victoria Harbour Lumber Company, Whitefish, Ontario, Oct. 11, 1911.
17. *Ibid.*
18. Public Archives of Canada, Frontier College Papers, 186, Miss McMechan to Alfred Fitzpatrick, Oct. 12, 1911.
19. Public Archives of Canada, Frontier College Papers, 11, H.N. Bethune to Miss McMechan, Nov. 12, 1911.
20. Fitzpatrick, "The Diffusion of Education", Public Archives of Canada, Frontier College Papers, 132, Annual Report, 1911.
21. Public Archives of Canada, Frontier College Papers, 11, H.N. Bethune to Miss McMechan, Nov. 12, 1911.
22. Public Archives of Canada, Frontier College Papers, 139, E. Bradwin to A. Fitzpatrick, Nov. 30, 1911.
23. Archives of Ontario, Records of the Education Department, 52, E. Bradwin to Instructors, Dec. 19, 1911.
24. Public Archives of Canada, Frontier College Papers, 11, H.N. Bethune to A. Fitzpatrick, Dec. 31, 1911.
25. Fitzpatrick, "The Immigrant", Public Archives of Canada, Frontier College Papers, 132, Annual Report, 1912.

26. Public Archives of Canada, Frontier College Papers, 11, H.N. Bethune to A. Fitzpatrick, Dec. 31, 1911.
27. Public Archives of Canada, Frontier College Papers, 186, A. Fitzpatrick to Miss McMechan, Feb. 16, 1912.
28. Public Archives of Canada, Frontier College Papers, 11, A. Fitzpatrick to H.N. Bethune, Mar. 14, 1911.
29. Public Archives of Canada, Frontier College Papers, 11, H.N. Bethune to A. Fitzpatrick, July 10, 1912.
30. Fitzpatrick, "The Diffusion of Education", *op. cit.*

* * *

Abstract

Frontier College, where Bethune served as a labourer-teacher from September 1911 to March 1912, was established in 1899, initially as the Reading Camp Association. Its founder, Alfred Fitzpatrick, had realized that a missionary's occasional sermon in a lumber camp in Northern Ontario was ineffective in instructing lumberjacks and miner, and that what was needed was instruction by someone who would live with them and teach them, too. For Fitzpatrick, educational work was "more or less religious" and the objective in life was to serve others. He worked tirelessly for this objective. Joined by Edward Bradwin, Fitzpatrick saw his work grow to such an extent that, by 1913, eight provincial governments were supporting his Reading Camps and 79 labourer-teachers were working in eight provinces in mining, lumber and hydro-electric camps. Fitzpatrick needed young educated men and women to provide a good influence supervising and teaching in the camp reading rooms, and one of these persons was Bethune. He joined a lumber camp near Whitefish, Ontario, and, working as a labourer, taught reading, writing and other subjects and gave religious instruction also. Bethune was recognized as one of a group of excellent labourer-teachers that the Reading Camp Association could rely on. Service to others and a readiness to share with others were evident in Bethune in 1911 and 1912, as they became increasingly later in his career.

Résumé

Norman Bethune travailla, de septembre 1911 à mars 1912, comme ouvrier-instituteur, au Frontier College *qu'Alfred Fitzpatrick avait fondé en 1899 sous le nom de* Reading Camp Association. *Fitzpatrick en était venu à la conclusion que les sermons que prononçaient les missionnaires de passage dans les camps de bûcherons du Nord de l'Ontario, ne contribuaient que fort peu à l'instruction des mineurs. Il paraissait plus fructueux de leur faire donner un enseignement soutenu par des maîtres qui partageraient leur vie au camp tout en leur enseignant. Pour Fitzpatrick, l'enseignement était une vocation à caractère quasi religieux et le dévouement la raison d'être de la vie. Il travailla sans relâche à cette cause. Assisté d'Edmund Bradwin, il vit son oeuvre croître à tel point qu'en 1913 ses* Reading Camps *recevaient l'assistance de huit gouvernements provinciaux; 79 travailleurs-enseignants étaient à l'oeuvre dans les camps de mineurs, de bûcherons et d'ouvriers des barrages hydro-électriques établis dans huit provinces. Fitzpatrick voulait des jeunes gens instruits qui exerceraient une bonne influence tout en enseignant dans les camps; Bethune fut un de ceux-là. Pendant six mois, il travailla comme journalier dans un camp de bûcherons près de Whitefish, en Ontario, tout en enseignant la lecture, l'écriture et d'autres matières en plus de donner des cours de religion. Il faisait partie d'un groupe de travailleurs-enseignants sur lesquels le* Reading Camp Association *pouvait compter. Son dévouement, son empressement à partager étaient déjà évidents en 1911 et 1912, comme ils continueraient de l'être tout au long de sa carrière.*

Frontier College Today:
From Norman Bethune's Times to the Present

Jack Pearpoint

In considering Norman Bethune's work as a labourer-teacher with Frontier College, which has been described in detail by Marjorie Zavitz Robinson[1], I relate experiences of early labourer-teachers, such as those of Bethune, to today's realities — parallel challenges faced by Bethune in 1911 and by the College in the 1980s. To do this I will share two simple fantasies. The first is that Frontier College had an important formative influence on Bethune. The history of Frontier College is an action statement of commitment to people — Canada's most underutilized renewable resource. The concept of the labourer-teacher, one of the delivery techniques pioneered by Frontier College, was an innovative response to one of Canada's most intractable educational shortfalls. My fantasy is that this concept, embedded in Bethune's consciousness, was part of the concept of the 'bare-foot doctor' — the 'worker-healer' — that has produced the most significant public health revolution of this century in the People's Republic of China. My second fantasy is that, were Bethune young today, he would re-apply to Frontier College. Perhaps this is more than a fantasy because the values upheld by the College since 1899 are unchanged. Programs have altered and technologic developments have been revolutionary, but many of the fundamental problems — the human problems — are still with us. Thus, Frontier College still offers programs in basic literacy and educational upgrading for workers in rail gangs, logging camps and mines. Remarkably, 1,000,000 adult Canadians still cannot read and write and another 4,000,000 have problems in functioning at the basic levels demanded by our highly technological society[2].

As we enter the 1980s, a "quantum" shift is underway in the world. Virtually every aspect of our society is under review and is being challenged — globally, nationally, provincially, and locally. Wherever and however the questions arise, they are fundamentally questions about our values and principles. What kind of people are we? What kind of society do we want? For many, the questions and the implications, the staggering imminence of what is presently the "unknown" and, often, the "unknowable", are frightening. We are conditioned by international information 'overkill' to react, to retract, and to be defensive. We are so overburdened with bad news that we are too exhausted to see the constructive, exciting and creative opportunities that are the *alter ego* of our global crisis. Frontier College is not exempt from these pressures. The whole field of education is traumatized, as a revolution in communications has outmoded fundamental components of the education structure before it even acknowledged the challenge. The learning needs of the next century are here two decades early, and no one of us is adequately prepared.

* * *

In this turbulent environment, Frontier College stands fast and unshaken, because the principles and values that Alfred Fitzpatrick, its founder, articulated in 1899 are still tried and true. He saw education as a "window on the world", and never limited his vision to mere "schooling". He spoke about literacy and about access to education as a way of giving people control of their lives. Frontier College programs were, and still are, an invitation to citizen participation. It was, and is, an organization committed to working with people: people who slip through the cracks; people whose needs are unmet; and people who are missed by the traditional system. Frontier College began with that commitment of *service to and with people.* From those principles evolved the labourer-teacher, the homestead visitors, correspondence education, regional and mobile libraries and community education. Although the list should not and will not stop now, there is no question that the work of the labourer-teacher is the most dramatic and undiluted application of the principles. But it is only one of the *techniques* of delivery of service developed and implemented by Frontier College today.

As technological developments rapidly alter the very concept of work, Frontier College once again is rising to the greater and more complex challenge of the 1980s, falling back to basic principles in order to redesign its delivery systems. It is not giving up on the labourer-teacher, because it works. Every summer sees the return of the rail gangs and of our sweaty workers who teach at the end of a day of arduous labour. But today there are other needy groups. The involvement in rail gangs, camps and mines was not focussed on railroads, forestry or mining corporations, but on the needs of people. The focus today is still on people's needs, though some of the people form new groups. Thus, the College works today with and for aboriginal Canadians. Responsive to their needs, we provide upgrading, teach management or help to initiate small businesses. In jails, which house another disadvantaged community, we are modeling a range of programs that ultimately lead to jobs. For injured workers, we have also piloted a program in trying to create educational alternatives for workers deprived of their livelihoods by accidents. And for the physically disabled, based on our experience in creating small businesses in Native communities and for ex-inmates, we are demonstrating business opportunities. Independent enterprises allow them to regain their self-confidence and independence, and to participate again as full human beings and citizens rather than as defective automatons requiring institutionalization. With this wider variety of needs and target populations, today's projects frequently require more specialized experience and longer service on the part of field workers, often up to 2 years. The statistics indicate a substantial interest in providing the appropriate educational service that will meet the needs of these largely neglected groups.

* * *

In 1980, from nearly 800 applicants, over 140 men and women, ranging in age from 18 to 73 years, worked with Frontier College and covered both the geographic and social frontiers of service. Basic upgrading and literacy programs were implemented for adults in locations as diverse as, for loggers and miners, the Queen Charlotte Islands, for women workers, Red Lake, Ontario and, for the physically disabled adults, metropolitan Toronto. Small business support has covered places ranging from Pelly Crossing on the Dempster Highway in the Yukon, to Stanley Mission in northern Saskatchewan, and to North West River in Labrador. The job placement program for ex-offenders in the Kingston area has completed 1,100 part-time and 400 full-time placements in 2 1/2 years, with only 15 people returning to jail. And, in Winnipeg, a juvenile diversion program has just been successfully handed over to the John Howard Society for long-term implementation.

The success of its new programs in the 1970s has accorded Frontier College fresh recognition of its capacity to adapt its educational and organizational methods to changing perceptions of need. This has been its role, in fact, since the beginning of the century — to initiate and innovate, to test new models and, in due course, to transfer responsibility for programs to others to apply it more widely. Recently, in order to plan its new projects most effectively, the College has been experimenting with arrangements to draw on the pooled wisdom of field workers and their regional supervisors, with their sensitive awareness of people's needs, along with the skills of innovative specialists in adult education and community development; the whole has been coordinated by an experienced administrative staff and backed by a supportive Board of Governors. With this combination, we are confident that the College will meet the new challenges that lie ahead, whether from the new educational electronics or changes in the social scene. The principles of Frontier College, therefore, are unchanged — only the details of our delivery have been updated. We believe that all people have the right to be full participants in their society — and with dignity. The fact that many of us failed to maximize our first opportunities is no reason to deny a second. Many of us did not learn to swim or drive on our first attempt — but we got a second chance. Frontier College is still committed to creating "second chance" learning opportunities. We can model and demonstrate by our *actions* what can be done.

No words better summarize what we are jointly grappling with than Fitzpatrick's on the profound philosophical challenge in the mandate of Frontier College. He believed that "wherever and whenever men shall have the occasion to congregate, then and there should be the time and means of their education"[3].

* * *

Frontier College was an inspiration to Bethune— as Bethune is to us today. Frontier College then was people, concerned about and involved with people, as it still is. A Chinese proverb sums up the intensely personal education philosophy that has universal validity, and on which Frontier College programs, old and new, are based.

Tell me — I will forget,
Show me — I may remember,
Involve me and I will understand.

* * *

REFERENCES AND NOTES

1. See this book, Marjorie Robinson, "Norman Bethune and Frontier College, 1911-1912", pp. 32-39.
2. Audrey M. Thomas, "Adult Basic Education and Literacy Activities in Canada, 1975-1976," World Literature of Canada, Toronto, April 1976.
3. Alfred Fitzpatrick, *University in Overalls,* Toronto, 1923.

* * *

Abstract

The concept of the labourer-teacher, which led Alfred Fitzpatrick to found Frontier College some 80 years ago, appealed to Bethune, and may even have influenced his approach to medical care in China, for the concept of the barefoot doctor was an analogous response to a shortage of personnel in health care. Today, 70 years after Bethune worked as a labourer-teacher with Frontier College, literacy programs are still brought to rail gangs, loggers and miners by the College's labourer-teachers, but their work is only one facet among many activities of the College. Frontier College now assists aboriginal Canadians, prisoners, injured workers and the disabled in upgrading their education and in finding them employment. Thus today, while the programs for delivering education and groups aided have evolved with the times, the principle underlying the work of Frontier has not: the College remains wholly committed to creating "second-chance learning" opportunities.

Résumé

Le concept du travailleur-enseignant, qui poussa Alfred Fitzpatrick à fonder Frontier College *au début du siècle, séduisit Bethune et influença peut-être son approche à la pratique médicale en Chine où le concept du médecin aux pieds nus formait une réponse analogue au manque de spécialistes de la santé. De nos jours, quelques soixante-dix ans après le stage de Bethune en tant que travailleur-enseignant à* Frontier College, *des programmes d'alphabétisme sont toujours offerts aux travailleurs des chemins de fer, aux bûcherons et aux mineurs, mais ils ne constituent qu'une facette des multiples activités du Collège.* Frontier College *aide maintenant les Amérindiens, les prisonniers, les accidentés de travail et les handicapés à parfaire leur éducation et à trouver de l'emploi. Ainsi aujourd'hui, alors que les programmes éducationnels et les groupes auxquels ils s'adressent ont évolué avec le temps, les principes qui inspirent le travail du Collège restent les mêmes: le Collège demeure entièrement engagé à procurer l'opportunité d'une "seconde chance d'apprendre".*

Battlefield Surgery and
the Stretcher-bearers' Experience

Charles G. Roland

When Norman Bethune wrote of "the blood-bespattered faces of the dead"[1], fallen in battle, he spoke of faces he knew. One year before graduating in medicine, Bethune enlisted at Valcartier on September 8, 1914, in the Field Ambulance, and with his unit reached France in February 1915[2]. Soon he saw his idealistic images washed away by the mud and blood of the trenches. "The slaughter," he wrote, "has begun to appal me... I see little of war's glory, and most of war's waste."[3]

The slaughter in the trenches of Flanders was exquisitely evident to the stretcher-bearers, committed to the most forward positions and constantly confronted with war's waste, as represented by maimed and broken bodies that must be carried to safety. This was the slaughter that Bethune recoiled from, during his short period of duty. For on April 29, 1915, at the Second Battle of Ypres — just 1 week after the Germans first used poison gas there — he was wounded by shrapnel in the left leg. Most combatants came to pray for a wound just serious enough to get them back to England — a "Blighty" as it was called. This was Bethune's "Blighty" that would take him out of the trenches. When he returned, in 1917, it was to much cleaner, if not necessarily safer, service as a surgeon in the navy.

* * *

Organization in the Field

The field ambulance to which Bethune was attached, a unit of recent birth, dated back in its modern form only to the Boer War. During the First World War, the field ambulance contained, at full strength, 9 officers and 238 other ranks, plus 15 riding horses, 39 draught horses, and 7 motorized ambulances[4]. Within the field ambulance, the men were assigned to one of two units, the stretcher-bearers or the tent division. Further subdivision permitted the function of three sections, containing members of both the bearer and the tent divisions, and each capable of setting up and conveying casualties to a hospital accommodating 50 patients. Thus the field ambulance as a whole could provide for 150 patients[5]; it was a mobile unit that moved with the front line and operated immediately behind it. In addition to manpower, transporting the wounded also was done with horsed and with motorized ambulances, both of which had special advantages and were used throughout the war[6].

But this organization was the second line of medical care. Regimental medical officers and regimental stretcher-bearers made up the first and most advanced line (Fig. 1). Each battalion had its own medical officers and its own stretcher-bearers. These front-line bearers might be volunteers or they might have been assigned to the task; they might have had some training prior to their service but usually had not[7]. But they were rank and file from the individual regiment and

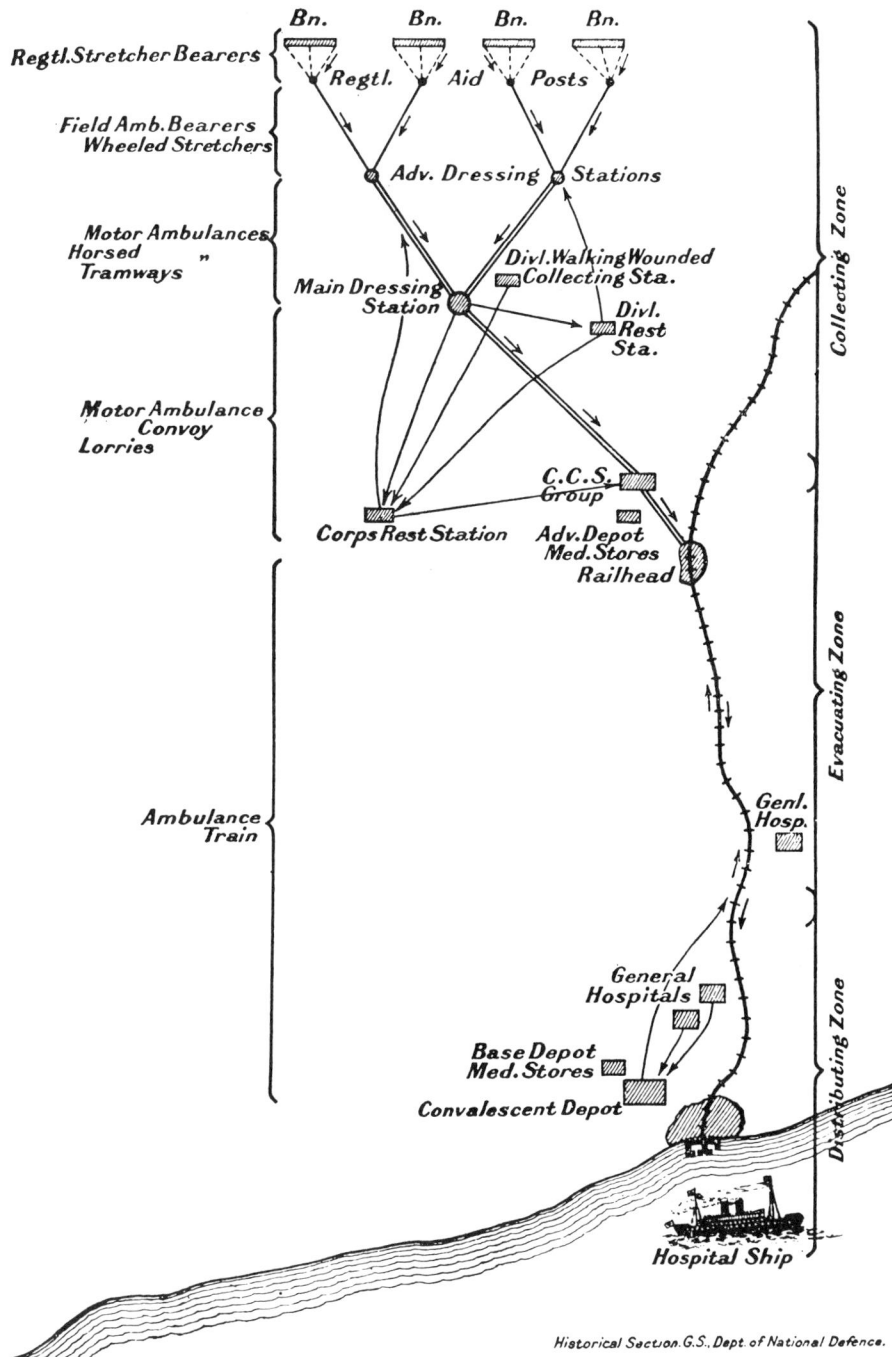

Fig. 1. Schematic diagram of medical arrangements in the field during World War I. (From A.E. Snell: *The C.A.M.C. With the Canadian Corps During the Last Hundred Days of the Great War*, Ottawa, 1924, p. 11.)

aided friends and comrades. Their chief responsibility was to deliver casualties to the Regimental Aid Post. Thereafter, casualties were the responsibility of the bearers specifically carrying out that role within the Canadian Army Medical Corps, the Royal Army Medical Corps, or analogous formation.

The Second Battle of Ypres, in which Bethune was wounded, may be used to illustrate the system of organization. Men wounded by enemy action would apply dressings themselves or have them applied by comrades or by the regimental stretcher-bearers. These men became skilled in such work — Macphail recorded that "it was quite common to pass patients all the way to the casualty clearing station without any disturbance of the first dressing."[8] These dressings were too small for many of the ghastly wounds inflicted, and the bearers supplemented their supplies by tearing up sheets and other materials[9]. A bearer wrote that "stretcher-bearers don't carry morphine; they carry — I carry — bandages, dressings (shell and field), iodine which I slosh liberally on every wound, a pair of scissors, and sometimes a little sal volatile. That's all."[10]

So expert did bearers become at dressing wounds that often they were employed at that task alone. Thus a battalion would at times retain the bearers in the forward trenches to apply dressings and would detail other men from the platoons to act as stretcher-bearers[11].

Casualties who were unable to walk would be carried by the regimental stretcher-bearers to the Regimental Aid Post. Bethune's unit, the 2nd Field Ambulance, served the 2nd Brigade on the right at Ypres; that brigade was holding its section of the line with two battalions, each of which would have a Regimental Aid Post, perhaps on Gravenstafel Ridge or in St. Julien (Fig. 2). At the Regimental Aid Post the regimental medical officer examined each patient and adjusted or changed his dressing, if necessary giving him morphine to relieve pain. The wounded man was tagged with his identity, diagnosis and medication, given hot drinks and stimulants, and made as comfortable as possible pending evacuation[12].

That evacuation would be made, often necessarily under the protective cover of darkness, to the Advanced Dressing Station. The Advanced Dressing Station of the 2nd Field Ambulance was located in the village of Wieltje, 2 miles from Ypres and about 3 miles from the trenches. Those who could, walked, and the remainder were removed on stretchers by men of the bearer's section of the field ambulance — Bethune and his mates — or in the motorized or horse-drawn ambulances. Wieltje is of interest in Canadian military history, for it was during this battle, on April 25, that a Montreal native, Capt. F.A.C. Scrimger, performed feats of gallantry in moving casualties through heavy shellfire to the Advanced Dressing Station at Wieltje, and became the first member of the Canadian Army Medical Corps to be awarded the Victoria Cross[13]. This same frightful battle gave rise to the most famous poem to come out of World War I, John McCrae's "In Flanders' Fields." There were 5,500 Canadian casualties during this battle[14].

After receiving appropriate treatment, the wounded next travelled to the

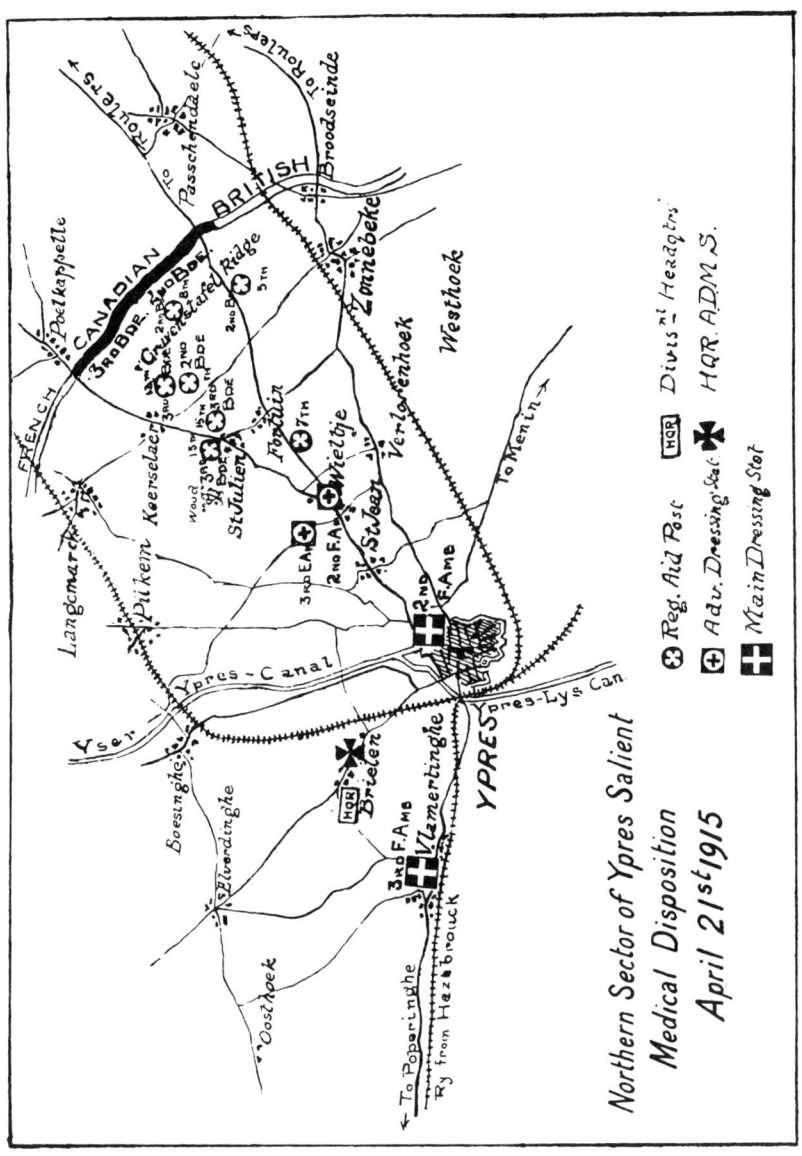

Fig. 2. Medical dispositions in the Ypres area, April 21, 1915. (From J.G. Adami: *War Story of the Canadian Army Medical Corps*, Toronto, 1918, facing p. 99.)

Main Dressing Station, recently evacuated from the outskirts of Ypres to the village of Brielen. From the main dressing station, the wounded would then be taken to casualty clearing stations and hence to general military hospitals.

Conditions in the dressing stations were appalling. One medical officer, after the Second Battle of Ypres, gave this account:

> ... one never-ending stream which lasted day and night for seven days without cessation: in all some five thousand two hundred cases passed through our hands. Wounds here, wounds there, wounds everywhere. Legs, feet, hands missing, bleeding stumps controlled by rough tourniquets; large portions of the abdominal wall shot away; face horribly mutilated; bones shattered to pieces; holes that you could put your clenched fist into, filled with dirt, mud, bits of equipment and clothing until it all became like a hideous nightmare, as if we were living in the seventh hell of the damned[15].

* * *

"Stretchers Stiff and Bleared with Blood"[16]

This was an officer speaking, an officer who served in the relatively protected area of a Main Dressing Station. What of the stretcher-bearers themselves? (Fig. 3). They laboured in situations almost indescribable. There was, of course, the endless cacophony of pistols and rifles, machine-guns, mortars, grenades,

Fig. 3 Stretcher bearers in Flanders. *Courtesy of Imperial War Museum, London* Q-1332.

bombs, and howitzers — noise so horrific that men often were deafened permanently. Nor did these deadly missiles spare the bearers. There is some evidence that, early in the war, the Germans avoided firing on stretcher parties, but this did not last many months. Soon, accounts were heard of stretcher-bearers pinned down, in a shell crater, with the wounded they sought to aid, for as long as 3 days before managing to escape[17]. Other confrontations ended more tragically. In one French company, a *poilu* (French soldier) was wounded while reconnoitering the German trenches; two comrades were themselves wounded while trying to aid him. After dark, two more men set out and were promptly wounded in turn, bringing to five the total of men "crying to their comrades to come and save them." The officer in charge forbade any further effort, but he had no control over two Red Cross *brancardiers* (stretcher-bearers). Now, the account concludes, "*seven* men are still there between friend and foe — but at peace now, God willing."[18] Frank Dunham noted in his diary that of 31 in his group of bearers only 6 survived unscathed; 8 were killed, 9 were wounded (of whom two lost legs), and 8 were taken prisoners of war[19].

Getting away from the front meant traversing a landscape of surrealistic danger and disorder. The mud pervades the recollections of most front-line soldiers (Fig. 4). In the Verdun area, the chaplain recorded seeing " ... the spectacle of a horse, still harnessed to its wagon, struggling in the mud of a huge

Fig. 4 No. 16 Canadian Machine-Gun Company, Passchendaele, November 1917. *National Photography Collection, Public Archives of Canada.* PA 2162.

crater. He had been there for two nights, sinking deeper and deeper, but the troops, obsessed by their own suffering, passed by without so much as casting a glance at the wretched beast."[20] On the Somme, trenches were knee-deep with gluey mud. The sides of the trenches were full of buried or partially buried corpses. The stench was revolting. The stretcher-bearer had a grim task:

> As one was carrying a wounded man down one perhaps got stuck in the mud, and staggered whilst one extricated one's self . . . You put out a hand to steady yourself, the earth gave way and you found you were clutching the blackened face of a half-buried German . . . Mingled with the odour of putrefying flesh was always the odour of powder; a heavy, sickening stench in itself. Sometimes we used to risk being shelled and got out on top[21].

But getting out on top carried obvious and often fatal risks. One Canadian stretcher-bearer tried to tell his wife what he was experiencing:

> I leave you to imagine what it's like, getting a wounded man out. The stretcher is wider than the trench. One night we got on top to carry; we stayed about a minute. The first flare to come over, and he got after us with both whizz bangs and heavies . . . Well, we got out. Our stretcher cases were alive, and our 'walkers' too. Going down the main trench, he shelled us all the way. It was the night of the relief, and we passed them coming up. Imagine that, too, if you can. The men hurrying, cursing, with sobbing breath, coming up; and we trying to get down with our stretchers. Telephone wires across the trench everywhere. I dunno' *how* it's done; but it is[22].

But sometimes it was not done. Sixty years and more later, workers in Flanders frequently find those still classified officially as Missing: " . . . half-hidden in a shell-hole the tableau of three skeletons — of two stretcher-bearers and the casualty they were carrying, all killed by the same shell."[23]

What is hardest to comprehend, perhaps, after all these years — as the ranks of those who were there thin rapidly — is the way it felt to a stretcher-bearer. We know that the illusions of glory faded quickly. Volunteering for the front was easy in Canada, much harder in England[24]. Being a stretcher-bearer was seen quickly to be a rotten job, but fortunately more than one man thought that he would be more use binding up wounds than "just carrying a gun in the ordinary way."[25]

One anonymous writer has described the physical strain that was so much a part of the job.

> Stretcher-bearing is a severe strain on a man's physique. It is no easy matter to carry a patient weighing twelve stones [76 kg] or more for a distance of over half-a-mile [approximately 1 km]. And when this is done all day and all night too, the whole body soon becomes a mass of aches and pains. The shoulders suffer most, becoming sore almost beyond endurance, and no adjusting of the slings will ease them. The wrists ache also and the hands develop an uncomfortable roughness. Then the leg muscles begin to give way, and at each step sharp pains are felt in the thigh and calf. As a last straw to the bearer's burden, his feet fail him, and blisters come to add to his torture. The strain on the nerves is no less severe. It is often necessary to walk along roads that are peppered by machine-gun fire, or to pass batteries which the enemy is shelling. If one were alone it would be possible to fall to the ground on first hearing the racket of the machine-gun or the whistle of the shell, or to run to shelter if the place became 'too hot.' But when carrying a case this cannot be done. One must keep hold of the stretcher and go slowly

and steadily, ignoring the impulses to fall or run. Thus, face to face with danger, the heart beats fast and the sweat oozes from the body, and, when the journey is over, sometimes the limbs tremble like young trees in the wind. These are the common, everyday trials[26].

* * *

Casualties

Several references have been made to the violent death of stretcher-bearers and other medical personnel. The casualty figures are expressive. In the Canadian medical services, 504 officers, nursing sisters, and other ranks were killed or died of wounds, and 694 were wounded; in a total group of 1198 casualties, the fatality was 42%. By comparison, of the total casualties to all Canadian forces overseas, the fatality was 28%[27].

From these figures one can, perhaps, conclude that the medical services were subject to unusually hazardous conditions. The statistics do not distinguish stretcher-bearers among the 1042 "other ranks" killed or wounded, but they certainly would be numbered in the hundreds; and these figures refer only to members of the Canadian Army Medical Corps. Regimental stretcher-bearers were included in battalion returns and were rarely identified as bearers; details pertaining to them thus are lost to statistical analysis. In Dunham's group, the casualty rate reached 80%; how typical this experience was, we do not know.

* * *

Norman Bethune's Experience

We also do not know where Bethune's experience in France coincided with this general description and where it did not. Any accounts of his months there seem to have gone unrecorded, or the record is lost. Certainly he saw some of these sights, felt some of these emotions. How was he affected?

He did write that he was appalled by the terrible waste. His professional career can be seen as a struggle to prevent such waste, both as a civilian surgeon and more particularly as a military surgeon. And it was in warfare that Bethune's international reputation was founded — ensuring blood for the wounded in Spain, operating upon the wounded in China. To this endeavour he brought not only his political commitment, his social convictions, and his professional training; he brought also an image of the shattered bodies at Ypres.

* * *

Acknowledgement

Some of the research for this chapter was supported by a grant from the John P. McGovern Foundation, Houston, Texas.

* * *

REFERENCES AND NOTES

1. Bethune's poem, "Red Moon," is quoted in F.H. Fish: "Dr. Norman Bethune, 1889-1939," *Calgary Associate Clinical History Bulletin* 10 (1946); pp. 151-159. See this book p. 107.
2. Roderick Stewart, Ted Allan and Sydney Gordon, *Bethune*. Toronto, 1973, p. 7.
3. Cited in T. Allan and S. Gordon: *The Scalpel, the Sword: The Story of Dr. Norman Bethune*, Boston, 1952, pp. 14-15.

4. Andrew Macphail, *Official History of the Canadian Forced in the Great War, 1914-19: The Medical Services,* Ottawa, 1925, p. 68.
5. *Ibid.,* p. 67.
6. *Ibid.,* p. 69.
7. For example, Frank Dunham, a private in the 1/7th London Regiment, responded to a call for specialists and became a bearer, in France, because he had obtained a first aid certificate from the British Red Cross Society. R.H. Haigh and P.W. Turner (eds.), *The Long Carry: The Journal of Stretcher Bearer Frank Dunham, 1916-18,* Oxford, 19, p. 9.
8. *Ibid.,* p. 134.
9. William Charles Adair, Interview recorded by C.G. Roland, Sunnybrook Hospital, 4 July 1979.
10. R.A.L., *Letters of a Canadian Stretcher Bearer,* Toronto, 1918, p. 222.
11. J.G. Adami, *War Story of the Canadian Army Medical Corps,* Toronto, n.d. [1918?], pp. 87-88.
12. G.W.L. Nicholson, *Seventy Years of Service: A History of the Royal Canadian Army Medical Corps,* Ottawa, 1977, p. 82.
13. *Ibid.,* p. 84.
14. Macphail, *op. cit.,* p. 35.
15. Cited *Ibid.,* p. 85.
16. R.W. Service, *Rhymes of a Red Cross Man,* Toronto, 1916, p. 7.
17. A. Jobson, *Via Ypres: Story of the 39th Divisional Field Ambulance,* London, n.p., 1934, p. 72.
18. Anonymous, *With the American Ambulance Field Service in France,* N.P., 2nd. edit., 1916, pp. 133-134.
19. Haigh and Turner, p. 44.
20. A. Horne: *The Price of Glory: Verdun 1916,* Harmondsworth, 1964, p. 199.
21. A. Jobson, p. 71.
22. R.A.L., pp. 194-195.
23. A. Horne, p. 352.
24. R.A.L., p. 15.
25. *Ibid.,* p. 107.
26. J. Telfer and A.V. Fox (eds.), *Splints and Splinters: Notes and Reminiscences of the 102nd Field Ambulance, R.A.M.C.,* Glasgow, n.d., p. 62.
27. Percentages derived from data in Macphail, pp. 248 and 250.

* * *

Abstract

In 1914, Bethune interrupted his medical studies to become a stretcher bearer with the Canadian army in France. After 3 months in the field he was wounded and invalided home, where he continued his studies. Although he left no record of his experiences in France, Bethune was appalled by the war's wastage of lives, and his work as a stretcher bearer inevitably influenced his later career in Spain and in China. He knew "the blood-bespattered faces of the dead" and the suffering of the wounded. He gained an understanding, too, of the problems of transporting the wounded from the front line to sites where they could be treated. Bethune served in the 2nd Field Ambulance, which served the 2nd Brigade during the second battle of Ypres; he found himself, therefore, in the thick of battle. Bethune's international reputation is based largely on his skill as a military surgeon in Spain and China, and to his work there he brought not only the political commitment, social convictions and professional training that informed his philosophy, but also the image of the shattered bodies imprinted in his memory from his experience at Ypres years earlier.

Résumé

En 1914, Norman Bethune interrompit ses études pour devenir brancardier dans l'armée canadienne en France. Après trois mois passés au front, il fut blessé et ramené au pays où il reprit ses études de médecine. Bien que Bethune n'ait laissé aucun témoignage sur ce séjour en France, il a été profondément marqué par le nombre impressionnant de pertes de vie et sa carrière a été grandement influencée par son expérience de la guerre, en particulier par celle qu'il a eue au moment de la guerre d'Espagne et du conflit sino-japonais. "Les visages des morts éclaboussés de sang" et les souffrances des blessés lui étaient devenus familiers. Il avait appris à organiser le transport des blessés, du front au poste de secours du régiment, de là au poste de secours avancé, puis au poste d'évacuation et, enfin, à l'hôpital militaire. Au cours de la deuxième bataille d'Ypres, Bethune avait été de service dans la deuxième ambulance de campagne attachée à la Deuxième brigade; il s'était donc trouvé au coeur de la mêlée. La réputation internationale de Bethune est due à la dextérité dont il a fait preuve comme chirurgien militaire en Espagne et en Chine. Son labeur dans ces pays s'est appuyé sur son engagement politique, ses convictions humanitaires et sa formation professionnelle, qui formaient les trois aspects de sa philosophie, ainsi que sur l'image des corps souffrants qu'il avait soulagés, plusieurs années auparavant, à Ypres.

From "A Social Disease with a Medical Aspect" to "A Medical Disease with a Social Aspect": Fighting the White Plague in Canada, 1900-1940

Katherine McCuaig

"To attack... the prevalence of tuberculosis," the Chief Medical Officer of the federal Department of the Interior, Peter H. Bryce, sternly instructed the Commission of Conservation for Canada in 1910, "is to lay down a programme dealing with milk and meat foods, the housing problem, and indeed, with every sphere of human activity...".[1] In the decade and a half before the First World War, anti-tuberculosis work in Canada was simply one more cause in an urban reform movement bent on improving all facets of Canadian society. Koch had isolated the bacillus in 1882, but as yet there was no vaccine, and the only cure consisted of Osler's "fresh air, good food, good houses and hope." It was preeminently, as he observed, "a social disease with a medical aspect."[2] With the First World War, however, this changed; the campaign became increasingly bacteriologically oriented, and the focus shifted to attacking the *germ* as the fundamental cause of the disease, so that by the 1930s Osler's dictum had been reversed: tuberculosis had evolved into a *medical* disease with a *social* aspect.

* * *

Beginning in 1896 with the National Sanatarium Association in Ontario, lay and medical reformers had begun to unite to form local voluntary societies across the country to tackle the problem, affiliating with the national organization, the Canadian Association for the Prevention of Consumption and Other Forms of Tuberculosis, founded in 1901. Chronically short of funds, but with a sense of mission, idealism and enthusiasm inspired by the social gospel, reformers usually focused first on erecting sanatoria, often little more than shacks and tents, but campaigned as well for legislation to eliminate first the germ, and, second, the social conditions that fostered the disease. Thus they waged an unceasing war against indiscriminate spitting, the common drinking cup, dry sweeping, flies, dip tanks and impure milk, as well as poor housing, long working hours, low wages, overcrowding, poor nutrition and alcoholism. And since nearly every Canadian was infected by adulthood but not all succumbed to the disease, it seemed obvious, as one Toronto physician observed, that the germ was merely "a cause", but not "the only cause" of tuberculosis[3].

With limited financial resources, anti-tuberculosis volunteers began to establish an institutional framework in which to carry out a simple treatment of fresh air, good food and, more important after 1910, rest. There were only 1800 sanatorium beds in Canada by 1914[4], but these were of no practical value to the urban poor, who could not afford to stop working and take the cure anyway, even if beds had been available; so the dispensary was developed to examine suspects, supervise the patient at home with a visiting nurse, and supply relief. Beginning in 1904 in Montreal, it became the bedrock of the campaign there, and extended to all major centres in the country. With the same cure in mind, "open air" classrooms, forest schools and preventoria were established toward the end of the first decade to improve the health of weak or susceptible children, in order that they might not fall prey to the disease. In sum, then, the prewar fight against tuberculosis was, as the superintendent of the Mountain sanatorium later commented, "primarily a humanitarian movement of lay people."[5]

The Great War profoundly altered the campaign, and emphasized the magnitude of the tuberculosis problem in Canada: while roughly 50,000 Canadian soldiers had been killed in action or had died of war wounds, at home almost the same number had died of the disease during the war period[6]. The more tangible results of the war, however, were the easily visible changes in diagnosis and treatment, and the expansion of institutional facilities. Soldiers were examined earlier than civilians generally were; and with complications resulting from gassing, war wounds, trench fever and even the influenza epidemic, an accurate diagnosis was not only more difficult, but more important, for fully one third of the tuberculous soldiers returned to Canada were later proven not to have the disease at all. And their disability pension depended on the doctor's decision[7].

The Military Hospitals Commission had arranged with existing sanatoria to treat tuberculous soldiers from their areas. To help deal with this sudden influx of patients, the federal government increased accommodation and laboratories, and radiographic, surgical and dental facilities, spending roughly $3,500,000 on capital account alone by 1925, and an additional half a million dollars for hospital equipment. It also pioneered occupational therapy, later extended to civilians, at a cost of $900,000, to reduce the tedium of the treatment routine, and so cut down on drunkenness and insubordination[8]. Federal involvement therefore not only added to postwar civilian accommodation and programmes, but was a factor changing the sanatoria from glorified summer camps into hospital-like institutions with specialized staff and departments; and, more important, it both permitted and encouraged the campaign in general to become more bacteriologically and technologically oriented.

Partly as a result of the war, there was a profound change in Canadians' attitudes. Science in general flourished in the 1920s, encouraged by the National Research Council; "as religion and the humanities declined in popular influence", noted W.L. Morton, "science succeeded them, not only as a material utility, but also as a world view."[9] The tuberculosis campaign's bacteriological and technological orientation, then, merely reflected the prevailing mood of the times. In addition, there was a growing acceptance, demonstrated by the passage of the Old Age Pension Act in 1927, that patchwork private charity was simply not enough. This, too, was mirrored in the anti-tuberculosis campaign — for the Department of Soldiers Civil Re-establishment's comprehensive care of tuberculous soldiers clearly showed what the government *could* do, if it so desired, as well as what *should* be done for Canadian civilians. "With this effective organization of treatment for military consumptives before our eyes," wrote the *Hamilton Times,* "it will be absolutely inexcusable if the country fails to organize an equally efficient campaign against the "white plague" among our people as a whole."[10] Associated with this concept of state duty and its responsibility for the public health was a new emphasis on the community rather than the individual, with the bacteriological approach — attacking the *germ* as the cause of the disease — now in the forefront.

Together these were probably the most important results of the war, for as far as tuberculosis was concerned these views were the fundamental attitudes that determined how the disease would be tackled in succeeding decades. No longer, as David Stewart, the superintendent of the Manitoba Sanatorium reflected in 1930, were related social reforms the primary concern of those leading the campaign:

> Twenty years ago or more the first question was, *what* made this man tuberculous — dingy house, foul factory, late hours, dust, drink, bad environment generally? Now the first questions are likely to be: *who* made this man tuberculous? Where has he already scattered his disease? What circle of contacts is he infecting? Then we thought first and foremost of the diseased person, but now usually first and most of the infected community... Cure for the sick man — compassion first — may make the stronger appeal, but cure for the infected community — safety first — pays the bigger dividends[11].

Instead of trying to alter the whole socioeconomic system, or optimistically dispensing relief, then, the specialists focused on eliminating the *germ,* using the growing number of specific techniques and equipment at their disposal. Prevention came to mean *not* the building up of an individual's resistance in an attempt to ward off disease, but the elimination of sources of infection.

* * *

To attack the disease in an organized fashion, however, there was first a stocktaking of the problem. This began with the Saskatchewan Royal Commission in 1921, which reported that, of 1700 children examined, 44% were infected by the age of 6, 60% by 14, and 76% by 18[12]. The Red Cross helped finance surveys of school children across the country from 1923 to 1925. The Quebec Board of Health, the Victoria Medical Society, the Montreal Health Survey Committee, a Health and Hospital Survey Committee in Manitoba and an Ontario Royal Commission on Public Welfare all reported on the tuberculosis problem throughout the decade, which led to a growing public awareness and a demand for solutions.

So specific, bacteriologically oriented, preventive work began. Travelling diagnosticians and extension clinics operating out of sanatoria examined contacts, suspects and select groups, such as school children, to uncover early cases; testing with BCG vaccine, first developed in France, began in infants in Quebec, in 1925; and tuberculin inoculation, a physical examination, a personal history, an examination of sputum, a barium meal, blood tests and, most important of all, radiography, all enabled the chest expert and his associates to pinpoint tuberculosis more accurately, and at an earlier stage. All patients with active disease had to be identified, segregated, and treated — not just for themselves, but to prevent them infecting others.

With regard to therapy, rest became *the* specific treatment: by 1924, 95% of the patients at Muskoka received bed care and, by 1928, a patient was advised to spend at least a year in bed[13]. With mothers' allowances hopelessly inadequate, for most such a period was a frightening prospect. Advocated in addition to bed rest were surgically induced rest for the lungs (therapy that Bethune himself underwent), and mental rest, through occupational therapy, to speed recovery.

With the aggressive case-finding and the emphasis on rest, sanatoria became more essential, and the additional beds available from the wartime building programme along with construction in the 1920s permitted and then reinforced this emphasis. They were fast becoming "big business". By 1927 there were over 5,000 beds in the country, and the estimated replacement value of tuberculosis institutions was $14,500,000[14].

Clinics in turn were evolving into referral centres for these hospital-like sanatoria, as well as following up ex-patients and supervising those who remained at home. They, too, had specialized departments for ear, nose and throat, dental and radiologic work, and for laboratories. Relief was becoming a minor part of dispensary work — its emphasis, like that of the sanatorium, was increasingly bacteriological and technological.

As the cost and size of the tuberculosis programme increased, and as the specialists now began to tackle the rural areas largely ignored in the urban reform era, those concerned with the programme clamoured for more state, particularly provincial, involvement. Volunteer associations could no longer alone support the expanded facilities that the federal government had built. Moreover, it only seemed fair, as Stewart reasoned in 1928, that "as the man is treated to make the state safe, the state should help with the burden of payment."[15] In the 1920s, the provinces were paying the greater share of the capital costs and, together with the municipalities, assuming more of the burden of maintenance costs. Saskatchewan and Manitoba introduced a pool system, which led in the former province to the extension of free treatment to all its residents in 1929. By the end of the decade, maintenance of indigents (which in a loose definition included most patients, as few could finance an extended stay in a sanatorium without help) was, together with a now seemingly chronic bed shortage, the thorniest problem. For Saskatchewan, with its low death rate, offered irrefutable proof that an effective campaign needed an adequate supply of beds maintained at public expense.

In 1932 Stewart estimated that tuberculosis caused Canada to lose 22 lives and one third of a million dollars a day[16]. And the Depression, the specialists gloomily predicted, could only worsen the situation. What it *did* do, however, was to demonstrate with startling clarity how far the campaign had come from the pre-war social reform "cures" of better housing, sanitation and a living wage. Tuberculosis workers were aware of the obvious connection between tuberculosis and poverty — as Grant Fleming observed with good sense in 1935, "anything which improves the economic status of the poor will reduce the number of cases of tuberculosis",[17] a view that Bethune himself held. Yet, as R.G. Ferguson, the medical director of the Saskatchewan Anti-Tuberculosis League pointed out bluntly, "this living standard method of combating tuberculosis has its limitations; it does not prevent infection."[18] It simply gave added protection to the more naturally resistant members of the community, and prevented small infections from developing into disease, but was little help to the non-resistant or those constantly exposed. Most would have agreed with the dogmatic assertion of one Ontario specialist in 1934:

> Tuberculosis comes from tuberculosis and not from coughs or colds or draughts or malnutrition or overcrowding, but from the tubercle bacilli roaming around in the fields of lowered resistance... Eliminate the bacillus and he cannot run amuck. Raise resistance and he finds the battle longer, harder, more expensive and the public pays. We must bottle up bacilli, kill them when we find them and put them out of business. That is our task[19].

As a result, tuberculosis workers, *although concerned as individuals,* left social service and relief work to social workers, service clubs, relief organizations and the government and, *as a group,* concentrated their energies instead on *reducing infection* to eliminate the disease.

* * *

Ironically, then, in the midst of the Depression, specific bacteriologically oriented methods of diagnosis and treatment were relied on more and more to control the disease. The case-finding work begun in the 1920s intensified, as the specialists worked to diagnose and isolate every sufferer with active disease. With the rate of infection falling faster than the death rate in those provinces with adequate accommodation — Saskatchewan, for example, reported that only 14% of urban school children and 7% of rural ones were infected by 1936[20] — tuberculin inoculation was becoming indispensable as a means of exclusion; but radiographs, too, were essential both to find early tuberculosis and to determine the extent of disease, and in these hard times their cost was often prohibitive. A sputum examination was important, not so much in aiding a precise diagnosis but, again, in determining infectivity; for an individual with consistently negative sputum or, better still, none at all, was usually considered to be non-infectious. And *this*, in turn, became important in deciding how long a patient was to be hospitalized. By the end of the decade, "No sputum, no tuberculosis" became for some the slogan of the campaign as more and more they attempted to treat the sick, not simply for the sake of the sick man himself, but to ensure the good health of the community[21].

But non-infection could be a mixed blessing, as the young nurses in training were proving. To the specialists' horror, a Saskatchewan survey revealed that the rate of these women who became ill from tuberculosis in general hospitals was 12 times greater than that of the general population, and 8 times that of normal school students; a New Brunswick study confirmed this[22]. When a person lacked even the dubious minimal resistance that universal infection had once conferred, "any stray outside infection," the superintendent of the Manitoba Sanatorium commented frankly, in 1936, "is a spark in dry grass, not a spark in the rather sodden grass of half or even a quarter of a century ago."[23] And tuberculosis was still the leading cause of death of those between 15 and 45[24]. As the campaign against the disease in the past was at least partially responsible in ensuring that these young adults had grown up unexposed and thus uninfected, the specialists considered themselves duty bound to make sure this protection continued.

Contacts were the most fruitful source of active disease, but there was a growing concern with industrial workers, Indians and hospital employees; at the same time, the more comprehensive investigations of existing programmes and facilities in a given area continued, notably in Vancouver and Montreal. And, although non-infection was the ultimate goal, BCG vaccine began to be used in areas where the campaign had lagged, or in groups particularly infected or exposed; in other words, Quebec, Indians in Saskatchewan, and hospital employees. The surveys of children, however, once so valuable, were fast outliving their usefulness in unearthing much unsuspected disease; by 1940 the Saskatchewan Anti-Tuberculosis League, always in the vanguard, had ceased sponsoring them.

Prolonged bed rest was still the basic treatment for arresting the disease in the 1930s, but it was collapse therapy, particularly artificial pneumothorax and thoracoplasty, that Bethune and other specialists relied on as never before. The development and increasing use of radiography, surgical instruments and techniques, anaesthetic agents and the availability of blood transfusion and facilities for supplying adequate oxygen made surgery not only more practical but more successful; the growing emphasis on non-infection, the high cost of sanatorium accommodation and the shortage of beds all encouraged a more extensive application of this treatment. Collapse therapy offered a speedier recovery, usually stopped hemorrhaging and rendered at least 50% of successful cases sputum-negative[25]. A 1934 study of 460 ex-patients of the Nova Scotia Sanatorium showed that 58% of the patients with moderatley advanced disease and 25% of those with advanced disease who had received artificial pneumothorax were well and working, while only 22% and 5%, respectively, of those who had not received the treatment were well[26]. Moreover, the extension of artificial pneumothorax to the treatment of patients with a relatively good prognosis permitted sanatoria to discharge patients earlier and give them refills as outpatients instead, thus extending their services to a greater number of victims: the Royal Ottawa Sanatorium, for example, reported in 1936 that it cared for almost 50% more than its adult bed capacity in this fashion[27]. Sometimes this was done through a stationary clinic, which was now slowly altering from a diagnostic centre to an institution that was as well a treatment centre for non-infective cases and a clearing-house.

While not a cure-all, then, collapse therapy was definitely advantageous; but not all centres used it as extensively as they should have, Montreal being a notable example. In that city, despite investigations and surveys carried out by various groups since 1910, the mortality from tuberculosis was the highest in Canada after Quebec and Halifax; the rate of 84.9 in 1937 compared particularly unfavourably to that of 35.6 for Toronto, 26.1 for London and 11.9 for Saskatoon[28]. The Tuberculosis Committee of the Montreal Medical Society pointed out that diagnosis here was often made too late for the treatment to be of value, while the serious lack of beds prevented patients from being institutionalized early enough to begin effective treatment. Collapse therapy, then, needed the support of all the other adjuncts to the Canadian Tuberculosis Control programme: beds, clinics, facilities and public health nurses. Where these were available, however, collapse therapy was quickly becoming, after rest, *the* specific treatment. Artificial pneumothorax was attempted in 60% of patients admitted to the Toronto Hospital for Consumptives in the 1930s, 52.8% at Tranquille, B.C., by 1938 and over 80% of the pulmonary patients at the Manitoba Sanatorium in 1936[29].

Sanatoria formed the bedrock of the campaign now, to treat and, most important, to isolate all active cases. The increased specialization and use of surgery had led to higher costs, so that by 1937 roughly $7,000,000 a year was spent on maintenance costs alone, mostly from public funds[30]. More intensive case-finding; a greater desire on the part of patients to be institutionalized when tuberculosis was diagnosed; the belief on the part of physicians that this was the best solution; and the emphasis on segregation to lower the rate of infection and the provinces and municipalities assuming the greater part of the burden for maintenance costs — all this fuelled the demand for more beds and aggravated the shortage. At the beginning of the decade the problem was acute in eastern Ontario, Vancouver, the Maritimes and Quebec, but by the end the situation was particularly serious only in Quebec (especially Montreal). Sometimes the emphasis on community safety had rather inhuman results. In 1939 the British Columbia Tuberculosis Division announced that the only patients to be admitted for treatment were those in whom an element of tuberculosis control existed — non-pulmonary cases, usually non-infectious, were excluded under this ruling[31].

* * *

The Depression brought the general issues of health and welfare to a head in the 1930s but, surprisingly enough considering the social upheaval, human misery and inadequate services, its effect on the anti-tuberculosis campaign was less than might have been expected. There was, understandably, a greater demand for public beds and free clinics, but the falling price of commodities, combined with some staff reductions and a stringent control of expenses, enabled most sanatoria to continue operating at the same level they had in the 1920s, and sometimes even to expand. More important, the Depression brought the problem of indigents and the issue of municipal responsibility and free treatment to a head. In all provinces it was becoming evident, if it was not so already, that municipalities were incapable of shouldering this burden. And it was both wasteful and stupid to pour money into case-finding if the newly discovered sufferers could not be treated. This was confirmed in Ontario where, despite available beds, only a disappointing 53% of the people dying of tuberculosis in 1936 had received sanatorium treatment[32].

Assessment at the end of the 1930s found the situation generally encouraging. Although the problems of accommodation and financing treatment had not been solved in the eastern provinces, particularly Quebec, free treatment had been extended in fact, if not in name, to the residents of Ontario, Manitoba, Saskatchewan, Alberta and British Columbia. Saskatchewan, with its Anti-Tuberculosis League, and Manitoba, with its Sanatorium Board, had already demonstrated the value of unification and central direction, and by 1938 provincial tuberculosis divisions had been established in Nova Scotia, Quebec, Ontario, Alberta and British Columbia to coordinate, organize and supervise tuberculosis services. There were over 10,000 sanatorium beds in the country; the problem of childhood tuberculosis was being reduced to a minor concern; cases were discovered earlier; and individuals were beginning to fall prey to the disease at a later age. But there was a new concern: unprotected youths, such as nurses, were being unwittingly exposed to disease. Rehabilitation still had to be dealt with. And with half of the total expenditure of provincial health departments being required to support the tuberculosis control programme in 1937, specialists were demanding federal grants[33]. Moreover, the optimistic predictions of public health workers in the social reform era that the elimination of tuberculosis, the scourge of youth, would automatically increase the life-span of an individual was not being borne out by the facts: although expectation of life at birth had increased over the past generation due to preventive medicine, the expectation of life for those over 40 had not[34]. Cancer and heart disease were killing increasing numbers.

Nevertheless, most would not have found R.G. Ferguson unduly optimistic in his remarks at the annual meeting of the Canadian Tuberculosis Association in 1936:

> Our first slogan was "Tuberculosis is Curable"; it is now "Tuberculosis can be Prevented", and, for the future, "Tuberculosis can be Eliminated"...
>
> It would seem evident now that the back of the tuberculosis problem has been broken and the way cleared for the final drive for the reduction of this disease to a minor cause of death[35].

* * *

Acknowledgement

I am indebted to Carman Miller for valuable criticism of an earlier draft of this paper.

* * *

REFERENCES AND NOTES

1. Peter H. Bryce, "Maintenance of Public Health, Part II", *Public Health Journal*, I (Nov. 1910), p. 534.
2. Quoted in Marjorie Freeman Campbell, *Holbrook of the San*, Toronto, 1953, p. 57, and Canadian Tuberculosis Association, *Annual Report* (hereafter *C.T.A.A.R.*), 1955, p. 102.
3. Edward Playter, *Consumption: Its Nature, Causes and Prevention*, Toronto, 1895, p. 63.
4. Campbell, p. 97.
5. J.H. Holbrook, "Forty Years of Advance," *Canadian Hospital*, 23, Nov. 1946, p. 30.
6. "Report of the Executive Council," Canadian Association for the Prevention of Tuberculosis, *Annual Report* (hereafter C.A.P.T.A.R.) 1919, p. 14.
7. D.A. Stewart, "Retrospect and Prospect: Tuberculosis Ten Years Ago, Today and Tomorrow", *C.A.P.T.A.R.*, 1920, pp. 21-2. Campbell, p. 137.

8. Public Archives of Canada, Canadian Tuberculosis Association (hereafter *P.A.C., C.T.A.*), II a, file 93, H. Sloman, "Memorandum", (May 4, 1925).
9. W.L. Morton, "The 1920s", *The Canadians: 1867-1967*, Part One, Toronto, 1968, p. 223.
10. "Secretary's Report," *C.A.P.T.A.R.,* 1917, p. 171.
11. Stewart, *Things Old and New*, reprinted from the *Canadian Medical Association Journal*, hereafter *C.M.A.J.,* 24 (1931), pp. 9-16), pp. 5-6.
12. "Report of the Royal Commission in Saskatchewan, Summary of Findings of the Commission in Regard to Tuberculosis," *C.T.A.A.R.,* 1922, pp. 110-111.
13. "Ontario," *C.T.A.A.R.,* 1924, p. 98; "The Laurentian Sanatorium," *C.T.A.A.R.,* 1928, p. 150.
14. "Resident Tuberculosis Treatment Institutions of Canada, 1927", Canadian Tuberculosis Association, *Bulletin* (hereafter *C.T.A.B.*), 7 (Sept. 1923), p. 3.
15. Stewart, "Anti-Tuberculosis Measures in Rural Districts," *C.M.A.J.,* 29 (1928), p. 674.
16. Stewart, "The Challenge of Tuberculosis," *Canadian Public Health Journal* (hereafter *C.P.H.J.*), 23 (1932), p. 113.
17. A. Grant Fleming, *What You Should Know About Tuberculosis*, Toronto, 1935, p. 44.
18. R.G. Ferguson, "Some Fundamentals in Tuberculosis Prevention," *C.P.H.J.,* 29 (1938), p. 204.
19. "Essex County Sanatorium," *C.T.A.A.R.,* 1934, p. 86.
20. "Saskatchewan," *C.T.A.A.R.,* 1936, p. 171.
21. A. Grant Fleming, "The Tuberculosis Problem," *C.T.A.B.,* 19 (June 1941), p. 5.
22. R.G. Ferguson, "Activities in a Province Wide Programme for the Control of Tuberculosis," *C.P.H.J.,* 26 (1935), p. 134; R.J. Collins and C.W. MacMillan, "Tuberculosis and the Student Nurse," *C.M.A.J.,* 34 (1936), pp. 649-54.
23. Stewart, "The Red Man and the White Plague," *C.T.A.A.R.,* 1936, p. 20.
24. Grant Fleming, *What You Should Know About Tuberculosis,* pp. 25-6.
25. *Ibid.,* p. 30. Fleming, "The Tuberculosis Problem," p. 6.
26. "Nova Scotia," *C.T.A.A.R.,* 1934, pp. 67-68.
27. "Royal Ottawa Sanatorium," C.T.A.A.R., 1936, p. 133.
28. "Public Support Sought," *C.T.A.B.,* 17 (June 1939, p. 4. "Tuberculosis in Montreal," *C.T.A.B.,* 17 (Sept.) 1938, p. 3. "Progress in the Cities," *C.T.A.B.,* 18 (Mar.) 1940, p. 3.
29. P.A.C., C.T.A., IIa, file 23, Montreal Medical Society, "Report of Tuberculosis Committee" (1936), pp. 2-3. Godfrey L. Gale and Norman C. Delarue, "Surgical History of Pulmonary Tuberculosis: The Rise and Fall of Various Technical Procedures," *Canadian Journal of Surgery,* 12 (Oct.) 1969, p. 381. D.A. Stewart, "What is New in Tuberculosis?" *C.M.A.J.,* 26 (1932), p. 38. "British Columbia," *C.T.A.A.R.,* 1938, p. 34. "Manitoba," *C.T.A.A.R.,* 1936, p. 60. "National Sanatorium Association." *C.T.A.A.R.,* 1935, pp. 110-111, 115.
30. "Ontario," *C.T.A.A.R.,* 1936, p. 130. "Brief Presented to Rowell Commission," *C.T.A.B.,* 16 (Mar. 1938), p. 3; Fleming, "The Tuberculosis Problem," p. 5.
31. "British Columbia," *C.T.A.A.R.,* 1939, p. 39.
32. Editorial, "Progress in Tuberculosis Control," *C.P.H.J.,* 29 (1938), p. 189.
33. Editorial, "The Need for Federal Government Assistance in Public Health," *C.P.H.J.,* 32 (1941), p. 478.
34. James J. McCann, "Some Public Health Activities and Needs in Ontario," *C.P.H.J.,* 25 (1934), p. 258.
35. R.G. Ferguson, "President's Address," *C.T.A.A.R.,* 1936, p. 16.

* * *

Abstract

In the late 1890s, tuberculosis was a social disease with a medical aspect, but by the end of the 1930s it was regarded as a medical disease with a social aspect. In half a century the approach to and the management of the disease changed, so that what had been tackled by lay and medical reformers in local voluntary societies devoted to a humanitarian activity became instead the concern of the state and especially the provinces. Prevention came to be thought of elimination of sources of infection as opposed to building up an individual's resistance; the community rather than the individual was emphasized; and a bacteriologic technologic outlook had replaced one based on the abolition of habits such as indiscriminate spitting and dry sweeping. What were the factors that brought about these changes?

At the turn of the century, the formation of the National Sanatorium Associa-

tion (1896) and the Canadian Association for the Prevention of Consumption and other forms of tuberculosis (1891) gave support to reformers who urged legislation to eliminate the tubercle bacillus and to ameliorate the social conditions that fostered the disease. Fresh air, good food and rest in a sanatorium constituted treatment. But even though by 1914 there were 1800 sanatorium beds in Canada, sanatoria were of no use to the urban poor, who could not afford to take the time off work in order to rest; the dispensary therefore was introduced. The effects of the Great War next influenced the anti-tuberculosis campaign. The need for accurate differential diagnosis in ill soldiers sharpened diagnostic techniques; many soldiers were treated in sanatoria; with federal help, institutional facilities were expanded; and sanatoria became more like hospitals than glorified summer camps. Attitudes towards tuberculosis became more scientific, and prevention took on a specific bacteriologic orientation; the tubercle bacillus was recognized as the specific cause of the disease. Case-finding was stressed, the process being facilitated by travelling clinics, and physical examination and radiographic facilities became available to a larger group of the population; BCG testing was begun and tuberculin inoculation programs were started; and active cases of disease were segregated in order to prevent the spread of infection. Treatment now comprised bed rest, mental rest (e.g. occupational therapy) and surgically induced rest of the lungs (collapse therapy). All this, however, meant increases in the cost and size of the anti-tuberculosis program and, in turn, demands for increased state and provincial involvement. Too, the Depression made itself felt, which brought such issues as indigent care and municipal responsibility to a head. Surprisingly, the effects of the Depression were less grave than might have been expected, partly because bacteriologically oriented methods of diagnosis and treatment were relied on more and more, and partly because decreasing commodity prices, staff reductions and control of expenses enabled sanatoria to operate at a satisfactory level. And so, by the end of the 1930s, the back of the tuberculosis problem had been broken: childhood tuberculosis was less serious a matter; cases of tuberculosis were being discovered more quickly and sooner; individuals were contracting the disease in adulthood rather than in childhood; the number of sanatoria beds exceeded 10,000; provincial tuberculosis divisions were being formed; and free treatment in fact, if not in name, was available to residents in several provinces. The way had been paved for the final drive towards reducing the gravity of the disease to one that was soon to become a minor cause of death.

Résumé

A la fin du siècle dernier, la tuberculose était regardée comme un mal social ayant une incidence médicale, mais à la fin des années trente, elle était devenue une maladie avec une dimension sociale. Dans l'espace d'un demi-siècle, la façon d'aborder et de traiter la tuberculose changea tellement que ce qui avait été jusque là confié à l'action des réformateurs, médecins ou profanes, réunis dans des organismes bénévoles locaux se consacrant aux activités humanitaires, devint la préoccupation de l'Etat, en particulier au niveau provincial. Les programmes de prévention se tournèrent vers l'élimination des sources d'infection, abandonnant le développement de la résistance individuelle, vers la communauté au lieu de l'individu; une perspective bactériologique et technologique remplaça celle qui s'attachait à éliminer la mauvaise habitude d'expectorer en public et le balayage à sec. Quels facteurs entraînèrent ces changements?

Au tournant du siècle, la fondation d'une Association nationale des sanatoriums (1896) et de l'Association canadienne pour la prévention de la consomption et autres formes de tuberculose (1901) encouragea les réformateurs qui insistaient pour obtenir des lois visant à éliminer les bacilles et à modifier les conditions sociales qui favorisaient la maladie. L'air frais, la nourriture saine et le repos en sanatorium constituaient le traitement. Bien qu'il y eut en 1914, 1 800 lits en sanatorium au Canada, ce traitement était peu utile aux pauvres des villes qui ne pouvaient se permettre de laisser leur travail pour se reposer. On introduisit alors les dispensaires. La campagne anti-tuberculeuse fut aussi affectée par la Grande Guerre. Le besoin de diagnostic précis pour les recrues entraîna l'amélioration des techniques de diagnostic. Plusieurs soldats furent traités en sanatorium. Avec l'aide fédérale, les institutions prirent de l'expansion et les sanatoriums ressemblèrent plus à des hôpitaux qu'à des colonies de vacances. Alors que l'attitude envers les tuberculeux devenait plus scientifique, la prévention prit une orientation plus spécifiquement bactériologique: le bacille tubercule fut reconnu comme la cause spécifique de la maladie. Le dépistage des cas acquit une plus grande importance et fut facilité par l'instauration de cliniques ambulantes, et par l'expansion des examens physiologiques et de la radiographie désormais accessibles à une plus grande population. La cuti-réaction au BCG et un programme d'inoculation à la tuberculine furent inaugurés et les cas actifs furent isolés pour éviter la contamination. Le traitement comprenait désormais l'alitement, le repos mental (thérapie occupationnelle, par exemple) et le repos des poumons par procédés chirurgicaux (collapsothérapie). Toutes ces mesures eurent pour résultat une augmentation des coûts pour le programme antituberculeux et, à la longue, des demandes d'aide accrue auprès de l'Etat, fédéral ou provincial. Il paraît aujourd'hui étonnant que les effets de la crise économique n'aient pas été aussi graves qu'on aurait pu s'y attendre. Ceci est dû en partie aux méthodes de diagnostic et aux traitements orientés de plus en plus vers la bactériologie. La baisse des prix, la réduction du personnel et le contrôle des dépenses permirent quand même aux sanatoriums de fonctionner à un niveau acceptable. A la fin des années trente, on avait cassé les reins à la tuberculose: la tuberculose infantile n'était plus un problème grave, la maladie s'attaquant plutôt aux adultes et le dépistage se faisant plus tôt et plus rapidement. Le nombre de lits dans les sanatoriums se chiffrait à 10 000, les provinces participaient à la lutte contre la maladie et le traitement gratuit était offert aux résidants de plusieurs provinces. Le mouvement de régression de la maladie était amorcé. Celle-ci ne serait bientôt plus qu'une cause mineure de mortalité.

Norman Bethune and Tuberculosis

G.J. Wherrett*

Dr. Wherrett died after a brief illness on February 27, 1981. For much of his life he was a leader in Canada and abroad in the campaign to conquer tuberculosis. After service in Saskatchewan and New Brunswick, he was Executive Secretary of the Canadian Tuberculosis Association for many years. He enjoyed wide respect around the world for his active roles in the International Union Against Tuberculosis, of which he was elected president in 1959, and in the Expert Committee of the World Health Organization from 1959 to 1972. An account of these and other developments in tuberculosis may be found in his The Miracle of the Empty Beds (University of Toronto Press, 1977).

— Eds.

My personal recollections of Norman Bethune are confined to the years he lived in Montreal, from 1928 to late 1936, when he left for Spain. Earlier, though, I had become familiar with Bethune's background before his arrival in Montreal, for several of my friends knew him then. One such friend was Dr. John Barnwell, who was a patient with Bethune in the sanatorium at Saranac Lake, and who became Bethune's close friend; I knew, too, Dr. Julie Wilson and Dr. David Smith, who worked in the laboratory at Ray Brook, near Saranac Lake, while Bethune was working there. Whenever I met these friends I learned much about this unusual and interesting Canadian. I gained more insight from Dr. Gabriel Nadeau's interesting paper, "A T.B's Progress," which outlined the outstanding features in Bethune's life: his medical history, his experiences with the microorganisms that cause childhood diseases and later his bout with tuberculosis[1]. Nadeau told how Bethune gave his own prognosis and predicted an early death from tuberculosis — this in a poem illustrated by murals drawn on the walls of his sanatorium cottage, the final one showing him in the arms of the Angel of Death. The following philosophical comment from this poem by Bethune shows his talent as a poet:

> Sweet Death! Thou kindest angel of them all,
> In thy safe arms, at last, O let me fall.
> Bright stars are out, long gone the burning sun;
> My little act is over and the tiresome play is done[2].

In those days — the 1920s and 1930s — tuberculosis was very much "the captain of the men of death," and when Bethune went to Montreal in 1928 for training in thoracic surgery under Dr. Edward Archibald, tuberculosis was a cause of serious illness and death. Thus my recollections of Bethune are interwoven with the picture of tuberculosis in Montreal, particularly, and of Canada, generally[3].

* * *

In 1930, at least 8,000 persons in Canada died from tuberculosis and another 40,000 persons had active disease, many with a "positive" sputum that was a source of infection for family and associates. Of all active cases only a small percentage were detected and reported to health departments. Few patients could be admitted to sanatoria for treatment; there were not enough sanatoria and treatment at home was often impractical and ineffective. Such were the problems that faced those who were concerned with the care and treatment of the tuberculous.

The ever-widening campaign against tuberculosis, however, engendered a feeling of optimism from the results of treatment of the disease. We saw, on every side, those who had recovered, and we saw many more doctors and nurses become part of the treatment service of the community — but we also saw the greater numbers who had lost their battle with tuberculosis. This was before the days of "miracle drugs;" not even penicillin had been recognized as having antibiotic properties.

Research was talked about in theoretical and almost evangelical terms. Thus Dr. Charles Parfitt, then president of the Canadian Tuberculosis Association, in 1925:

> Research may be regarded as the spiritual side of medicine. It is faith in the future to be revealed by endeavors. It is the substance of things hoped for, the evidence of things not seen, for altho' we see through a glass darkly, we cherish always the hope that something may be found which will cure or hasten the cure of tuberculosis[4].

Who would have thought in 1930, least of all Bethune, that in 20 years we would embark on a programme of chemotherapy with three new drugs — available to everyone in Canada who had tuberculosis and that this would empty all those sanatoria that had been built at great expense and effort? The miracle of the empty beds became a reality, and the possibility of complete control of the disease came within our reach. This was the faith that every tuberculosis worker carried in his heart.

This was a time when tuberculosis divisions were being set up in departments of health, when clinics and nursing services were being expanded and when the building of sanatoria was being encouraged. Routine sanatorium treatment was augmented by the use of measures to collapse the lung such as pneumothorax, interruption of the phrenic nerve and thoracoplasty; later, diseased parts of the lung were resected and lobes, even whole lungs, were excised. During Bethune's Montreal years these surgical measures were being used more and more frequently, and Bethune was very much a proponent of such active treatment. He favoured lung collapse especially, because his own health had rapidly improved after the use of pneumothorax had been used to rest his lungs while he was a patient at Saranac Lake.

* * *

I remember particularly two surgeons in Montreal. One was Archibald, the teacher who had made surgery a safe and useful addition to sanatorium treatment[5]. Recognized during his lifetime as the Father of Thoracic Surgery, he received the Trudeau Medal of the National Tuberculosis Association and the Bigelow Medal of the Boston Surgical Society. A cultured and kindly gentleman who, by his quiet research and careful surgical work, founded the school of chest surgery, Archibald is revered wherever thoracic surgery is discussed. His qualities were well portrayed by Dr. William Howell at a dinner he gave to honour

Archibald on the occasion of his receiving an honorary degree from the University of Paris. During a speech Howell recited these lines of verse that he had written to Archibald:

> You've only brains and industry,
> Good breeding, kindness, modesty,
> The faculty of making friends
> With ne'er a thought to serve your ends;
> Sound judgement, sympathy and skill
> To comfort and to heal the ill.
>
> O Edward, You would be sublime
> If only you could be on time[6].

Bethune was the other surgeon, the newcomer who went to Archibald for training. He literally burst upon the scene, and in a few years he was well known in both Canada and the United States as a former tuberculosis patient who had a wide interest in the disease. As a surgeon, he was concerned with getting the patient treated; as an activist, his inclinations impelled him to participate in all phases of the campaign against tuberculosis, and he never lost an opportunity to prod and encourage all those responsible for the different aspects of the campaign, be they physicians or lay persons.

Bethune used whatever means he could in the fight against tuberculosis. He used the radio for public education and wrote plays for this medium. And in a speech to the Progress Club of Montreal, he entertained his audience with an inquiry into the death of a fictitious John Bunyan who died of tuberculosis. Bethune constructed the "inquest" to point out that many people, organizations and institutions were directly responsible for Bunyan's death: Bunyan himself, for not having had sufficient interest in his health to consult a doctor earlier in his illness; the doctor, for not recognizing the disease and not referring his patient to a clinic for tests; and the community and the province, for not providing sanatorium beds for treatment, and the lack of any financial plan to lower the cost of treatment[7]. So many were guilty! This clever device of an inquest received much notice in the Montreal papers.

Bethune's interest and his activist tendency made him a useful member of the anti-tuberculosis hierarchy. He attracted attention in whatever group, medical or lay, he attended. Not only his style as a participant in discussions attracted attention; his style of dress certainly caused comment. Instead of wearing the usual conservative attire of the medical fraternity of that time, he would appear at the most prestigious meeting in coloured shirts and pants and an unusual hat — all of which would attract attention even today.

As a surgeon Bethune promoted collapse therapy and as a literate surgeon he composed "The Compressionist's Creed," a parody of the Apostles' Creed. Published in the *American Review of Tuberculosis*, it pleased some and scandalized others. It ran as follows:

> I believe in Trudeau, the mighty father of the American Sanatorium, maker of a heaven on earth for the tuberculous; and in Artificial Pneumothorax, which was conceived by

Carson, born of the labours of Forlanini, suppressed under Pompous Pride and Prejudice, was criticized by the Cranks whose patients are dead and buried; thousands now will, even in the third stage, rise again from their bed; ascending into the Heaven of Medicine's Immortals, they sit on the right hand of Hippocrates our Father; from thence they do judge those pthisiotherapists quick to collapse cavities on dead or their job. I believe in Laennec, Bodington, Brehmer, Koch and Brauer, in Murphy, Friedrich, Wilms, Sauerbruch and Jacobeus, in the unforgiveness of sins of omission in Collapse Therapy, in the resurrection of a healthy body from a diseased one and long life for the tuberculous with care everlasting. Amen[8].

Bethune's career as a chest surgeon and his espousal of collapse therapy attracted some and repelled others. Discussions with him brought forth this reply: "I know I'm always in a hurry but I come by this trait honestly. My father was a Presbyterian minister who joined the Moody and Sankey evangelical movement. Their slogan was 'the world for Christ in one generation,' and that is my slogan, whether people like it or not."

* * *

Whatever his political philosphy, Bethune had many friends and supporters and an equal number who considered him an actor in everything he did. That appeared to be the feeling when he rather suddenly left to join the movement for aid to loyalist Spain. There his organization of the blood transfusion service was a superb effort, an aspect of his work that is seemingly in constrast to his work in Montreal.

Bethune's career was changing, and it changed again when he left for China, even more distant from Montreal and his work for the tuberulous. If Bethune was an actor, it was in China that he played out his final scenes — as a hero of the revolution, acknowledged by Mao Zedong and never to be forgotten by the Chinese people.

* * *

REFERENCES AND NOTES

1. Gabriel Nadeau, "A T.B.'s Progress: The Story of Norman Bethune," *Bulletin of the History of Medicine*, 8 (1940), 1135-1171.
2. Norman Bethune, "The T. B.'s Progress," *The Fluoroscope*, 1 (August 15), 1932. pp. 1-10. The story of the murals and their accompanying verses was related by Nadeau (op. cit. pp. 1139-1143) and summarized by Ted Allan and Sydney Gordon in *The Scalpel, the Sword: The Story of Dr. Norman Bethune,* Toronto, 1971 (revised edition), pp. 33-34. The full text of Bethune's article, with illustrations, is reproduced in Roderick Stewart's *The Mind of Norman Bethune*, Toronto, 1977, pp. 14-17. An enlarged reproduction of the ninth drawing, related to the verse quoted herein, is included among the illustrations following page 50 of Stewart's *Bethune*, Toronto, 1973.

    The Fluoroscope was a short-lived publication of a sanatorium in Michigan. A copy of the first issue, which contains "The Compressionist's Creed" (see also reference 8 below), is among the papers of Roderick Stewart that have been deposited for research purposes in the Osler Library, McGill University, Montreal.

    See, for a detailed treatment of Bethune as a poet, the chapter by Lee Thompson in this book pp. 104-113.
3. For a detailed account of tuberculosis in Canada in the early part of the 20th century, see the chapter by Katherine McCuaig, pp. 54-64.
4. Charles Parfitt, Public Archives of Canada, Canadian Tuberculosis Association, Annual Reports, 1925.
5. Edward Archibald's contributions to thoracic surgery are discussed in detail by H. Rocke Robertson on pp. 71-78 of this book.

6. Wilder Penfield, "Edward Archibald, 1872 - 1945", *Canadian Journal of Surgery*, 1 (1958), p. 169, and *No Man Alone: A Neurosurgeon's Life*, Boston, 1977, pp. 354-355.
7. Cited by Roderick Stewart in *Bethune*, Toronto, 1973, pp. 70-71 and 180; see also *Montreal Gazette*, Apr. 11, 1934.
8. There may be three versions of this parodic creed. The first one appeared under Bethune's authorship in *The Fluoroscope* (see reference 2). The second one was published in the *Journal of Thoracic Surgery*, 5 (1936), p. 330, on the urging of the then editor, Dr. Evarts Graham; it followed a surgical paper by Bethune published in that journal. A third version was attributed by the present author to the *American Review of Tuberculosis*, though a current search of the literature has failed to verify this. The 1932 version opens with the words, "I believe in rest the restorer, mighty maker of fibrosis (healing scar tissue) and health," followed by criticism of "the cranks of exercise therapy." The opening of the third version is identical to that of the second: "I believe in Trudeau, the mighty father of the American Sanatorium". In the 1932 version the pioneers "suffered under pompous pride and prejudice," while in the 1936 and in the third version the alliterative words were capitalized — the present author using the verb, "suppressed." Finally, the Greek word for tuberculosis, or consumption — *phthisis* — has given rise to interesting confusion. Originally, Bethune wrote the two words "phthisis therapists"; in 1936, the single word "pthisiotherapists" appeared, as used also by the present author; and since then we have seen "phisiotherapists" too. Except, however, for Bethune's change in emphasis in the opening sentence, the other versions may be the result only of slips or whimsy.

* * *

Abstract

Since tuberculosis was so common a cause of death in the 1930s, and since Bethune was identified so strongly with the fight against the disease, personal recollections of Bethune are interwoven with the picture of tuberculosis of that era, both in Montreal and in Canada. In 1930, in Canada, at least 8,000 persons died from tuberculosis and another 40,000 had active disease. Treatment of tuberculosis was problematical: the antibiotic era had not dawned, beds in sanatoria were too few and treatment at home was impractical and ineffective. Bethune was one of the few thoracic surgeons who had been trained to face such problems; his chief, Edward Archibald, was another. Bethune differed greatly from Archibald, however; Bethune's temperament, skills and philosophy were those of an activist, which Archibald was not. Bethune prodded and provoked others in the campaign against tuberculosis, and used all means at his disposal to encourage all to fight the disease. Although his views repelled some of his colleagues, he had many friends and supporters, though some saw him as much an actor as a physician. Bethune was always in a hurry, as he himself admitted; he hurried from Montreal to Spain and then to China. In China, he played out his final scenes and, in so doing, became a hero of the Chinese people.

Résumé

Comme la tuberculose était souvent mortelle durant les années trente, et comme le souvenir de Bethune est fortement lié à la lutte contre cette maladie, les retours personnels sur sa vie font souvent référence à la situation de la tuberculose à Montréal et au Canada à cette époque. Au Canada, en 1930, 8 000 personnes moururent de la tuberculose et 40 000 en furent atteintes. Le traitement de cette maladie, à l'époque, était douteux: l'ère des antibiotiques n'était pas commencée, les lits dans les sanatoriums trop peu nombreux et les soins à domicile inefficaces et impraticables. Bethune fut un des rares chirurgiens du thorax ayant la formation pour faire face à la situation. Son maître, Edward

Archibald, le père de la médecine thoracique en Amérique, partageait cet intérêt. Bethune et Archibald étaient pourtant très différents; le tempérament de Bethune, sa dextérité, sa philosophie, étaient ceux de l'homme d'action, ce qui n'était pas le cas pour Archibald. Bethune provoqua et stimula l'intérêt de plusieurs personnes pour sa campagne contre la tuberculose et employa tous les moyens à sa disposition pour encourager la lutte contre cette maladie. Si ses idées éloignèrent de lui certains de ses collègues, il conserva beaucoup d'amis et de partisans, dont certains voyaient en lui l'acteur autant que le médecin. Comme il le reconnaissait lui-même, Bethune était toujours à la course. Sa course l'amena de Montréal en Espagne, puis d'Espagne en Chine. C'est là qu'il joua sa dernière scène devenant ainsi un héros du peuple chinois.

Edward Archibald, The "New Medical Science" and Norman Bethune

H. Rocke Robertson

When Norman Bethune was plotting the course that he was to pursue following his release from the sanatorium at Saranac Lake, McGill University's star was in the ascendancy. It had not always been so. Though the spirit and the reputation of the medical faculty had been well sustained over the years, there was a period just before, during, and after the First World War when McGill University lagged sadly behind others in the surge of scientific enterprise that prevailed in the early years of the new century and that has, indeed, continued to the present.

* * *

From its humble beginnings in 1829, which resulted in Canada's first medical graduate (William Logie, M.D. 1833, the only member of the graduating class)[1], the Faculty made steady progress. Forty years later its teaching was of such quality as to induce the young William Osler to abandon his studies at Toronto in order to come to McGill where, as Cushing put it, "the clinical opportunities in Montreal hospitals far exceeded those which Toronto offered."[2]

These clinical facilities and the medical staff were sufficient to enable McGill to keep pace with the other universities during the latter half of the 19th century. It was a magnificent era and the published record indicates that McGill, if it played no part in actual discoveries, was at least progressive enough to take an early advantage of them.

But after the initial excitement that accompanied the adoption of new and enormously successful methods there came a time for sober reassessment, questioning, investigation — in short, research. While this was the normal pursuit of basic scientists, it was not then that of clinicians, all of whom were dependent for their living on the earnings from private practice. Few clinicians could afford to devote time to anything else, and so were slow to progress scientifically; indeed one is tempted to draw a mischievous parallel between chemistry, which had made no progress as long as men were concerned immediately to convert base metal to gold[3], and clinical medicine, in which progress was slow as long as doctors were sustained by the transmutation of patient care into gold.

The first move on this continent to correct this situation was made when the new medical faculty at Johns Hopkins University in Baltimore appointed full-time clinicians to the hospital staff. Later, following Abraham Flexner's highly critical report of the standard of teaching and research in many schools on this continent, most of the leading schools started to invest energy and money in staff and facilities that would further the scientific side of medical practice — though, as things turned out, the scientific aspect of medical practice eventually was overemphasized at the expense of the human aspect.

Now McGill began to fall rapidly behind the other universities. However great the energy in the Faculty, it lacked the money — or thought it did. Sir William Osler, who had long since left McGill but had not lost interest in his alma mater, sensed this keenly. In 1919, in an open letter to the Dean, he urged the organization of university clinics at McGill. "The matter", he wrote, "is urgent if the school is to keep in the van."[4] Spurred by this letter and aided, no doubt, by the authority it carried, the Dean was able to convince the powers of the day, and soon McGill made its move by establishing the University Clinic at the Royal Victoria Hospital with Dr. Meakins in charge. By 1925 the Clinic was, according to the Principal's Annual Report, "running in a very satisfactory manner."[5] By 1928, when Bethune arrived, the Clinic had settled down to a steady pace of productive activity. Much of the research was in the respiratory field, which must have appealed to him.

The Department of Surgery, in which Bethune enlisted, was less advanced from an organizational point of view. But by virtue largely of the efforts of one man, it had, by the time Bethune arrived, established a firm base of clinical and laboratory research.

Edward Archibald was one of the exceptions to test the rule that those who live on their earnings from private practice have no time for research. He showed his colours early: he published his first paper, a case report, a year after his graduation from medical school. During the next 47 years he published an average of more than two papers a year — some of them extensive and many important[6]. His investigations covered a wide range. Versatile in his clinical and research accomplishments, his interests ranged far wider, as is evident in his writings on non-medical subjects, which revealed an extraordinary depth of insight and knowledge. His intellectual curiosity drove him to examine his own experiences critically and to test his ideas in the experimental laboratory.

Archibald's two great medical interests were pancreatitis and thoracic surgery. To the understanding of pancreatitis, his main laboratory activity, he made some very important contributions; and in thoracic surgery, he was a veritable pioneer. By the time Bethune arrived, Archibald had published 27 articles covering a wide span of topics related to the investigation and treatment of respiratory disease. His clinical experience was extensive and clearly he took great pains to assess the results of his efforts as described in his reports. One that is particularly pertinent is his 1928 paper on a follow-up study of 149 patients with pulmonary tuberculosis who had been treated (117 of them by thoracoplasty) in his clinic up to that time[7]. His main laboratory work on thoracic problems centred on the investigation of the effects of coughing, and he produced the rather surprising results of this work in 1928[8].

Thus the Montreal stage that Bethune entered in 1928 was active indeed. On the medical side the clinic was well established — already a number of full and part-time faculty had been appointed (by 1930 they numbered 17). In that year members of the department of medicine at McGill published 84 papers — several of them in the respiratory field— and their surgical colleagues published 20, 6 of which were Archibald's. Added to the ferment in these two departments were the exciting first moves that led to the establishment of the Montreal Neurological Institute.

There were facilities, albeit primitive, for surgical experimentation, and the hospital was fully equipped to enable its staff to treat and to follow the course of patients under study. There was, unquestionably, an atmosphere of intense eagerness and enthusiasm. McGill again was abreast of the times. It had entered the era of the so-called new medical science, which was characterized mainly, in the present context, by the systematic study of various categories of disease by bringing together the clinical and the basic scientists to study the causes, the course and the factors that influence the course of diseases.

* * *

Bethune was 38 years old when he came to Montreal to start a new life that, I have no doubt, he hoped would be less disturbed than his previous one. Time and again his career had been interrupted. War and illness had repeatedly cut him short just as he seemed to be settling down. The story is well told by his biographers; suffice it here to point out that up to this time his actual practical medical experience from the time of graduation amounted to a year and a half in the Royal Naval Medical Service, 3 years of training in hospitals in London, 6 months of general practice, 2 years on the surgical staff of a large city hospital (Detroit), and 3 months in laboratory research — this last immediately before coming to Montreal.

For those days and for any person this was a considerable experience. While it was not ideal training for the so-called academic surgeon, for one of Bethune's capacity and versatility it fitted him well for the post of first assistant to the new clinic, the Medical-Surgical Pulmonary Clinic.

What, then, did he contribute to it? Let me examine this question under the headings of research, clinical practice and "stimulation".

His formal research that led to publication was mainly in the field of bacteriology, to which he had been introduced before he came to Montreal by his involvement in an excellent study at Ray Brook. He collaborated in the publication of an important paper on the subject of the spontaneous development of pulmonary disease in the rat[9]; this paper served, no doubt, to caution those attempting to produce lesions experimentally, as he did later himself with spirochaetes[10] and fungi[11], in studies that clearly revealed an inquiring mind and a fine, direct pen[12].

In his fourth published experimental study he investigated, using dogs and cats as the subject, 21 different methods of creating pleural adhesions, 5 of which were of his own devising[13]. The paper is a model of simplicity of concept and description leading to the conclusion that he had discovered a useful method — which, indeed, he had.

His stay in Montreal being relatively short and interrupted by the move from one hospital to another, it is not surprising that Bethune did not publish any analyses or follow-up studies of the results of the routine clinical work with tuberculous patients that occupied so much of his time. He did not, however, miss the opportunity of reporting the unusual— to wit, the use of maggots in the treatment of chronic infections in the chest[14]. The somewhat scornful challenge to his paper, which he read to an august society, evoked, from Bethune, a delightful sally of repartee, so different from most of the content of the stereotyped surgical literature.

One has to conclude that Bethune's research effort during these 8 short years was creditable, particularly if one counts the informal and unpublished research that is described in anecdotal form by his biographers. And while some questioned the profoundity of imaginativeness of some of his research, his forte in mechanical invention was fully acknowledged; and there is every reason to say that amongst his colleagues in clinical surgery he pulled his weight in the field of investigation.

With respect to clinical practice, having only the conflicting opinions of others to go on, I am cautious in trying to judge Bethune's surgical abilities. On the one hand, one reads a former student saying that Bethune "was a hell of a good surgeon, there is no doubt about of that . . . fast and brilliant," while someone else is quoted as saying that he "an excellent operator and . . . exhibited sound surgical judgment . . ."[15]. On the other hand, a young surgeon who frequently worked with Bethune opined that he was "brilliant, no question about that, and he had technical skills, but the kind of technical skill that kills people because he liked to go too fast" — a statement that is followed by a bone-chilling description of a performance that could only be termed irresponsible showmanship[16].

Archibald, himself a daring, if slow and methodical, surgeon was critical of Bethune's work. A pioneer chest surgeon— he undertook cases and procedures from which others would shrink, and his crowning achievements were to be the first on this continent to perform a thoracoplasty and the first in the world to carry out a pneumonectomy successfully in one stage[17] — Archibald considered Bethune quick, rough, untidy and "a little dangerous".[18] Above all, Archibald criticized Bethune's judgement. Thus he wrote:

> In surgical judgement, as to whether the patient had sufficient resistance to stand the proposed operation, I found him really lacking. His mind was set on the mechanical possibility too much, and on the degree and character of the tuberculosis . . . too little. His brain was active and exploring; he was full of hunches; but I usually had to sit on his hunches because they lacked solid foundation knowledge of the human material. In short, he was an inventor, not a 'great surgeon'. But he deserved, and won, a reputation through his inventions; that was carried over by the general run into the real thing of Thoracic Surgery, which, I think, was not really deserved[19].

Archibald's opinion on the question of judgement was supported by a lowly, but so often percipient, observer — a clinical clerk. One is quoted as saying, "I became aware that Dr. Bethune's patients had a rocky time recovering from surgery more frequently than those of Dr. Archibald or Dr. MacIntosh . . . in spite of our best care we are losing patients operated on by Dr. Bethune at an unusual rate".[20]

Bethune's response to criticisms of his judgement, particularly his selection of cases for operation, was that in the long run more lives would be *saved* by the radical rather than the conservative approach; that to refuse to operate on advanced cases was to deprive them of their one chance of survival. "More lives would be lost but still more would be saved" he argued, "by doing more operations on the more seriously ill than by 'playing it safe'."[21]

These are some of the pros and cons. Can one say that Bethune's daring did more harm than good in the long run, or vice versa? There cannot be any firm answer to this. Only results of long-term follow-up studies of comparable groups of patients managed conservatively and radically could tell the tale, and there are, so far as I know, no such figures available from this clinic. One's answer can be no more than one's guess.

Is it possible that Bethune's detractors were jealous, or that they were venting their disapproval of Bethune's other activities by lifting over their critisisms into a field in which their opinions would likely find more respect? Of course it is. Perhaps it is fruitless to try to determine how good a surgeon (using the word surgeon in its broadest sense) Bethune was; but, on the basis of the available information I would support Archibald's view that Bethune's claim to fame, which is undisputed, should not be based upon his abilities as a thoracic surgeon; his performance in other fields was more than sufficient to justify the recognition that at long last was accorded to him. I do, however, have to admit some bias. I was a student of Dr. Archibald's, and in numerous encounters with him and close association with several of his colleagues I developed a great admiration for his ability and his integrity. I doubt very much that his judgement was influenced in any way by pique or jealousy; I am certain that it was based on careful observation of Bethune's work.

One more point in this connection concerns Bethune as a military surgeon. It is entirely possible that the very qualities that caused some of Bethune's colleagues to criticize his work in chest surgery — his speed of hand and decision — may have rendered him a superb military surgeon. Whereas in peace-time surgery there is a place — even a need, usually — for cautious judgement and methodical operating, in times of active warfare the requirements are very different, and the quickest surgeon may be the most effective. Here Bethune's speed of thought and action served him — and others — well.

As for stimulation, Bethune without question, stimulated those around him. We read of how he affected students and internes: "He was informal, outgoing, dynamic in speech and body movements . . . he seemed to stimulate in us quickly a sense of person to person contact with him . . . a response he evoked also from patients . . . his gifts as a teacher came out most strikingly."[22]

Clearly the combination of great intellectual capacity and extraordinary powers of expression mobilized by an irrepressible urge to doubt, to criticize and to confront made him a most attractive, and probably, most effective teacher, for to students no one is more appealing than the accomplished iconoclast, the balloon-pricker. Those whom he taught suggest that he had an extraordinary ability to explain, to teach; indeed, his discussion of problems that mystified students seemed to produce an effect like that of developing fluid on film — to produce a clear picture out of blankness.

But evidently Bethune's penetrating mind and intolerance of those he considered fools caused some difficulties. "His vision", wrote Archibald, "was keen but narrow. He wore blinkers. He trod on many toes often without knowing it or caring if he did know it."[23] Others said he picked fights[24] and that "he would put forward his own views in an extreme way to cause discussion..."[25]; and "unable to conceal his feelings he was hostile and cruel in sometimes juvenile ways".[26]

Whether or not such ill effects as these goadings and criticisms may have had on his surgical colleagues were balanced, or more than balanced, by Bethune's injections of new ideas or new ways of looking at things is a moot question. But what was Bethune's effect on the "new medical science", on this strongly advancing tide? It may be — indeed I think it likely — that he forced his colleagues to think more deeply than they would have without his challenging. Perhaps he turned off some people who, fearing his barbs, would not do as well as they might have otherwise. It is conceivable that he had no significant influence — that his needlings and provocations were lost in the whirlwind of talent around him — but I think this is highly unlikely. Archibald, however critical he may have been of some of Bethune's work, conceded that he did a lot for the clinic. He wrote that "he kept it together, devoted his whole time to it, was enthusiastic...", and later Archibald "recognized his ability and was sincerely grateful for this enthusiastic work...".[27]

Thus in answer to the question that I put earlier one can say confidently that Bethune contributed a great deal to the Clinic. This is an inescapable conclusion. Enthusiasm is a word that occurs often in all writings about him, just as do brilliance, intelligence, impatience, action; and such qualities that, combined in an individual as they were in Bethune, could hardly fail to render him enormously useful to the group with which he was working.

There was a real place for the revolutionary too, and this he surely was, having no respect for tradition and authority and being determined to set them aside in order to improve things. By the time he arrived in Montreal, affairs in the hospital and the medical faculty had progressed well for a few years and doubtless the dangerous seeds of self-satisfaction were beginning to sprout. At the same time the vines of science were beginning to strangle humanism in medicine. I have no doubt that Bethune served by disturbing these growths.

* * *

An old saw about revolutionaries, ascribed to Bernard Shaw, goes this way: "Though revolutionaries seldom do much good, they sometimes do a lot of very refreshing harm!". To apply this to Bethune would obviously do him less than justice, but it does evoke the thought that repeatedly comes to mind as one reads of Bethune, and even more so when one reads what he wrote, the thought of refreshment — of the breath of fresh air that moved with him.

* * *

REFERENCES AND NOTES

1. Barbara Tunis and E. H. Bensley, "William Leslie Logie: McGill University's First Graduate and Canada's First Medical Graduate", *Canadian Medical Association Journal*, 105, (1971), pp. 1259-1263.

2. Harvey Cushing, *The Life of Sir William Osler,* Oxford, vol. 1, 1925, p. 66.
3. Abraham Flexner, *Universities American, English, German,* Oxford, 1930, p. 14.
4. D.S. Lewis, *Royal Victoria Hospital, 1887-1947,* Montreal, 1969, pp. 69-70.
5. McGill University Annual Report, 1925.
6. The topics of Archibald's varied papers concerned the diseases and surgery of the gastrointestinal tract, pancreas, thyroid and respiratory organs.
7. E. Archibald, "The Surgical Treatment of Pulmonary Tuberculosis," *Canadian Medical Association Journal,* 18 (1928), p. 3.
8. Archibald and A.L. Brown, "Cough. Its Action on Material in the Tracheobronchial Tract. Experimental Study," *Archives of Surgery,* 16 (1928), p. 322.
9. D.T. Smith, N. Bethune, and J.L. Wilson, "Etiology of Spontaneous Pulmonary Disease in the Albino Rat," *Journal of Bacteriology,* 20 (1930), pp. 361-370.
10. N. Bethune, "Note on Bacteriologic Diagnosis of Spirochaetosis of the Lung," *Canadian Medical Association Journal,* 20 (1929), pp. 365-368.
11. Bethune and W. Moffatt, "Experimental Aspergillosis With Aspergillus Niger: Superimposition of This Fungus on Primary Tuberculosis," *Journal of Thoracic Surgery,* 3 (1933), pp. 86-98.
12. For more detailed discussion of Bethune's medical papers see the chapter in this book by David Shephard (pp. 92-103).
13. Bethune, "Pleural Poudrage. — A New Technic for the Deliberate Production of Pleural Adhesions as a Preliminary to Lobectomy," *Journal of Thoracic Surgery,* 4, (1935), pp. 251-261.
14. Bethune, "A Case of Chronic Thoracic Empyema Treated With Maggots", *Canadian Medical Association Journal,* 32 (1936), pp. 301-302; "Maggot and Allantoin Therapy in Tuberculosis and Non-Suppurative Lesions of the Lung and Pleura, Journal of Thoracic Surgery, 5 (1936), pp. 322-328. See also in this book (pp. 92-103) by David Shephard for additional comments.
15. Roderick Stewart, *Bethune,* Markham, 1975, pp. 51 and 50.
16. Stewart, p. 47.
17. John J. White, "Edward Archibald and William Reinhoff, Jr.: Father of the Modern Pneumonectomy— An Historical Footnote," *Surgery,* 68 (1970), pp. 397-402.
18. Archibald, Letter to T. Allan, Apr. 24, 1942.
19. Archibald, Letter to T. Allan, Apr. 24, 1942.
20. Stewart, p. 49.
21. Wendell MacLeod, Libbie Park and Stanley Ryerson, *Bethune: The Montreal Years,* Toronto, 1978, p. 58.
22. MacLeod, Park and Ryerson, p. 41.
23. Archibald, Letter to G. Nadeau, Dec. 27, 1940.
24. Stewart, p. 65.
25. Stewart, p. 40.
26. Stewart, p. 41.
27. Archibald, Letter to G. Nadeau, Dec. 27, 1940.

* * *

Abstract

In 1928, when Bethune arrived in Montreal to work under Edward Archibald, the prominent chest surgeon, the Montreal medical stage was an active one. Basic scientists cooperated with clinical scientists in the study of disease and so contributed to the "New Medical Science". Physicians, both internists and surgeons, were researchers as well as busy practitioners, and the university medical-surgical clinic recently established at McGill University provided an academic support for everyday clinical work. Bethune spent 8 years in Montreal and, during this period, made his own contributions to medicine there and influenced his medical colleagues in these specific ways. First, working with Archibald, himself a notable researcher, Bethune produced his own creditable research. Second, in clinical practice he was recognized as an innovative surgeon, though his speed of mind and hand, which more certainly suited Bethune later as a military surgeon, was sometimes adversely contrasted with Archibald's slow and careful manner. And, third, Bethune's approach to all he did was always his own and, in stimulating his colleagues, elicited a response that was favourable in some and adverse in others. The Montreal medical scene would have been different without Bethune: he forced his colleagues to think more deeply than they would otherwise have done, and he disturbed the growth of the vines of science that were tending to strangle the flowers of humanistic medicine.

Résumé

En 1928, lorsque Norman Bethune arriva à Montréal pour travailler sous la direction de l'éminent chirurgien du thorax, Edward Archibald, le monde médical de Montréal était des plus actifs. Scientifiques et praticiens unissaient leurs efforts dans l'étude de la maladie et contribuaient ainsi à la création de la "nouvelle médecine". Internistes et chirurgiens s'adonnaient aussi bien à la recherche qu'à la pratique. La clinique de médecine et de chirurgie qui venait d'être établie à l'Université McGill fournissait le support académique au travail quotidien accompli en clinique.

Bethune passa huit ans à Montréal; pendant cette période, il y fit sa marque dans le monde médical et exerça une influence sur ses collègues de trois façons: d'abord tout en travaillant avec le chercheur de renom qu'était Archibald, Bethune poursuivit ses recherches personnelles. Deuxièmement, comme clinicien dans le service d'Archibald, il fut reconnu comme un innovateur en chirurgie, même si sa vivacité d'esprit et sa rapidité d'exécution — qui le servirent si bien plus tard dans la vie militaire — contrastèrent parfois à son désavantage avec les manières lentes, réfléchies et appliquées d'Archibald. Et finalement, dans tout ce qu'il entreprit, Bethune eut son style bien à lui; sa présence fut un stimulant pour ses collègues, mais la faveur de ces derniers ne lui fut pas toujours acquise. Sans Bethune, la scène médicale montréalaise eut sans doute été différente. Il força ses collègues à plus d'approfondissement; il émonda les vignes de la science qui commençaient à étouffer les fleurs de la médecine humaniste.

The Royal Victoria Hospital, Montreal: Common Diseases in the 1920s and 1930s

Jessie Boyd Scriver

The illnesses that were treated in hospitals in the 1920s and early 1930s presented a very different picture from that of those seen in today's hospitals. Progress in medicine and in health care over half a century has been remarkable, and many infectious diseases and nutritional deficiency disorders that were common 50 or 60 years ago are now either rare or much less serious than they used to be. The general public, however, can have no conception of the extent of this progress and what has lain behind it, and for this reason I will describe some of the diseases that I saw as an intern in Montreal in 1922, and comment on their rarity today. In the context of Norman Bethune's times and of his legacy this will not only give some idea of the extent of medical progress in the past half century, but also enable us to gain insight into the health environment with which Bethune was so dissatisfied.

* * *

I was the first woman to become an intern at the Royal Victoria Hospital in Montreal; that was in July, 1922. The five women, including myself, who were the first to graduate from McGill University in medicine, had graduated that spring after 5 years of medical studies unmarred by any need for an aggressive attitude on our part. Acceptance at the hospital was the next question, but when I reported for duty the welcome was cordial. I was assigned to the paediatric service, where I would see so many of the diseases that characterized medicine of that era.

The "Royal Vic" enjoyed an enviable reputation in medical circles. A general teaching hospital, its paediatric service was located in a partly cubicled ward of 40 beds. New patients were admitted to cubicles for assessment and for protection of non-infectious patients, and critically ill patients were also assigned cubicles. Of critically ill patients we had many: that summer, over half the patients on the service were infants who were suffering from severe gastroenteritis with dehydration and often extreme malnutrition. Treatment for this disease was very different from the treatment given today. The standard form of treatment on admission of a patient was to give castor oil by mouth and a Murphy "drip" by rectum and then, when vomiting had ceased, small quantities of a weak formula. Results of treatment were less than satisfactory and many of the infants did not survive. At about that time, however, the results of investigative studies of body fluids and electrolyte balance became available, and Dr. Graham Ross, who had participated in some of those studies at Baltimore's Johns Hopkins Hospital, returned to the Royal Victoria Hospital and instituted appropriate treatment for loss of body fluids and for electrolyte imbalance. At first, fluids were given subcutaneously; later, they were given into the peritoneal cavity; and, later still, they were given intravenously. As always, appropriate tools and skills have

The Royal Victoria Hospital, Montreal, Drawing, M. Dobie Munroe, 1932.

L'hôpital Royal Victoria, Montréal. Dessin, M. Dobie Munroe, 1932.

brought about a vast change in treatment methods, and today the intravenous route only is used, so that in even the smallest premature infant administration of fluids can be maintained by means of a scalp vein infusion if necessary.

A different form of malnutrition affected the fat, white baby, often the proud mother's joy yet presenting for treatment with an alarmingly low concentration of hemoglobin in the blood— even as low as 4 grams per cent. This type of baby became ill after taking for a prolonged period an exclusively milk diet. Through the years there has been progress: we no longer see the fat, white baby.

Again in the nutritional group, vitamin D-deficient rickets was prevalent in the 1920s and 1930s and became less common only when public health teaching reached more of the population. Today, of course, milk is fortified with vitamin D, and we are unable to demonstrate active rickets to medical students, except in a rare and atypical biochemical condition associated with a congenital defect or with abnormal kidney function. Scurvy, frequent in the 1920s and 1930s, also is rare today, again because of the improved knowledge and eating habits of the population.

What is the story of infections other than gastroenteritis? A brief review of deaths in the province of Quebec in infants under 1 year of age in 1930 is pertinent[1]. First, though, to emphasize the fact that gastroenteritis has become much less serious, note that, in 1930, 2,730 infants died of diarrhea and enteritis — and that, in 1974, the death rate was only 1 in every 100,000 live births.

From pneumonia, 271 infants in the first year of life died. On one hospital ward, where we probably saw the more seriously ill infants, empyema complicated pneumonia in about 50% and, of these infants, nearly one half did not survive. But, as with gastroenteritis, the results of treatment of pneumonia and of bacterial meningitis have greatly improved since the advent of antibiotics. From diphtheria in 1930, 18 infants under the age of 1 year died, and among persons aged 0 to 40 years, 309 died. Today, however, diphtheria is so rare that we are unable to show a case of this disease to our medical students; similarly, many younger physicians have neither seen the dirty grey membrane nor smelled the characteristic foetid odour from the throat of a child with diphtheria. This remarkable progress in the prevalence of diphtheria we owe to the immunization programmes of the past 40 years.

In 1930 also, whooping cough killed 345 infants in Quebec and measles, 163. Immunization has made these infections fast disappear and we hope that poliomyelitis, too, has all but disappeared.

Two other common conditions in our clinics were congenital syphilis and typhoid fever, but education and social responsibility, both for the individual and the community, have, with diligent medical care, been instrumental in virtually eradicating them. A friend of Bethune, Dr. Aubrey Geddes, directed the congenital syphilis clinic in our paediatric service, seeing between 80 and 100 children, from newborns to early adolescents, who were under treatment for congenital syphilis. Obstetricians were urged to diagnose syphilis in the pregnant woman, and at first they checked all the public patients that came to the outpatient clinic; but then they were reminded that the Colonel's Lady and Judy O'Grady were the same under the skin — and so they insisted on blood tests for all pregnant women, with the diagnosis made and treatment started before the need arose for them to be admitted to hospital. The result was that if intrauterine syphilis was treated by the fourth month a normal baby was delivered.

A major epidemic of typhoid occurred in Montreal in the late 1920s, many of the patients being children. The source of the infection was traced to one of the dairies in the city; the pasteurization plant had broken down and no one had corrected the fault. The calamity could have been prevented, if the public had been educated to understand how typhoid fever is transmitted and if the staff of the dairy had been socially responsible enough to realize that pasteurization is essential for the public's protection. It is only with constant vigilance that we can hope to maintain standards of safety and thus freedom from disease.

* * *

What has wrought this extraordinary change, this remarkable degree of progress in medicine and health care? Two factors: the application of the results of patient and meticulous research in investigative projects, and the education and the social responsibility of the public. Credit must also be given to government provision of medical care, which the health care system has placed within reach of all the country's citizens. But there is still much to be done and this is no time to reduce either effort or facilities. The continuing occurrence of tuberculosis illustrates this.

In 1930 in Quebec, 32 infants under 1 year of age and 196 children from 1 to 14 years of age died from tuberculosis. Every year we saw several cases of tuberculous meningitis, which was invariably fatal until the advent of streptomycin. (It was dramatic to see Dr. Harold Cushing stand at the bedside and ask the intern about a child with tuberculous meningitis, "When did you say this child took ill?" Cushing would pause and then tell the intern that the patient would die on the 21st day of illness — and would invariably be right.) And even today tuberculosis still kills, though in 1976, in Quebec, among persons of all ages, there were only 20 deaths, with an average age of 67 years. This shift in mortality from childhood to older age groups is a striking piece of evidence of progress, but the battle is not over. In 1977 in Quebec, among persons from birth to the age of 4 years, there were 10 new cases, and among those aged 5 to 14 years there were 19 new cases[2]. Diagnosis, treatment, assessment of the environment and follow-up are all necessary to achieve the desired result, but we cannot afford to relax our vigilance.

* * *

What has all this to do with Bethune? Bethune was decades ahead of his time, in his understanding of the causation of disease and in his sense of social responsibility. He was flamboyant, yes; we remember him walking through the corridors of the hospital with that characteristic stride, the scarf flying out as he strode to his ward — a very dramatic person! A surgeon, though not of the calibre to head an academic department of surgery, he was different, unfortunately, from many surgeons. Bethune was a surgeon with compassion; when a patient with tuberculosis required a chest operation, Bethune asked pertinent questions: Why did this patient develop *this* case of tuberculosis? Was he hungry? Was he poorly housed? Did he live in contact with a relative or others coughing out tubercle bacilli? And there grew, among those who listened, a sense of social responsibility that was translated into action.

In Bethune, thought was translated into action in ways both small and large. An example of a small way lies in the rib shears he invented; he realized the need for an adequate instrument to facilitate thoracotomy, and thought became action in the form of the Bethune Rib Shears. But we remember Bethune more for thought and action on a larger scale. Bethune has been described as "an angry man, a man roused to anger by stupidity, by bureaucracy, tyranny, brutality, by the contradictions and absurdities of the society around him".[3] And so the loss of lives resulting from delay in transport from battlefield to hospital prompted the organization of blood transfusion in the field in Spain; and in China, when fully trained personnel were in pitifully short supply, Bethune trained an auxiliary force, thereby saving many lives.

It is no wonder that, by his selflessness in thought and action, Bethune became such a hero to so many.

* * *

REFERENCES AND NOTES

1. Canada, Dominion Bureau of Statistics, Tenth Annual Report, Ottawa, 1933. Other sources consulted include the Canada Year Book and the Quebec Year Book. These three reference texts have provided the information relating to most of the incidence rates quoted herein.
2. The information relating to 1977 incidence has been kindly provided by Dr. Helen Freedman Brickman.
3. Wendell MacLeod, Libbie Park and Stanley Ryerson, *Bethune: The Montreal Years*, Toronto, 1978, p. 8.

* * *

Abstract

In the past 50 years, progress in medicine and improvements in the public's health have been remarkable. In the 1920s and 1930s, infectious diseases such as gastroenteritis, pneumonia, diphtheria, whooping cough, measles, typhoid fever, tuberculosis and congenital syphilis were common, and their mortality and morbidity were high. In Quebec, in 1930, as one example, 32 infants under 1 year of age and 196 children aged 1 to 14 years died from tuberculosis. Nutritional disorders like rickets and scurvy, too, were common and debilitating. Today, all these conditions are uncommon; some are so rare that medical students never see them. This improvement in health is attributable to two factors. One is the patient and meticulous medical research over the years, with the application of such research to clinical practice; the other is the growth of the public's knowledge and sense of social responsibility regarding the health of the community. These two factors were understood by Bethune, who never failed to consider social and environmental aspects of a patient's illness. Yet, while such progress has been remarkable, some of the diseases of the 1920s and 1930s still cause appreciable mortality and morbidity. Thus, in Quebec, in 1976, 20 persons died from tuberculosis — admittedly their ages averaged 67 years — so that it remains essential to be ever vigilant regarding the public's health.

Résumé

Durant les cinquante dernières années, les progrès de la médecine et l'amélioration de la santé publique ont été remarquables. Au cours des décennies de 1920 et de 1930, les maladies contagieuses — gastro-entérite, pneumonie, diphtérie, coqueluche, rougeole, fièvre typhoïde, tuberculose et syphillis congénitale — étaient chose courante et maintenaient la morbidité et la mortalité à un niveau élevé. Par exemple, au Québec en 1930, 32 enfants de moins d'un an et 196 de un à quatre ans, sont morts de tuberculose. Les troubles dus à la malnutrition, comme le rachitisme et le scorbut, n'étaient pas rares et leurs effets étaient débilitants. Aujourd'hui, ces maladies sont peu fréquentes, certaines sont tellement rares que les étudiants en médecine n'en ont presque jamais d'exemples sous les yeux. Ces améliorations remarquables de la santé publique sont attribuables à deux facteurs: d'abord les recherches patientes et méticuleuses effectuées durant plusieurs années dans le domaine médical et la mise en application clinique des découvertes; ensuite, une meilleure connaissance et une meilleure compréhension de la part du public, de ce que sont la santé et la maladie, ainsi qu'un sens plus aigu de la responsabilité collective en matière de santé commu-

nautaire. Norman Bethune avait lui-même très bien compris l'importance de ces deux éléments. C'est pourquoi il prenait toujours en considération la dimension sociale et environnementale de l'état de santé d'un patient. Toutefois, malgré ces progrès marqués, certaines maladies répandues durant les années vingt et trente, contribuent encore aujourd'hui à accroître le taux de mortalité et de morbidité. Au Québec, en 1976, vingt personnes sont mortes de tuberculose (même s'il faut tenir compte de leur âge moyen qui était de 67 ans). Il est donc essentiel de continuer à exercer une vigilance constante dans le domaine de la santé publique.

Norman Bethune:
l'influence de l'hôpital du Sacré-Coeur
Pierre Delva

Ce chapitre est divisé en deux parties: la première concerne l'hôpital du Sacré-Coeur, et la deuxième quelques activités de Norman Bethune depuis son arrivée à l'hôpital en février 1933 jusqu'à sa démission et son départ pour l'Espagne en octobre 1936. On ne peut comprendre l'évolution de Norman Bethune pendant cette période sans connaître aussi l'histoire de l'hôpital.

* * *

"Quelques filles pieuses et charitables", selon un texte officiel de 1951, commencèrent à accueillir "des malades pauvres, cancéreux, tuberculeux, infirmes, incurables ou totalement invalides" dans une maison de la rue St-Charles-Borromée le 1er juin 1898, jour de la fête du Sacré-Coeur. Le 4 décembre 1899, ce travail fut confié aux Soeurs de la Charité de la Providence par l'archevêque Paul Bruchési et toute l'oeuvre fut transférée dans un deuxième local situé rue St-Denis. La communauté acheta alors le monastère des religieuses du Précieux-Sang à Notre-Dame-de-Grâce, y fit des transformations, et inaugura, le 23 avril 1902, l'hôpital des Incurables dont la capacité était de 350 à 375 lits. A la suite d'un incendie, le 15 mars 1923, on décida de bâtir un nouvel hôpital sur le site actuel, à Cartierville: l'hôpital du Sacré-Coeur reçut ses premiers patients le 27 janvier 1926. On pouvait y hospitaliser six cents malades. Tout en continuant de recevoir les cancéreux et les patients atteints de maladies chroniques nécessitant des soins médicaux, l'hospitalisation des tuberculeux, dont les besoins étaient urgents, devint l'oeuvre principale: le travail adopta un caractère nouveau et scientifique. Des services médicaux s'organisèrent peu à peu, ainsi qu'une nouvelle école d'infirmières.

En février 1931, on créa un service d'orthopédie sous la direction du docteur J. Édouard Samson. Dans le rapport de l'assemblée des médecins de l'hôpital, tenue le 27 février 1932, on peut lire: "le docteur G. Mignault aborde la question du chirurgien en tuberculose pulmonaire et pose en principe que ce service particulier de la chirurgie ne doit être confié qu'à un expert spécialisé ... il expose devant le bureau médical que le docteur Bethune, assistant du professeur Archibald, est une valeur réelle comme chirurgien, bronchoscospiste et aussi clinicien". Et dans celui de l'assemblée du 26 novembre 1932, la "Révérende Soeur Supérieure communique à l'assemblée le rapport de son entrevue avec le docteur Bethune qui accepterait la position de chirurgien sans nomination spéciale avec l'intention de former un jeune chirurgien canadien-français; le bureau médical après avoir considéré les rares applications, décide de mettre le docteur Deshaies à l'essai; si le travail l'intéresse et qu'il semble montrer des aptitudes, le Bureau médical plus tard proposera une nomination universitaire". En janvier 1933, Norman Bethune devint donc le premier chef d'un nouveau service de chirurgie pulmonaire et de bronchoscopie. Jusqu'alors, dans les

Sacré-Coeur Hospital, Cartierville, Quebec, ca 1930.
Public Archives of Canada PA 116907

L'hôpital du Sacré-Coeur, Cartierville, Québec, vers 1930. *Archives publiques du Canada.* PA 116907

hôpitaux francophones, la chirurgie thoracique était du domaine de la chirurgie générale. Bethune devint donc le premier chirurgien qualifié en chirurgie thoracique nommé dans un hôpital francophone.

Février 1934 marque l'ouverture d'un dispensaire anti-tuberculeux, et la clinique externe d'orthopédie, établie à la maison-mère des religieuses en septembre 1930, fut transférée à Cartierville le 16 mai 1938. En 1943, l'hôpital ne recevait plus que des tuberculeux et des cas d'orthopédie. En 1956, il devint un hôpital général multidisciplinaire de plus de sept cents lits, et en 1972 un hôpital universitaire de soins tertiaires au même titre que les trois autres hôpitaux généraux de soins tertiaires à Montréal affiliés à l'Université de Montréal, soit l'hôpital Notre-Dame, l'Hôtel-Dieu de Montréal, et l'hôpital Maisonneuve-Rosemont.

Voici en bref quelle était l'organisation des services de chirurgie en 1933: en orthopédie, le docteur Édouard Samson avait comme assistant le docteur Ulric Frenette. On comptait deux autres orthopédistes, les docteurs Maurice Fortier et Antonio Samson. Deux jeunes chirurgiens, les docteurs Georges Deshaies et Gérard Rolland assuraient les services de chirurgie générale et voulaient se spécialiser en chirurgie thoracique. Le docteur Georges Cousineau apprenait l'anesthésie à l'hôpital Royal Victoria et à l'hôpital du Sacré-Coeur sous la tutelle de l'anesthésiste Édouard Samson. Les docteurs Norman Bethune, Georges Cousineau, Georges Deshaies et Gérard Rolland formaient l'équipe de chirurgie thoracique. Il y avait deux salles d'opérations qui fonctionnaient surtout les lundi, mercredi et vendredi. Les opérations thoraciques incluaient des pneumonectomies, des lobectomies, des compressions de poumons avec de l'huile minérale. Les anesthésies étaient réalisées de façon élémentaire à l'aide de chloroforme, d'éther, d'oxygène et d'hydroxide d'azote. L'intubation n'était pas encore utilisée et on commençait à peine à pratiquer l'anesthésie par voie intraveineuse (Évipal). Les opérations pouvaient durer jusqu'à dix ou onze heures et tous les patients recevaient automatiquement les derniers sacrements avant l'opération. Le taux de mortalité en chirurgie thoracique était de 50%. Les patients qui devaient subir une opération étaient donc très anxieux et ce n'est qu'après le départ du docteur Norman Bethune que la routine religieuse fut changée.

* * *

Ce qui précède est important, comme je l'ai indiqué précédemment, pour comprendre l'évolution des idées de Norman Bethune entre 1933 et 1936. L'hôpital Royal Victoria, d'où venait Bethune, et l'hôpital du Sacré-Coeur étaient deux mondes différents. Le premier, un hôpital universitaire d'une des facultés de médecine les plus prestigieuse d'Amérique du Nord, dépendait de l'*establishment* anglophone. Le travail s'y faisait en fonction de la médecine dite scientifique, des besoins des professionnels; le deuxième était un hôpital francophone tout neuf et le travail s'y faisait en fonction des soins à long terme, surtout pour les tuberculeux, service dont avait surtout besoin la population francophone. Cette même différence d'orientation se retrouvait au Royaume-Uni entre les *Voluntary Hospitals* privés qui contrôlaient les écoles de médecine et les *Public Hospitals* qui essayaient de subvenir aux besoins de la population en matière de services hospitaliers; ceux-ci étaient toujours dépourvus financièrement et souffraient de pénurie de médecins. L'hôpital Royal Victoria était une copie à tout point de vue du Royal Infirmary à Edimbourg, un *Voluntary Hospital* affilié à l'Université d'Edimbourg. Il devait être difficile pour un chirurgien thoracique à l'hôpital Royal Victoria de comprendre l'impact d'une maladie comme la tuberculose sur la population, compréhension qui allait de soi. Les statistiques qui suivent présentent aux lecteurs les problèmes de la tuberculose à l'hôpital du Sacré-Coeur.

En 1927, il y avait six cents lits à l'hôpital du Sacré-Coeur, pour 1 187 admissions, 725 sorties et 377 décès. En chirurgie, il n'y eut que 61 opérations, (dix laparotomies, trois thoracoplasties, cinq phrénicectomies, et 42 ponctions, curetage osseux, et ouverture d'abcès). En orthopédie, on fit en plus onze "appareils plâtrés" et il y eu "neuf guérisons". Quinze patients tuberculeux reçurent 390 insufflations.

L'année 1933 est la seule des quatre années passées par Bethune à l'hôpital du Sacré-Coeur pour laquelle l'auteur a pu découvrir des statistiques valables. Celles-ci sont divisées en six chapitres: la tuberculose, le cancer, la médecine, la chirurgie générale, l'orthopédie et le laboratoire. Seule la tuberculose sera considérée ici: on peut voir au tableau 1 la distribution des patients à l'hôpital pendant l'année 1933. Il y eu 667 admissions, 421 sorties et 235 décès. Il y avait à peu près quatre cents patients tuberculeux à l'hôpital le 1er janvier des années 1933 et 1934. Au tableau 2, on peut voir que 52% des admis avaient trente ans ou moins, ce tableau montrant le nombre d'admissions en 1933 par sexe et par âge. Le tableau 3 montre la condition des patients à la sortie: moins de 9% des patients étaient guéris, et 41% sortaient de l'hôpital sans amélioration; 52% des patients prirent congé sans autorisation médicale ou furent expulsés pour indiscipline!

TABLEAU 1
La distribution des patients pendant l'année 1933

	Hommes	Femmes	Totaux
Malades hospitalisés le 1er janvier 1933	211	184	395
Admissions en 1933	321	346	667
Totaux	532	530	1 062
Sorties	218	203	421
Déçès	117	118	235
Totaux	335	321	656
Malades hospitalisés le 1er janvier 1934	197	209	406

TABLEAU 2
Admissions en 1933 selon l'âge et sexe

Age	14-20	20-30	30-40	40-50	50-60	60-70	70-80	80-90	Totaux
Hommes	41	108	77	52	35	6	1	1	321
Femmes	56	139	100	29	14	7	0	1	346
Totaux	97	247	177	81	59	13	1	2	667

TABLEAU 3
A. Condition des patients à la sortie — 1933

	Apparemment guéris	Maladie non-progressive	Maladie apparemment non-progressive	Au repos à la maison	Améliorés	Non-améliorés	Totaux
Hommes	13	14	10	14	78	89	218
Femmes	24	10	20	8	58	83	203
Totaux	37	24	30	22	136	172	421

B. Raisons de congé non-associées avec la tuberculose — 1933

	Non-tuberculeux	Partis sans congé	Indisciplinés
Hommes	14	115	14
Femmes	18	87	4
Totaux	32	202	18

TABLEAU 4
Interventions chirurgicales en 1933

Bronchoscopies	15	Pleuroscopies	6
Costotomies	11	Plombage	1
Jacobeus	11	Pneumolyse	1
Laryngoscopies	1	Ponctions	10
Lavage des plèvres	11	Poudrage pleuraux	3
Lipiodols	53	Thoracoplasties	60
Lobectomies	3	Thoracoscopies	10
Phrénemphraxis	4	Transfusions	7
Phrénicectomies	43	Totaux	250

Le dernier tableau montre le nombre et la qualité des interventions chirurgicales complétées en chirurgie thoracique à l'hôpital du Sacré-Coeur pendant l'année 1933: il y en eut 250, dont soixante thoracoplasties, trois lobectomies, et sept transfusions. Ce dernier fait est intéressant: le docteur Norman Bethune introduisit au Sacré-Coeur la transfusion sanguine de personne à personne, et l'hôpital devint un des premiers à Montréal à avoir sa propre banque de sang. Le docteur Gérard Rolland devait organiser la "mécanique" de la transfusion: le donneur de sang venait souvent de l'extérieur de la ville, et l'opération était quelquefois remise à une date ultérieure, ce qui était très fâcheux pour lui. Bethune donnait de temps en temps des "opérations démonstrations" pour des visiteurs de l'extérieur, et l'horaire des opérations était alors établi en fonction de ces visiteurs. En général il opérait une journée par semaine. Il était très attaché aux enfants, et on pouvait souvent le trouver sur l'étage dans une chaise berçante avec un enfant sur ses genoux; après le décès d'un patient il devenait très déprimé pour quelques jours; mais il était inquiet quand il avait guéri l'un deux estimant que le retour dans son milieu amènerait une rechute suite au contact direct avec d'autres tuberculeux.

* * *

Entre 1933 et 1936, les activités de Norman Bethune étaient vraiment incroyables: comme enseignant en chirurgie et aussi en peinture pour les enfants du quartier; comme peintre de murales et de tableaux — de fait pendant un hiver il avait loué une chambre près de l'hôpital du Sacré-Coeur dont les murs se couvrirent de murales au grand désaroi de la propriétaire; comme écrivain tant dans le domaine de la médecine que de la prose non-médicale ou de la poésie; comme inventeur d'instruments chirurgicaux, tel l'interne de fer; comme chirurgien; comme initiateur de techniques nouvelles. Il a aussi probablement été le premier chirurgien à faire des thoracoplasties bilatérales; le premier au Canada à faire une pneumonectomie chez un enfant de dix ans; le premier à faire des transfusions sanguines à l'hôpital du Sacré-Coeur. De plus, il participait activement au travail des sociétés scientifiques. Il devint, par exemple, membre de l'exécutif de l'association américaine de chirurgiens thoraciques et visita la Russie avec Hans Selye et Fred Banting en 1935 pour y examiner de plus près les services de santé et assister au congrès international de physiologie. Comme omnipracticien, il avait organisé une clinique médicale gratuite pour les chômeurs. Mais le plus important fut son propre développement au niveau social: sa conviction que le niveau de santé d'une population dépend tout autant des conditions socioéconomiques que des services de santé, car pour la population québécoise, la médecine n'avait qu'une influence très limitée sur la tuberculose. Il y avait une tuberculose des riches et une tuberculose des pauvres. Il devint ainsi intéressé au développement des systèmes de santé. A Noël 1935, il forma un groupe d'étude dont il fut l'animateur et le secrétaire, le *Montreal Group for the Security of the People's Health*. Une deuxième version du rapport du comité fut publiée en août 1936, avant l'élection provinciale, et envoyée aux professionnels de la santé. Un résumé fut remis au premier ministre Godbout, au chef de l'opposition monsieur Duplessis, à chacun des candidats pour l'élection provinciale, et aux maires et échevins de la ville de Montréal: rien ne changea. Bethune partit alors pour l'Espagne et la Chine: il avait compris l'importance de l'engagement politique pour résoudre les problèmes médico-sociaux affectant les populations.

On pourrait donc diviser la vie de Bethune en quatre parties: sa période de formation de 1890 à 1926; son apprentissage personnel et médical des problèmes de la tuberculose de 1926 à 1933; sa période d'activités multiples et de développement social personnel pendant son temps à l'hôpital du Sacré-Coeur, et finalement la période d'intenses activités médico-chirurgicales en Espagne et en Chine.

* * *

J'aimerais faire mention de plusieurs conversations qui j'ai eues avec les docteurs Rolland et Cousineau, et avec soeur Ena Charlant, étudiante infirmière en 1933 et ensuite chef des services infirmiers en chirurgie thoracique: les deux hommes vénèrent le nom de Norman, comme ils l'appellent (les anglophones parlent toujours de Beth), et soeur Charland, en voyant pour la première fois l'affiche qui annonce ce congrès, s'exclama "Oh! il a ses yeux carrés"; c'était apparemment une expression courante voulant dire que Norman travaillait d'une façon concentrée: il fallait faire attention! Soeur Charland n'avait pas revu cette expression de visage depuis les années trente; elle parle de Norman avec admiration, sincérité et amour, comme tous ceux avec qui, à l'hôpital du Sacré-Coeur, il avait travaillé.

* * *

RÉFÉRENCES
1. Archives, hôpital du Sacré-Coeur.
2. Archives, maison-mère, Soeurs de la Charité de la Providence.
3. Communications personnelles: soeur Ena Charland; docteurs Georges Cousineau et Gérard Rolland; le docteur Roger Alarie, Directeur des Services Professionnels, hôpital du Sacré-Coeur; Irene Kon, dont le père était un ami de Bethune (Louis Kon), elle-même amie de Bethune.

Résumé

Pierre Delva situe Norman Bethune dans le milieu hospitalier où il a oeuvré de 1933 à 1936. D'abord un hôpital pour incurable et cancéreux fondé en 1898 par les Soeurs de Charité de la Providence, l'hôpital du Sacré-Coeur occupe son site actuel à Cartierville depuis 1926. En 1931, l'assemblée des médecins de l'hôpital décide d'engager un spécialiste en chirurgie pulmonaire et en janvier suivant Bethune devient le premier chef de chirurgie thoracique. Georges Cousineau, responsable de l'anesthésie, ainsi que Georges Deshaies et Gérard Rolland complètent l'équipe de Bethune qui, trois jours par semaine, effectue des lobectomies, pneumonectomies et compressions de poumons à une époque où les chances de succès atteignent à peine 50%.

C'est Bethune qui introduisit la transfusion sanguine de personne à personne et, grâce à son initiative, le Sacré-Coeur devint un des premiers hôpitaux montréalais à avoir sa propre banque de sang.

Pendant cette période extrêmement fertile de sa vie, Bethune fut à la fois chirurgien, enseignant, inventeur d'instruments chirurgicaux, écrivain, artiste et engagé dans un groupe d'étude sur la santé communautaire qui deviendra le Montreal Group for the Security of the People's Health.

Abstract

The medical environment in which Bethune worked from 1933 to 1936 was l'hôpital Sacré-Coeur. Established in 1898 as a hospital for incurable and cancer patients by the Sisters of Charity of the Providence, the hospital has occupied its present location in Cartierville since 1926. Following a decision in 1931 by the assembly of doctors of the hospital to hire a specialist in thoracic surgery, Bethune became the head of this service in 1933. George Cousineau, in charge of anaesthesia, Georges Deshaies and Gerald Rolland made up Bethune's team which, three days a week, performed lobectomies, and pneumonectomies and instituted pneumothorax — all this at a time when chances of success from radical surgery reached only 50%.

Bethune introduced person-to-person blood transfusion, and, thanks to his initiative, Sacré-Coeur became one of the first hospitals in Montreal to have its own blood bank.

During this extremely fertile period of his life Bethune was not only a surgeon, inventor of surgical instruments and teacher, but also a writer and artist. He also became involved in a group discussing public health that was to become the Montreal Group for the Security of the People's Health.

Creativity in Norman Bethune:
His Medical Writings and Innovations
David A.E. Shephard

The context of this discussion of Norman Bethune is threefold: his experience of tuberculosis, both as a patient and as a physician; his medical writings and his work as an innovator in thoracic medicine and surgery and as an inventor of medical and surgical instruments, particularly in relation to the management of patients with tuberculosis; and, as the end-point in discussion, the quality of creativity that made Bethune the man he was.

My primary sources have been chiefly the 14 medical articles that Bethune wrote between 1929 and 1936[1]. Each sheds light on Bethune but three are of particular importance. These are, first, "A Plea for Early Compression in Pulmonary Tuberculosis", published in the *Canadian Medical Association Journal* in July 1932; second, "A Phrenicectomy Necklace", which can be read in the *American Review of Tuberculosis* of September 1932; and third, his final work, "Some New Thoracic Surgical Instruments", published in the *Canadian Medical Association Journal,* December 1936. Of value also have been two texts of John Alexander: *The Surgery of Pulmonary Tuberculosis* (1925) and *The Collapse Therapy of Pulmonary Tuberculosis* (1937). As secondary sources the several biographies of Bethune have provided a valuable overview of Bethune himself.

Bethune and Tuberculosis

A turning point in Bethune's career was his reading, while a patient in Trudeau Sanatorium, of Alexander's *The Surgery of Pulmonary Tuberculosis*. Bethune was profoundly influenced by Alexander's message, which was simply that *surgical* treatment of tuberculosis, an uncommon practice in the 1920s, provided the tuberculosis patient with "an excellent chance to escape a certain tuberculosis death and to become permanently well".[2] Bethune resolved to specialize in thoracic surgery and soon, in his turn, came to advocate surgical treatment of tuberculosis.

His well-argued paper, "A Plea for Early Compression in Pulmonary Tuberculosis",[3] is an example of such advocacy, especially in Canada. Thus he wrote, in authoritative vein, that

> no sanatorium today can call itself modern which does not have some form of collapse therapy, a distribution of say 30 percent pneumothoraces, 15 percent phrenicectomies, and 5 percent thoracoplasties or extrapleural wax fillings, etc.

And, in more vociferous vein, that

> optimism as to the outcome in cavity cases when treated conservatively is not only fatuous but unjustifiable. That many cases will recover and few cavities close without surgical intervention no one will deny, but when sanatoria show in their records on discharge only 25 percent arrested minimal cases, and only 2 to 5 percent of arrest in the moderately and advanced groups, one begins to wonder if this is good enough.

This paper is interesting for another reason: it points to Bethune's growing awareness of the importance of socioeconomic factors in the prevention and causation of tuberculosis. Although he wrote in the same paper that "we, as physicians, can do little to change the environmental forces which predispose to re-infection", in reference to "poverty, poor food, unsanitary surroundings, contact with infectious foci, overwork, and mental strain", he clearly understood the socioeconomic aspects of the disease and the need for the medical aspects to be considered in relation to the socioeconomic aspects. Three sentences from his paper, which was primarily a medical paper, foreshadow his later journey into the common territory bordered by social, economic, political and medical lines:

> Lack of time and money kills more cases of pulmonary tuberculosis than lack of resistance to that disease. The poor man dies because he cannot afford to live. Here the economist and the sociologist meet the compressionist on common ground.

Bethune experienced the illness of tuberculosis as a patient and as a surgeon. He was, therefore, unusually well qualified to speak about the various factors that related to causation, pathology and treatment of tuberculosis. But of greater significance in this discussion is the fact that, in this context as in others in his life, he went beyond simple lip-service acceptance of the relevant factors. He did more: he asked himself how *he* might counter these factors, what he, in his position, might do to make life better for his patients. This combination of understanding, realization of the obligation to act, and then action underlay his creativity, whatever his endeavour.

Innovations in Thoracic Technique, and Surgical and Medical Inventions

Among innovations in thoracic technique that we associate with Bethune's name was, then, his advocacy of various forms of surgical treatment for pulmonary tuberculosis. Especially important among these forms of treatment was collapse therapy. Alexander, in his textbook on collapse therapy, wrote that this form of therapy was "the only important addition to the treatment of pulmonary tuberculosis since the sanatorium was introduced ... [and that it had] revolutionized the management of phthisis".[4] Bethune was one of a handful of thoracic surgeons on this continent who followed Alexander's lead, and in Canada Bethune vigorously shared this lead, first at the Royal Victoria Hospital and then at l'Hôpital Sacré-Coeur.

"A Plea for Early Compression in Pulmonary Tuberculosis", well argued in its development and convincing in its rhetoric, was the paper of an advocate, but Bethune's detailed suggestions for collapse therapy were the work of an educator also. Thus he provided guidelines for *phrenicectomy* (both temporary and permanent), for *scaleniectomy*, for *pneumothorax* (both unilateral and bilateral), for *wax filling* of cavities, and for *thoracoplasty*. Published in Canada's national general medical journal, this paper presented the simple message that "tuberculosis can be cured, not only clinically but often anatomically, if properly treated in its early acute stage". He listed ways in which this message might be spread: "better education of doctors, public education to the point of phthisiophobia, enforced periodic physical and x-ray examinations, early diagnosis, early bed rest, early compression, isolation and protection of the young".

* * *

Three examples of Bethune's management of pulmonary tuberculosis are worth brief discussion: his use of cotton-seed oil in oleothorax; his unusual choice of maggots as therapeutic agents in pulmonary infection; and his research into and use of the technique of pleural poudrage.

Cotton-seed oil for oleothorax

One of the problems in treating a patient by means of artificial pneumothorax was general loss of space, consequent on the pathological process of progressively obliterative pneumothorax, which could be filled with air that would rest the lungs. In 1922, Bernou in France had introduced gomenol as an alternative to air for this purpose, but this agent had never become popular in the North American continent. Bethune suggested commercial cotton-seed oil as a cheap, pure and effective alternative.

In his 1932 paper entitled "Cotton-seed Oil in Progressively Obliterative Artificial Pneumothorax",[5] Bethune described his use of cotton-seed oil. He found that "it was definitely less irritating than 5 percent gomenol or liquid paraffin" and reported its use in three cases. His was a small study but his documentation was diligent and his period of follow-up consistent with that of the careful clinician.

Maggots for Treatment of Lung and Pleural Infections

Quite different were Bethune's reports of treatment of purulent lesions of the lungs and pleura with maggots, but again they illustrate his originality of thought. The case he described in the *Canadian Medical Association Journal* in March 1935[6] seems to have been the first such case to be reported in the literature of chronic recurrent empyema and the painstaking and serious report contained in the *Journal of Thoracic Surgery*[7] for February 1936 was leavened with a pleasing strain of humour.

The humour arose in the discussion that was appended to this 1936 paper, in which he described use of maggots in seven patients. An American member of the audience concluded "from the presentation . . . [that] there is certain indication for treatment of this sort," but the discussant went on to report having been unable "to train the maggots sufficiently well to stay in the wound"; he wondered therefore whether "Canadian maggots are more easily trainable and more easily hypnotized". To which Bethune enjoined: "they were not Canadian-born maggots; they were American maggots naturalized" — in reference to the source of the maggots he used.

Pleural Poudrage

More memorable than maggot management was the technique of pleural poudrage, in which talc was blown into the pleural space. Bethune's paper,

Pleural Poudrage — "A New Technique for the Deliberate Production of Pleural Adhesions as a Preliminary to Lobectomy"[8] (1935), represents Bethune the investigative surgeon and physician author at his best. The problem (how to fix one part of the lung during resection of another) was clearly stated; the limitations of previous work were outlined; his own research, both experimental and clinical, was detailed, in particular the technique of pleural poudrage that required specially designed instruments; the follow-up period was 10 months or longer; and the writing was clear and direct yet also imaginative.

This was good work, good enough to become known as the Bethune method. Archibald reportedly claimed that pleural poudrage was "a distinct advance", and that this and other of Bethune's contributions" make Bethune's genius in mechanical inventions an established fact".[9]

* * *

With respect to his inventions, Bethune gave much thought to the design of the instruments he used, and he always stressed craftmanship. His 1936 paper on surgical instruments[10] and his 1932 paper entitled "A Phrenicectomy Necklace"[11] provide us with insight concerning two key aspects of Bethune the inventor.

A passage from the 1936 paper underlines Bethune's view of surgical inventions from a historical perspective:

> Surgical instruments in use today are a curious collection of the awkward heirlooms of the past, mixed with the new, delicate and efficient tools of contemporary technology. As a general statement, few will deny that many surgical instruments could be vastly improved upon . . . Just as the inventor of the first primitive wheel can be held responsible . . . for the very mixed blessings of modern machinery, so that unknown genius who hinged together two knives to make the first pair of scissors, is the true father of modern surgical instruments.

This demonstrates Bethune's lineage as an inventor, but the three sentences that follow this passage point to the dimension of Bethune as creator as well as inventor:

> The mind of the modern inventor . . . is in tune (perhaps he sets the tune) with the spirit of his time. His dissatisfaction with the old, impatience with slowness and inefficiency, are characteristics of his age. Even variation for its own sake, as an artistic gesture of freedom from conventional design, is quite in the modern manner.

This is a key passage, to be set alongside the passage about the ground shared by the economist, the sociologist and the compressionist. Bethune was an inventor but he had the qualities of a da Vinci rather than an Edison.

Of his many inventions (Table 1), I will select seven for brief comment: the pneumothorax apparatus, and the pleural fluid aspirator and aspirating foot pump described in his 1936 paper; the scapula lifter and retractor, rib shears, rib stripper and periosteum elevator also described in this paper; and the phrenicectomy necklace described, in his 1932 paper.

Pneumothorax Apparatus, Pleural Fluid Aspirator and Aspirating Foot Pump

As Bethune wrote in the 1936 paper, "the injection of air into the space is such

TABLE 1
Bethune's Surgical Inventions

Lipiodol oil-gun
Pneumothorax apparatus (several designs)
Aspirator and aspirating foot-pump for pneumothorax apparatus
Scapula lifter and retractor
Chest rests
Rib shears
Rib stripper, periosteum scraper
Lobectomy tourniquet
Transilluminator (for intrathoracic work), trocar and annula, clip applicator
Pleural powder blower
Air-tight pneumatic empyema tube
Phrenicectomy retractors, hook, and avulser

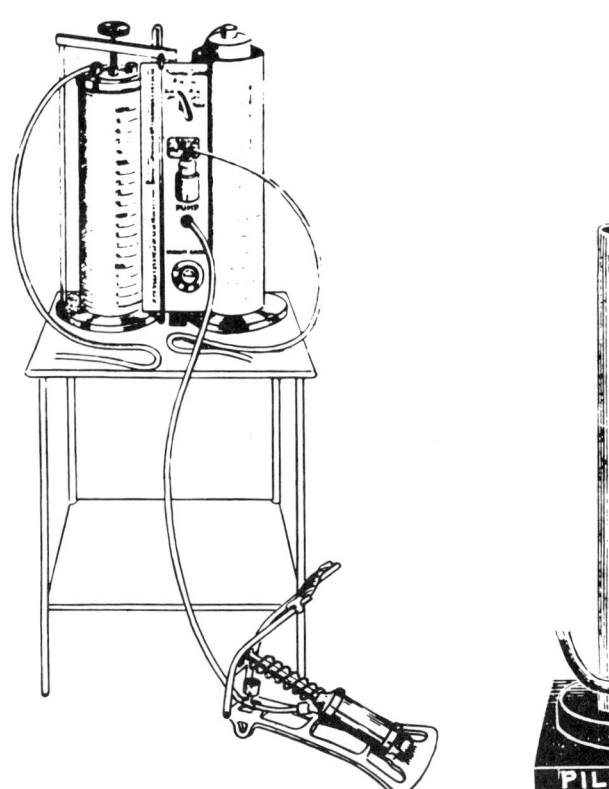
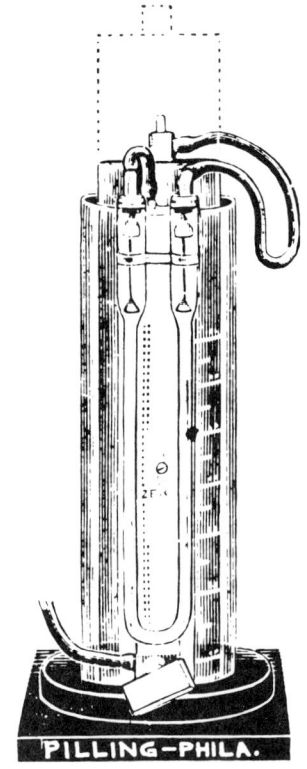

Fig. 1. Bethune's pneumothorax apparatus, constructed of two cylinders. See text for full description. (Courtesy, *Canadian Medical Association Journal.*)

Fig. 2. Bethune's pneumothorax apparatus, the entire unit, including the Bethune Foot Pump, assembled. (Courtesy, *Canadian Medical Association Journal.*)

a simple affair, mechanically considered, that it lends itself to a large number of possible variations". He noted that some 25 types of machines had been described since Forlanini proposed the technique in 1882; he designed his own, as was his wont in general, "to improve craftmanship".

The pneumothorax apparatus he described in 1936 (Fig. 1) made use of the gasometer principle, which Murphy had relied on in designing his apparatus 40 years earlier though Bethune was not aware of Murphy's design until after he had invented his own in turn. The way Bethune's apparatus worked is best understood from his 1936 article:

> Two transparent jars of unbreakable pyralin are inverted, one inside the other. The outer jar is filled three-quarters full of ordinary tap water. The trapped air is thus under a pressure corresponding to the weight of the inverted inner jar. This has been fixed, arbitrarily, at plus 10 c.c. of water, as a working head of pressure. It can be varied easily by lifting up the inner jar with two fingers, so that a negative pressure of minus 15 c.c. or lower can be obtained, or by pressing down with one finger, so that positive pressure up to plus 20 c.c. is obtainable... For initial injections, the inner jar is run down until the enclosed air is at zero pressure. Two hundred c.c. of air can be sucked into the pleural cavity by virtue of its own negative pressure. There is only one tap to manage. This controls the air flow from the jar to the needle. The water manometer has no tap and cannot be cut off, and registers at all times one of three possible pressures. (1) When the tap is "off" the manometer registers the pressure at the point of the needle. (2) When the tap is "on" and the air is flowing from an unobstructed needle it registers an intermediate pressure between the pressure at the point of the needle, and the head of pressure of the air in the jar. (3) When the tap is "on" but air is not flowing, owing to needle obstruction, it registers the head pressure in the jar only... When the tap is off these fluctuations immediately fall in total pressure, but increase in swing and show at once the true intra-pleural pressure. Both ends of the manometer are protected by small valves which cut off automatically wide excursions in either direction of the water column, such as are produced by coughing or very high or low pleural pressures. These valves drop back of their own weight when the pressure causing them to close is relaxed.

His apparatus was simple and worked well. That it was useful not only to Bethune is evident from the fact that Alexander paid Bethune the compliment of an eponym, referring to the foot pump as the Bethune Foot Pump[12] (Fig. 2). Alexander referred in fact not only to the pneumothorax apparatus itself but also the pleural fluid aspirator and the aspirating foot pump that Bethune added to the pneumothorax apparatus. Alexander explained the need for the whole apparatus: "in active pneumothorax clinics, it is convenient to have set aside in readiness special apparatus for fluid aspiration and for the management of a ruptured lung".[13] Bethune's entire apparatus was an advance on Potain's aspirator: with the latter one could not determine the negative pressure in the aspirator jar but with Bethune's, as he himself explained, "the gauge on the pump informs the operator at all times of the negative pressure in the jar": one stroke gave "about five inches of partial volume". Bethune's foot pump was simple and freed up an operator's hand; in Bethune's hospital it was named "The Nurses' Friend".

Scapula Lifter and Retractor, Rib Shears, Rib Stripper, and Periosteum Scraper (Fig. 3)

Another useful piece of apparatus Bethune invented, this time nicknamed "The Iron Intern", was the *Scapula Lifter and Retractor*, also described in the 1936 paper. "This instrument", wrote Bethune, "lifts and holds the scapula up and forwards, off the chest wall, during an upper stage thoracoplasty". He added that "a really extraordinary range of movement is obtained by three universal ball and socket joints". The apparatus was humanoid: "it consists of an 'arm', a 'fore-arm', and a 'hand'. The joints are the 'shoulder', the 'elbow', and the 'wrist'. And "to operate", Bethune explained, "place the clawed hand beneath the scapula, lift the fore-arm up, pull back the arm, and tighten both screws".

Again, simple and practical. It seems to have been Bethune's own invention: as he wrote, "this instrument was invented because its originator acted for one year as second assistant, with the job of scapula retractor... [and] he [Bethune] was the one who was the most fatigued at the end of an operation.

Modifications of "The Iron Intern" are still in use today.

Also in use today are the *Bethune Rib Shears*, which are his most enduring and most probably his most original invention: surgical instrument catalogues illustrate nothing similar to Bethune's. Bethune's own description in the 1936 paper explains the background and value of his rib shears:

> My original model of 1928 was a copy of a leather-cutting shears made by the United States Machinery Company. The only alteration made was to blunt the points. Two years later it was remodelled, using a stiffer steel (the first was too flexible), and putting rubber grips on the handles. For ordinary use it is still my favourite. The ratio of jaws to handle length is 3.5 cm. to 29.5 cm. This gives tremendous leverage; most ribs can be cut with one hand. It is as powerful as a double-action shears and is lighter and more graceful in manipulation. It takes the hard work out of rib work.

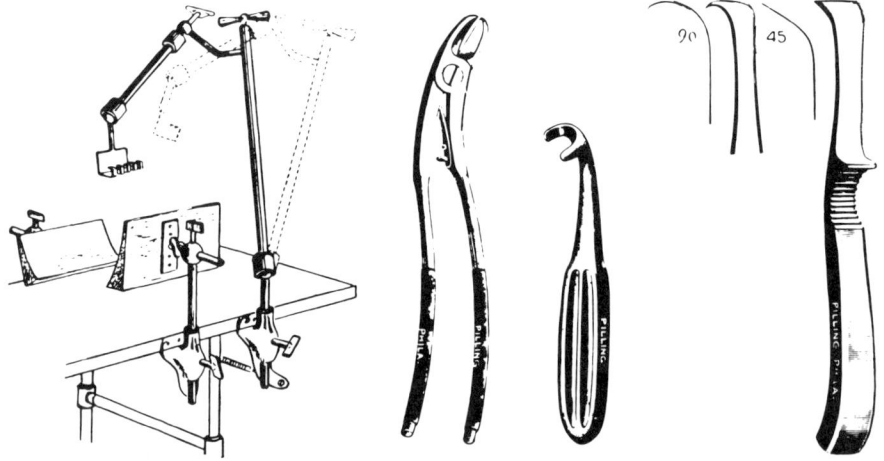

Fig. 3. Bethune's scapula lifter and retractor, rib cutter (or shears), rib stripper, and periosteum scraper. (Courtesy, *Canadian Medical Association Journal.*)

The *Rib Stripper* and *Periosteum Scraper* are worth mention for two reasons. First, the rib stripper was a modification of an instrument already in use, but Bethune observed that he made the modification to suit his "own particular fancy". In other words, he knew precisely what he wanted in a surgical instrument and designed what he wanted. Second, although he modified both the rib stripper and the periosteum scrapers from instruments designed by others he was careful to give credit to the original designers — in the first case, Matson and Plenk, and in the second Faraboef [sic].

The Phrenicectomy Necklace

In Bethune's day, phrenicectomy was a common operation. The rationale was interruption of the phrenic nerve and thus rest of the diaphragm it innervated, and consequently of the lung itself. Bethune used it both to mark the site of incision and then to permit the patient to disguise the scar of the phrenicectomy wound (Fig. 4). Use of the necklace is best described in Bethune's own words, taken from his 1932 paper:

> Take an ordinary bead necklace of the "choker" type (a 10¢ one from Woolworth's is excellent) and, after removal of a few beads from the string, introduce a thin, slotted, flexible, silver bar, 1 1/2 inches long and 1/4 inch wide. A short link of silver chain, 5 inches long, is placed at one end of the necklace from 12 to 16 inches . . . This bar has a slot 1 inch long and 1/8 inch wide. The necklace, is placed in position with the patient sitting upright, head to the front . . . The adjustable clasp is fastened and the bar is then placed in the correct position by palpating the anterior scalene muscle which is felt below. With a small applicator dipped in mercurochrome, one then can draw a line on the skin through the slot in the bar, without disturbing the beads. The necklace is then

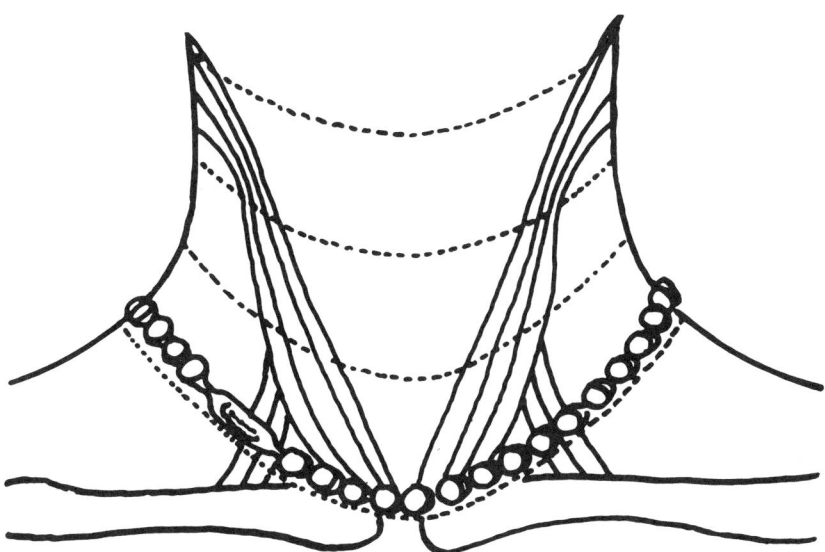

Fig. 4. Bethune's phrenicectomy necklace. See text for full description. (Courtesy, *American Review of Tuberculosis.*)

removed and the patient placed in the operating position. The incision is made through the red line. After the operation the patient is informed that a necklace of such and such a length (say 14 inches) will hide the scar from view.

To this description were added the words of Bethune the man as much as Bethune the surgeon: "strange to say, this seems to fill the female breast with the most profound gratitude".

Even though Bethune himself referred to this device as no more than an "amusing little trinket", the invention leads us to comment on no less than the creative impulse in Bethune. For in this brief report on the use of the necklace Bethune does more than address a relatively minor surgical issue. His writing here makes one realize that Bethune was not only a surgeon committed to the practice of surgery but also a man who recognized that his work to a large degree was informed by a commitment to the creative impulse:

> Bound by the rigid and inexorable laws of his medium, the human body, the surgeon is permitted but few of the liberties his fellow craftsmen may take who work with stone, wood or metal . . . He is not allowed the exhibition of playful fancies, wit or humour, which often has the soul of a creative artist, although the nature of his plastic medium restricts the free play of his artistic nature. Like most other men, his creative force is confined to one channel and allowed but one escape . . .

Synthesis: The Creative Impulse

Most surgeons are craftsmen and many are highly skilled in the practice of their craft, but few have "the soul of a creative artist"; rare is the surgeon who is concerned with "creative force". Such a concern is one of many aspects of Bethune's personality that made him a singular man, and in order to understand fully his approach to the surgical art it is necessary to consider some aspects of creativity.

Creativity was one of the forces that motivated Bethune. It is, of course, apparent in his various innovations and inventions but it equally informs many — so many — other interests of Bethune. Let us consider just four examples of these interests[14]. First, his somewhat utopian design for a model city for tuberculosis patients, though merely an idea, was a most creative one. Second, as a physician-citizen of Montreal in 1935 and 1936, his increasing concern about the people's health care led him to put forward some creative ideas relating to health care plans for Quebec. Third, as a physician-author, while usually direct and matter-of-fact in his approach, he occasionally wrote with pleasing imagery. Thus in his paper entitled "The Silver Clip Method of Preventing Hemorrhage While Severing the Interpleural Adhesions", he described in unusual terms the use of a special transilluminator instead of a thoracoscope to illuminate the pleural cavity:

> The thoracoscope with its own light is rather similar to a man entering a small wood carrying a lantern in his hand. With the separate and far-away transilluminator light, the view obtained is similar to that of a man walking towards one in the same wood with the trees thrown into bold relief[15].

And, as the fourth example of creativity, one can refer to Bethune's interest in art and literature; his nine-scene mural, an allegorical view of his own susceptibility to the tubercle bacillus painted while he was a patient in Trudeau Sanatorium, is of extraordinary interest in this respect, as are his poems.

Bethune clearly acknowledged the power of the creative force, and it is reasonable to suppose that it was the creative force that made Bethune the person he was. In this way, rather than either idolize or reject Bethune, perhaps we can come to evaluate Bethune as a human being in terms of what he *created*.

Let us, then, think about Bethune in the context of creativity defined by Carl Rogers and by Walter Pater, thinking in particular of Bethune as a human being who lived through his experiences.

First, the context of Carl Rogers' view of creativity:

> The creative process is . . . the emergence in action of a novel relational product, growing out of the uniqueness if the individual on the one hand, and the materials, events, people, or circumstances of his life on the other . . .
> The mainspring of creativity appears to be . . . *man's tendency to actualize himself, to become his potentialities* . . . when the individual is 'open' to all of his experiences . . . then his behavior will be creative . . . To the degree that the individual is open to all aspects of his experience, and has available all the varied sensings and perceivings which are going on within his organism, then the novel products of his interaction with his environment will tend to be constructive both for himself and others[16].

If we assume that some individuals are more open to their experiences than are others, Bethune was surely one of those who was acutely aware of what he experienced throughout his life. As a physician he was surely more open to all that he experienced around him than were most of his professional colleagues. And as a human being it was to society — the world society — that he decided to make available his understanding and his talents. In this light, Bethune was most certainly "constructive" and therefore creative.

The second context is that of Walter Pater, whom Bethune greatly admired. One statement by Pater crystallizes the experiential approach, an approach that seems the essence of Bethune's philosophy:

> Not the fruit of experience, but experience itself is the end . . . To burn always with a hard, gemlike flame, to maintain this ecstasy, is success in life[17].

Bethune *lived* his life fully, *creatively;* the 'hard, gemlike flame' that was Bethune warmed and illuminated life around all who responded to him.

In these terms Bethune was as much as any of us can hope to be, both constructive and "successful". His times are long past but the legacy he *created* continues to move and to motivate us.

* * *

REFERENCES AND NOTES

1. These 14 papers are listed on page 236 of this book. Of these papers, in this chapter I cite only those that are of immediate relevance to the present topic.
2. John Alexander, *The Surgery of Pulmonary Tuberculosis,* Philadelphia, 1925, p. 17.
3. Norman Bethune, "A Plea for Early Compression in Pulmonary Tuberculosis," *Canadian Medical Association Journal.* 27, (1932) pp. 36-42.
4. Alexander, *The Collapse Therapy of Pulmonary Tuberculosis,* Springfield, 1937, p. 3 (hereinafter referred to as *Collapse Therapy*).

5. Bethune, "Cotton-seed Oil in Progressively Obliterative Artificial Pneumothorax," *American Review of Tuberculosis*, 26 (1932), pp. 763-770.
6. Bethune, "A Case of Chronic Thoracic Empyema Treated With Maggots," *Canadian Medical Association Journal*, 32 (1935), pp. 301-302.
7. Bethune, "Maggot and Allantoin Therapy in Tuberculosis and Non-tuberculosis Suppurative Lesions of the Lung and Pleura," *Journal of Thoracic Surgery*, 5 (1936), pp. 322-328.
8. Bethune, "Pleural Poudrage.— A New Technic for the Deliberate Production of Pleural Adhesions as a Preliminary to Lobectomy," *Journal of Thoracic Surgery*, 4 (1935), pp. 251-261.
9. Ted Allan and Sydney Gordon, *The Scalpel, The Sword: The Story of Doctor Norman Bethune*, Toronto, 1971, p. 54.
10. Bethune, "Some New Thoracic Surgical Instruments", *Canadian Medical Association Journal*, 35 (1936), pp. 656-662.
11. Bethune, "A Phrenicectomy Necklace," *American Review of Tuberculosis*, 26 (1932), pp. 319-321.
12. Alexander, *Collapse Therapy*, p. 231.
13. Alexander, *Collapse Therapy*, p. 231.
14. For more detailed comment on the model city, see the chapters by Libbie Park (pp. 138-144) and Katherine McCuaig (pp. 54-64); on the concern about the people's health care in Montreal, the text by Park; and on Bethune's interest in art and literature, the text by Charles Hill *et al.* (pp. 114-128), and Lee Thompson (pp. 104-113).
15. Bethune, "The Silver Clip Method of Preventing Hemorrhage While Severing Interpleural Adhesions. — With a Note on Transillumination," *Journal of Thoracic Surgery*, 2 (1933), pp. 302-306.
16. Carl Rogers, "Towards a Theory of Creativity," in P.E. Vernon (ed.), *Creativity*, Harmondsworth, 1970, pp. 139-140.
17. Cited by Allan and Gordon, p. 17.

* * *

Abstract

The quality of creativity in Bethune's medical writings and medical-surgical innovations can be considered from three standpoints: his experience of tuberculosis, both as a patient and as a thoracic surgeon; his dissatisfaction with current techniques and instruments and his desire for improved craftsmanship; and his own ideas about creativity itself. With respect to tuberculosis, Bethune followed the lead of Trudeau and Archibald in advocating collapse therapy (which Bethune himself had experienced as a patient), and some of his innovations in instrumentation were related directly to his determination to facilitate treatment (the technique of pleural poudrage, his pneumothorax apparatus and Bethune rib shears evidenced his innovative approach). Bethune saw himself as an innovator; he had the mind of a inventor, being dissatisfied with inefficient and poor craftsmanship. Some instruments he designed in order to make the surgeon's work easier and more efficient — witness the scapula lifter and retractor, in addition to the rib shears. But Bethune had, especially, the mind of a creator, and he recognized the gifts of the surgeon who was endowed with "creative force". Indeed, creativity is one of the qualities that made Bethune a singular man and a surgeon who was concerned not only with medical writing and medical-surgical innovations but also with matters more removed from surgery, such as the concept of a model city for tuberculosis patients, plans for a health care system in Quebec and art and literature as aspects of everyday life. Perhaps the secret to Bethune as a creative man is this: when an individual is open to all his experiences, that person's behaviour, in Carl Rogers' view, will be creative; when that individual emphasises the importance of experience, the "hard, gem-like flame" of experience in Walter Pater's words, the preservation of this flame is success in life. Bethune was open to all his experiences, and he lived his life fully; in this he was a successful human being.

Résumé

Les qualités créatrices de Bethune dans ses écrits médicaux et ses innovations médico-chirurgicales peuvent être envisagées sous trois aspects: l'expérience que Bethune a eue de la tuberculose, d'abord en tant que patient et ensuite comme spécialiste de la chirurgie thoracique; son insatisfaction devant les techniques couramment employées et les instruments de médecine et de chirurgie; et finalement ses propres vues sur la créativité. Dans le traitement de la tuberculose, Bethune a d'abord suivi les traces de Trudeau et d'Archibald qui préconisaient la collapsothérapie, qu'il avait lui-même expérimentée en tant que patient. Ses propres innovations — appareils pour pneumothorax, costotôme — découlaient directement de son désir de faciliter le traitement. Bethune se percevait comme un innovateur. Il avait l'intelligence d'un inventeur, qui ne se satisfait pas de ce qui existe, et qu'impatiente le travail inefficace et bâclé. Certains de ses instruments visaient à rendre plus facile et plus efficace le travail du chirurgien. C'est le cas, par exemple, de son costotôme. Bethune avait un esprit créateur et démontrait des dons de chirurgien doué d'une "force créatrice". En fait, la créativité est le trait de caractère qui fit de Bethune un être spécial, un chirurgien non seulement intéressé à écrire des articles médicaux et à inventer des instruments, mais aussi captivé par le projet d'une cité modèle pour tuberculeux, par l'élaboration d'un plan d'assurance-santé au Québec, par le développement de la littérature canadienne. Le secret de la créativité de Bethune réside peut-être dans ce qui suit: selon Carl Rogers, quand un individu est attentif à toutes ses expériences, son comportement devient créateur; quand un individu met en valeur l'importance de l'expérience, "la forte et précieuse flamme" de l'expérience comme le dit Walter Parer, la préservation de cette flamme est un gage de succès dans la vie. Bethune a été attentif à toutes ses expériences et il a vécu pleinement sa vie. En ce sens, c'est un être humain qui a réussi.

Norman Bethune and His Brethren: Poetry in Depression Montreal

Lee Briscoe Thompson

When I began my research on Canadian poetry of the Depression, I expected to find a thousand poetic equivalents of Norman Bethune — a throng of poets angry with the conditions of that terrible decade and railing against the status quo with all their poetic strength. In time I came to discover quite the contrary: crisis did not necessarily encourage innovation, Bethune was unique and his poetic brethren were a mere handful. The frustration of Bethune battling the medical establishment of Montreal — their often unexamined assumptions, the frequent smug self-satisfaction, the reliance on obsolete techniques and equipment — closely parallels that of Montreal's modernist and socialist poets. As Bethune became celebrated for throwing clumsy instruments across operating rooms, so the members of what has come to be known as the Montreal Group or the McGill Movement tossed aside 19th century clichés of poetic diction and traditional notions of the "proper" subjects of poetry. Similarly, Bethune's eager adoption and invention of new surgical techniques correspond to these poets' enthusiastic taking up of free verse and unconventional rhythms, of colloquial "unpoetic" language and of inelegant, even sordid or pathological, imagery. Conservative practitioners of the medical arts clung to received ideas of physiology and treatment; the traditionalists of Montreal verse, most prominently clustered beneath the roof of the Canadian Authors' Association, Montreal branch, stood as steadfastly and with equal moral certitude by the metre and diction of their forefathers, by sublime rather than pedestrian topics, by celebration and stoicism rather than protest and indignation. Like Bethune, the avant-garde writers of Depression Montreal were at pains to respond directly to modern life and to reflect it accurately — as it was seen, not as wishful thinking could make it.

* * *

Regarding the majority traditionalist stance, I for one was long in danger of cavalierly dismissing it entirely as evidence of brain damage. It seemed incongruous to me to encounter so many sonnets to a Westmount daffodil or quatrains of devotion to God and Mount Royal in the face of crushing unemployment, massive social disorientation, and the fact as well that modernist verse had already been accepted in Great Britain for at least a decade. It was only in the reading of some 15,000 of such verses that it became possible for me to appreciate conservative rationales.

Certainly there was the ostrich impulse: ignore trouble and expect it to go away. Widespread, too, was the escapist response: tacitly acknowledge the times but see no reason for a poet to stick around and be miserable with the heavens of poesy at hand. Leave the dirty work to the prose writers and dramatists, was the implication. There was, as well, in a culture dominated by an academic and ecclesiastical elite, a visceral distrust of proletarian poetry and free verse as radical, communist, totalitarian, anarchist — anathema. Anxiety and an instinctive rejection of the new and threatening were part of the response; with a conservative city in a conservative country, one is not surprised to note the dimensions of these reactions. In a world changing too quickly and an alarmed bourgeois society frantically seeking order — recognized order — modernism in poetry represented all that traditionalists saw going awry. Practitioners of free verse, of *vers libre,* for example, were often mocked as "verse libertines". (Until comparatively recently the popular 'wisdom' survived that free verse was like playing tennis without a net.) Conservatism was massively and predictably reinforced in versifiers by the strains of Depression, the repercussions of Western drought and the betrayal of the puritan ethic.

Depression themes seemed to many traditional Montreal poets inappropriate in view of the reasonable certainty that God's face was not permanently averted from His children, that the Depression *would* pass. What then would be the point of gloomy poems decrying specific abuses, documenting transitory problems and perceptions, brooding on the ephemeral and the quickly dated? For the traditionalist poet as fully as the visionary socialist, better times lay just around the corner; where the socialist might attain them by overthrowing the present system, the traditionalist would simply let things happen in their natural, God-ordained way. The impression of Canada as a nation and of Montreal as a city in fear of the Lord is borne out by the impressive amount of religious, consolatory verse written in that harsh decade. Such Montreal unknowns as Minton Johnston and Hazel Wanklyn drew from their own funds to publish poetry aimed at preserving the belief in a loving God despite the reality of a monumentally unloving world[1].

Other notions of responsibility militated against much radicalism in Montreal poetry in the 1930s. The traditionalists were heir to a simple version of Horace's doctrine that the functions of art were to instruct and to delight. They were committed to a vision of the poet as priest, as one who helps others to see, and in this belief they harmonized perfectly with their radical colleagues, including Bethune. Both schools proclaimed the artist's duty to improve and uplift his society; both wanted the best of human virtues to survive. To these ends the modernists attempted to expose societal and individual blemishes, but conventional tactics tried instead to elevate man's thoughts, to remind him of the godhead within, to woo him to greatness. A happier Canada, preservation of Poetry's sublimity, retention of values for better years, and even the fate of civilization were perceived to hang upon the success of this high goal.

* * *

Literary historians have tended to dismiss this substantial majority of Montreal's (and Canada's) Depression poets — the largely second-class versifiers, of course, but also the men in the street moved to express themselves more often than not in carefully regular metre, rhyme and sentiment. Interest has focussed instead, understandably, on the minority, the trailblazers, the innovators, the

Bethunes of poetry. Montreal had, in the mid-1920s, become the cradle of a modernist movement in Canadian poetry, led by Leo Kennedy, A.M. Klein, F.R. Scott, and A. J. M. Smith. All four were in vocal revolt against what they scorned as the Maple Leaf School of Poetry, and they used the short-lived periodicals, the *McGill Fortnightly Review* and the *Canadian Mercury,* to demand "the emancipation of Canadian literature from the state of amiable mediocrity and insipidity in which it now languishes".[2] Neither colonial nor Canadian chauvinist, the group worked to promote cosmopolitan Canadian writing, comparable in excellence and range of technique to the offerings of any other nation.

These concerns continued forcibly in Montreal of the Great Depression but merged increasingly with a social imperative. One might stick with his odes and rondeaus, but it became difficult not to challenge those artists who, in an era of widespread suffering, Quebec's increasing fascism, and the coming of another "war to end all wars", could (in Leo Kennedy's so quotable words) "blithely comb their woolly wits for stanzas to clarify intimate subjective reactions to Love, Beauty, the First Crocus, Snow in April and similar graceful but immediately irrelevant bubbles".[3] In the same article in *New Frontier,* Kennedy opined that "the function of poetry is to interpret the contemporary scene faithfully; is to interpret especially the progressive forces in modern life which alone stand for cultural survival".[4]

"Cultural survival" — we see here an instance of the many ways social poets turned the traditionalists' terms upon themselves. For example, if a poet were traditionally to be the "unacknowledged legislator of the world",[5] he must keep up to date, planned obsolescence being for automobiles and toasters, not for immortal bards. Fixed in a given timespan and a specific city rather than a timeless void, and blessed with the power of *poesis*, Montreal's new Adam must seize his opportunity to remake the universe — concretely. Next, charged as a humanitarian with being his brother's keeper, the poet became at once implicated in the class struggle. Asked, in the centuries-old phrase, to hold a mirror up to nature, the poet was obliged to reflect accurately the complexion of the modern age — one of smoke and steel and human sweat. Expected traditionally to concern himself with man's spiritual condition, a conscientious poet found it inextricable from economics and was inevitably drawn into contemplation of current, temporal conditions. Life was everywhere asserting itself, its power and its vitality and its pain. The coincidence of the Mass and the Masses was no accident; both were sacraments. And so it went, the rationales for a new poetry demonstrating a striking affinity with and clever use of the traditional frames of reference. Here, it is impossible to attempt anything like a proper review of Depression Montreal's major poets. The four most important were A.J.M. Smith, F.R. Scott, A.M. Klein, and Leo Kennedy. (Dorothy Livesay lived in Montreal only in 1933 and 1934.) Severe financial strictures on publishing, combined with the notorious timidity of Canadian publishing houses, forced almost all of these poets to forego producing individual volumes until the 1940s.

They turned, therefore, to periodicals outside of Montreal — *The Canadian Forum* and later *New Frontier* in particular — as rather sophisticated, leftist outlets for their work. A Montreal chapter of the Progressive Arts Club promoted literature in tune with the times, although admittedly with less success than the group in Toronto.

In an examination of Montreal's leading social poets (here firmly excluding Livesay), it seems fair to generalize that their main point of commonality was a lack of interest in actual revolution. They might dream of the millennium, turn to Marxist rhetoric, richly satirize and ruthlessly expose social injustices and political corruption, but the majority were essentially reformers intent upon the improvement of society by positive non-violent means. This does not mean they never foresaw violence; it simply suggests that they did not usually advocate it as an inevitable part of the class struggle. Nor, for that matter, was "class struggle" an invariable part of their thinking. In the matter of form these poets all attempted experimental verse of one type or another. But, again, they were consistent in their ability to handle traditional prosody, frequently combining it with a new, plain and often terse diction, irony, precise images, and realistic depiction of urban scenes. A third point of commonality was that all defended the place of social concerns in literature but, in theory and practice, placed their ultimate priority on Art over Cause. In retrospect it is indisputable that, by the end of the Great Depression, this nucleus of Montreal poets, in conjunction with fellow poets and periodicals in Toronto and of course the severity of the times, had brought Canadian poetry into the 20th century.

* * *

The alliteration of my title, "Bethune and His Brethren", was meant at first as an English-Canadian pun on the well-known epic poem by E. J. Pratt, "Brébeuf and His Brethren". At a more serious level, however, it attempts to suggest the kinship of innovators, a fellowship of creative spirits: Bethune in medicine, his friends in the arts. These remarks lead me not, as they might well have done, into comparisons of Brébeuf and Bethune — the epic scope, the heroic action, the stunning self-sacrifice — but instead into a realm where Bethune and his artist-friends converged: the writing of poetry.

The best known poem by Bethune, "Red Moon", was published in *New Frontier* in 1936:

>And this same pallid moon tonight
>Which rides so quietly, clear and high —
>The mirror of our pale and troubled gaze,
>Raised to a cool, Canadian sky,
>
>Above the shattered Spanish mountain tops
>Last night, rose low and wild and red,
>Reflecting back from her illumined shield
>The blood bespattered faces of the dead.
>
>To that pale disc we raise our clenched fists,
>And to those nameless dead our vows renew,
>Comrades who fall in angry loneliness,
>Who died for us — we will remember you[6].

The title, "Red Moon", yoking the political and the natural, anticipates the direction of the poem. Its form is quite traditional: three quatrains, tetrameter and pentameter lines, with alternate end rhyme. And the structure is far from free: a disciplined progression from pale austerity through red passion to a final merging of the two. The imagery starts with the "pallid moon", "quiet — clear and high", reflecting our "pale" gaze from "a cool, Canadian sky". The second, contrasting section plunges into the shattered, red wildness of Spain's civil war, where the moon, reduced to an unromantic disc, now reflects the "blood-bespattered faces of the dead." Then in each of the concluding four lines Bethune establishes a powerful juxtaposition of images: the pale passive moon versus the angry gesturing fist; the lifeless anonymity of the nameless dead versus the poet's renewed personal vows; comrades versus loneliness; and the death of loyalists for us versus our remembrance and memorial for them. The tone throughout is impassioned but controlled, bitter yet idealistic, graphic in its immediate effect while romantic in its vision of a solemn oath, of a covenant with the moon and the slain, of the fallen "illumined" by the shield-bearing moon, itself a warrior in the end. The poem captures Bethune at his most committed and charismatic; it has weathered well as an effective, moving exhortation to Canadians, already appropriately "troubled", to become involved in the pains and struggles of the modern world.

Scholarship of recent years has made public two other Bethune poems, of a personal nature, dedicated to an unidentified artist friend. The first, untitled, reads:

> STRIKE, if strike you must
> But warm us first, t'was better so to die
> Beneath your fierce flames than perish in the shade,
> Cold and alone.
> Perhaps, a miracle as happened once, should come again[;]
> That golden glare were made to stand
> And never sink and never leave the land
> Desolate and dark,
> But stay, suspended overhead,
> High, serene and clear
> Perpetuate[7].

Its imagery is dramatic, its form a very free verse within a formal tone and diction. The poem begins sharply, with such crisp and intense monosyllables as "strike", "fierce", "flames", "cold"; then its second stanza, opening with the tentative "Perhaps", shifts from striking and perishing to miracles and a vision of serenity. The pace is slowed by polysyllables down to the purity of a single, long, lingering, one-word final line, "Perpetuate." Lyrical qualities are achieved in a short space by such alliterations as "golden glare", "Desolate and dark," "stay suspended", "leave the land", and "fierce flames", and rhythm is accentuated by repetitions: "STRIKE, if strike you must," "never sink and never leave".

The other poem, "Remembrance", speaks with a considerably different voice:

> I can't pretend
> I think of you every hour, why
> Such dull days, I'm not aware of you at all,
> Any more than the beating of my heart. Thru,
> A young tree in the wind.
>
> A white flower in the grass,
> A quick bird in flight,
> A breath of sun-named air,
> And the whole world is emptied of delight
> Like a cup turned upside down
> And I am hollowed and sick for my love,
> But I can't pretend
> This happens every day,
> My Pony[8].

"Remembrance" demonstrates an alternation between romanticism and cynicism that seems to me an apt mirror of dichotomy in Bethune's own character — in one incarnation, literally a swashbuckling hero on a white horse; in another, the initiator of a venereal disease clinic for Detroit's working girls. Bethune here creates a similarly dual persona, he of the "dull days" when he thinks not at all of his love and he of the "hollowed" heart, "sick for my love" (a phrase reminiscent of troubadours and the Song of Songs). The rash of traditional poetic images and the lover's lament are played off for effect with the deliberately insistent descent from romanticism — "But I can't pretend/This happens every day" — and the two faces are slyly linked at the conclusion by the use of that absurd, sweet, private pet name.

Worth mentioning primarily for their fun and inventiveness are the verses of Bethune's "The T.B.'s Progress, a Drama in one act and nine painful scenes".[9] All but the first are quatrains, scanning fairly regularly as three-and four-beat lines, the rhythms in other words, of much popular verse such as limericks. Modelled on Hogarth's *The Rake's Progress,* Bethune's version was composed to accompany that memorable mural he painted at the Trudeau Sanatorium, Saranac Lake. This takes him through his prenatality, birth, childhood, and early manhood, plunges him into the Abyss of Despair, depicts his gaze upward from the capital "D" Depths, his return to the evil City, his search for health and happiness in the South-West, and his final embrace with the kindly Angel of Death. The action, expressed with a mock heroic flourish of capitalized nouns, features such Spenserian defenders as Sir S[c]hick who fights off the Dragon Dipth[eria] and Odysseyan Sirens (Fame, Wealth, Love and Art) who seek to swamp his ship. With black humour, Bethune chronicled his own demise from tuberculosis — "And so the plains got his remains/ For his disease deceased him" — and concluded stoically, even prophetically:

> Bright stars are out, long gone the burning sun,
> My little act is over, and the tiresome play is done.

Here again he has moved metrically from short irreverent bursts at the start to lengthy pensive lines at the end.

Genre theorists might question my mentioning prose in talking about Bethune's poetic efforts, but, in these times of "found" poems and a renewed interest in narrative verse, the presence of music, of lyricism, seem justification enough. "Spread" this poem on your mental page:

> Mud walls
> Mud floor
> Mud bed
> White paper windows
> Smell of blood and chloroform
>
> Cold
>
> Three o'clock in the morning....
> Men with wounds.
> Wounds
> like little dried pools
> caked with black-brown earth
> Wounds
> with torn edges
> filled with black gangrene
> neat wounds
> concealing beneath the abscess in their depths
> burrowing into
> and around
> the great firm muscles
> like a damned-back river
> running around
> and between the muscles
> like a hot stream
> wounds
> expanding outward
> decaying orchids or crushed carnations
> terrible flowers of flesh
> wounds
> from which the dark blood
> is spewed out in clots
> mixed with the ominous gas bubbles
> floating on the fresh flood
> of the still-continuing
> secondary
> haemorrhage[10].

This was Bethune writing a prose account of the Eighth Route Army in North China for the People's Relations Association. The rest of the article is equally vivid and moving. This was obviously not the scribbling of a Montreal Sunday poet, no simple exercise in egotistic self-expression. Here was poetry in a pure sense, articulating deeply and unconscious of self, naturally in touch with well-springs of rhythm in part because of innate oratorical gifts, in part because he cared so profoundly.

* * *

It is not my intention to try to drum these few verses and passages into a poetic cannon, to resurrect Bethune the Bard in any substantial way. What I think these pieces *do* amply display, however, is Bethune's imagination, his sensitivity to sound and image, his ease with modern as well as traditional techniques and themes in verse, and his capacity for the sort of truth-telling in art that he was so insistent upon in other fields, indeed as a principle of living. His verse was consistent with the ideas of a man who saw creativity as a natural part of being, who rejected compartments — doctor/poet/painter/social reformer/designer/ military strategist — and felt himself free to do a little or a lot of each. His medical advice that the doctor must be master of many skills found its parallel in his spontaneity with modern and conservative poetry, and both roles — artistic and medical — served as models for the versatility that Bethune was certain the new age would demand.

* * *

REFERENCES AND NOTES

1. Minton C. Johnston, *The Still Small Voice* (Montreal: Author, 1938). Hazel Wanklyn, *The Flower Within* (Montreal: Private printing, 1936). Johnston and Wanklyn are representative of this phenomenon not only in Montreal but throughout Canada.
2. Editorial, *Canadian Mercury*, 1 (December 1928), 3.
3. Leo Kennedy, "Directions for Canadian Poets," *New Frontier*, 1 (June 1936), 21-4.
4. *Ibid.*
5. Percy B. Shelley, "A Defence of Poetry".
6. Norman Bethune, "Red Moon," *Canadian Forum*, 17 (July 1937), 118. A slightly different version is given in Ted Allan and Sydney Gordon, *The Scalpel, the Sword: The Story of Dr. Norman Bethune* (1953; Toronto: McClelland & Stewart (revised edition), 1971; New York and London: Monthly Review Press, 1971), p. 107. These authors' phrasing suggests that their version, which I vastly prefer, was the original form, perhaps altered by the *Forum* editors. Poet Dorothy Livesay, writing of "Canadian Poetry and the Spanish Civil War," *107*, no. 2 (May 1976), 12-16, favours this version.
    And this same pallid moon tonight,
    Which rides so quiet — clear and high —
    The mirror of our pale and troubled gaze,
    Raised to a cool, Canadian sky,
    Above the shattered Spanish mountain tops
    Last night rose low and wild and red,
    Reflecting back from her illumined shield
    The blood-bespattered faces of the dead.
    To that pale moon I raise my angry fist,
    And to those nameless dead my vows renew:
    Comrades who fall in angry loneliness,
    Who die for us — I will remember you.
7. Bethune, untitled poem ("STRIKE, if strike you must"), in Roderick Stewart, *The Mind of Norman Bethune*, Toronto, 1977, p. 31.
8. Bethune, "Remembrance," in Stewart, *op. cit.*, p. 31.
9. Bethune, "The T.B.'s Progress, A Drama in one act and nine painful scenes," in Stewart, *op. cit.*, pp. 13-17. The book includes photographic reproductions of eight of the nine drawings. The mural and accompanying verses are briefly described in Allan and Gordon, *op. cit.*, pp. 33, 34, and described and illustrated (one drawing) in Stewart's *Bethune*, Toronto, 1973, p. 29f, p. 50 (vi).
10. Bethune, "Wounds," in Stewart, *The Mind of Norman Bethune*, pp. 122-123. Available also, albeit hard to locate, reprinted, is entitled "Dr. Bethune in China," in *Ideological Forum*, I (10.8.1968), 23-25, which cites its source as *Progressive Worker*, Vol. 3, no. 12, and reports that the article was originally written by Bethune for *China Today* (Yenan, China: People's Relations Association, March 1940).

* * *

Abstract

Among Bethune's Montreal friends were many artists, and with some of them he shared an interest in poetry. The Montreal Group (or the McGill Movement) of poets brought Canadian poetry into the 20th century, often by refuting 19th century clichés of poetic diction and traditional notions of subject matter and by using modern poetic techniques in responding directly to modern life and reflecting it accurately. Poets like Leo Kennedy, A.M. Klein, F.R. Scott and A.J.M. Smith promoted Canadian writing that was cosmopolitan and strove for excellence and a range of technique comparable to those qualities in poetry elsewhere. Their task in moving Canadian poetry away from the 19th century is paralleled, in the frustration they felt, in Bethune's frustration in battling the established views of Montreal's medical orthodoxy; their acceptance of new poetic techniques parallels Bethune's adoption of new techniques and devices in medicine and surgery. These poets' goals struck a chord in Bethune; Leo Kennedy, for example, held that poetry should interpret the contemporary scene faithfully and also the progressive forces that would ensure cultural survival. This response on the part of Bethune is surprising, for he was a sensitive poet, as "Red Moon", "Remembrance" and other poems show. His sensitivity to sound and image was consistent with his view that creativity is a natural part of being. His poems are characterized by a dramatic and powerful juxtaposition of images and lyricism; their tone is impassioned yet controlled, bitter yet idealistic, and their combination of romanticism and cynicism mirror the dichotomy in Bethune himself. His medical advice that the doctor must be master of many skills found its parallel in his so easily accepting both modern and conservative poetry. The artistic and medical aspects of Bethune that enabled him to be poet and physician served as a model for the versatility that be was certain the new age would demand.

Résumé

Dans son cercle d'amis de Montréal, Norman Bethune comptait de nombreux artistes et avec quelques-uns d'entre eux, il se mit à écrire de la poésie. Le Groupe des poètes de Montréal (qu'on appelle aussi l'École de McGill) faisait accéder la poésie canadienne au XXe siècle en abandonnant les canons usés de la poésie du XIXe siècle et ses thèmes traditionnels au profit de techniques poétiques nouvelles qui correspondaient mieux à la vie du temps et l'exprimaient fidèlement. Des poètes comme Leo Kennedy, A.M. Klein, F.R. Scott et A.J.M. Smith voulaient créer une poésie canadienne plus universelle, comparable par son excellence et la diversité de ses techniques, à celle de n'importe quel autre pays. On retrouve dans leur volonté farouche de rompre avec les valeurs poétiques du siècle passé la même inspiration qui a amené Bethune à s'opposer à l'establishment *des milieux médicaux de Montréal. Ils embrassaient les nouvelles techniques de l'écriture poétique aussi spontanément que Bethune adoptait les techniques nouvelles en médecine et en poésie. Les conceptions de ces poètes trouvaient un écho chez Bethune. Comme Leo Kennedy, par exemple, il croyait que la poésie devait interpréter fidèlement le monde contemporain et les forces de progrès de la vie moderne qui devaient assurer la survivance culturelle. Il n'y a pas à s'en étonner puisque Bethune lui-même était poète, comme* "Red Moon", "Remembrance" *et plusieurs autres poèmes en font foi. Il était sensible aux sons et aux images, lui qui tenait la créativité comme composante naturelle de tout être humain. La poésie de Bethune se caractérise par une puissante et dramatique juxtaposition d'images et par son lyrisme. Son ton est passionné mais contrôlé, amer mais idéaliste, et le mélange de romantisme et de cynisme qu'on y retrouve reflète la dualité de la personnalité de Bethune. En médecine, Bethune croyait important que le praticien maîtrise de nombreuses aptitudes; en poésie, il acceptait à la fois la poésie moderne et la poésie traditionnelle. Artiste et médecin tout à la fois, il a été lui-même un de ces hommes aux talents variés dont il croyait que les temps nouveaux avaient besoin.*

"They could split rock ...":
Painting in Montreal in the 1930s, and the Children's Creative Art Centre — A Conversation Piece

Charles Hill, Louis Muhlstock
Marian Scott, Leo Kennedy

Norman Bethune was a talented and understanding artist as well as a skilled and dedicated surgeon. Common to both these roles was a highly developed creative spirit, which for Bethune was a natural motivating force in humankind. Bethune himself painted, he befriended many artists and, with Fritz Brandtner, he organized the Children's Creative Art Centre in order to facilitate the development of the creative faculty in children, especially disadvantaged children. Some aspects of Bethune's interest in art were discussed during the 1979 conference by two contemporary artists and a writer and the Curator of Canadian Art, National Gallery of Canada, in an informal conversation, the spontaneity of which, we hope, has been preserved in the following rendering. — Eds.

Louis Muhlstock (LM):

I knew Norman Bethune — and yet I did not know him. He wasn't easy to get to know, and I wasn't in his milieu often enough to be able to say that he was my "friend". We just knew one another. I knew him through his association with Fritz Brandtner, through the art classes he had organized for children, and through his visits to exhibitions; and because he was interested in art and because he painted. I remember only one of his paintings, a water colour of one of those round-bellied Quebec stoves, with quite delicate colours. But because we were of the same era and experienced many things in that age of depression, I will tell you what it was like to be a painter in Montreal during the Depression.

Born in a small town in Galicia, part of Austro-Hungary, I was only 7 years old when I arrived in Montreal. We first lived in a 14 dollar-a-month unheated house on St. Dominique, in the slum part of the city. Our house was on the west side of the street, and we lived in the basement, where no sunlight ever shone in; and for about 14 years we lived in that kind of ambience. My first images, of course, were those of St. Dominique Street and Demontigny Street, and Cadieux Street, and the lanes in that slum section. Later, we moved to Upper St. Dominique, near Duluth Street, where the rent was $20 a month. Now we lived on the east side of the street, and on the second and third storeys; it was beautiful because the sun came in to the house. We made sure that we would get as much sun as we could: we had no curtains and we saw to it that the shutters were open. So we enjoyed living on upper St. Dominique Street; it was like Westmount for those who had known only Demontigny Street, St. Dominique Street, and Grubert Lane and Leduc Lane.

While I was at high school, I worked for 6 years as an assistant bookkeeper at $14 a week, but slowly worked up to $20 a week and then $30, which enabled me to save some money. At the end of the 6 years I had saved over $2,000 and I felt that I had had enough of working for someone else. During those years I had attended art classes, three or four nights a week after a full day's work, and I had taken no holidays of any kind. So with my savings I bought a ticket for Paris, where I lived for 3 years.

I returned to Montreal during the Depression. In 1935 I had an exhibition at the Art Association of Montreal (now the Montreal Museum of Fine Arts). I thought it an excellent exhibition of some 60 or 70 works — out of which exactly three items were sold, for $90; and these were framed, too, which gives an idea of the state of the art world for us. Much later the National Gallery made up for part of this because, with Charles Hill's advice, it bought some of these drawings, and so has one of my drawings of the Depression period. Regrettably, some of my Depression drawings were stolen from my house; and though I lost more than 200 works, I am said still to have the largest collection of original Muhlstocks in the world!

We couldn't afford frames or canvas, and little paint, so we drew on Kraft wrapping paper that we obtained from friends who had factories, and we painted on stretched-out sugar bags (each costing 10¢) that we treated with a coat of size; I still have a few paintings done this way. Nor could we afford models, so our models were the homeless people of Fletcher's Field — the ones who had nowhere to sleep. In summer, especially, they would make use of Mount Royal,

Fig. 1. *Homeless* — Fletcher's Field, Montreal. Louis Muhlstock, c. 1932.

Fig. 1. *Sans abri* — Fletcher's Field, Montréal. Louis Muhlstock, v. 1932.

Fig. 2. *The Last Supper.* (The last meal ticket). Louis Muhlstock, 1932. Ink.

Fig. 2. *La dernière cène.* (Le dernier bon de secours). Louis Muhlstock, 1932. Encre.

Fig. 3. *Untitled sketch* — Louis Muhlstock, c. 1936.
Following the Japanese invasion, refugees from China arrived in Montreal around 1936.

Fig. 3. *Sans titre,* v. 1936.
Des réfugiés chinois, chassés de leur pays par l'envahisseur japonais, débarquent à Montréal vers 1936.

Fig. 4. *William O'Brien Unemployed.* Louis Muhlstock, c. 1935. Charcoal and brown chalk on Kraft paper.

National Gallery of Canada. No. 17668

Fig. 4. *William O'Brien en chômage.* Louis Muhlstock. v. 1935. Fusain et craie brune sur papier Kraft.

Galerie nationale du Canada. N° 17668

covering themselves with their few belongings, a coat or a jacket. They were never aware of being looked at, so I would walk about with a sketch pad or paper and a folding stool; and when I spotted a model, such as one resting beautifully, I would sneak up quietly and draw. These were spontaneous things that I experienced and enjoyed. And I would also go to hospital clinics and use the rows of waiting people as models, stealing my notes while hidden behind a newspaper or magazine (Fig. 1, 2, 3, 4).

Charles Hill (CH):

Let us try to understand Bethune's own personal vision, in terms of art, and the development of his taste, and also the quite radical change in his attitude to art over a period of about 8 years. We should also consider the influence of his own paintings, though very few of them have been reproduced, and I have seen only one. Roderick Stewart mentions Bethune's buying paintings when he lived in Detroit and his interest in art early on[1]; however, I am not aware of the kinds of paintings he bought or of his interests.

Bethune certainly was a friend of many artists from an early period in his life, besides being an amateur artist himself — his earliest known works being the murals he painted while he was a patient in the Trudeau Sanatorium. One of his friends was John Lyman, a Canadian artist, born in Montreal, who had studied in France. He had studied with students of Matisse, and his exhibition, held in Canada in 1913, corresponded in time with the lambasting that the Armory Show was being subjected to in New York. The Montreal critics picked up on the New York criticism, and Lyman was so disgusted that he left Canada, returning to reside here only in September, 1931. Lyman founded a school with Hazen Sise (the architect, who went with Bethune to Spain), George Holt, Elizabeth Frost and André Bieler. He would hold open house for friends, mostly painters and writers.

Marian Scott (MS):

The Lymans' evening functions were often referred to as the Lyman Salon and it was at one of them where I first met Bethune. I only got to know him well, though, while crossing the Atlantic by boat — he bound for Russia, to attend the International Physiological Congress in August 1935.

CH: What were Bethune's attitudes to art? Which artists did he know?

MS: Bethune had been very impressed by Brandtner, but other artists he mentioned were his friends Jean and Jori Palardy; Graham Norwell, with whom he painted and shared a cottage; and Harold Beament. From having had family conservative views (he had been to classes by Sherriff Scott at one time), he had become interested in the more creative attitudes towards painting. Certainly he talked often about Brandtner, who stimulated Bethune with feelings of creative energy, of daring, of adventure, and Bethune enjoyed discussions with him.

CH: What were Brandtner's views?

MS: If you were a critic, you would say he was an expressionist. He didn't talk so much about painting; he *painted.* And his paintings were full of vitality and colour.

Leo Kennedy (LK):

I once asked Brandtner about a painting I had bought from him. I asked him, "What does it mean?" He simply replied, "I don't know." But it is a beautiful picture!

CH: Is there a parallel in the personalities of Bethune and Brandtner? For Bethune was such a creative person, moving from one thing to another with so many diverse interests and involvements, and Brandtner too worked at so many projects and in so many media.

MS: Brandtner was much more the professional painter, but, through the two of them coming together and through the friendship that developed the idea of the Children's Creative Art Centre emerged. The idea was to encourage creative qualities in children. They were both very fond of children, particularly Bethune. And other artist friends of Bethune's helped; for example, Pegi Nichol, who, while staying with her husband, Norman MacLeod, at Bethune's, made a linoleum poster for a party to raise funds for the Centre; she also made portrait sketches at the party for $5 each.

CH: Did Bethune's ideas influence Brandtner? I noted, when going through the works that Brandtner had exhibited, that it was only during and after August 1935 that the works for which he is often known were painted — the studies of victims and gas attacks and of the unemployed, for example. In terms of Bethune and Brandtner, August 1935 coincides with Bethune's visit to Soviet Russia; so, did Bethune's political attitude have any influence on Brandtner?

MS: Friends do influence each other. Brandtner had come from Germany and had been influenced by the Expressionists, who were concerned by the coming war and by the devastation of the Great War.

CH: Let us think about them and the Children's Art School — or, more correctly, the Children's Creative Art Centre — and the work of Bethune and Brandtner there.

MS: There is a difference in the two names. Mainly, the Centre was not so much a place for teaching, as a place where children could enjoy painting, where they could develop their imagination and creativeness. We only helped with method and technique when we were asked or when we thought this was needed.

The Centre grew out of the friendship of Bethune and Brandtner, out of their love of children and young people, and out of their deep belief in art as a great and good force in life. Brandtner knew of methods of releasing creative energy in children, with wonderful results, for he had studied under Cizek in Vienna, who had developed these methods. And Brandtner's influence was growing; in Montreal alone, I had been deeply impressed by the painting being done in the classes of Ann Savage and Arthur Lismer, both of whom had been influenced by him.

The children painted in Bethune's studio-apartment. On Saturday mornings, they went on expeditions to various places, including art galleries, and these expeditions often became the subjects of their later paintings.

CH: In terms, now, of art in Montreal in the 1930s, one of the areas Bethune figured in was the politicization of artists. One thinks of a parallel with the art unions in Great Britain and in the United States, yet there doesn't seem to have been any effort in that direction among Canadian artists. Why?

LM: The only group that existed at that time was the organized group known as the Royal Academy. The Art Association of Montreal had an annual exhibition in the Spring, and there were only two public galleries in Montreal — the Watson Gallery, and the Johnson Gallery, which mostly did framing. Most of the artists were loners, who worked independently; so there was no meeting place of the artists. That didn't exist until 1941, when the Federation of Canadian Artists was formed.

In contrast, Toronto artists met each other at the studio where artists like the Group of Seven worked; they were in and out of each other's studios and knew what each other was doing. In Montreal, we had no studio but just continued as best we could. Some didn't paint at all because of job commitments. Brandtner worked for the T. Eaton Company on window displays; some artists did commercial art; and others, when they were fortunate, had teaching jobs. So there was no such thing as politicization — though some of us were politically aware and would attend political meetings, often radical in purpose. We certainly became involved and lived in that kind of atmosphere, but we were not really organized. There was, though, one combined effort of Montreal artists: the exhibition of Soviet art, sponsored by the Friends of the Soviet Union — though Bethune was not one of the sponsors; Louis Kon and Robert Ayre were involved in it.

MS: Most of us felt that we couldn't use paintings for political purposes.

CH: But, Louis, you often did drawings of the unemployed.

LM: As an individual artist, I was interested in people, and I was able to reach out for the unemployed, who, for the dollar or two that we could afford to pay, were happy to sit for us. I was glad I had these people. I could visit the soup kitchen; I saw them in the parks and I would befriend them and they were happy. They had contact with another human being; otherwise they were alone, just moving from spot to spot, by the thousands. One of them sat, all alone, on a bench one day; when I asked him why he sat by himself and not with the others, he replied, "Ah, oui, ce n'est pas de conversation." So he apparently preferred to be alone, though when I got him to my studio he did have something to do.

MS: But that is certainly not what I meant by "using art". Louis' work came out of his compassion and fellow feeling. Let me explain by quoting my own words to express my thoughts as a painter in the 1930s:

The inner necessity to paint was there, in spite of the times, in spite of the misery, the growing fear of fascism and war. I found that I could not (or should not) 'use' my painting directly, but I could use some of myself, some of my time.

A number of us worked to collect funds for the Committee to Aid Spanish Democracy, and the Canadian League Against War and Fascism (later the League for Peace and Freedom.)

Of course my painting was 'affected' by the times. How much? How should I know? More stark, more 'public' than it might have been?

Figures being moved up and down escalators, figures on outside stairways, 'cement', 'dock' — and when I allowed myself to paint plant forms, it was with the knowing that they could split rock[2] (Fig. 5, 6, 7).

CH: In terms of Bethune's own thoughts as a painter and of his views on art and creativity, a letter he wrote from Spain is of great interest[3].

MS: Although it is difficult to describe Bethune — and to pass on ideas of what Bethune was like — it becomes easier if one reads this letter from Spain. In it, Bethune was talking not only about art and the artist, but about *himself*. He thought of himself as an artist. Even though he didn't paint very much, even as a doctor he had this feeling of creativeness, that an operation could be a work of art. He ended the letter with the words, "the creative spirit that is in the soul of man".

Fig. 5. *Park.*
Marian Scott, 1935. Watercolour

Fig. 5. *Le parc.*
Marian Scott, 1935. Aquarelle

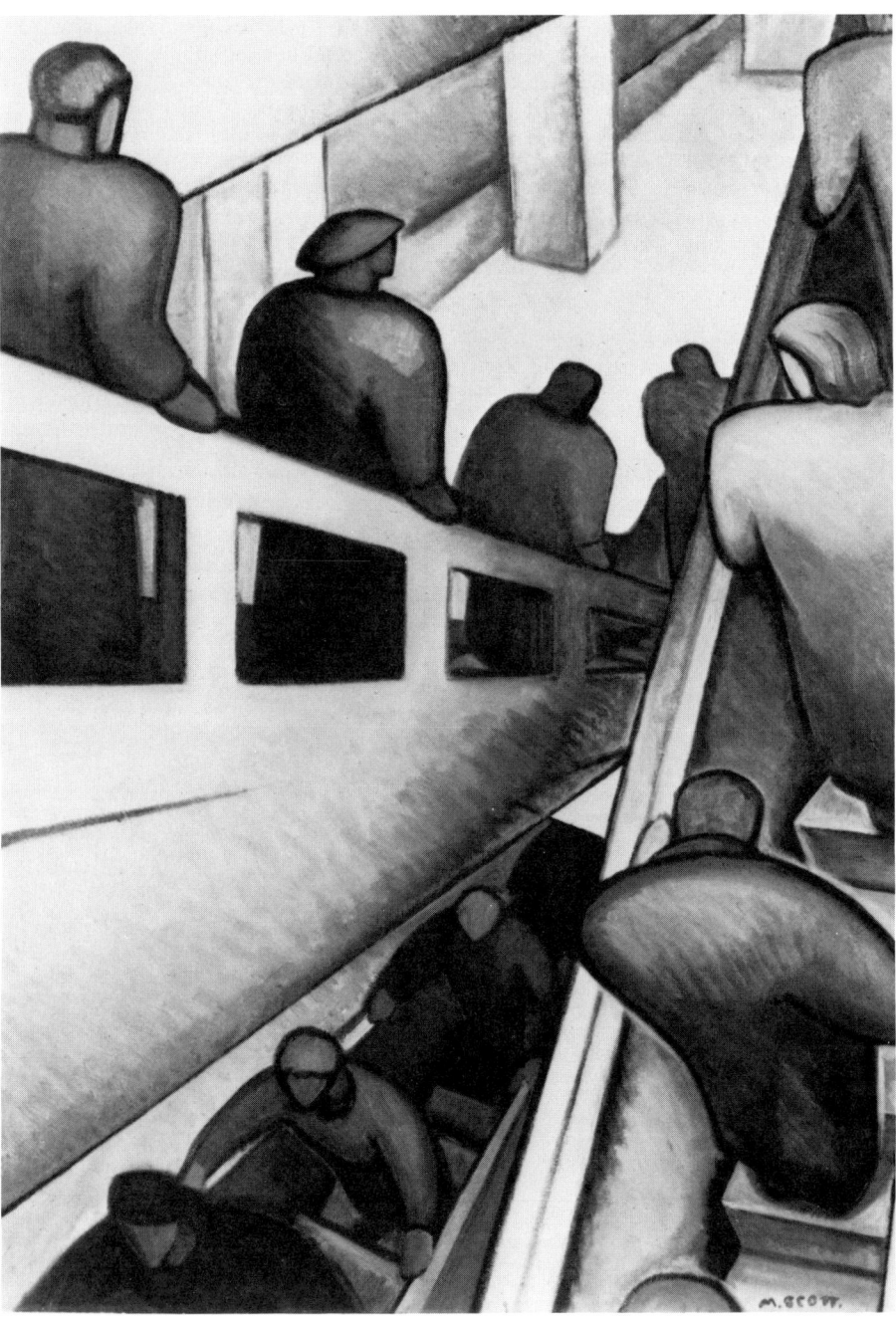

Fig. 6. *Escalator.*
Marian Scott, 1938. Oil

Fig. 6. *Escalier roulant.*
Marian Scott, 1938. Huile

Fig. 7. *Crocus.*
Marian Scott, 1938. Oil

Fig. 7. *Crocus.*
Marian Scott, 1938. Huile

CH: Certainly for Bethune "the creative spirit of life *working in* the soul of man" — the creative spirit that David Shephard sees in Bethune's medical writings and inventions and innovations[4] and that Lee Thompson sees in his poetry[5] — and the relationship of creativity and art — the visual arts — are very much part of his own creativity.

But I wonder, though, whether Bethune was just talking about art in that letter, or, in a way, about creative life also. Consider the words he used: "in the bright banal glare of day, [the artist] enjoys the purification of violence"; "the catharsis of action"; "his appetite for life is enormous"; and [he] "makes uneasy the static, the set and the still. In a world terrified of change, he preaches revolution — the principle of life. He is an agitator, a disturber of the peace." Indeed, Bethune could well say of the artist that "he is the creative spirit of life working in the soul of man" (Fig. 8, 9, 10).

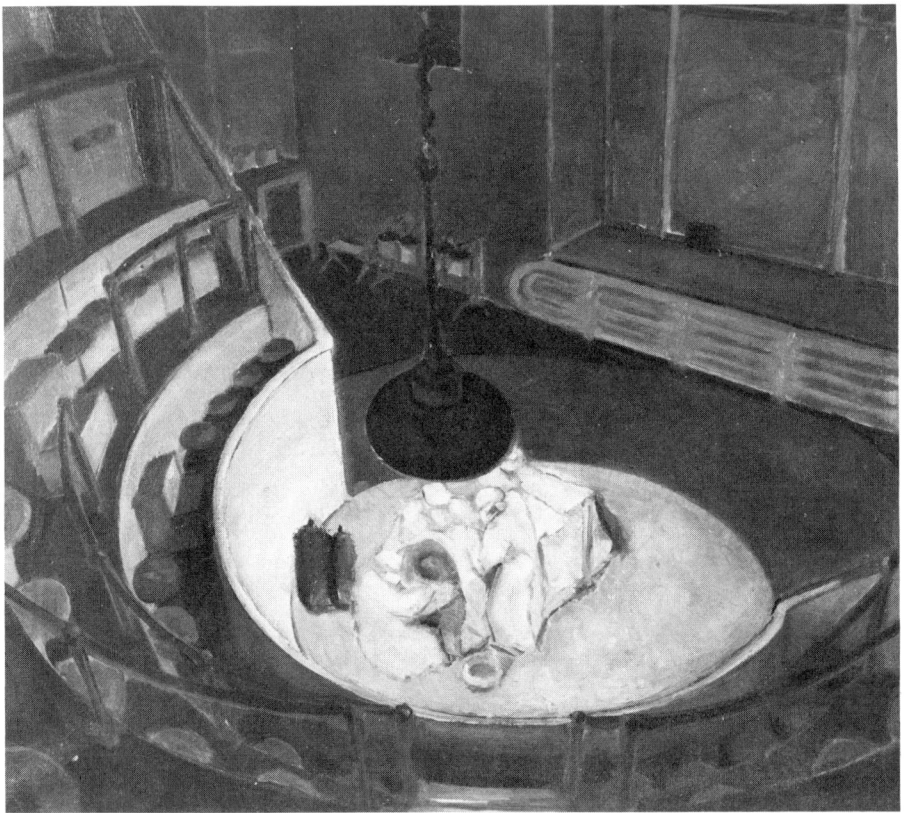

Fig. 8. *Night Operating Theatre.* Norman Bethune, c. 1934. Oil.
Public Archives of Canada, National Film Board Collection. PA 116910

Fig. 8. *Salle d'opération, la nuit.* Norman Bethune, v. 1934. Huile.
Archives publiques du Canada, Collection de l'Office national du film, PA 116910

Fig. 9. *Frances Campbell Penney.* Norman Bethune, 1933. Portrait of wife. Oil.

Public Archives of Canada, National Film Board Collection. PA 116911

Fig. 9. *Frances Campbell Penney.* Norman Bethune, 1933. Portrait de sa femme. Huile.

Archives publiques du Canada, Collection de l'Office national du film, PA 116911

Fig. 10. *Norman Bethune, 1934.* Self-portrait. During his second year at Sacré-Coeur Hospital.

Public Archives Canada, National Film Board Collection. PA 116909

Fig. 10. *Norman Bethune, 1934.* Auto-portrait. Durant sa deuxième année à l'hôpital du Sacré-Coeur.

Archives publiques du Canada, Collection de l'Office national du film. PA 116909

MS: Richard Allen has referred to one of the developments from Presbyterianism — this feeling of the unity of art, science and religion[6]; and I immediately thought of Bethune. He had this conviction: he talked of "the Immortal Tree of Art", that the paintings of a certain generation were just "the fruits of that Immortal Tree."

CH: As part of growth, a continuing growth.

MS: For me, too, it had that religious element to it.

CH: It surprised me how very brief this passage was. But in Bethune's life, apart from the period of his medical career, which goes back much earlier, the period of his much more active involvement in society, of his stirring up, of his role as a catalyst, was really very brief. Yet in art, as in other aspects of his life, Bethune had a great deal of influence in awakening energy in a lethargic community.

* * *

REFERENCES AND NOTES

1. Roderick Stewart, *Bethune*, Toronto, 1973, p. 17.
2. Marian Scott — From notes of Marian Scott.
3. Norman Bethune, "An Apology for Not Writing Letters," Madrid, May 5, 1937. Reproduced in part by Allan and Gordon, *The Scalpel, the Sword: The Story of Dr. Norman Bethune*, Toronto, 1971, pp. 156-157; in full by Stewart, *The Mind of Norman Bethune*, Toronto, pp. 69-72.
4. See pages 92-103 of this book for a discussion of this aspect of Bethune's work.
5. See pages 104-113 of this book for further treatment of this topic.
6. See also pages 22-31 of this book.

* * *

Abstract

Norman Bethune befriended many artists who lived in Montreal in the early 1930s and was a painter himself. One painter he knew well was Fritz Brandtner, with whom Bethune founded a centre where they and others could help children develop their creativity. Like Bethune, Brandtner was a man of great creative energy, whose life was characterized by daring and adventure. The two loved children, and Brandtner had studied in Vienna under Cizek, who had learned how to release creative powers in children. Bethune was always deeply interested in creativity and saw creativeness in his medical work as well as in his painting and writing. He envisioned the artist as "the creative spirit of life working in the soul of man" and as "an agitator, a disturber of the peace." And in Montreal in the 1930s, Bethune and artists such as Louis Muhlstock and Marian Scott, in whom the creative spirit moved forcefully, were sensitive to the immense social problems, and each faced them in their own ways. Some were politically oriented; others were less so. But all knew that the growth of their work, like the growth of plants, in the end "could split rock."

Résumé

Norman Bethune, peintre lui-même, se lia d'amitié avec plusieurs artistes habitant à Montréal au début des années trente. Parmi ceux-ci se trouvait Fritz Brandtner avec qui Bethune et quelques autres fondèrent un centre d'art où les enfants pouvaient venir développer leur créativité. Brandtner, comme Bethune, était doué d'une grande énergie créatrice et menait une vie de risque et d'aventure. Tous deux aimaient les enfants et Brandtner avait travaillé à Vienne avec Cizek, qui avait appris à libérer le pouvoir créateur des enfants. Bethune fut toujours intéressé à la créativité et voyait la possibilité de créer à la fois dans son travail médical et dans la peinture et l'écriture. Il envisageait l'artiste comme "l'esprit créateur de la vie travaillant sur l'âme de l'homme" et comme un "agitateur, un perturbateur de la paix." A Montréal, pendant les années 1930, Bethune et des artistes tels Louis Muhlstock et Marian Scott, tous fortement animés d'un esprit créateur, étaient sensibles aux immenses problèmes sociaux et essayaient d'y faire face chacun à leur façon. Certains adoptaient une orientation politique, d'autres y croyaient moins, mais tous savaient que leurs oeuvres, comme la croissance des plantes, parviendraient un jour à "fendre la pierre".

The Health of the People: Montreal in the Depression Years

Terry Copp

Both society's collective memory and the categories used by historians have firmly established the view that the 1930s were a distinct period in Canadian history. No doubt in many ways the "dirty thirties" deserve this special treatment, but studies that focus on the decade frequently obscure elements of continuity in our history that need to be understood. Certainly no enquiry into the health of the working class in Montreal can isolate the Depression years, and in this account I summarize the basic trends in health issues both before and after the Depression so that the particular circumstances and issues of the 1930s can be understood; a fuller account of the health question in Montreal during the first 30 years of this century has been published elsewhere[1].

* * *

Perhaps the first point that should be established is that, relative to other major North American cities, Montreal's hospitals and medical practitioners both were first-rate. At no time in the 20th century was this city deficient, by contemporary standards, in ideas or expertise on medical and public health questions.

The second point may be bluntly stated. Few North American cities — perhaps none — had a worse record than Montreal in caring for the health of its working class population. Its mortality and morbidity rates were notoriously high, and public health measures had been scandalously neglected throughout most of the city's history.

The most outrageous problem was infant mortality. As late as 1922, this was as high as 213 deaths per 1000 live births in working-class wards, when it was under 60 per thousand live births in the better residential areas. The major medical cause of infant deaths was "disease of the digestive system usually classified as diarrhoea and enteritis"[2].

Montreal had begun to tackle this problem before the First World War by establishing *Gouttes de lait*, or pure milk depots, in the areas of highest infant mortality. *Gouttes de lait*, combined with well-baby clinics and the pasteurization of milk, began to break this vicious cycle and the rate decreased steadily through the 1920s and 1930s. This decline in fact accelerated during the 1930s, the overall rate per thousand decreasing from 133.7 in 1928 to 59.3 in 1940[3]. Most of this change occurred among the working class population. There the 1928 rate had been as much as four times higher than that of upper-class groups but by the late 1930s it was only twice as high.

Why? No final answer can be given but several interesting points can be made. First, the pressure exerted by the Montreal Anti-Tuberculosis and General Health League in the late 1920s had stirred city council to increase the number of well-baby clinics from 23 to 37[4]. Next, the proportion of pasteurized milk sold in the city exceeded 90% in the early 1930s. Also, intensive work on the treatment of gastroenteritis in the 1930s reduced the mortality from this disease. A fourth point is that expenditure on child hygiene by the Montreal Health department doubled between 1928 and 1930 and increased slowly throughout the decade[5].

A similar pattern emerges from the study of diphtheria morbidity and mortality. Montreal had lagged behind all other North American cities in developing anti-diphtheria immunization. In wealthier areas of the city diphtheria had all but disappeared by the 1920s, yet, in 1927, in working class areas, 1,826 cases with 219 deaths were recorded. As a direct result of a privately financed immunization program begun in 1926, the civic authorities finally tackled diphtheria and the incidence of the disease decreased sharply, the mortality decreasing from 29.9 per 100,000 to just 2.1 in 1933 and 1.2 in 1940[6].

With respect to tuberculosis, the death rate in Montreal declined steadily from 1929 to 1934 and then rose slightly to 1937, when it again declined. Leonard Marsh, the distinguished Director of Social Research at McGill University in the 1930s, concluded in 1938, after a careful study of the available statistics, that "it is not possible to gauge whether the depression in its later years has widened the incidence of the 'white scourge'"[7]. The statistics from 1938 on suggest that it had not. The tuberculosis death rate decreased steadily in the 1940s[8].

Mortality from the other communicable diseases that had plagued the working-class population of Montreal and that could be lessened by even marginal improvements in public health delivery systems also declined steadily in the 1930s. This was no small matter. In 1927 a typhoid epidemic had doubled the average number of deaths from infectious diseases to over 1,200. In the late 1930s fewer than 200 people a year died from diseases such as typhoid, measles and scarlet fever[9].

The term, 'health of the working class', of course, encompasses many issues other than mortality rates. Indeed, changes in mortality rates may not be a good guide to general health conditions. Regarding Montreal, however, two things seem clear. Reforms in public health administration and financing, begun in the late 1920s, were carried forward into the 1930s. Expenditure on public health was increased in the early 1930s and was maintained at the new levels. The success of this modest example of public health reform was particularly striking when compared with other areas of Quebec, where no such breakthrough occurred until functional public health units were established in the 1940s.

Another important interpretive question must be considered. Marsh collaborated with Dr. Grant Fleming in a 1938 study entitled *Health and Unemployment*. He worked through some of the statistical material I have summarized and cautioned his readers against "an optimistic deduction". Marsh warned that "reserves of ill-health may have been built up in recent years in spite of the downward tendencies in mortality and other indices ... An increased amount of sickness during bad times may lead to higher death rates a sufficient number of years ahead"[10]. For the record, it is important to establish that this possibility Marsh raised did not come about. Mortality and morbidity rates of the kind we have been discussing continued to decline after 1940.

On the question of mortality from disease, there is, therefore, no doubt that substantial progress was made throughout the 1930s due to improvements in public health and that this trend was not reversed by "reserves of ill health" built up during the 1930s.

* * *

Marsh was mainly concerned with the effects of unemployment and extended dependence on relief upon the general health of the population. Before we turn to this aspect of the problem, however, we must examine the impact of the Depression on Montreal's working class.

By June 1, 1931, 20% of the male labour force and 10% of the female labour force were without work. During the winter of 1931-32 more than 100,000 Montrealers were on relief[11].

The main emphasis of federal, provincial and municipal unemployment relief during 1930 and 1931 was on public works projects, though provision was made for minor amounts of direct assistance. Montreal borrowed over 20 million dollars at the very high rate of 6% to pay its share of expenditure on relief projects during the two years[12]. Mayor Houde and his associates spent public works money with a fine disregard for administrative niceties such as adequate accounting practices. Work projects were oriented towards maximizing employment, and by 1932 Houde claimed that 18,000 additional workers, "the majority taken from the ranks of the unemployed"[13], were at work on city-initiated public works.

The federal Unemployment Relief Acts had made provisions for small amounts of direct relief in 1930 and 1931. In Montreal such assistance was channelled through the traditional private denominational organizations, which distributed funds according to their own procedures. The St. Vincent de Paul Society maintained its responsibility for the French-Catholic community, 60% of the population, and by the end of 1932 it was providing support for an average of 34,000 families a month, mainly the same families in each month. The Society was dispensing close to 1 million dollars each month and more than 3,000 volunteers were spending their evenings trying to maintain the policies outlined in the *Manuel du Visiteur du Pauvre*[14]. The *visiteurs* were supposed to try and tailor their assistance to family needs and apparently did so. *Bons,* or vouchers, redeemable at local stores, were issued. Other *bons* for rent, fuel, clothing, and even school books were provided. The Society continued to visit the sick, provide counselling, help families find new accommodation, and serve as a buffer between the needy and their creditors.

Within the Protestant community, direct relief to the able-bodied unemployed was provided by the Emergency Unemployment Relief Committee, an organization established in the winter of 1924 to cope with seasonal unemployment. This Committee worked in conjunction with the Protestant Employment Bureau and relief was available so long as the head of the family reported to the Bureau every second day and had his card signed weekly by his local church minister. By 1933 between 4,000 and 5,000 thousand families were receiving rent assistance, a fuel allotment and a weekly ration of the following composition:

9 lbs. stewing beef	2 lbs. sugar
¾ lb. salt pork	½ lb. cheese
20 lbs. potatoes	2½ lbs. beans
4 lbs. carrots and onions	2 lbs. prunes
4 lbs. rolled oats	1 lb. peanut butter
2 lbs. rice	2 lbs. Lassie's syrup
3 bars Lennox soap	

This was supplemented by bread and milk to a maximum of two loaves and two quarts a day[15].

When the civic authorities took over relief administration in August 1933, some 60,000 names were on the various relief rolls and an estimated 205,000 persons were dependent on direct assistance[16]. Since these figures apply to the City of Montreal proper and not the Metropolitan area, they represent just less than one quarter of the 874,000 residents of Montreal. The winter of 1933-1934 was the worst period of the depression, with the total of municipal relief dependants reaching the 250,000 mark, 28% of the population.

A survey of the occupational background of relief recipients prepared in the winter of 1932-1933 indicates that the distribution of the burden of unemployment had remained heavily skewed towards hourly wage earners. Professionals accounted for just 2.6% of the total, other white collar workers for 10.1%, with the remaining 87.3% being made up of wage earners[17]. (Blue-collar workers accounted for approximately two thirds of the 224,000 males in the Montreal labour force.) In late 1933, then, one in every four males in the labour force was on relief, but more than one in every three male wage earners was on the dole. These figures also suggest that French-speaking Montrealers, heavily over-represented in the unskilled and semi-skilled occupations, bore a disproportionate share of unemployment and were much more dependent on relief than the English-speaking population. By the spring of 1934, with one quarter of the population on relief, Montreal was barely maintaining basic services. Relief cheques were not sent out in April because the Federal Government refused to forward further funds until errors and irregularities in Montreal's accounts were corrected. Many landlords had not been paid in months and hundreds of evictions were reported[18]. The city's streets had deteriorated and no money was available for repairs or street cleaning.

A new Unemployment Relief Commission moved quickly to set up a highly organized relief system. By mid-1935 there were more than 800 full-time employees working at the central office and in 20 district bureaus.

A force of 100 inspectors ran constant checks to ensure that no one was violating the rules, and much stress was placed on the penalties that would be incurred for giving a false oath or defrauding the city. In the first year of the Commission's existence, 866 cases were pursued by the investigators and 691 of these were cut off from relief or had their allocations reduced. Since more than 40,000 cheques were being issued each week, the number of cases of "fraud" uncovered by the vast investigating force seems quite small[19]. However, as the Depression continued, it became increasingly harder to get onto the relief rolls in the first place and the investigators were strongly criticized for their inflexible interpretation of the rules.

Two categories of "employable unemployeds" were recognized by the Commission. Unattached men and women could obtain an allowance of $1.80 per week plus $1.38 as a rent allowance. The allotment for a family of five totalled $38.58 in the summer and $41.38 in the winter; these amounts covered food, clothing, rent, fuel and electricity[20].

Relief was paid by cheque with direct payments to landlords and the Montreal Light, Heat and Power Company. A medical fund based on a city contribution of 25¢ per relief recipient was created and a panel of doctors recruited. The head of the household was allowed to earn up to $3 a week without penalty and the wife and children could seek employment, as long as 50% of their earnings was contributed to the family[21].

Unattached men who were eligible for municipal relief found themselves under enormous pressure to enrol in the Dominion Government's relief camps. In 1934 there were 8,614 bachelors, widowers and separated husbands on the city lists. In less than a year that number had been halved. As the Commission explained it, conditions of life in the camps might not be ideal but they were, "at any rate, a great deal better than life in the city at $1.80 a week"[22]. Perhaps, but when the King government cancelled the program in 1936, lifelong residents of Montreal found that they had lost their residency status and could not get back on to the municipal rolls.

The Commission also enforced strict residency requirements insisting that only persons resident in Montreal on May 1, 1933 were eligible for relief. During the winter of 1935-1936, the *Montreal Star* carried this account of the plight of "transient families":

> Denied the dole because they arrived here after May 1, 1933, at the mercy of charity which has not the funds to maintain them, between six and seven thousand families embracing twenty thousand souls are in a desperate plight and the city administration is baffled because at least five hundred thousand ($500,000) would be required for winter food, fuel, and shelter and the aldermen hesitate to tax real estate owners further for the benefit of people who drift during the crisis. Most of the families are from rural Quebec and in their home towns or villages there is no dole because their local communities cannot support it, so they filtered to the Metropolis in the hope of finding work or getting on the dole rolls[23].

At first City Council accepted the Commission's ruling but in January, 1936 the residence requirement was moved forward to May 1, 1934, thus adding additional thousands to the city's relief rolls.

The system of public relief developed by Relief Commission was roughly comparable to the schemes in existence in other large Canadian cities. Toronto had established a municipal Department of Public Welfare in 1931, when it became apparent that the need for public assistance was likely to be prolonged. Relief assistance rates were generally higher in Toronto than in other Canadian cities, but the amount of unemployment in the city was much lower and its financial resources were much greater than in any other large Canadian urban centre.

In 1938 the Provincial Government decided to remove female heads of families with young children from relief rolls since such women were not employable. In addition it was suggested that the needy would be taken care of under the provisions of the new Mother's Allowance Act passed by the legislature in March 1937. In fact, the first payments under the Act were not made until December 1938 and then only to mothers having two or more children. The average monthly payment under the Act was $30 — a bitter joke indeed[24].

Approximately 3,000 women were declared ineligible for relief in the spring, including "females incapable of producing work, those living in a state of concubinage, unmarried mothers, widows with young children, and women with husbands in jail." A demonstration by 75 women at City Hall led to a temporary restoration of relief funds entirely at city expense, but after suggestions of Communist influence behind the demonstration and a commitment from Quebec to make such women eligible for assistance under the Quebec Public Charities Act, they were permanently removed from the rolls[25].

* * *

Approximately one third of the population of Montreal had been engaged in a desperate struggle for survival in the Depression. How had this affected their general health? Marsh put it this way:

> For the population subject to unemployment, even morbidity and mortality measurements together may not reflect the full effects of the Depression. The economic consequences of unemployment are food restrictions, inadequate housing, overcrowding, insufficient clothing and exposure... all of them undermine general health and weaken resistance to disease... Poor nutrition can be a handicap to health and employability long before it is revealed by the onset of specific deficiency diseases[26].

Marsh reported on an investigation of a sample of 1,003 adult male relief recipients. Unfortunately this study was heavily weighted towards the English-language population. A control group of employed workers was also examined. The results were interesting. Malnutrition, clinically defined, was higher among unemployed white collar workers than among the unskilled. Even more striking was the presence of as much malnutrition among employed workers as among the unskilled unemployed[27]. Nutrition is a very difficult subject for laymen (and, I often suspect, for doctors) to deal with. Marsh could fairly conclude that overall malnutrition was more common among the unemployed; he could guess that white collar workers had to spend a higher proportion of their income on appearances, but there were many unexamined variables and too many unexplained problems to allow him to say much more.

An investigation of infant weight gains, in terms of four categories of income groups, showed that general standards had not fallen during the first 3 years of the Depression[28]. A similar study of the weight and height of school-age children did show a strong correlation with income groups, but the children had been born in 1926 and the poorer groups had lagged behind the better-off group in both "prosperity and depression"[29].

Other specific studies revealed shocking levels of dental, skin and vision problems in the unemployed population, but pointed to the existence of a substantial measure of the same difficulties among the employed.

Marsh had, I think, expected to find much more striking evidence of the effects of unemployment on the health of the population. But it turned out that what he was observing was a health crisis of long duration, which had in some ways been made worse by Depression conditions and in other ways had actually been lessened by improvements in public health.

* * *

There is a clear moral to this story. The society may or may not have had the capacity to tackle the economic crisis of the 1930s, but it clearly had, as Bethune recognized and strove to make known, the capacity to reform the health system in quite fundamental ways. A few halting steps had been taken in the late 1920s, steps that paid rich dividends during the 1930s and the 1940s. An enormous amount remained to be done, but unfortunately further reforms were very slow in coming.

* * *

REFERENCES AND NOTES

1. Terry Copp, *The Anatomy of Poverty: The Condition of the Working Class in Montreal 1847-1929*, Toronto, 1974. (Published in French as *Classe ouvrière et pauvreté*, Montreal, 1978).
2. *Ibid.*, p. 93.
3. *Annual Report of the Montreal Board of Health*, 1929-1940.
4. *Ibid.*, 1932, p. 108.
5. *Ibid.*, 1929-40. In per capita terms expenditure rose from 34 cents in 1926 to 61 cents in 1930 and 67 cents in 1939.
6. *Ibid.*, 1940.
7. Leonard Marsh, *Health and Unemployment*, Montreal, 1938.
8. *Quebec Statistical Yearbook*, 1940, p. 143.
9. *Ibid.*, p. 138.
10. Marsh, p. 26.
11. *Census of Canada 1931*, vol. 6, p. 1268.
12. Montreal, *Report of the Director of Finance*, 1932, p. 4.
13. *Montreal Star*, March 25, 1932, p. 3.
14. Peter Kralik, *The St. Vincent de Paul Society in Montreal during the Depression*, Unpublished Research Essay, Concordia Univ. 1974.
15. *Montreal Star*, May 16, 1931, Cited in Sally Jones *Unemployment and Relief in Montreal 1930-1933*, Research Essay, Concordia Univ. 1974.
16. E. B. de Panet, *The Work of the Unemployment Relief Commission 1934-35*, Montreal 1935, p. 4.
17. Leonard Marsh, *Canadians In and Out of Work*, Oxford and Montreal, 1936, p. 356.
18. *Montreal Star*, Feb. 24, 1934.
19. Panet, p. 4.
20. *The Realities of Relief*, A report submitted by the Unemployment Study Group of the Montreal Branch of the Canadian Association of Social Workers, Montreal 1938, mimeographed.
21. *Ibid.*, p. 31.
22. Panet, p. 5.
23. *Montreal Star*, Feb. 9, 1935, Cited in June Macpherson *The Administration of Unemployment Relief in Montreal 1930-1941*, Research Essay, Concordia Univ. 1975.
24. *Quebec Statistical Yearbook*, 1942, p. 229.
25. Macpherson, p. 54-55.
26. Marsh *Health and Unemployment*, p. 28.
27. *Ibid.*, p. 28.
28. *Ibid.*, p. 152.
29. *Ibid.*, p. 154.

Abstract

Long before the Depression, Montreal had first-rate hospitals and physicians, yet a poor recording health care of the working class. Mortality and morbidity were high (in 1922, infant mortality was as high as 213 deaths per 1000 live births among the working class, but 60 per 1000 among the higher classes), and public health measures had been neglected. In the 1920s, however, advances in health care did begin to alleviate this serious situation. Among beneficial measures were pure milk depots, pasteurization and milk, well-baby clinics, diphtheria immunization (albeit after an initial phase of private funding) and reforms in public health administration (including increases in expenditures on child hygiene). These improvements were carried forward into the 1930s, and other advances, such as research into gastroenteritis during the 1920s, augmented the slow but steady ameliorative public health measures. Infant mortality, for example, relating to gastroenteritis decreased to 59.3 in 1940. Thus when the Depression made its effects felt in Montreal, the public's health was not as severely affected as this might have been. Such effects are difficult to assess, though, because many variables must be considered. While malnutrition was, perhaps, made more severe in the Depression — about one third of the Montreal population was engaged in a desperate struggle for survival, and one in every three of male wage earners was on the dole — it was as common among employed workers as among the unskilled unemployed. A fair conclusion is that what occurred in Montreal in the 1920s and 1930s was a health crisis of long duration, which in some ways worsened with the Depression yet which in other ways did not, owing to improvements in public health antedating the Depression. While the society of Montreal might or might not have been able to tackle the economic crisis of the 1930s, it still was able to reform the health care system in fundamental ways. A few halting steps had indeed been taken, albeit late, and these steps of the 1920s did pay rich dividends in the succeeding two decades.

Résumé

Bien avant la crise, Montréal était dotée d'hôpitaux et de services médicaux de première qualité. Pourtant l'état de santé de la classe ouvrière restait déplorable. Les taux de mortalité et de morbidité y étaient élevés: en 1922, la mortalité infantile atteignait 213 morts pour mille enfants nés vivants dans la classe ouvrière et 60 pour mille dans les classes plus aisées. Les mesures d'hygiène publique avaient longtemps été négligées. Dans les années vingt, cependant, certains progrès dans le domaine de la santé commencèrent à porter fruit et des mesures bénéfiques furent prises: services de distribution de lait, pasteurisation du lait, cliniques pour nourrissons, immunisation contre la diphtérie (d'abord financée par l'entreprise privée), enfin, réformes de l'administration et du financement de l'hygiène publique et en particulier augmentation des fonds pour l'hygiène infantile. Ces améliorations, qui se poursuivirent jusque dans les années trente, et d'autres développements, comme la recherche intensive sur la gastro-entérite déjà entreprise dans les années vingt, contribuèrent à rehausser lentement mais sûrement le niveau de l'hygiène. C'est ainsi que le taux de mortalité infantile due à la gastro-entérite tomba à 59.3‰ en 1940. Lorsque la crise se fit sentir à Montréal, ses effets ne furent pas aussi graves qu'on aurait pu le craindre. Ils demeurent cependant difficiles à évaluer puisqu'il faut tenir compte de plusieurs facteurs. La malnutrition qui augmenta alors, puisqu'environ un tiers de la population montréalaise devait lutter pour survivre et un tiers de la main-d'oeuvre dépendait des secours publics, se fit sentir aussi bien chez les travailleurs que chez les chômeurs. La situation difficile que connaissait depuis longtemps Montréal, dans le domaine de la santé, s'aggrava donc sur certains plans pendant la crise tout en continuant à se résorber grâce aux progrès de l'hygiène publique. Si la population de Montréal ne put résoudre la crise économique, elle put continuer à profiter des réformes touchant la santé publique. Bien qu'un peu tard, on avait déjà fait quelques pas dans la bonne direction et les mesures prises dans les années vingt continuèrent à faire sentir leurs effets pendant les deux décennies suivantes.

The Bethune Health Group
Libbie Park

Just why a group of persons in Montreal in late 1935 should have been concerned about problems of public health may be made clear from well-documented accounts of health in Montreal in the 1930s[1]. The group, now often referred to as the Bethune Group, became known at the time as the Montreal Group for the Security of the People's Health. Though clumsy, the title is descriptive and expressed our reaction to the conditions and circumstances of people in Montreal during the Depression years of 1935 and 1936.

* * *

The group was organized through the initiative of Norman Bethune in December, 1935, shortly after his return from attending the International Physiological Congress in Moscow and Leningrad in the summer of 1935. I was a graduate of the Montreal General Hospital School of Nursing and in 1935 was working part-time in the eye clinics at the Montreal General Hospital and the Montreal Western General Hospital. I met Bethune first at a meeting organised by the Friends of the Soviet Union, at which he spoke, and we kept in touch. At that time, Bethune was developing ideas of a "model city" for tuberculous patients who would have just spent a period in hospital undergoing treatment. The Model City was to be a complete rehabilitation centre, fully equipped with clinics, living accommodations, recreation areas, parks, shops and workshops. He gave much thought to the project he was proposing. He and his friend, the artist Fritz Brandtner, sketched a design for the Model City in pastel colours, and debate and discussion about it led him to think in terms of an overall health plan that would permit people to escape from what he and the group's members thought was an intolerable situation: for want of funds, people suffered and died from diseases that were curable, that could have been prevented had sufficient money been available.

A wealth of scientific knowledge existed but the lack of money made it impossible to use this knowledge for the benefit of the patient. As one writer put it, "dollarless doctors faced penniless patients"[2]. Bethune was determined to do what he could to change the situation, and he invited a few young and interested doctors to become the nucleus of what he saw as an expanding group of doctors, nurses, social workers and dentists that would work out a proposal for medical and health care in Quebec. I was invited and accepted.

* * *

The nucleus met for the first time at Bethune's apartment on Fort Street, at the corner of Tupper Street. Present at that meeting were Dr. Hy Shister, then in cardiology at the Women's General (now Reddy Memorial) Hospital; Dr. Wendell MacLeod, a young doctor in private practice in Montreal; Bethune, then head of thoracic surgery at l'Hôpital Sacré-Coeur; and myself.

Bethune had been investigating the problems of health care. He had been in touch with Dr. I. S. Falk in the United States (author of a pamphlet *The Present and Future Organization of Medicine*[3] and several books); he had received copies of the programme and principles of the Medical League for Socialized Medicine in New York; and he had started to read material on systems of medical care from Britain and European countries. He understood, too, something that not all doctors at the time would have accepted: the group he was forming was not to be just a medical group, a group of doctors; it was to be a medical and health group, to include members of all the allied health professions, all of whom, if possible, should be included in working out a health plan.

The group would grow, the original members would attract others. Public meetings would be arranged, but the main line of action would be to study and analyse medical and health services in developed countries and the relationship of these services to the state. From this analysis would come the basis for proposals on medical and health services in Quebec, support for these services being rallied by the group. But study and discussion alone did not interest Bethune; they were to be followed by action, and at the first meeting of the group Bethune outlined his proposals along those lines. We were in general agreement and we considered how to expand the group and to divide the work.

By the second meeting we had added Kay Dickson, of the Victorian Order of Nurses, Dr. Moe Bronstein and Dr. R. Gottlieb. Dr. Francis McNaughton joined us later, as did Dr. Ruth Dow, an intern at the Montreal General Hospital. An actuary helped us work out cost comparisons for various health programmes.

At later meetings, the number present varied; usually we had not more than 10 or 12, but more often there were fewer. Among Bethune's papers is a list from a desk pad with 16 names of persons, apparently to be called for meetings. The names include those of Florence Pike, a social worker, and of Dr. H. N. Segall, who has recorded an interview about the group meetings. At least two women were nearly always among the members, sometimes more.

A problem was where to meet. Bethune's Fort Street apartment was too small, and for the first few months members with accessible and roomier homes came to the rescue. In the spring of 1936, however, Bethune moved into a flat on Beaver Hall Square, which was conveniently central and had a large studio, and here we then met regularly.

The group was an unstructured one in which Bethune was very much the leading spirit. Though no minutes seem to have been kept, meetings were business-like, starting at about 8:30 p.m. and ending at about 11:00 p.m. They were not social events, but they were not dull — they were lively and exciting. We were all busy people, concerned about doing the job we had undertaken, and only those who cared about the subject attended. One became a member by invitation or by simply attending and taking part in the discussions. A member would give a paper on the country the member was studying, and discussion followed. Someone else would volunteer for the next meeting. Occasionally a guest would attend sometimes from out of town, and the meeting would be larger; I remember visitors from Detroit and Chicago.

Bethune was a popular public speaker and often accepted speaking engagements. His wide reading, his interest in health care and his personality made him a lively and attractive speaker. On at least two occasions after the group had begun its work, Bethune spoke as an advocate of socialized medicine. One speech was delivered in February, 1936, at Memphis, Tennessee, to the Mid-South Medical Assembly; another was given on April 17, 1936, when he was one of the speakers at a symposium on medical economics organized by the Montreal Medico-Chirurgical Society, of which he had just been elected a Fellow. The Society's minutes show that 128 physicians were present, an unusually large number[4]. At the Montreal meeting he announced that a group had been studying plans for the security of the people's health already in effect in other countries, and he offered to provide further information about it to anyone interested.

* * *

Two events gave us a new sense of urgency and direction. The first was the setting up in June, 1936 of the Unemployment Medical Relief Commission in Montreal, as a subcommittee of the Montreal Relief Commission. The second was the announcement of a provincial general election to be held on August 17, 1936 — the election that brought Duplessis to power for the first time. We wanted to comment on the Unemployment Medical Relief Commission and particularly to put a health plan proposal before the public and the political parties and the candidates in the election. The Depression had hit Montreal hard — in March, 1936, 170,000 persons were on relief, out of a population of 985,000 — and the city at long last proposed to set up a fund of 25 cents per month for each person on relief. This would amount to $500,000 a year, from which doctors, dentists and druggists, who provided services or medical supplies to those on relief, would be paid. The city's plan was an important step, even if inadequate, but we were concerned that it might not survive the election. We were particularly anxious that any plan be made province-wide, and that the allotment of funds per person be doubled.

We set to work at increased tempo to produce a document setting out our proposals. The first draft of our position went out in mimeographed form to the medical, dental and nursing societies under a covering letter from Bethune dated July 27, 1936; the same material appeared in the *Canadian Medical Association Journal* for August[5]. A second, much enlarged, version was mailed to doctors, candidates and political figures on August 10, 1936 (see Appendix C). The first version drew extended coverage in the *Montreal Gazette* — a lengthy news story and editorial comment[6].

It was when we came to put out this material that we had to choose a name for the group. Bethune favored using the words 'socialized medicine' in the name, but the group did not agree. It was not that we were disagreeing about the nature of our proposals; the question concerned the name for ourselves as the persons putting forward the proposals. What Bethune was calling socialized medicine was in fact a system of public medicine that could operate under the existing economic system. Moreover, the words 'socialized medicine' were ambiguous, for they could refer to a social as distinct from an individual approach to the practice of medicine, or to medicine as organized in a socialist society. Finally, we agreed that the best solution was a more unifying, descriptive title, accurate even if cumbersome — The Montreal Group for the Security of the People's Health — and our letters with Bethune's signature were sent out under that title.

Both our documents began with a detailed examination of the Unemployment Medical Relief Commission as proposed by the city. This dealt with a problem that was very much on our minds at the time, and we devoted far more space to it than we did to our own proposals for a health plan for the province. We wanted medical relief expanded to include surgical and dental treatment and home nursing. We called for a City Medical Planning Board and a City Nursing Planning Board — and, above all, we took the position that the plan should be made province-wide and that the amount of money devoted to it should be doubled.

For our proposal, we borrowed an idea from the Ontario Medical Association, which had recently suggested that experimental programmes be set up in that province. We suggested four plans as being typical of what was being discussed and debated, to be tried out in carefully selected areas in Quebec and judged on the basis of results. (For further details, see Appendix C.)

1. Plan One we described as *Municipal Medicine*. A dedicated team of doctors, dentists and nurses, representing all specialities, should be named by a Provincial Medical Planning Board. The team would be provided with a small modern hospital and would be responsible for health protection and for the cure of disease in the entire municipal area chosen. All members of the team would be paid a salary. The total cost would be borne by municipal taxation and a provincial grant. (In his speech to the Montreal Medico-Chirurgical Society, Bethune had stated that, if $3,000 a year was taken to be an adequate income, 40% of all physicians in the United States were earning less than that in 1933.[7])
2. Plan Two we termed *Compulsory Health Insurance.* Discussion concerned whether health insurance should be compulsory or voluntary, and whether the premiums should be paid by the individual or the state or shared. We proposed that a municipality with a fairly homogeneous economic pattern be selected, one with a minimum of relief recipients. All wage earners would be included in a plan of health insurance, regardless of their incomes, and the true actuarial cost would be determined.
3. Plan Three we referred to as *Voluntary Hospitalization and Health Insurance*, to be applied in a selected urban municipality of from 5,000 to 10,000 persons.
4. Plan Four was different in character: it was a proposal for a province-wide plan to deal with medical care for the unemployed. This was an urgent matter: Quebec, with 12% of the population of Canada, had 28% of all unemployed and the highest proportion of unemployables — 48% of the total in the country.

As far as Plans One, Two and Three were concerned, Two and Three each moved further away from what the group itself thought desirable. Our aim was to get away from a debate over terms by putting the alternative plans into practice in different localities under controlled conditions, to be judged by results and public reaction.

Our first document ended with an appeal for a mass meeting of all the health professions — English and French — plus social workers, and the Trades and Labour Council, to form a United Professional Front and to put forward the demands of the professions. "Action" (surely a Bethune touch) was to be "immediate, united and decisive." The second document expanded the argument, improved the presentation, made some corrections, and ended with an appeal for the calling of a Congress of French and English doctors and members of related health professions, social workers and trade unionists. It appealed to persons in the health professions to join their local professional societies; to urge verification of French and English doctors, dentists and nurses; to fight racial and professional isolation; and to unite in a common cause — health security for the people, and economic security for the professions. (While our group was at least aware of the importance of unity among the professions, neither of the documents seems to have been issued in French, and neither was noticed in the French-language press.)

* * *

What was the importance of the group's work? Looking back, it is not easy to assess it. Yet we were pioneers, not in initiating discussions about health insurance — that was well underway — but in involving all the health professions in matters that until then had been the concern mainly of the medical associations. In this, the influence of the group was felt much beyond its membership. Politics in the narrow sense did not enter into our work; we were all professional people, dealing with matters in which we had a common interest and concern, and we did not argue with each other about our personal political or philosophical beliefs — which certainly would not have been identical.

Bethune's biographers have not done justice to the period Bethune spent in Montreal. Allan and Gordon have captured the feel of the times and the spirit of Norman Bethune as we knew him, but they are weak on details and dates; thus they referred to "one hundred" doctors, dentists, nurses and social workers who joined the group[8], though if there were as many as 20 who could be called members I would be surprised. Stewart has broadened our knowledge of the details of Bethune's life, but he stated that the group decided to "lay out a detailed plan for a policy of socialized medicine"[9], but that was never our plan, no matter how one defines socialized medicine.

In a personal sense, as I have tried to show in *Bethune: The Montreal Years*[10], work in the group was intense and happy experience in a joint effort, and when Bethune left for Spain in October, 1936, and I left for Toronto in the autumn of that year, the group did not dissolve — the work of the group was carried on in Montreal by Wendell MacLeod, Kay Dickson and Francis McNaughton, among others.

As for Bethune, the group, like everything he took part in, was a means to provide a practical answer to a practical problem, an answer that could be acted on.

Spain became for him a practical problem of direct concern, and he acted accordingly.

The cause of the Chinese people was to him a call to action, and he responded.

Some have seen Bethune in 1936 as a desperate man, running away from a Montreal that rejected him. We who worked with him in the group would not agree.

He did what he felt he had to do; he could not have done otherwise.

* * *

REFERENCES AND NOTES

1. The chapter by Terry Copp in this book pp. 129-137 is a well-informed source of information; the chapter by Jessie Scriver pp. 79-84 is also informative.
2. Myron Weiss, "Dollarless Doctors and Penniless Patients", *Canadian Medical Association Journal*, 35 (1935), p. 673.
3. I.S. Falk, *The Present and Future Organization of Medicine* (pamphlet), New York, 1934.
4. The minutes of the Montreal Medico-Chirurgical Society are held in the Osler Library, McGill University.
5. "Proposed Plans for the Security of Health in the Province of Quebec" *Canadian Medical Association Journal*, 35 (1936), p. 205.
6. Montreal Gazette, July 30, 1936; Aug. 10, 1936.
7. Norman Bethune, "Take Private Profit out of Medicine", Canadian Doctor, 1937 (January), p. 11.
8. Ted Allan and Sydney Gordon, *The Scalpel, The Sword: The Story of Norman Bethune*, Boston and Toronto, 1952, p. 91.
9. Roderick Stewart, *Bethune*, Toronto, 1973, p. 74.
10. Wendell MacLeod, Libbie Park, Stanley Ryerson, *Bethune: The Montreal Years*, Toronto, 1978, pp. 73-134.

* * *

Abstract

The Bethune Health Group (the Montreal Group for the Security of the People's Health) was organized in December 1935 by Bethune, soon after his return from attending the International Physiological Congress in Russia. At this time he was developing the concept of a Model City for the tuberculous, and discussions led to the concept of an overall health care plan for Quebec that would allow people to escape from an intolerable situation in which lack of money caused suffering and death from diseases that were, in fact, curable and preventable; morever, the scientific knowledge was available but a lack of money prevented its application. Bethune knew about health care systems elsewhere, and invited people he knew to form a group to study systems of health care in various countries, out of which might come a proposal for medical and health care in Quebec. Bethune always stressed the need for action, but, soon, two events gave urgency to the group's work: the setting up in June 1936 of an Unemployment Medical Relief Commission, and the call for an election in Quebec on August 17, 1936. The group wanted to comment on the plan for the Commission and to put forward a health care plan for Quebec, to be considered by the political candidates. The proposal comprised four plans, each to be tried in a different area under controlled conditions and the value of each to be judged in due course. The group also called for mass meetings of health professionals and social workers and the Trades and Labour Council; also for a Congress of French and English doctors and for meetings of health care professionals and trade unionists. In their work the group, which comprised doctors, dentists, nurses, social workers and others, pioneered, not discussions on health insurance but involvement of all *health care professionals in matters that, until then, had been the concern mainly of the medical profession.*

Résumé

Le groupe pour la santé organisé par Bethune (The Montreal Group for the Security of the People's Health*), fut mis sur pied en décembre 1935 peu de temps après son retour du Congrès international de physiologie, tenu à Moscou et à Leningrad, au moment où il travaillait à la conception d'une Cité modèle pour tuberculeux. Les réflexions autour de la Cité modèle eurent comme corollaire la discussion d'un programme général de santé destiné à permettre aux gens d'échapper à cette situation intolérable où le manque d'argent semblait lié à la présence de maladies souffrantes et parfois mortelles, alors qu'elles étaient curables et évitables. Même les connaissances scientifiques acquises ne pouvaient être mises au service des patients à cause du manque d'argent. Bethune, qui était au courant des systèmes d'assurance-santé en vigueur dans d'autres pays, invita donc des gens de sa connaissance à former un groupe de spécialistes — médecins, infirmières, travailleurs sociaux, dentistes et autres — pour étudier ces différents systèmes et élaborer un plan de soins médicaux pour le Québec. Bethune mettait toujours l'accent sur l'action et bientôt deux événements vinrent rendre le travail du groupe plus immédiatement tangible: l'établissement, en juin 1936, de la Commission des secours médicaux pour les chômeurs et l'élection provinciale d'août 1936. Le groupe voulut plus spécialement se prononcer sur l'établissement de la Commission: il reconnaissait le bien-fondé de sa mise sur pied mais craignait qu'elle ne survive pas aux élections. Le groupe élabora donc un plan en quatre points: médecine municipale, assurance santé obligatoire, hospitalisation et soins médicaux pour les sans-travail. Le plan devait être mis à l'essai dans diverses localités, dans des conditions contrôlées afin de pouvoir être évalué par la suite. Le groupe proposa de tenir une assemblée de tous les professionnels de la santé, des travailleurs sociaux et des membres du Congrès des Métiers et du Travail. Il proposa aussi la tenue d'une congrès pour médecins anglophones et francophones et de réunions entre professionnels de la santé et syndicalistes. Par son travail, le groupe fut l'instigateur non pas tellement de discussions sur l'assurance-santé, mais de la mobilisation de tous les professionnels de la santé à propos de questions restées jusque là l'apanage de la profession médicale.*

Political Commitment in the 1930s

Stanley B. Ryerson

In seeking to understand Norman Bethune, it is a little as though we are all trying to decode a message — the message of a life. We are also, seemingly, hunters in search of a legacy. The message is addressed to us, who are in some way his heirs. But how can this be? And what *is* a life that is itself a message?

For that life to speak to us, which is a life no longer but a memory, and for it to reach us, it must somehow involve us. It must be decipherable, translatable — at least approximately.

If he were to see us rack our brains so earnestly about him, Bethune would surely have chuckled — he who was possessed of a sense of humour not without its sting. "But look!", he would have burst out, "it's so damned simple, really: the sick suffer from bacterial infection and at the same time from a sick society that has all of us in its grip. The health of individuals is inseparable from that of society as a whole; it cries out for therapy and surgery; and it has reached the doors of Emergency".

Daniel Longpré, a doctor with a social conscience if ever there *was* one, who looked after the children of workers, the families of the working-class East End, said of Bethune, "He was above all *honest*." What Bethune felt as truth, was an imperative to act.

* * *

A life that is a message must be one that involves those to whom it speaks; it does so because we, the recipients, share in some way the core experience of the sender. It is our life as much as his that is enmeshed in the tangle of a historical experience common to both. So the key words in the message that was Bethune's life and that we are seeking to decipher — sometimes faint and all but illegible, or perhaps in other tongues (Spanish, Russian, Chinese?) — are still charged with meaning for us all.

His was a life lived in alignment, increasingly, to the end, with the great thrust of a world awakening — awakening to the social realities of work and property and power, and a historic possibility of choice and change. Such a choice is hard to make, hurtful perhaps to the point of death, yet impossible to evade indefinately, in our inmost self.

The issues Bethune faced — with explosive honesty— are with us still, however changed their secondary symptoms, or the terms in which they present themselves. One example may suffice. In the essay, "Wounds", Bethune excoriated the eminent and eminently respectable beneficiaries of "free enterprise" corporate business, charging them with responsibility for the mass casualties of war and poverty[1]. *"It is these men who make the wounds";* men for whom *private profit* was the be-all and end-all of their lives. That axis of all our social arrangements is no less a determinant now than in the 1920s and the 1930s. Thus a questionnaire addressed to 200 heads of corporations in Quebec by Pierre

Fournier, a political scientist, included the innocent query, "What do you consider to be the most important objective of business?" and elicited these replies: profitability, in 70%; growth of the economy, 20%; and social objectives, 5%[2]. Such ethical priorities can hardly be uninfluential in the society that business dominates and shapes in its own image. Issues of housing, health, pollution, community needs, must be, and are, pervaded — and perverted — by them.

Bethune was one of us. Like a growing number of fellow Canadians in the early and mid-1930s, he had joined the Left (in the broad sense of that term) because he had grown convinced of two pressing truths. One was that an industrial private enterprise society with vast productive powers, which stalled periodically and led to unemployment, poverty and insecurity for millions of working people, was going to have to be replaced by a society arranged quite differently. Only a radical turn-over to a new social order would suffice, one based on planned, participatory communitarian ownership and management of the gigantic modern technology of mass production. Acceptance of this vision of an alternative future involved a change of mind, of world outlook, that was for Bethune, as for the rest of us, a revolutionary turning point. I am reminded, for instance, of his delight at discovering the conception of dialectical change — change through internal conflict of opposites — as the medullary substance of historical process, the very marrow of personal and community life.

At the core of change stood the fact of social class, as the expression of historically evolved relations of work, and property, and power, in the setting of the grand metabolism of human society interacting with the physical world of nature. A pitting of social class against social class, seen not as some artificial artifact of agitators, but as the organic concomitant of property accumulation by the few at the cost of deprivation of the many. Mass struggles in the 1930s of workers without work, of exploited factory hands, miners, loggers, from Cape Breton to the Queen Charlotte Islands, had their impact on the consciousness of intellectuals and professionals.

To be a social revolutionary meant, in the 1930s, becoming a communist. As to what that implied in those days and, in the light of Bethune's own party and military experience, what makes the matter more complicated in today's world context, I have tried to suggest in *The Montreal Years*[3]. But the fundamental crux — of changing the social system through social struggle — remains inescapable.

Equally important as the long-range, structural socialist prospect, for Bethune and all those who thought like him, was a second proposition: the democratic majority of Canadians would be won over to agreement with that perspective only through their own lived experience of collective action and its results, with practice vindicating theory. Moreover, the dream of a future society, restructured to a new freedom, had to face up to a present that threatened all its prospects — a present charged with the twin nightmares of mounting fascism and oncoming universal war.

In his leadership of the community-political work for the security of the people's health, in Montreal, as in the anti-fascist, anti-imperialist medical army service in Spain, and then in China, which was to cost him his life, Bethune expressed in action the world-view he had made his own.

The drawing of lessons from that experience, now, nearly half a century later, is still only just beginning. Recognition of what he *did* is yet to be completed by understanding of *what it meant*, for his time and for ours. The challenge to deepen that understanding touches on two areas at least of progressive-democratic and socialist thought. One is that of the connection between ends and means, the "what is to be done" to respond to the present in such a way as to embody at the same time consciousness of the future society, its nature and its needs. The second, linked with this, is the overcoming of a crisis, in Marxism and the Left, that will have to include unravelling a core of democratic dedication from the stubbornly encrusted, conflict-ridden integuments of a diversity of state-power, military-political interests on a planetary scale.

Lent to Bethune by Louis Kon, in the very early days, was an old, battered book by Julius Hecker — *Moscow Dialogues: Discussions of Red Philosophy*[4]. This book bore a dedication by the author to a theologian, leader of the peace movement in the United States, Dr. Harry Ward: "Friend and Comrade in the struggle for a social order where the strife of class and race shall be no more, and where truth, goodness and beauty shall be the share of all." So dreamed Bethune, also.

That dream is out of reach, so long as the twin horror-shadows of nuclear war and of pollution-induced self extermination of the species continue to close in on us with the passing days. The poisoning of the Mediterranean beaches with titanium dioxide[5], to the nuclear nightmare of Three Mile Island and Mississauga's chlorine gas — the international corporate powers of consolidated profit are "those that make the wounds". Their dislodgement from military, social, political power is the price of human survival.

The legacy, then is a challenge. But the message remains a question.

* * *

REFERENCES AND NOTES

1. Norman Bethune, "Wounds"; see Roderick Stewart, *The Mind of Norman Bethune,* Toronto, 1977, pp. 31.
2. Pierre Fournier, *The Quebec Establishment, The Ruling Class and The State,* Black Rose Books, Montreal, 1976, pp. 44.
3. Wendell MacLeod, Libbie Park and Stanley Ryerson, *Bethune: The Montreal Years,* Toronto, 1978, pp. 143-156, especially.
4. Julius Hecker, *Moscow Dialogues: Discussions of Red Philosophy,* Chapman and Hall, London, 1933. Reprinted, Hyperion Press, Westport, CT, 1980.
5. Christian Huglo et René Cenni, *Une société de pollution,* Jean-Claude Cimoën, Paris, 1977.

* * *

Abstract

Though Bethune died more than 40 years ago, and though he faced issues of and suggested solutions for the 1930s, the problems of society that he identified and described, with explosive honesty, are with us today. We share in the historical tangle of experience that Bethune knew and the message of his life is therefore relevant to us, his heirs, today. Bethune lived his life in alignment to the thrust of a world awakening to the social realities of work and property and power and to the historic possibility of choice and change. Free-enterprise corporate business was charged, in Bethune's eyes, with the responsibility for the mass casualties of war and poverty, and, because Bethune felt as truth the imperative to act, he committed himself to finding solutions and insisting on the need for them. For Bethune, an industrial private-enterprise society, which stalled periodically and led to unemployment, insecurity and poverty must be replaced by a very different social order, one that was not based on social class. A new order could only arise if the lived experience of collective action and its results won a society's citizens over to agreement and to this perspective, and this dream of a future society, in Bethune's day, had to face up to mounting fascism and an oncoming universal war. So his dream was not to be realized, at any rate in Canada and the West. And for us today, who observe that the profit motive overrides social objectives, solutions are no easier, for the axis of our social arrangements are still determined as they were in the 1930s; problems of housing, health, environment and community welfare are perverted by ethical priorities based on capitalism. Moreover, the dreams of a new social order free of stripe of class and race remains out of reach as long as the twin horrors of nuclear war and pollution close in on us. Yet realising the meaning of what Bethune did is a start and a path to finding the social order that lies beyong the horizon.

Résumé

Bien que Bethune mourut il y a plus de quarante ans et qu'il rencontra des problèmes et proposa des solutions pour les années 1930, les problèmes sociaux qu'il identifia et décrivit avec une puissante honnêteté sont toujours parmi nous. Nous partageons l'enchevêtrement historique dont Bethune fit l'expérience et pour nous, ses héritiers, le message de sa vie est toujours pertinent. Bethune vécut sa vie aligné sur l'élan d'un monde se réveillant aux réalités sociales du travail, de la propriété et du pouvoir, et de la possibilité historique du changement. L'entreprise privée des corporations d'affaires portait, aux yeux de Bethune, la responsabilité des pertes causées par la guerre et la pauvreté, et, parce qu'il considérait la vérité comme un impératif pour l'action, Bethune s'engagea à trouver des solutions et à insister sur leur nécessité. Pour Bethune, une société d'entreprise privée industrielle, périodiquement en panne et cause de chômage, d'insécurité et de pauvreté, devait être remplacée par un ordre social très différent, un ordre n'étant pas basé sur les classes sociales. Un nouvel ordre social ne pouvait s'implanter que si l'expérience vécue de l'action collective et de ses résultats poussait les citoyens d'une société à se mettre d'accord dans cette *même perspective. Ce rêve d'une société future, à l'époque de Bethune, devait faire face à la montée du fascisme et à l'avènement d'une guerre universelle. Son rêve ne s'est pas réalisé, tout au moins au Canada et en Occident. Et pour nous, aujourd'hui, qui observons que le profit a précédence sur les objectifs sociaux, les solutions ne sont pas faciles car les axes des dispositions sociales sont toujours déterminés comme ils l'étaient pendant les années trente: les problèmes de logement, de santé, d'environnement et de bien-être communautaire sont pervertis par des priorités basées sur le capitalisme. De plus, le rêve d'un nouvel ordre social libre des considérations de classe et de race demeure hors de portée aussi longtemps que la double horreur d'une guerre nucléaire et de la pollution nous menace. La réalisation du sens de ce que fit Bethune est cependant un début et une voie pour parvenir à l'ordre social qui se trouve au-delà de l'horizon.*

L'engagement politique après les années trente: l'organisation des travailleurs

Madeleine Parent

Rapidement, après le début de la deuxième grande guerre le problème du chômage massif au Canada se résorbait. En peu de temps, presque toute notre capacité de production industrielle était mise à profit et on construisait de nouvelles usines pour répondre à la demande de production de guerre. Un pays, hier incapable de produire, paralysé par la crise économique, devenait maintenant un vaste arsenal. On avait les moyens; on n'avait pas voulu s'en servir. Et dans ce vaste arsenal des années 1940, on invitait les femmes. Elles avaient, depuis le XIXe siècle, formé une main d'oeuvre à bon marché, le *cheap labour* des usines de textile, qui travaillait dans des emplois restreints traditionnels, mal payés. Ces femmes étaient en demande pendant la guerre dans toutes les industries, dans les usines de munitions, dans les industries lourdes; on en faisait des machinistes, des soudeurs, des menuisiers, des camionneurs. Il n'y a rien que les femmes ne pouvaient pas faire au travail pendant ces années de guerre.

* * *

Au Québec, le nombre de travailleurs industriels a doublé de 1939-1943. Mais s'il n'y avait désormais à peu près pas de chômage, les conditions de travail dans les usines de guerre et surtout dans les usines traditionelles comme le textile laissaient beaucoup à désirer. Les salaires étaient bas; il n'y avait presque pas de bénéfices, de congés, de vacances payées, de plans de santé. Les heures de travail étaient longues. Chez nous, dans le textile, les femmes et hommes travaillaient 55 heures par semaine, 10 heures par jour. Quelques hommes, et même beaucoup, travaillaient 12 heures la nuit; et le samedi, pour les employés de jour, était une journée de travail. Les accidents industriels, dans une industrie en expansion rapide, étaient très nombreux. On ne s'occupait pas des accidents et même des mortalités dans la force de travail. Les droits des travailleurs à l'ancienneté, à la protection en emploi étaient très minimes. Ce qui fait que, dans ce vaste arsenal de guerre qu'était maintenant le Canada industriel, ceux qui faisaient l'effort, ceux qui faisaient les sacrifices, c'étaient les travailleurs gagnant peu d'argent pour de longues heures dans des conditions difficiles. Les patrons, dirigés par Mackenzie King et son lieutenant C.D. Howe, produisaient avec le coût de leur production garanti et une marge généreuse de profit toujours garantie. Il n'y avait pas de risques pour les patrons en période de guerre; le profit était certain.

Poussés à bout, les travailleurs dans ces industries se sont syndiqués. Ils avaient moins peur, il n'y avait presque pas de chômage. Il y eut alors une vague montante de syndicalisme de 1942-1943 jusqu'aux premières années de l'après-guerre. Comme exemple, citons l'organisation des travailleurs dans les usines d'amiante au Canada, au Québec, en Ontario, dans les Maritimes. Les travailleurs de l'aluminium à Arvida dans le lac Saint-Jean s'organisaient. Les travailleurs de l'International Nickel dans le nord de l'Ontario dans la région de Sudbury s'organisaient par milliers. Il en était ainsi des travailleurs dans les usines d'équipement électrique General Electric, Westinghouse, ici à Montréal à RCA Victor et ailleurs, de ceux des chantiers maritimes qui construisaient les navires de guerre, et aussi des marins qui étaient sur ces navires et qui, eux aussi, en haute mer, prenaient des chances énormes, tout comme de nos forces armées, pour transporter l'équipement de guerre aux alliés.

Il se trouva que dans cette montée du syndicalisme au Canada, beaucoup de travailleurs dans les industries traditionelles comme le textile ont repris courage encore une fois et se sont organisés. Les revendications des travailleurs en temps de guerre étaient modestes: d'abord, Mackenzie King s'en était occupé, les salaires étaient gelés. On nous permettait seulement de gagner une petite partie de ce qu'on devait gagner: c'était la loi. En plus de ça, des grandes fédérations ouvrières, celles des États-Unis, dominées par les Américains, avaient fait la promesse qu'il n'y aurait pas de grève en temps de guerre. Que ce soit une bonne idée ou une mauvaise, malheur aux militants à l'intérieur de ces grandes fédérations qui auraient prôné la grève. Dans une période de confrontation, ils auraient été attaqués avec beaucoup de force pas seulement par les gouvernements mais aussi par les dirigeants des fédérations ouvrières et cela aurait été le coup qui aurait porté le plus. Dès l'après-guerre, d'autres grèves marquèrent la continuité du mouvement d'organisation syndicale. Les patrons dans plusieurs industries ont exécuté de vastes mises-à-pied. Beaucoup de gens étaient encore dans l'insécurité, et les travailleurs ont senti qu'on voulait les retourner aux années de la misère, aux années de la grande crise, et surtout leur faire sentir qui était le maître au Canada, c'est-à-dire le grand patron et ses lieutenants à Québec, à Ottawa et ailleurs, les Duplessis, les Mackenzie King, les Louis Saint-Laurent.

Les travailleurs se sont organisés, face à ce défi. Il y a eu une continuité dans la campagne d'organisation et il y a eu de grandes grèves, surtout dans les années 1946 et 1947. Les travailleurs dans l'équipement électrique, à la Westinghouse à Hamilton, dans les usines d'acier à la Stelco, qui avaient été précédés d'ailleurs par les grévistes de la Ford à Windsor, les travailleurs dans le textile, les marins canadiens, se sont élevés pour revendiquer des conventions collectives, des conditions décentes et un après-guerre où les ouvriers et leurs familles pouvaient dire "ces années ont signalé des victoires très importantes pour le mouvement ouvrier!"

La riposte des patrons s'est fait sentir non seulement tout de suite après la guerre, mais elle s'est développée, elle s'est raffinée dans les années de la guerre froide inspirée par le vaste mouvement anti-communiste aux États-Unis par les sénateurs McCarthy et tous leurs alliés. On décida que ceux qui combattaient pour la justice, pour une vie meilleure, étaient tous des communistes et devaient être poussés à l'extrême, et isolés autant que possible. Ce mouvement pendant la guerre froide a été secondé malheureusement par les grands bureaucrates des fédérations ouvrières au Canada qui, eux aussi, se sont attaqués aux militants dans le mouvement syndical. Dans le Congrès canadien du travail on s'est attaqué, par exemple, à l'Union de l'électricité, à l'Union des pêcheurs, à l'Union des mineurs et les grands chefs de nos syndicats ont soutenu un agent secret de la police américaine comme S. Baron qui, au sein du Congrès, faisait des discours passionnés pour s'attaquer à la gauche du mouvement syndical, pour tâcher de détruire le mouvement. Cet homme a été appuyé non seulement par les chefs du gouvernement, mais aussi par les grands bureaucrates dans les unions à dominance américaine. Dans le congrès auquel je faisais partie, le Congrès des Métiers et du Travail, cela a été la même chose. Il y a eu une lutte énorme pour expulser le syndicat canadien des marins et c'était le précurseur de la destruction de la marine marchande canadienne en haute mer, que nous n'avons pas reconstruite encore aujourd'hui. Ça été le chemin ouvert pour amener au Canada un gangster américain du nom de Hal Banks que Mackenzie King et Saint-Laurent ont placé à la direction du mouvement syndical chez les marins canadiens pour que ceux-ci ne puissent plus se défendre. Cela a été une période honteuse dans le mouvement des travailleurs alors qu'on cherchait à nous retourner aux années d'avant-guerre, aux années de crise, en désarmant les travailleurs eux-mêmes et le mouvement qu'ils avaient bâti pour protéger leurs intérêts.

* * *

Cependant, pendant que la guerre froide se déroulait, et qu'au Québec on vivait les années noires du duplessisme, les syndicats catholiques, qui autrefois avaient été domestiqués par les prêtres et les patrons, étaient enfin devenus un mouvement beaucoup plus militant qui se basait sur les revendications des travailleurs et une confrontation avec les patrons. Quatre ans après que notre propre syndicat du textile, qui était d'allégeance américaine, même si on menait notre barque chez nous, avait finalement été brisé par les patrons et les chefs américains en 1952, les syndicats catholiques confrontaient la Dominion Textile dans les usines des villes industrielles du Québec. Ils ont ainsi continué pendant une bonne période la lutte que nous avions entreprise dix ans plus tôt.

Auparavant, en 1949, les travailleurs dans les syndicats catholiques ont livré la grève contre les patrons dans l'amiante lors de la grève d'Asbestos, dont tout le monde se rappelle, ou tout au moins a entendu parler.

Avec cette montée plus militante du syndicalisme catholique au Québec, devenu de moins en moins catholique et de plus en plus ouvrier, il y avait aussi une montée dans les unions industrielles du Québec. Elles avaient formé une fédération provinciale, la F.U.I.Q. qui, en alliance avec les militants des syndicats catholiques, développait un programme d'action pour les travailleurs, avec le but de former un parti des travailleurs et de leurs alliés un peu plus tard. Dans ce programme, on préconisait le retour à l'État des ressources naturelles pour que les patrons ne les gèrent plus. On réclamait un programme de santé universel. On demandait l'instruction gratuite et beaucoup d'autres réformes qui étaient en avance sur leur temps.

Quand on voulut développer un parti politique chez les travailleurs et leurs alliés au Québec, il y eut deux grands obstacles au développement et à la continuité de ce travail politique: premièrement, les chefs des grandes fédérations ouvrières américaines craignaient avant tout que les travailleurs au Québec forment un parti politique québécois. Ils ont tout fait pour empêcher le succès d'un parti politique au Québec. Deuxièmement, monsieur Pierre Elliott Trudeau, un intellectuel de la gauche en ces temps-là, bien vu parmi beaucoup de militants, prêchait le rassemblement des forces démocratiques au Québec. Cela sonnait bien mais c'était très vague. Il voulait rassembler les forces démocratiques pour battre Duplessis aux élections. Or, il y avait, selon lui, seulement le parti libéral qui pouvait battre Duplessis aux élections. Donc, avec un syllogisme très fin: pas de parti politique des travailleurs, mais appuyons plutôt les libéraux pour que Duplessis soit battu. Comme quoi M. Trudeau n'a pas tellement changé dans vingt ans.

* * *

From the times of Bethune until to-day, organized workers in Quebec and all of Canada went from the crisis of the 1930s, with its massive unemployment, a period of desperate and militant struggles, to the buoyant union organizing campaigns of the war years that continued into many campaigns in the immediate after-war years and many victorious struggles, several of them conducted in strikes. Then there were the difficult critical years of the Cold War when the American influence on our economy, on our government, and the American influence on our trade union movement, cost the workers of Canada many a bitter battle, where our leadership in the trade unions with few exceptions, was regressive and worked in collaboration with American employers, with governments that were anti-labour. Then there followed a new wave of organization amongst the workers of Canada. The 1960s saw organization of public workers throughout this country and particularly in Quebec, in their hundreds of thousands. These public workers are giving a new face to the labour movement of Canada because they are setting up Québécois or Canadian labour unions, not American-dominated labour unions. So that, thanks to them, to-day the majority of the organized workers in Canada are in unions that are run and conducted directly from this country where the rank and file has a much greater say. These service workers, these public service workers, particularly the postal workers, are threatened by the employers, but so are the members of the Canadian Union of Public Employees, who are not only under attack from employers, and administrators in government, but also under attack from to-day's big American bureaucrats in the labour movement such as the Dennis McDermotts. But these people are growing in number. They are determined in their fight, they have greater powers, and I think their future will be a better one because we have growing ranks of people in a fighting movement who, through our experience and theirs, through their understanding of the forces standing before them and opposite them right now, are determined to bring about a better world, the kind of world Norman Bethune fought for, and that many others have, and are fighting for, but which will come about with the future generations.

* * *

Résumé

La prospérité des années de guerre a succédé à la dépression économique mais n'a pas résolu tous les problèmes de la classe ouvrière. L'absence de chômage a pu placer les syndicats dans une position de force, mais le besoin de main-d'oeuvre a conduit à une plus grande utilisation de main-d'oeuvre bon marché, en particulier féminine, dont l'organisation restait à faire. Cette organisation syndicale s'est poursuivie après la guerre pour se buter au mouvement de répression qui a marqué la guerre froide et dont l'aile radicale du mouvement ouvrier a dû faire les frais. Au Québec, cette période vit une sécularisation du syndicalisme catholique et une augmentation du militantisme qui ne parvient cependant pas à déboucher sur l'action politique. Pendant les années 60 le mouvement syndical a rejoint les travailleurs dans la fonction publique et ses succès font qu'aujourd'hui la majorité des travailleurs appartiennent à des syndicats canadiens. Ces travailleurs s'efforcent de réaliser un monde meilleur, ce monde meilleur pour lequel Bethune avait déjà combattu.

Abstract

Wartime prosperity succeeded the economic depression but failed to solve all the problems of the working-class. Full employment may have placed the unions in a position of strength, but the need for workers led to a greater utilisation of cheap labour, mainly women, whose organization remained to be done. Union organization went on after the war only to meet the repression that marked the Cold War and for which the radical wing of the labour movement paid the highest price. In Québec, the post-war period witnessed the secularization of catholic syndicalism and an increase in militantism, though it did not succeed in the political arena. During the 1960s unions reached public servants and their recent success mean that, today, most workers belong to Canadian organizations. These workers strive to establish a better world, the kind of world for which Bethune was fighting.

Spain/Espagne
1936-1937

And this same pallid moon tonight
Which rides so quickly — clear and high . . .

Above the shattered Spanish mountain tops
Last night rose low and wild and red,
Reflecting back from her illumined shield
The blood-bespattered faces of the dead.

— Norman Bethune
From "Red Moon"

Source: Canadian Forum, 17 July 1937, 118

Henning Sorensen to Graham Spry: A Letter

Henning Sorensen, who worked with Bethune in Spain, was unable to come to Montreal to share his reminiscences. This letter from him was read by Graham Spry, moderator of the session on Spain and author of the script for the radio dramatization entitled Canada in Spain *(see Appendix D).*

Henning Sorensen
1806 Cliffwood Road   6 November 1979.
North Vancouver, B.C.

Dear Graham:

   We have met only once. That was in September 1936, the night before I left Montreal for Spain. You may remember you came to my apartment together with Frank Scott and Jacques Bieler. You had learned I was going to Spain and you came to ask me to act as an agent for a newly created Committee to Aid Spanish Democracy. This led to my association with Norman Bethune in Madrid later that fall. So, you see I owe you a debt of gratitude — or at least one third of the debt, since there were three of you. I became Bethune's interpreter in the blood transfusion unit created by him.

   The Bethune Foundation has done me the honour to ask me for a message to the conference in Montreal, What can I say that has not already been said? I think those who were associated with Bethune, those who received the impact of his personality, have never been quite the same since. There is a little Norman Bethune inside all of us reminding us of what we might be if we had his drive and passion. There is a little bit of shame that we manage to put into a mental drawer.

   When I look upon the life of Norman Bethune, it seems to me to be one long preparation for the final period — his life and work in China. In Canada he had achieved success but he could not rest on his laurels. In this impatient, passionate man there was a deep concern for mankind. As he grew older the anger inside him became more intense — his anger against social injustice and hypocrisy, and so did his impatience with inefficiency, procrastination and opportunism. A vision had been growing in his mind, a vision of a world where men would be brothers, exploitation of man by man eliminated, where selfish aspirations and violence would be abhorred. He had come to the conclusion that he must dedicate the remainder of his life to the struggle toward that final and supreme goal. He wanted his life to be in harmony with his convictions. In China, in the midst of the stress and the almost unbearable toil and fatigue, he felt he had at last achieved that harmony. I feel fortunate that my life was touched by his.

                                                                    Henning

With Norman Bethune in Spain
Ted Allan

I first met Norman Bethune when I was about 17 years old, in the mid-1930s. Hitler was already in power and Naziism was well-established. I was then a young communist; Bethune, though not yet a communist, was involved in left-wing political activities and was well known to me not only as a famous thoracic surgeon, but also through his reputation in organising free medical clinics for the unemployed, being involved in eviction cases, and advocating socialised medicine. I knew he had been to Russia. For me, Bethune was a star, but we had never met. Then, one day, Bethune telephoned me just to tell me that he very much liked my short story in *New Frontier*. I was thrilled. He was enthusiastic and then invited me to a party he was about to give. Overwhelmed by his flattery, his praise and his attention, I made my way to that party on Beaver Hall Hill, where he had his apartment.

The party had a political reason that I cannot remember, but most of the left-wing writers of prominence, painters and intellectuals were there. He greeted me warmly, and took me immediately to his bathroom, which puzzled me; but on his bathroom wall hung all the diplomas that he had received at various universities and various awards — and also hand-prints. He put my hand into a plate of water-colour paint, then put it against the wall and then said, "Now, autograph". I did, and he said "All right, you're now among my friends". I felt favoured and honoured, and in a short time he became a sort of surrogate father to me.

* * *

Bethune was the most exciting man I had ever met. At the time he was a new world to me. I came from a very poor Jewish family; he was a of Presbyterian Scottish-Canadian stock — his grandfather a surgeon, his great-grandfather a minister. There was an aura of not only success about him, but wealth also, and he impressed me on many levels. His encouragement was incredible for me because at the time — maybe it is still a Canadian trait — young writers and artists did not get much encouragement from their fellow Canadians; yet Bethune not only encouraged me, as a young writer, but also other writers and painters. He would buy their work just to encourage them.

It was at this party that I met a lovely woman whom he introduced to me, saying, "This is my wife Frances"; she smiled and replied, "I'm not his wife — we've been divorced twice". Bethune then rejoined, "I do not give my wife, I only lend her." This gives us a hint of the complexities of that very complex relationship. It was a relationship that may give some insight not only into heroes, but into men generally of our period. (By our period I mean the last few thousand years, and perhaps the next few thousand years.) Bethune's dependency on Frances was deep. But perhaps this dependency in Bethune began with his mother, who was a Presbyterian missionary (his father was a Presbyterian minister). She was a powerful lady, and her son must have grown up trying consciously and unconsciously to fight this dependency on his mother and then to transfer this to the fight against a dependency on any woman. So Bethune's need of Frances, and his inability to admit this dependency, or be conscious of it, was the clue to his relationship with Frances and it seems to be the clue, perhaps, to much of his behaviour.

I met Bethune again in Spain. I was in the International Brigade, and had been transferred from a fighting unit to the blood transfusion service to investigate rumours of big problems within the unit. When I arrived, he greeted me like a long lost brother, or perhaps a son, hugging me and saying, "God, I need you." Right then and there he appointed me political commissar. This was confirmed officially by the Brigade.

* * *

Bethune's work in blood transfusion is too well known for me to discuss[1]. (He was the first man to introduce the mobile blood bank to a battlefield. A blood transfusion service had already been organized in Barcelona by the Catalan doctor, Duran Jorda, who gave Bethune much advice about blood storage, but this Barcelona blood transfusion unit was far from any of the fronts and the wounded did not get transfusions immediately on being wounded. This was Bethune's genius that he saw the need for the mobile transfusion unit at the front[2].) I would like to concentrate instead on some of the personal events that took place between us.

The danger of hero worship is that it can turn into its opposite. And because Bethune drank a lot in Spain, I became disillusioned. He disturbed me. He did not act as a hero is supposed to act, and he did not act as *my* hero was supposed to act. I did not understand *why* he drank. It took a long time for me to understand what had happened. Bethune had come to Spain in a wave of that idealistic fervour that brought so many of us to Spain, to devote ourselves to the fight against Hitler, and to the fight against fascism. He had had a rather idealized concept of what a communist should be, and not all the doctors who were assigned to the blood transfusion unit fitted that picture. The Spanish doctors were average human beings; not all of them were communists, who were supposed to be the most dedicated and most committed of the anti-fascist fighters. Some were republicans, some were anarchists, and some were right-wing socialists. Whatever the spectrum, there they were; and they had their disagreements, and some of them had large egos, and they did not work the way Bethune, who did not sleep much, was used to working. Bethune said that he did not need as much sleep, but I suspect that he suffered from insomnia. He also had nightmares, which I believe now were connected with his dependency problem, and when things went wrong he tried to get to Frances. Frances was not there, and so he lost his temper often because his Spanish colleagues did not do what he wanted them to do, nor did they work as hard as he expected them to work, and so he was disturbed.

He was not necessarily disillusioned, but he was disturbed, and this was reflected in his behaviour. It was reflected also in my disillusionment, and, with myself playing the sometimes rather heavy role of the political commissar, we ended up arguing. After a while I began to insist that he go home, and that he conduct a propaganda tour of the U.S.A. and Canada, because I felt he would be more useful at home than he was becoming in Spain. He had done his work. He had organized a mobile blood transfusion service. Blood was now being delivered to all sectors of the central front, but he was unhappy, because I do not think the Spanish made him feel that they needed him. Neither did they make him feel their total commitment and dedication. So he was bitter and unhappy.

Other things were going on in Spain that we only "smelled" at the time. The murderous purges had begun in Russia, the Bakuninites and the Trotskyists were being accused of being facists and agents of the Imperial powers. This was vicious nonsense but it was reflected in Spain because of the influence of the Russian Communist Party. It confused both of us and did not enhance the general atmosphere. Meanwhile, Spanish democracy was losing, and we were affected by that.

I was mainly responsible for his going home, for which, I believe, he never really forgave me. After he left, our relationship cooled. I was caught in the retreat at Brunete, hit by a tank and badly wounded. After I had returned home, Bethune examined my foot, and made sure that I saw him regularly, that I was taken care of, and that the recuperation of my wound was satisfactory. A sort of reconciliation took place, but our relationship was never quite the same, for he felt I had let *him* down, and I felt he had let *me* down. Then we talked of China. He was excited about going to China; he had read Edgar Snow's recently published *Red Star Over China* and was excited by Snow's descriptions of a Mao Zedong and of egalitarianism, the behaviour of the communists in China. And so, he went to China, and we were never in touch after he went there.

* * *

He had an equally significant effect on the Chinese, for he had an incredible combination of gifts. It is as though a writer not only writes a script, but writes it, directs it, produces it, acts in it — and invents the camera to make the movie. This is what Bethune did. He trained peasants to become doctors and nurses; he wrote textbooks; he created a school; he created a hospital and he created mobile medical units; he taught as he went along; and he transformed the entire medical services of the communist armies. On top of that he set an example of such self-sacrifice, such devotion, that he became a living legend; and, if the word "hero" means anything, he became a hero of enormous proportions to the Chinese. Bethune is the first foreigner in the history of China to be so revered. As far as the Chinese are concerned he died for them.

* * *

In that he died for the Chinese, there is something saintly, Christlike, in the Bethune story. Yet Bethune was very human. He adored women. The idea of calling him a womanizer, though, is old-fashioned: he loved women and women loved him; he loved to be loved and he loved to love. He drank too much before he went to China, and he used to lose his temper. In China he did lose his temper but there is no evidence of his *ever* drinking once he arrived in Yenan and went on to the mountains of Wutai Shan, or of the need for drink. Bethune also had a wanderlust. In Madrid he disappeared for weeks at a time, because he had a compulsion, a need just to go when he felt like it. The same temptation must have come to him in China but he had simply too much work to do. He hoped, however, to go home to Canada for a Christmas visit in 1939 and to return with badly needed supplies.

Of his period in China he can be criticized for not knowing how to pace himself because he really exhausted himself; he drove himself and worked in such a way that he could not resist the infection that killed him. Perhaps, then, his example is that he was a human being who became a hero, and, when we see his failings and his weaknesses, we perceive that perhaps all of us can become heroes.

As for myself, I loved him. I loved him as a father and as a friend, and he became an inspiration in my life's work. When we remember Bethune, I wish I had the wisdom to explain what we should remember specifically about him; yet I do not know — and I have only spent 30 years trying to understand it. His love for people, his creativity, his imagination — these perhaps; but certainly he is someone we should think about, and not only once a year. His life, the meaning of his life, and of his behaviour — all this is something we should not only be inspired by, but also we should learn from.

* * *

REFERENCES AND NOTES

1. Bethune's work in blood transfusion was never described in detail by Bethune himself, but it is considered at some length by both myself and Sydney Gordon in *The Scalpel, The Sword* (Toronto, 1952) and by Roderick Stewart in *Bethune* (Toronto, 1973). See also the chapters in this book by Hasen Sise (pp. 162-169) and Paul Weil (pp. 177-180).
2. A formal account of Duran-Jorda's work in Barcelona was published under the title of "The Barcelona Blood-Transfusion Service", an article that appeared in the leading British medical journal, *The Lancet*, on April 1, 1935 (vol. 1, pp. 773-775). By January, 1939, the service had obtained no less than 9,000 litres of blood and had studied and classified a list of 28,900 donors.

* * *

Abstract

Bethune's work in Spain, particularly in blood transfusion, is well known, and a personal account of his life there will complement accounts of his work there as a physician; it will also indirectly shed light on his greater success in China. As many others did, Bethune went to Spain in idealistic fervour in the fight against fascism. For Bethune, who had visited Russia, communists were the most committed of antifascists; but not all the Spanish with whom Bethune worked fitted his picture of an antifascist; nor did all of them make him feel that they were totally committed to the cause. As well, the Spanish republicans, notably Duran Jorda, had set up their own blood transfusion service and some of them may not have made Bethune feel that they needed him. Bethune became bitter and unhappy, a state that was reflected in a need for alcohol and in insomnia; and the growing storm elsewhere in Europe deepened his unrest. But his later work and personal involvement with the Chinese was a different matter; they did fit his image of ideal antifascists — they were like the communists he dreamed communists should be like. Their effect on Bethune transformed him; his effect on the Chinese influenced them too. His dedication as a physician and his self-sacrifice and devotion to the Chinese cause made him a Chinese hero, the more because he died for them. A Canadian, Bethune became the first foreigner to be so revered by the Chinese. Today, the thought that Bethune was a man with failings and weaknesses, yet became a hero may suggest to us that each of us, too, can become a hero.

Résumé

L'oeuvre de Bethune en Espagne, particulièrement en ce qui concerne les transfusions sanguines, est bien connue. Un récit personnel de sa vie là-bas vient compléter les témoignages sur son travail de médecin dans ce pays; indirectement, ces propos jetteront de la lumière sur ses plus grands succès en Chine. Comme plusieurs, Bethune alla en Espagne mû par une ferveur idéaliste pour la lutte contre le fascisme. Pour lui, qui était déjà allé en Russie, les communistes étaient les plus engagés des antifascistes. Ce ne sont pas tous les Espagnols avec qui il travailla, cependant, qui répondaient à l'idée qu'il se faisait de l'antifasciste, et ils ne lui semblaient pas tous entièrement dévoués à la cause. De plus, les républicains espagnols, en particulier Duran-Jorda, avaient monté leur propre service de transfusion sanguine et certains d'entre eux ont probablement fait sentir à Bethune qu'ils n'avaient pas besoin de lui. Bethune devint amer et morose et son besoin d'alcool et ses insomnies reflétaient son état. La tempête qui montait ailleurs en Europe contribuait à augmenter son malaise. Plus tard, cependant, son travail et son engagement personnel en Chine furent tout autre chose: les Chinois correspondaient à l'image qu'il se faisait de l'antifasciste idéal, ils étaient tels qu'il avait imaginé les communistes. Leur influence sur Bethune le transformèrent et les Chinois se ressentirent aussi de son influence. Son dévouement en tant que médecin, son esprit de sacrifice et son abnégation pour la cause chinoise en ont fait un héros en Chine, en particulier parce qu'il donna sa vie pour eux. Canadien, Bethune fut le premier étranger à être aussi vénéré par les Chinois. Aujourd'hui, l'idée que Bethune était un homme avec ses défauts et ses faiblesses qui, malgré tout, devint un héros peut suggérer que chacun de nous peut aussi parvenir à l'héroïsme.

The Vivid Air Signed With His Honour: In Memory of Norman Bethune

Hazen Sise*

*This essay by the late Hazen Sise, now published posthumously, consists of two pieces he wrote about Bethune. The first part dates from 1940, and was written for the first anniversary of Bethune's death. His recollections of Bethune were fresh, even alive, and his insight into his character was based on their intimate and arduous wartime experience together. The second part was prepared in 1971 for the Norman Bethune symposium held on November 25 of that year at McGill University, Montreal.

It is a privilege to be able to include this memoir, never before in print, in this book. The 1979 conference was, in a sense, a tribute to and a consequence of the effort of Hazen Sise in founding in 1971 the Bethune Memorial Committee, now the Bethune Foundation, and it is therefore most appropriate that Hazen Sise's essay be published here.

— Wendell MacLeod, Hilary Russell.

A challenge is always an uncomfortable thing. Whether implicit in an idea or a man's life, we usually resent its rude assault and, for protection, shrink back into our cozy citadels of self-esteem, re-wrapping ourselves more snugly than ever in our crazy quilts — patched with conventional myths, slogans and excuses.

No one who ever knew him will deny that Norman Bethune was an uncomfortable sort of person to have around. He fairly bristled with challenges and had no qualms about expressing them. Though frequently illogical and inconsistent as to details and with sometimes a breezy disregard for petty accuracies, the sum total of his attack was none the less devastating and was the more so for being launched through an exceedingly attractive, not to say exciting, personality.

He could alternately charm and exasperate his friends; nor was it only his opponents — Tories and philistines — who might, by some smug remark, earn his mocking laughter. Those who came into close contact with him were never quite the same again; few even wanted to be. Why?

I think it was because there had been glimpsed several rare qualities combined in the same man; and, despite certain irritating discords, they were harmoniously combined. First, in a world riddled with neuroses, it was a delight to find a man capable of so happy and spontaneous an outpouring of energy. Bethune radiated energy and enthusiasm at such a high potential that it often appeared to casual acquaintances that he was putting on an act. It seemed, nevertheless, contagious enough to quicken their pulse rates; even the more morose would brighten up when he entered the room.

I remember once what a girl had to say about Bethune as a companion: "Even to go shopping with Beth was somehow a memorable and exciting experience. It was not only his gaiety; he was able to invest everything he did — every object that interested him — with a sort of heightened reality. It was not just enthusiasm, but something more ... vivid." That just about defines it. But Bethune had another, more important, trait for which there is no adequate word in English. Call it "integrity" — but something more than integrity: the ability remorselessly to base his beliefs on reality rather than prejudice or self-interest, coupled with the even rarer ability to pass quickly from thought to action; to live in the light of his beliefs.

* * *

That quality, a quality of greatness, led him step by step on the path, first of seriously questioning the conventional ideology of his day, then into opposition to it. Then action: the foundation and leadership of a research group for socialized medicine, dangers and hardships in Spain, a continent-wide lecture tour (which he hated) to stimulate medical aid for Spain, and finally the long trek to North China, to even greater dangers and hardships — and death. As he wrote from North China on the evening of August 21, 1938, he would not have had it otherwise:

> I have operated all day and am tired. Ten cases, 5 of them very serious. The first was a fracture of the skull with the brain exposed. It was necessary to remove four loose pieces of bone and part of the frontal lobe. I hope he lives as he is a regimental commander. Tonight he looks very well, is conscious and without paralysis. It is true I am tired but I don't think I have been so happy for a long time. I am content. I am doing what I want to do. Why shouldn't I be happy? — see what my riches consist of. First, I have important work that fully occupies every minute of my time from 5:30 in the morning to 9 at night. I am needed. More than that — to satisfy my bourgeois vanity — the need for me is expressed. I have a cook, a personal servant, my own house, a fine Japanese horse and saddle. I have no money nor the need of it — everything is given me. No wish, no desire is left unfulfilled. I am treated like a kingly comrade, with every kindness, every courtesy imaginable. I have the inestimable fortune to be among, and to work among, comrades to whom Communism is a way of life, not merely a way of talking, or a way of conscious thinking. Their Communism is simple and profound, reflex as a knee-jerk, unconscious as the movements of their lungs, automatic as the beating of their hearts. Here are found those comrades whom one recognizes as . . . quiet, steadfast; wise, patient; with an unshakeable optimism; gentle and cruel; sweet and bitter; unselfish, determined; implicable in their hate; world-embracing in their love[1].

Those who are tempted to think that this is a bravura piece, written with an eye to its propagandist effect, should read, or re-read, Edgar Snow's magnificent piece of reporting, *Red Star Over China*. The above extract was taken, as a matter of fact, from a private letter that would have remained private had not death, half-expected, overtaken him at last. (He died of blood poisoning, probably from an infected wound, and the knowledge of this danger must have been with him for over a year.) The letter is continued the next evening:

> The little boy with his leg off and the colonel are both doing well, so I am happy. I have an infected finger — it's impossible to avoid them, operating without gloves in these dirty wounds. This is the third in two months.
>
> The partisans are great people. Not regular soldiers, but 'workers in uniform'. The average age of a soldier in the Eighth Route Army is 22, while among the partisans many are 30 and over — up to 39 or 40. They are often big fellows — six feet sometimes, with strong, burnt-black faces; quiet, purposeful movements and an air of determination and courage. It's a pleasure to work with them. After I dress their wounds they rise and bow profoundly, with an inclination of the body from the waist. The father of the little boy knelt with his head at my feet to thank me.

Bethune was a Marxist. He was not generally known as such but it appears that his last request, when leaving for China, was to have his membership in the Communist Party publicly announced on news of his death. Moreover, for those who have known and worked with Bethune, it will explain a great deal about him. For Marxism, with its scientific temper, insistence on the "unity of theory and practice" and rejection of philosophic idealism must inevitably have been a powerful stimulus for a man whose scientific training, focussed on surgery, was naturally biased towards action.

More important still was the fact that he was temperamentally incapable of theorizing *in vacuo*. Action followed thought with bewildering and frequently dismaying rapidity. This trait was at once his chief glory and his greatest source of weakness; for once convinced that something or other should be done, his tremendous energy and enthusiasm would frequently lead him to overlook or impatiently brush aside all those petty obstacles that inevitably crop up and that, however irritating, have sooner or later to be dealt with. He was thus the terror of bureaucrats and a considerable source of anxiety to his more pedestrian friends, who were continually being put in the position of saying, "Yes, yes, Beth; that's a good idea, and perfectly sound. But —." Then, after a picturesque and explosive dissertation on the timidity and small-mindness of our puny, petty-bourgeois selves, he would thrust his hands in his jacket pockets and stride out of the room, holding himself grim and erect.

He would go out and somehow or other, get the thing done. Toes might be trod on, officials outraged, the sound and the fury might echo for months afterwards but *he would get the thing done.*

Let us avoid the temptation to remember him merely with an indulgent smile. He was in reality far too big a man for that. His is still a name to conjure with. His work may not often be mentioned in polite society — but notice the uneasiness of certain people when his name does crop up. Though they may try and ignore it or rationalize it away, few are unaware of the challenge. In the years when we could have avoided the present catastrophe[2], the question, "Am I my democratic brother's keeper?" secretly worried more people than we can imagine. Bethune fairly shouted "Yes!" and backed it up with 3 years of heart-breaking and dangerous work — and finally with his life.

His influence still seems to worry his opponents. How else can one explain the deliberate assertion in a Montreal editorial that "the politics behind the wars in which so many of his years were spent meant nothing to him"[3]? Here Canadian journalism hit a new low, for the fact that he was a militant anti-fascist was the one thing about him that was inescapable.

Herein lies the essence of his merit as a man and his challenge as a symbol: in a world disintegrating under the stress of class conflicts, submerging the really basic human values which self-styled democrats prate about in speeches while betraying in practice in this depressing world, Bethune was one of those who had the essential honesty to smash through our tattered fabric of outworn beliefs and win through to recognition of the underlying realities, stark and unlovely as they are.

On those realities he acted and the fact that he became a communist in the process, though interesting, is less important than the pattern he set. History may well record that, if the democratic world had produced a few thousand more Bethunes in the years between 1936 and 1939, events might have taken a turn closer to heart's desire.

* * *

A great deal more will no doubt be written about him, for he will be remembered by hosts of humble people, not only in Canada, and remembered among

The names of those who in their lives fought for life
Who wore at their hearts the fire's centre.
Born of the sun they travelled a short while towards the sun,
And left the vivid air signed with their honour[4].

Those are Stephen Spender's words. It is fitting that he and Bethune once met — in Madrid.

* * *

November 1940 was a time of peculiar bitterness for those of us who had tried to help the Spanish Republic during its long agony. Not only was Spain lost to the democratic cause, but Abyssinia, Albania, Greece, Czechoslovakia, Hungary, Poland, Holland, Denmark, Norway, Belgium and finally France had by that time crumbled under the onslaught of the Axis powers. China had for several years been invaded by the third Axis partner — Japan. The chickens were certainly coming home to roost with a vengeance.

Bitterness may not be an attractive human condition, but we had a right to feel that way. For if we had been asked to state in a few words what we had hoped to accomplish in Spain, we would have replied that we hoped *to prevent the Second World War*. We sincerely believed that a victory for the Spanish Republic was the first essential step towards uniting Europe against Hitler. With easy triumphs blocked, internal opposition would have eroded Hitler's power. The post-war revelations of the German generals have indicated how easy that might have been in 1937.

Since the argument has a good deal to do with our estimate of Bethune as a thinker and doer, I will give it in briefest outline — not certainties, of course, but probabilities of reasonably high degree. If the Spanish Republic had won, as it came close to doing in 1937, the event would have constituted the first political and, above all, *military* defeat for Hitler and Mussolini, who were, despite the non-intervention agreement, heavily backing Franco not only with arms, but with troops and airmen. The victory would have immediately stiffened anti-fascist sentiment and resistance all over Europe. And a vital spin-off would have been the strengthening of the rather wobbly Popular Front government in France. With a strong and more resolutely anti-fascist French government, the British Conservatives could not have got very far with their policy of appeasement, which led to Munich and a whole sequence of calamities.

What I have been giving you is a sort of domino theory in reverse. I realize that the so-called domino theory, as concocted by the Americans to justify their military interventions in South-East Asia, is today in considerable disrepute, but that does not mean that a domino theory in reverse is an invalid guide to the political dynamics of the 1930s. The crux of the matter lay in the denial of the right of the Spanish Republic to buy arms to defend itself against the revolt of a military junta; and it is nowadays conceded by many historians that with arms they would have won, probably in 1937[5]. Being the democratically elected and legally constituted government of Spain, the Republic was certainly entitled, under international law and usage, to buy arms abroad. In particular, France was bound by solemn treaty to provide them. But arms were denied by the non-intervention agreement, forced on a confused French government by Britain.

So, on the international scene, the Spanish Civil War became a war for men's minds — an attempt to bring about a reversal of public opinion and a revulsion of sentiment sufficiently potent to force the Great Powers and particularly France to sell arms to the Republic. A tall order, you will say, but not impossible. For in recent years we have witnessed a tidal wave of revulsion in the minds of the American people towards the war in Viet Nam. But in regard to Spain, unhappily the reversal of opinion was only partial. It did not go fast enough or far enough — and we were all the losers.

But, in this war for men's minds, it is worth noting that Bethune was a remarkably skilful warrior. It is too much to say that no other *individual* was more effective in bringing home to Canadians — and even Americans — the hard realities, and the implications for all of us, of the Spanish Civil War.

He did it partly by instinct or, shall we say, by following the dictates of his own turbulent nature. Rather than agitate verbally, he acted. He committed himself and went to Madrid. There he quite quickly shaped his commitment into a form that was bound to have a strong emotional effect — *blood for the wounded*. There is absolutely no question but that a mobile blood transfusion service was urgently needed on the Madrid front. But he was a surgeon, and experienced surgeons were in short supply because the bulk of the Army Medical Corps had joined Franco's side. Medicine *tends* to be a rather conservative profession! At any rate, Bethune found himself under very strong pressure to become a military surgeon. Moreover, he knew little of the detailed technicalities of blood transfusion; it would mean starting afresh in a new field of specialization. But he stubbornly resisted all blandishments, perhaps because of a growing realization that blood transfusion not only would have a strong, universal appeal, but also would provide the Spanish Medical Aid Committee back at home with an identifiably Canadian and easily publicized objective for fund-raising. This was, after all, a matter of considerable practical importance.

* * *

And so it came to pass. The Hispano-Canadian Blood Transfusion Institute at Madrid soon became world-famous. Not because we were able to add any technical innovations to the art; we simply followed the normal practice of the day, using rather primitive equipment, which was all we could lay our hands on in Madrid, plus some blood syringe-pumps and blood needles brought in from Paris. Besides the appeal of "blood for the wounded", what was widely recognized and publicized as being truly innovative was that this was a *mobile* blood transfusion service — we delivered the blood to as close to the front line as possible; to the front-line hospitals and sometimes even to the casualty clearing stations. Here, incidentally, was the origin of Bethune's famous slogan in China: "Doctors! Go to the wounded. Do not wait for them to come to you!"

And so, when Bethune returned to Canada in June, 1937 to undertake a nation-wide fund-raising tour, he found that he had become famous and was being treated as a hero. Despite superficial impressions to the contrary, he was a genuinely humble person and I suspect that the adulation embarassed him. But there is no doubt that he eagerly welcomed his popularity as a means of reaching even greater masses of people with his message. That message was not just stated in humanitarian and philanthropic terms; it was also and quite deliberately political. He was out to rouse the sleeping Canadians to the dangers for Canada implicit in the rising tide of fascism in Europe. "Fascism means war" was certainly not an empty slogan. Nor was his clenched-fist salute to the great crowds — the Popular Front salute — just a theatrical gesture. It pointed to the type of political coalition — the alliance of political tendencies from extreme left to liberal centre — that appeared to be the surest means of checking fascism. And the crux of his message was another valid slogan, "Spain could be the tomb of fascism" — if arms could be supplied to the Republic.

The tour was a great success. Large sums were raised for the transfusion service and for refugee childrens' hostels in the Pyrenees that he had promoted before leaving Spain. More important, his political message had reached a surprisingly large number of Canadians.

But, towards the end of the tour, Bethune became more and more appalled at the increasing momentum of the Japanese attack on China. It preyed on his mind as being a parallel to the attack on Republican Spain — and again he raged at the indifference and inertia of the democratic powers. At the end of the tour he was approached by the China Aid Council in New York with the suggestion that he could be even more useful in China than in Spain. Specifically, it was pointed out to him that Mao Zedong's Eighth Route Army, based on Yenan, seemed to be the only Chinese army effectively fighting the Japanese — but that its medical facilities were almost non-existent. True to his nature, he did not hesitate very long. Again, he committed himself and this time he paid for his convictions with his life — as he had all along been willing to do.

But before he died, selfless devotion to the wounded and his tireless efforts to train medical personnel and establish hospitals earned him the undying gratitude of the Chinese people. Today his name in the Chinese form of Pai-Chu-En (meaning, appropriately enough, "White-Seek-Grace") is a household word because of Chairman Mao's moving tribute to him in the little red book — said to be one of the three most constantly read articles in China.

* * *

What is it that we can learn from Bethune? What was the heart of his message? We can find an important clue in an article he wrote in Madrid, shortly before he returned to Canada. With a good deal of justification, he thought of himself as an artist and this excerpt from the article is a sort of meditation on the role of the artist in society.

> The true artist lets himself go. He is natural. He swims easily in the stream of his own temperament. He listens to himself. He respects himself . . . . .
>
> He comes into the light of every-day like a great leviathan of the deep, breaking the smooth surface of accepted things, gay, serious, sportive. His appetite for life is enormous. He enters eagerly into the life of man, all men. He becomes all men in himself.
>
> The function of the artist is to disturb. His duty is to rouse the sleepers, to shake the complacent pillars of the world. He reminds the world of its dark ancestry, shows the world its present, and points the way to its new birth. He is at once the product and preceptor of his time. After his passage we are troubled and made unsure of our too-easily accepted realities. He makes uneasy the static, the set and the still. In a world terrified of change, he preaches revolution — the principle of life. He is an agitator, a disturber of the peace — quick, impatient, positive restless and disquieting. He is the creative spirit working in the soul of man[6].

That he was a great humanitarian I think everyone will agree. Indeed, there have been many attempts to draw his sting by depicting him as a humanitarian pure and simple. But for me his claim to greatness lies in the fact that his humanitarianism was never neutral — it always had a direction to it, a political direction if you like, seeking always to release liberating and constructive forces latent in quite ordinary situations and people. He indeed entered eagerly into the life of all men he encountered. He served the people — responsibly and warm-heartedly.

* * *

REFERENCES AND NOTES

1. Norman Bethune, Entry in diary and letter to a friend, Aug. 21, 1938.
2. "The present catastrophe" refers to World War II, for this part of the essay was written in 1940.
3. *The Montreal Star*, Editorial, Nov. 28, 1939.
4. Stephen Spender, "I think continually of those who are truly great". In *Collected Poems, 1928-1953*, London, 1955.
5. Hugh Thomas, particularly, has written an authoritative account of the Spanish Civil War: *The Spanish Civil War*, 3rd revised and enlarged edition, Harmondsworth, 1977..
6. Bethune, Letter from Madrid, May 5, 1937.

* * *

Abstract

Bethune, an artist as well as a physician, held that the function of the artist was to disturb society, "to rouse the sleepers, to shake the complacent pillars of the world". In this role Bethune made many around him uncomfortable; he bristled with challenges and had no qualms in expressing them. At the same time he was an attractive and exciting person, whose spontaneous outpouring of energy always affected others. He was a man of great honesty, with an unfailing perception of the realities in the world. Action followed thought and questioning about the directions his colleagues, his fellow citizens and even those in other countries were taking; he was never neutral and so his humanitarianism always had direction. Bethune matured in the 1930s, when the threat of fascism, in Spain and in China, was real but recognized only by a few, such as Bethune. He felt strongly the need to warn North Americans of the implications of the Spanish Civil War, which was a war for men's minds and a turning point, potentially — if this had been recognized widely enough — in a tide against Hitler and Mussolini. No other individual in North America did as much to show that "Spain could be the tomb of fascism". Thought led to action; he committed himself to the republican cause and he took blood to the wounded in Spain. Later, he committed himself to the cause of the Chinese in their struggle against the Japanese, whose attack on China he saw as a parallel with the attack on Republican Spain. Bethune was ever a man of integrity who lived, and died, in the light of his beliefs.

Résumé

Bethune, artiste et médecin, maintenait que la fonction de l'artiste était de perturber la société, d'éveiller les dormeurs, d'ébranler les piliers suffisants du monde. Dans ce rôle, Bethune incommoda plusieurs membres de son entourage. Il relevait tous les défis au sujet desquels il s'exprimait sans aucune réticence tout en étant un être séduisant et stimulant dont les élans spontanés d'énergie n'étaient jamais sans affecter les autres. C'était un homme d'une grande honnêteté avec une perception sûre des réalités de ce monde. Sa pensée et ses doutes sur les actions prises par ses collègues, ses concitoyens, et même les habitants d'autres pays entrainaient toujours l'action; il n'était jamais neutre et son humanitarisme était toujours d'inspiration idéologique. Bethune atteignit sa maturité dans les années 1930 quand la menace fasciste, en Espagne et en Chine, quoique réelle, n'était reconnue que par quelques uns, dont lui-même. Il ressentait fortement le besoin d'avertir les Nord-Américains des implications de la guerre civile espagnole laquelle était une guerre idéologique et qui, si elle avait été ainsi perçue par un plus grand nombre, aurait pu devenir un point tournant dans le mouvement contre Hitler et Mussolini. Aucun autre individu en Amérique du Nord n'a fait autant pour montrer que "l'Espagne pouvait être la tombe du fascisme". La pensée débouchait sur l'action: il s'engagea dans la cause républicaine et fournit du sang aux blessés d'Espagne. Plus tard, il prit parti pour la cause chinoise dans sa lutte contre le Japon dont il considérait les attaques sur la Chine semblables à celles dirigées contre les républicains espagnols. Bethune ne cessa d'être un homme d'intégrité qui vécut et mourut à la lumière de ses croyances.

The Spanish Civil War: Reminiscences of a Veteran of the Mackenzie-Papineau Battalion

Ross Russell

The Mackenzie-Papineau Battalion of Canada of the International Brigades[1] was an organization of over 1,200 Canadians who went to Spain to fight against fascism[2]. More than half never came back. Canada, with its relatively small population, had the second largest number of volunteers per population (second only to France, which has a common border with Spain) of any country in the world. Norman Bethune was a volunteer, too, and I hope that some method will be found that will make it possible for future generations of Canadians to learn about Bethune. Let me illustrate my point by saying that when I went to school I was told that William Lyon Mackenzie was a pretty bad character (and that's why they made him Mayor of Toronto, finally); that Papineau was a very bad character; and that Riel was *really* a very bad character and we had to hang him — and that therefore, it is of tremendous importance that we start working now, to ensure that Bethune is recognized. For Bethune is, generally speaking, not recognized in Canada. He is not very well known in Spain either, and only in China is he revered, as I discovered when I visited there in 1960 with a trade union delegation; everywhere I went, I heard repeatedly the name of Bethune. We were introduced as Canadians, and whether we went to kindergartens or to factories, or wherever we were, they knew Bethune. Bethune is a Canadian, first and foremost, and we have a responsibility to inform Canadians about him.

* * *

I first met Bethune in 1935. Born in Toronto of parents who had been born in the United States, I had gone to work at a fairly early age — in 1929, the year that ushered in the decade of the Depression. I worked for F.W. Woolworth, and after little more than a year I was transferred to Montreal. That was, of course, quite a period. In Europe, Hitler had come to power, and with him the terrible atrocities that Naziism was creating; and Mussolini, with his black-shirts, was using the most modern war weapons, including poison gas from airplanes, on people who were probably living still in the feudal system. And in Canada the Depression struck our country with perhaps a million unemployed, and deepening every day, every month, and every year.

This went on for a number of years, and I did not understand what was going on. I was looking for answers. When I was younger I asked my father certain questions, such as why there was anti-semitism, why black people were discriminated against so badly in the States. We had travelled to the States and I was aware of this as a young man — why there were rich people and poor people. My father did not understand these questions and his answer was, "You know, it's always been like that." As a young man he was an amateur boxer so he used terms like, "You know, you've got to roll with the punch. You shouldn't get into the thing." Without saying so in so many words, his general idea was that a young man should go out and make money because people who had a lot of money were smart, and those who were poor were not smart, maybe even stupid.

And so, while I did not understand what was going on, I was looking. I have always been very fortunate in meeting people who influenced me — people who understand and who helped me — and one such man as that was Louis Kon. Louis became like a father to me. There were no questions he did not have an answer to. He knew everything about everything, and could explain things so that you could understand them. So, as a young man, I began to understand and listen to him and others, and through him I met others; and finally, with all these terrible things going on in the world, these contradictions during the years from 1933 to 1935, when the picture began to become more clear, I went to a meeting where I met Bethune.

At that meeting, held soon after Bethune had returned from the Soviet Union, he spoke about preventive medicine — and he spoke in such a descriptive manner. I knew there were tens of thousands, hundreds of thousands of Canadians who were so destitute, so poor, that they were not getting, could not get, any medical attention in this country, but Bethune described the need for it here, what it would do for the people. He had the ability and the words to describe a problem in some detail, and what he was saying made a lot of sense to me.

Not only was fascism and Naziism on the rise on a world scale, but it was on the rise in Quebec. The rise of fascism and Naziism were manifest very clearly after July, 1936, when the democratically elected government of Spain was attacked from the outside. Let us never have any illusion on that question. Some people say that it was a civil war, that the people were divided, but this is not so. Franco was certainly a Spaniard, but Franco would never have got out of Morocco, let alone create a war. War material was supplied to him by Hitler and Mussolini.

Then things began to happen quite quickly. The man I knew a little bit about, Bethune, went to Spain. While he was in Spain, the Spanish democratic government sent a committee over to Canada to plead their cause. I remember two people who made up part of the committee: one was a Franciscan priest, another was a woman who was a socialist member of parliament in Spain. We had our fascists here too, with their red berets and with encouragement from the Catholic Church here in Quebec, which said publicly and in the newspapers that this priest was not a real priest. The hierarchy of the Catholic Church here upheld the position that Franco was taking. In regard to the church — and I may be wrong in this and I hope I will be corrected — in Spain itself, during the war, the hierarchy of the church took a forthright position for Franco, yet subsequently they apologized to the Spanish people for how they had acted in that period — but I am not aware that the church in the Province of Quebec ever apologized to the Quebecois or the Canadian people for the position that they took.

Here was a situation in which a government, duly elected, democratic — a long way from a communist government — was made up of Left Republicans, or what we would call Social Democrats, with only one or two cabinet ministers who were communists out of a large number. Here was a duly elected government that had in their treasury two thousand million gold pesetas and one thousand million silver pesetas, and all they wanted to do was to take this money and purchase war material from countries that had it — such countries as France, which was on their border, Britain, which was not far away, United States, Canada, and others — social democratic countries.

But a conspiracy was set up. A phoney non-intervention committee was organized by Neville Chamberlain in Britain, Léon Blum in France, and others. Our government, of course, had something to say, and Mackenzie King fell into line, and passed the Foreign Enlistment Act, 1937, the effect of which was to tell Canadians that they dare not go to Spain to help, and that if one did, one would be subject to 2 years' hard labour, or a $2,000 fine, or both. But it did not work. Canadians went anyway, in quite substantial numbers — and not one of them was prosecuted, for the simple reason that the people of Canada supported the actions of the men who went to Spain.

* * *

I am asked two questions frequently: "Why did you go to Spain?" and "How did you go to Spain?" We went because of the terrible condition that prevailed in Europe, the obvious situation in which the Nazis, in particular, with their Condor Division in Spain, and Mussolini, with his blockades and submarines, were preparing and testing for a second world war. They would not permit the people's will to be expressed through a democratic election; they were going to have the kind of government they wanted in a given country, or else they were going to do it by arms. This meant the likelihood of, or possibly even the inevitability of, a second world war.

At this period Bethune was in Spain. Statements were coming back through the press: he was a great inspiration. Although I cannot speak for the whole 1,200 or so Canadians who went to Spain, I can speak for myself and I can say, without any shadow of a doubt, that he was an inspiration to me. Here was a man so well known, so well established, and here I was, a sort of a nobody. He was prepared to go there, in the circumstances that existed, and surely he acted as an inspiration to me and to many others.

We became the vanguard, the vanguard of the Canadian army that ultimately had to go to fight against Hitler and against Mussolini. We fought with antiquated equipment against the most modern equipment that had been seen until then. The Nazis tested what was then a new gun, the 88-mm gun that took a wide variety of shells and was deadly accurate. That gun, which was mounted on tanks, which was used against aircraft and also against tanks, had a multiplicity of uses; that gun, combined with their dive-bombing tactics, particularly dive-bombing civilians so that the roads were plugged, spreading terror — this combination was the basis of the blitzkrieg, which was even effective against modern weapons held by France, Britain, and the Soviet Union. Imagine, therefore, what hope there was for those in Spain, for the Spaniards, who were not equipped with modern weapons. And then, at the end, the Spanish government was in great difficulty. The war was going badly, and so a kind of an arrangement was made — similar to an arrangement made by strikers: when losing the strike you make the best deal you can. They agreed to pull out the International Brigades in the hope that world opinion would force the Nazis and the Italian fascists to withdraw, but they did not, of course. But we were withdrawn.

I came out late because I was in the south. In that part of Spain, the night that Franco literally cut the country in two, I was on a hospital train of about 13 cars going north. Every car had a white spot on the top of the roof and we stopped for a whole day — I am certain it was sabotage — so that the red crosses that were on the top of each car could be washed. The red crosses, of course, made clear targets that night for the planes that bombed the train, and we never did get through. Hundreds of the men on stretchers and others on that train were wounded or killed, and I myself was wounded again on that train.

Finally, those of us who were cut off went by boat to Barcelona. It was 1939, early in February. In Barcelona, not unlike Montreal, a mountain, Montjuich, overlooks the city; a fort stands on the top of the mountain — and here I and some comrades, while waiting to leave, and with not much to do, were looking down. We saw, approaching towards us, several thousand persons. We went down to meet them, and found that they were soldiers, except that they had no guns, having run out of everything. They were defending a front not too great a distance away, but they had absolutely nothing — not even shoes, and this was February, and cold. Most were with canes and homemade crutches. They told us a terrible story: they had not even bullets left — this characterized the situation in Spain at that time — they were out of everything.

I walked through the tunnel, finally, into Cebère in France, which is about 250 miles [400 km] from Paris. We travelled north in a "sealed" train, with Senegalese guards; if you tried to stick your nose out, you soon found a bayonet in you. The train travelled slowly, often being pushed off to a siding, to let other trains go by. For almost the entire distance, from the border of Spain, right up to Paris, we could see that railroad sidings were packed with cars that were loaded, obvious to the naked eye, with war material. There were flat cars with anti-tank guns, with tanks, with anti-aircraft guns, with airplanes with the wings folded back. There were box cars with the doors open so that you could look inside and see that all of this material had Russian markings. There was no other way to ship, except by land, because everything that went by boat in the Mediterranean belonged to the man who made trains run on time, and would have been sunk — between the Italian navy and the German navy and the willingness of Britain to do nothing about it. So it was necessary to ship by land. But here was millions of dollars worth of war material, and the very things that would have made it possible to hold out, all on the other side of the border. It is unlikely to be any one man's responsibility alone, but one does tend to think of Léon Blum as the head of the French government — a socialist, as he called himself, a Jew, all of the reasons why he should have helped this government, helped the situation in Spain, and yet that material was not allowed to cross the border.

* * *

I have said *why* I went to Spain. The *how* should be made equally clear. There were a great many people who wished to assist the Spanish government in various ways here in Canada, people like Graham Spry and T.C. Douglas. But the fact was that, if you wanted to go to Spain, there was one place you could go, and the only place that I knew of, near me in Montreal was the communist party which had an office on St. Lawrence Main and, as a political organization, they were the organization that made it possible for you to go to Spain.

In 1978 my organization, the Veterans of the International Brigade and Mackenzie-Papineau Battalion, started to plan for something that we should have been given years ago. We tried to achieve recognition by our government. Throughout the Cold War period we were viewed as outlaws and pariahs, but in the past few years the situation has changed. We have been invited to speak at universities. We have been invited to speak at high schools. The whole climate has changed and here again, as in the case of Bethune, there is a vacuum in our history. People talk about World War II as if it just grew up out of nowhere. Of course, it did not. We, who went to Spain to fight, believe that this recognition is important, but not just for us. We are a dying organization; we do not know how many of us there are left, but a rough approximation is 150 or less. So we planned steps to try to bring about a situation in which our government would give the recognition that they should give to those men who so bravely went there, many of whom died. So we planned a trip back to Spain in 1979.

We were fortunate in that a friend of ours, Gloria Montero, who was the inspiration for the Canadian Committee for Democratic Spain in Canada, had returned to Spain to live. She was told of our plans and worked with the people in Spain. Some 30 of us, along with wives, made a total of 48 who went back. The reception that we received was splendid. We were received in chambers, in city halls, by the Mayor of Barcelona, by the Mayor of Albacete, by the President of the province of Albacete. We met with the leaders of the trade unions, the socialist trade unions, the worker's commission, the communist-led trade unions, the leaders of the communist party (people like Marcos Ana[3]) and the leaders of the socialist party. Most important, all of these meetings were emotional meetings, but none of them surpassed the emotion when we met with those who had been either prisoners of war or political prisoners. Those who had been prisoners of Franco, who had fought in the Republican army, and those who were political prisoners — men and women — we met these people, some of whom had been in jail for 25 to 30 years. One woman described how she brought up her children in a period of more than 25 years in jail.

* * *

I conclude, then, on the note that we look for help and support in our call to the government for recognition. I still have a document that was sent to me in 1979 by an association of former prisoners of Franco who fought in the Republican army, and political prisoners. The first paragraph, translated, reads as follows:

> As of the 11th of September, 1979, through official notification of the Minister of the Interior, it has been communicated to the Executive of this association that it has been legalized and inscribed in the official registry according to the law of associations of 1964 in the order of the 26977.

If that can happen in Spain, *surely* it can happen here in Canada. I believe that it will, with the help of the people just as they helped us in the old days. I am sure they will help us again.

* * *

REFERENCES AND NOTES

1. Victor Hoare and Mac Reynolds, *The Mackenzie-Papineau Battalion: Canadian Participation in the Spanish Civil War*, Toronto, 1969.
2. Many useful texts are available in English on the subject of the Spanish Civil War. A useful starting point is Hugh Thomas's *The Spanish Civil War* in the revised and enlarged edition of 1977 (Harmondsworth).
3. Marcos Ana, poet, jailed at the end of the war when he was 17, was held prisoner for 23 years. An international campaign on his behalf preceded his release.

* * *

Abstract

Despite the structure of the Foreign Enlistment Act that was passed in Canada in 1937, over 1290 Canadians went to Spain to join the fight against fascism in Spain. The Mackenzie-Papineau Battalion of the International Brigades constituted the Canadian force, more than half of whom never returned. These Canadians had realized that Hitler and Mussolini were preparing and testing for a second world war, the former with the Condor Division and the blitzkrieg technique and the latter using submarines and a naval blockade. The Nazis and Italians sought to prevent the people's will in Spain from being expressed through a democratic election, and they supplied Franco, in Spain, with war material. Bethune was an inspiration to Canadians who went to Spain and who understood the threat of fascism. But the Canadians fought an uphill battle, with antiquated equipment no match for the modern equipment of the forces opposing them. Eventually, the Spanish Government found itself in difficulty and the International Brigades were withdrawn in the hope that world opinion would force the withdrawal of the Nazis and the Italians; but this did not happen. Now, half a century later, not more than 150 veterans of the International Brigades, Mackenzie-Papineau Battalion remain. Their great hope continues to be recognition by the Canadian government, which has until now been lacking.

Résumé

Malgré l'interdit de la Loi contre l'enrôlement à l'étranger promulguée en 1937, plus de 1 290 Canadiens s'embarquèrent pour l'Espagne pour participer à la lutte contre le fascisme. Les forces canadiennes constituèrent le bataillon

Mackenzie-Papineau des Brigades internationales et plus de la moitié y laissèrent leur vie. Ces volontaires avaient réalisé que Hitler et Mussolini se préparaient et faisaient des essais en vue d'une seconde guerre mondiale, le premier avec la division condor et la technique du blitzkrieg, le second à l'aide de sous-marins et du blocus naval. Les Nazis et les Fascistes italiens tentèrent d'empêcher l'expression de la volonté populaire en Espagne par des élections démocratiques et équipèrent Franco en lui fournissant du matériel de guerre. Bethune était une inspiration pour les Canadiens qui allèrent en Espagne et qui comprirent la menace fasciste. Mais ceux-ci dûrent mener une bataille ardue avec de l'équipement périmé qui ne pouvait se mesurer avec les armements modernes des forces rebelles. Finalement, le gouvernement espagnol en difficulté demanda aux Brigades internationales de se retirer dans l'espoir que l'opinion mondiale forcerait le retrait des troupes nazies et italiennes, c'était un vain espoir. Aujourd'hui, un demi-siècle plus tard, il reste à peine 150 vétérans du Mackenzie-Papineau. Leur plus grand souhait est d'obtenir la reconnaissance du gouvernement canadien qui, jusqu'à date, leur a été refusée.

The Canadian Blood Transfusion Service. From right, Sise, Bethune and Sorensen, Madrid, 1937.

Public Archives of Canada, National Film Board of Canada. PA 116904

Le Service de transfusion sanguine. De droite à gauche: Sise, Bethune et Sorensen. Madrid, 1937.

Archives publiques Canada, Collection de l'Office national du film. PA 116904

Norman Bethune and the Development of Blood Transfusion Services
Paul Weil*

*At short notice the late Dr. Paul Weil prepared and presented the paper on which this chapter is based, in place of Dr. Valentin de la Loma of Madrid, the Spanish doctor with whom Bethune had worked most closely in the Canadian-Spanish Blood Transfusion Service in 1937. A sudden illness prevented Dr. de la Loma from leaving Spain, and he died on the day the Montreal conference opened. Dr. Weil died suddenly in Montreal on October 13, 1980. As a medical student at McGill University, he was taught by Bethune, whose inspiration led him into significant research on the role of the adrenal cortex in resistance to shock and related problems in military medicine. During World War II he was seconded as Major, Royal Canadian Army Medical Corps, to the Transfusion Service of The Canadian Red Cross Society, as Technical Advisor. He was a co-founder of the Bethune Memorial Committee, later the Bethune Foundation. — Eds.

Three scientific discoveries in the first third of this century have made blood transfusions possible, safe and effective. The first was the discovery of blood groups. Prior to Karl Landsteiner's demonstration that individuals could be divided into four groups, depending on a factor in the red blood cells arbitrarily called A, B, AB or O, a transfusion could be lethal if blood of one group were to be transfused into a patient whose blood was of another group[1]. Each person has agglutinins in his blood serum corresponding to the blood group factor, called antigen, that is absent from his red blood cells. This relationship is as follows:

Antigen (in red blood cells)	Agglutinin (in serum)
A	anti B
B	anti A
AB	neither
O	both

Thus if blood from a group A person is infused into a group B individual, the blood of donor A containing factor A will be acted upon by the anti-A agglutinins in the blood serum of the group B patient. The interaction takes the form of agglutination or clumping, a process that destroys the red blood cells, releasing subtances toxic to the kidneys. The kidney damage may be fatal. (Discovery of the Rhesus and other groups came later, but may, for completeness' sake, considered as part of the primary discovery of the blood groups.)

Group AB blood contains no agglutinins. Because of this reciprocal relationship, persons with group AB blood are known as universal recipients: they can receive blood from those of any group without any reaction taking place. By the same token, those whose blood group is 0 are called universal donors because their red blood cells contain neither A nor B anitgen to be agglutinated by a patient whose serum contains either anti-A or anti-B agglutinins.

The next advance was the introduction of anti-coagulating agents. The addition of such substances, notably the harmless sodium citrate, prevented clotting of the blood. This made transfusions possible, for obviously if infusions are to be feasible, blood has to be liquid and free-flowing.

The third significant finding was that the addition of the preservative, dextrose — an academic name for the household substance usually called sugar — would prolong the life of the blood to 3 weeks if kept in the cold just above freezing[2].

The first two discoveries came in time to be applied during World War I, but because of reasons that may have to do with either the belligerents' belief that it would be a short war with few casualties — the previous German invasion in 1870 was just such a war — or because of a lack of understanding that blood loss was the cause of often fatal, wound shock, transfusions were not provided for in the plans of the high commands. They were, however, used by a few medical officers acting on their own initiative. So, hours before an offensive was to begin, blood would be taken from previously grouped non-combatant soldiers and stored in a cool place in the trench or dug-out to be ready when the casualties began coming in[3].

Bethune's genius lies in the fact that not only did he recognize, when few others did, the role of haemorrhage in wound shock but also he devised means for making transfusions available in forward areas of the Spanish Civil War front, thereby saving valuable time between blood loss and its replacement. He and his colleagues in the Canadian-Spanish Blood Transfusion Service were also the first to organize a blood donor service. In order to have blood available for transfusions it must first be obtained. One must have donors — a lot of them — to bleed[4]. At the time, giving blood was a relatively new concept. There was the occasional paid-for donation to be used in hospitalized patients, but that was all. The Canadian unit in Spain developed also the idea of free civilian donations on a large scale, which was not only new but also highly successful.

Bethune described his concept and its development as the first unified blood transfusion service in army and medical history, supplying blood to the entire Spanish Republican Army[5].

His experiences with the transfusion service undoubtedly played a part in the later formulation of the dictum that won him renown in China: "Go to the wounded; don't wait for them to be brought to you". In a monthly report to his regional military commander, General Nieh, he wrote that "the time is past and gone in which doctors will wait for patients to come to them. Doctors must go to the wounded and the earlier the better"[6].

In World War II the Western Allies adapted the Spanish experience to their own requirements. The Axis Powers made little or no use of it.

In the early 1930s the Russians had developed a technique of using cadaver blood[7]. It never caught on, although it is still in use at the hospital where it was introduced in Moscow.

* * *

There was another surgeon whose life resembled Bethune's. Charles Drew graduated from McGill University and interned at The Montreal General Hospital, where he established what was probably the first burn unit when several of the maintenance men were seriously burnt in a transformer accident. Drew went on to a surgical residency in New York City, where he later carried out studies in surgical shock. During the Battle of Britain he opened a clinic for donors whose blood was sent to Britain. This Blood for Britain project continued until the United States entered the war. He later was appointed professor of surgery at Howard University in Washington, DC, where he continued to make contributions in his specialty until his premature, accidental death.

In partial atonement for its socioeconomic inactivity, which had been responsible for the conditions that led to the riots in Watts, Los Angeles, and as a gesture of good will to the blacks of that community, the Los Angeles establishment built a hospital and medical school which bears the names, The Charles Drew and Martin Luther King Post-Graduate Medical School and Hospital.

* * *

I am sure that Drew was as influenced by Bethune, as I was, in the work we were both doing — he in New York City and I at the Royal Victoria Hospital, Montreal, where one of the first blood banks anywhere was established. I had returned to Montreal the month after Munich, October 1938, to pursue postgraduate studies and soon got involved in war research. Shortly afterwards, I met Hazen Sise, who had returned from Spain. We became friends and we would often discuss his transfusion experiences and my research on shock and transfusion.

After the war was over and I had retired from the army, I returned to the Royal Victoria Hospital Blood Bank, which was still the only one in the city of Montreal. We supplied blood to other hospitals regardless of race, religion, language or colour; the Red Cross was not organized in Montreal until several years later. So I came to know the satisfaction of running a life-saving service and, although there were problems, both large and small, the work of obtaining and distributing blood — work that Bethune had done so superbly in Spain, and that had influenced me — was always an extraordinarily rewarding one. It was not difficult to understand how Bethune had found it satisfying, too.

* * *

REFERENCES AND NOTES

1. Karl Landsteiner, in 1901, described three groups that were then labelled A, B and C ("Über Agglutinationserscheinungen normalen menschlichen Blutes", *Wiener Klinische Wochenschift.*, 14 [1901], pp. 1132-1134), while his pupils A. Von Decastello and A. Sturli, soon thereafter, identified the rare fourth group, now known as AB ("Über die Isoagglutinine in Serum gesunder und Kranker Menschen," *Münchener Medizinische Wochenschift.*, 26 [1902], pp. 1090-1095).
2. The use of sodium citrate and of dextrose was initiated within a 2-year period, 1914-1915, and work on blood transfusion advanced rapidly with the outbreak of war. For details of key advances in this aspect of blood transfusion, see the following: A. Hustin, "Principe d'une nouvelle méthode de transfusion muqueuse," *Journal de Médecine de Bruxelles*, 12 (1914), pp. 436-439; L. Agote, "Nueva procedimento para la transfusion de sangre," *Anales Instituto Modelo Clinico Médico*, 1 (1915), p. 25; R. Weil, "Sodium citrate in the transfusion of blood," *Journal of the American Medical Association*, 64 (1915), pp. 425-426; and R. Lewisohn and N. Rosenthal, "Blood transfusion by the citrate method," *Surgery, Gynecology and Obstetrics*, 21 (1915), pp. 37-47.
3. The first military medical officer to have used transfusions in World War I appears to have been a Canadian, Dr. O.H. Robertson. He introduced the use of a citrate-glucose solution of the same volume as the blood being collected and found that it could be stored for 21 days (O.H. Robertson, "Transfusion with preserved red blood cells," *British Medical Journal*, 1 (1918), pp.

691-695. Dr. Robertson's contributions are commemorated by a plaque in the entrance to Toronto's Sick Children's Hospital.
4. A member of the British Ambulance Unit in Spain, Dr. R.S. Saxton, stated, in an article published on Sept. 4, 1937, entitled "The Madrid Blood Transfusion Institute", that there were "about 800 donors on the books" and that "some 20 more are added each day". The rate of supply of blood was 400 litres of blood per month. The chief of the Blood Transfusion Service of the Spanish Republican Army, Dr. F. Duran Jorda, whom Bethune knew, had a list of 28,900 donors; between August, 1936 and January, 1939. 9,000 litres of blood were obtained from donors. See: "The Madrid Blood Transfusion Institute", *Lancet*, 2 (1937), pp. 606-607, and "The Barcelona Blood-Transfusion Service", *Lancet*, 1 (1939), pp. 773-775.
5. Norman Bethune, *Daily Clarion*, Feb. 17, 1937.
6. Bethune, *November Report of the Canadian-American Mobile Medical Unit to General Nieh*, Yang-chia Chuang, Dec. 7, 1938.
7. S.S. Yudin, "Transfusion of Stored Cadaver blood", *Lancet*, 2 (1937), pp. 361-366.

* * *

Abstract

Key developments in the practice of blood transfusion were the discovery of blood groups, the introduction of anticoagulants (e.g., sodium citrate) and the use of preservatives (e.g., dextrose). These became known just before World War I, during which the need for a ready supply of blood in treating the wounded became recognized. A further development, especially in military surgery, was the organization of a mobile *blood transfusion service, whereby blood could be taken to the wounded rather than the wounded being taken to distant places where blood was stored. In this last development Bethune played a major role; he described the concept and its development in Spain during the Spanish Civil War as being the first unified blood transfusion service in army and medical history. Also important was the concept of a civilian panel of donors, which the Canadian transfusion unit in Spain developed on a large scale. Bethune's experience in Spain influenced his later career as a military surgeon in China and his formulation of the dictum that "doctors must go to the wounded and the earlier the better".*

Résumé

Les développements-clés dans la pratique de la transfusion sanguine furent la découverte des groupes sanguins, l'introduction d'anticoagulents comme le citrate de soude et l'usage de préventifs tel le dextrose. Ils furent connus juste avant la première grande guerre pendant laquelle on constata la nécessité d'approvisionner rapidement en sang les blessés. Le développement qui suivit, surtout en chirurgie militaire, fut l'organisation de services de transfusion sanguine mobile par lequel le sang pouvait être acheminé vers les blessés plutôt que d'avoir à transporter ceux-ci vers les dépôts, généralement éloignés. Bethune joua un rôle majeur dans cette dernière innovation; il en décrivit le concept et son application en Espagne pendant la guerre civile comme étant la première unité mobile de services de transfusion sanguine dans l'histoire militaire et médicale. D'importance égale fut l'idée d'un groupe de donneurs civils, développée sur une grande échelle par l'unité canadienne de transfusion en Espagne. L'expérience de Bethune en Espagne influença sa carrière subséquente comme chirurgien militaire en Chine et sa formulation de la maxime selon laquelle "les médecins doivent aller aux blessés et le plus tôt sera le mieux".

China/Chine
1938-1939

... 'twas better so to die
Beneath your fierce flames than perish in the shade,
Cold and alone.

— Norman Bethune
From an untitled poem

Source: Stewart, The Mind of Norman Bethune, p. 31

Norman Bethune in China

Ma Haide (George Hatem)

In the areas of China that are now beginning to be called "Bethune Country", the rugged countryside in the northern part of China, the people remember Norman Bethune well. Here it was that the Canadian surgeon worked, was happy and made his now legendary contribution to the Chinese people's struggle during a critical period in their history. Bethune had become a legend during his own lifetime. When I revisited this part of the country, the people and some of the veterans of the anti-Japanese war in this area recalled for me some of the slogans of those days — slogans like "Attack fearlessly, fear not being wounded, Bethune and his team are behind us, to take care of you", which raised the morale of the Eighth Route Army and guerillas fighting under extreme difficulties.

I met Bethune when he came to Yanan in 1938. This was China's most bitter hour, with a vast Japanese army advancing on all fronts. He came with his team sent by the Canadian and American people. From Yanan he went directly to the front lines in the mountains of East Shanxi. Showing a remarkable capacity for growth, he learnt much from the Eighth Route Army, and in turn gave an example of complete devotion to the task in hand, which made him a model for revolutionary fighters all over the land — a lasting model, an example to the millions of youth that are now grown up, and a memory not likely to be dimmed in China by the years. China hopes that in Canada it will not be lost either, for his spirit of internationalism is a precious thing to hold, for all people. And Bethune, as a down-to-earth, determined Canadian, has become a true internationalist in the minds of so much of the world. His star grows ever brighter. There has never in China been a greater show of respect for him and his memory as there was on the 40th anniversary of his passing. The mass meeting of thousands of representatives from all circles that was held in the Great Hall of the People and the myriads of meetings all over the country, especially in medical circles, attest to this. A respect is accorded that will become ever deeper, a love that will be abiding.

It is not easy for folk abroad to imagine the difficulties Bethune faced in those bitter days. He had to withstand the hard, barren hills of Wutai Shan, the deep stony valley high in the mountains of Tangxian, the stark poverty of the people and the need to work with insufficient drugs or surgical instruments. But his sacrifice stands in bold relief, encouraging many since his death.

* * *

Forty years ago I was among a group of medical, army and government cadres with representatives of the local population who welcomed Bethune and his medical team. We gathered near the ancient south gate of Fushih, a walled country town in the northwest of China, later known as Yanan. It served as the capital of the Shanxi-Gansu-Ningxia Border Region as well as the centre of the

Chinese Communist Party Central Committee and Eighth Route Army Military Headquarters. The welcoming banners and slogans decorating the road spoke of the "Great International Anti-Fascist Fighter", "Veteran of the Spanish Civil War", "World Famous Canadian Surgeon and Friend of the Chinese People". Crowds along the street held little paper flags inscribed with further welcoming sentiments. Little did I realise that this was an historic occasion. I regretfully did not keep a diary and memory dims, but the sight of that ramrod straight grey-haired figure striding purposefully towards the welcoming groups remains fresh among my impressions.

This was my first sight of Bethune and a first handshake between Canada, China and America's people. Bethune had come to China through Hong Kong and to Wuhan in 1938 as his first major stop. Here he met with and was received by Wang Bingnan, now Chairman of the Chinese Peoples Association for Friendship with Abroad, who was impressed with the directness and energetic approach that Bethune showed from his earliest contacts. He thought of the hidden power under the surface of that tall wiry figure. And it was Wang Bingnan that introduced the good doctor to Zhou Enlai, who was at that time in charge of the Eighth Route Army and the Chinese Communist Party office in Wuhan. In spite of Zhou's tremendous responsibility and immense work load, he found a midnight hour for a talk with Bethune. The discussion was warm, direct and friendly right from the start, centering on the anti-fascist experiences of Bethune in Spain and the war in China as its continuation. The situation at the front in both the Kuomintang areas and in the Eighth Route Army liberated areas behind the Japanese lines was outlined and the program, policies and organization of the Communist Party and its role in the Anti-Japanese War were clearly explained by Zhou Enlai. He tried to impress on Bethune the difficulties in the areas behind the lines and prepare him for the difficulties of the struggle and obstacles ahead. He even suggested that Bethune work for a period in the areas around Wuhan in Central China, further away from the front to give him a chance to get used to China conditions. Bethune refused bluntly and flatly. He was impatient to get to the front, not any front but the lines where the Communist armies were fighting in North China. The comrades were impressed with Bethune's determination. Wang Bingnan, in talking to me of the Wuhan days, said that he could see that Bethune, fresh from the Spanish Civil War, was a dedicated antifascist fighter, as eager to use his skill and scalpel as his gun in this battle. Wang Bingnan said that in watching and listening to Bethune in his talks with Zhou Enlai and later in his own talks he recognized a man matured in struggle and committed to fight staunchly for what he believed in. On Zhou Enlai's orders, "I expedited Bethune's trip to Yanan," Wang said.

When Bethune arrived in 1938, Yenan was in springtime glory. China had been fighting against Japanese aggression for nearly a year; the Kuomintang government of Chiang Kaishek and their armies were retreating on all fronts. Chinese Communist armies infiltrated the occupied areas to organize and mobilize the people for a protracted struggle. Bethune was welcomed warmly and escorted to quarters in the centre of Yenan. The best available compounds of the Eighth Route Army Logistics Corps were turned over to his team. As foreigners were rare, there were no guest houses in those days. Later on, as the war continued, many medical workers from abroad followed in Bethune's footsteps — medical doctors and surgeons, nurses and technicians from Austria, Canada, Germany, India, Indonesia, Japan, Korea, Malaya, the Philippines, the Soviet Union and the United States of America. But Bethune was among the first.

Accompanied by his operating room nurse, Jean Ewen, and by Dr. Richard Brown, who worked for 3 active months with him, Bethune was impatient. Although the comrades were solicitous of his comfort and his wishes, the conditions at the front were in a state of flux and travel across the lines not opportune at the time. He had been bombed on his road to Yenan when he diverted his team to cross the Yellow River to find a short cut to the front — "according to the map" he told me — and described his experiences and even pictures of the devastation to the carts carrying his supply. He spoke angrily about the bestiality of the fascist enemy, just like that of the enemy in Spain.

He recounted to me some of his Spanish Civil War experience. We talked for many hours about the war, the situation in China, life and the future. He also did his first of several operations in our Yenan Cave Hospital located just below the famous pagoda. Some of our Chinese surgeons and I assisted him. We recognized that he was an extremely able surgeon, competent, skilled and fast in his operating technique. He was also considerate and concerned for his patients.

* * *

Bethune brought with him the latest scientific knowledge and broad experiences in war surgery and care of the wounded. He had an extensive knowledge of blood transfusion service in the field, and he understood the need and urgency of immediate operation for the wounded, the value of control of shock and bleeding, the need for intravenous fluids, the importance of control of pain and the role of fixation and plaster casts for open fractures, osteomyelitis and similar injuries. This was the pre-antibiotic era. His experiences of military surgery in the Spanish Civil war enabled Bethune to convey all this knowledge to his colleagues. He used the training classes that he organized and in his mobile surgical teams to pass on this useful knowledge.

From our frequent talks and discussions with Chinese medical workers, he could appreciate in the Eighth Route Army the difference in the needs and conditions of guerilla war, with its need for speed and mobility, the use and dependence on the peasantry for the source of transportation, and provision of paramedical personnel. The peasantry provided homes for wards, transport of the wounded and the formation of underground hospitals. We showed him our rear hospitals in caves and in peasant homes. Bethune noted that, even under relatively primitive conditions and with little equipment and poor housing without hygiene facilities, medical and surgical military services could be carried on. We also showed him some of our training schools and medical classes with very little teaching equipment, much of it hand-made. Many of the texts for teaching and medical books were mimeographed or even hand-copied. We also introduced him to our war-time medical factories, where a combination of Western and Chinese herb preparations, mostly the latter, were made for both civilian and military uses. Many of the pills, powders and extracts were made from Chinese herbal plants according to well-tried traditional prescriptions — antipyretic and anti-diarrheal medications and pain relievers. Bethune became acquainted with the military and civilian integrated medical delivery systems that were developed by the Chinese Communist Armies during the 1920s and 1930s. Bethune quickly grasped and understood the method of the war being waged and the medical organization needed to serve it. In his later concrete work he incorporated his extensive modern military knowledge with the similarly extensive guerilla military medical work in our wartime services. He found that the Eighth Route Army had drawn on the experiences of its Red Army and its Long March fighting days to develop a military and civilian medical service suited to the Chinese conditions of guerilla warfare and care of the civilian population, to ensure that necessary relationship with the peasantry and acquire its support. At this time Bethune also noted the various principles of hygiene and prevention and measures used in military and civilian hygiene and in the training of the medical staff and the population itself.

Reaching the front behind the lines, travelling long distances and visiting and operating in the various rear hospitals on his way from Yenan to the Chin-Cha-Chi liberated area in North China, Bethune tried to pass on his surgical knowledge and modern medical techniques. Later he wrote illustrated textbooks and lectures for teaching. He worked with carpenters and blacksmiths to improve equipment for travelling surgical units that could transport medicines, supplies and instruments, and also serve as an operating table when this was removed from the pack animal that carried it. Bethune was a man of many ideas and talents. He worked and taught and led mobile surgical teams, frequently participating in close support to battle lines operating on the wounded practically at the front. Many other surgical teams improved their work and technical ability after training by Bethune and the associates he trained as teachers. Bethune set a fast hard pace and this example was followed by others melding with the tradition of hard work and self-sacrifice of the Eighth Route Army.

In the period of over a year that Bethune worked in the Shanxi-Chahar-Hobei liberated area, he not only did a tremendous amount of teaching, travelling, operating but spread by his own example a worthy style of work, raising the level of the medical work and the morale of the fighting forces.

The story of Bethune's work in the mountains and plains of North China behind the Japanese lines in the liberated areas is well documented and known. His mobile surgical teams operating near the front and under all conditions, in temple and huts, his school and hospital, his training classes, his care and tenderness to the wounded and the local population have all served as a source of inspiration. And many of the well known principles, ideas, policies and guidelines for organization and delivery of medical health services to both the military and civilian population in China today owe much to the earlier experiences and methods that existed in embryonic form 40 years ago.

* * *

Bethune arrived in China at a time when his political understanding had matured. I realized this in our late evening talks in the Yanan caves sitting on the brick-mud "Kang" sipping tea. He spoke passionately on how the world in general was unaware of the dangers of the Tokyo-Rome-Berlin axis then in formation. He said the lessons of the Spanish anti-fascist war, and the need for world-wide united front against the coming fascist onslaught, had yet to be learned. He recounted his own experiences in Spain, in Canada and in the U.S.A. Already he had arrived at certain conclusions about politics, social problems and society from his experiences with poverty, ill health, working class struggles, and medical work in the first World War, the Spanish Civil War and urban hospital work.

He realized that the people would suffer more bitter lessons before they rose in their might and anger to wipe out fascism. (Are there parallel lessons for us today regarding hegemonism, aggression and the danger of war?) Bethune understood that China was in the forefront of the antifascist struggle. Even though poorly equipped and supplied, the Chinese Communist armies were marshalling the people of their country to resist the Japanese fascist invaders. The Eighth Route Army, made up of battle-hardened Long Marchers, had won the first vital victories in the resistance war at the famous battle of Pingxinguan, in which they destroyed a crack Japanese brigade and then later destroyed part of the Japanese airforce on the ground in a night raid on an enemy airfield.

With such a background, Bethune understood the political situation in China. Chairman Mao Zedong had had a warm and lengthy talk with Bethune before he left for the front. Much of the ground covered was political. The Chairman outlined the future difficulties and conditions that Bethune would be working under. Mao had outlined also the policies, programs, and plans of the Chinese Communist Party for the period. He asked Bethune about his experiences in the Spanish Civil War, his medical ideas for work in the front. He urged Bethune to voice his opinions about the medical situation at the front. The reports Bethune sent back were full, vivid and constructive as he carried on his work at the front later.

Bethune then left Yanan, travelled across the lines to Shanxi-Suiyuan liberated area and then to the Shanxi-Chahar-Hobei and Hobei Central plains areas. When Bethune and his surgical team with Chinese comrades and staff from the Eighth Route Army Rear Hospital set off for the front, I was not given permission to be part of the group — "our two foreign doctors could not be all in one area".

In the course of his work in Shanxi-Chahar-Hobei (Chin-Cha-Chi), Bethune saw how Chairman Mao Zedong's development of Marxism as applied to the concrete conditions in China was being carried out. Bitter fighting and struggles in the mountains and plains of North China tempered Bethune; he learned how to be an effective surgeon and indomitable antifascist fighter. Bethune was deeply affected by the bravery and courage of the ordinary Eighth Route Army fighters and commander. He was struck by the army's selflessness and self-reliance, by their militancy and commitment to serving the people. As he operated on their wounded bodies with the limited anaesthesia available, he marvelled that they never complained of the pain, never made demands. How spartan their life, how warmly concerned about each other as only class brothers are; how eager and spirited they were; how they hated the enemy and loved the people — all this with clear understanding of the world wide implication of their struggle. And he deeply appreciated how they accepted him as one of their own. His own feelings of deep internationalism received intensive support from the reality of his day-to-day experience.

Bethune and his companions fought the powerful foreign invader. Bethune worked with the army so poorly armed and with inadequate medical supplies and medical facilities. His greatness lay both in his unflagging confidence in the world of the future and in his capacity to learn how to serve the Chinese people under all adverse conditions. He died at his post, a martyr for the lack of a few grams of penicillin that China now produces by the ton. All efforts to save his life at that time were of no avail. Bethune was buried among the people he loved; his final resting place today is a memorial park for martyrs and heroes in Shihjiazhang, provincial capital of Hobei. Dr. K.S. Kotnis of India, who took over the hospital work and teaching of Bethune later, died in the same area and lies in the same memorial park with the Canadian hero. At Chin Min when the Chinese people "sweep the graves" of their dead, tens of thousands of people visit Bethune's grave and pay their respects. In 1978, there were over 150,000 such visitors.

In his famous article, "In Memory of Dr. Norman Bethune"[1], Chairman Mao Zedong called him a true communist and a true internationalist, calling on all Chinese Communists and people to learn from him. He held up that son of the Canadian people as a lesson in internationalism for the whole Chinese people to follow, the internationalism that we set against both narrow nationalism and narrow patriotism.

I recently paid a visit to the areas in Hobei, Tangxian County, where Bethune fought and died. Many of the villages he worked in and the rooms he used as operating rooms, wards and classrooms are still preserved and the small room in a peasant home where he died is now a virtual shrine. The older folk of these villages — Huang Shiko, Huaper, Ho Chiachuang — still remember Bethune; some had been treated by him, others worked with him and some nursed him in his last illness. We also found the countryside much transformed from the barren, fought-over land where the Eighth Route Army fought the aggressor, to a beautiful prosperous and terraced farm country, with surfaced roads leading to the villages. The autumn crops were being taken in or drying. The famous dates (jujubes) and persimmons, which served as food and medicine in those hungry days, were to be seen everywhere, much of them being shipped out to other parts of the country. The people, and especially the children, looked well fed and healthy, red-cheeked and happy. This was in contrast to the past times when most children were undernourished thin and many with swollen abdomens. The people are living memorial to the people who gave their lives to make today possible, and Bethune was in the front ranks.

All over China, Bethune's life is well known in communes, factories and amongst the people's armed forces, indeed everywhere, even in the smallest out-of-the-way places. Today, when I travel to various parts of the country with our medical teams, I am naturally taken to be a fellow countryman of Bethune. The people solicitously enquire about my family in Canada and want me to send "greetings to the Canadian people" on their behalf. I am glad that finally I have this opportunity to be able to fulfill their request in person. My usual denials that I am not a Canadian do not register. How could a Western doctor working among the people in China not be a Canadian? I gratefully accept the reflected glory.

In the past 40 years numerous books, paintings, stories, commemorative stamps, articles and children's picture books and posters have found their way to all parts of China. Recently a full-length feature film has gone to all areas of China. Each year in medical institutions and hospitals and wherever groups of medical workers are concentrated there is usually an annual commemorative meeting to recall Bethune's life, his contribution to China and his qualities that should be emulated. These occasions help Chinese medical workers to review their own work, and to recall their own traditions during the revolutionary years, the history and contributions of their forerunners. It inspires the Chinese people to keep alive the traditional qualities of self-reliance and of serving the people, which are the hallmarks of former revolutionaries in the war days. It helps to keep fresh the example of internationalism.

* * *

China, in the 40 years since Bethune's death, has made great progress and is now on a new Long March to socialist modernization. This has included the medical work and the work in promoting the health of the people. I will review briefly the state of China's medical health care and progress as it is today and compare this with the past of Bethune's day. Before Liberation in 1949, China was regarded as the sick giant of Asia, both figuratively and literally. Epidemics were rampant, infant mortality was extremely high, nutritional diseases were common and famines, and floods were a regular occurrence. There were few medical services and fewer medical personnel. There was a dying population, affected by starvation and frequent nation-wide natural disasters. The poor and the labouring people had nowhere to turn for help or any government that had their welfare in mind. In all of China of those days there were only a miniscule number of qualified medical doctors and physicians, mostly concentrated in the cities. There were few hospitals and most of the beds were in the urban areas. There were only 80,000 beds in 1949, for 500 million people. Mortality and death figures were high and life had no security.

With the formation of the People's Republic of China and under the leadership of the government and Party, the medical workers and public health personnel, together with the people, set up a health delivery care system to serve the whole population. The scourges of smallpox, plague, cholera, venereal disease, trachoma and kala azar were practically eradicated. Many other acute and endemic diseases were brought gradually under control. Many parasitic diseases such as malaria, schistosomiasis and those due to intestinal parasites were attacked and morbidity rates reduced. Over two thirds of the schistosomiasis cases have been treated. Infant mortality was reduced and child and maternal health care was given high priority. New midwives were trained and the old village accoucheurs were retrained in modern aseptic and sterilizing techniques. The training of medical, public health and paramedical health workers was one of the early measures used to quickly build up an army of health professionals. At the end of 1978 there were 3,800,000 health workers, including 1,600,000 barefoot doctors and 700,000 midwives; 358,520 doctors graduated from medical colleges. In 1978 there were 1,856,000 beds, of which 700,000 were in the cities. As in Bethune's day, today many temporary wards and beds are set up as needed in local premises. China is nearly self-sufficient in pharmaceuticals, antibiotics, vaccines and other biological products, contraceptives and herbal medicines.

A three-tiered national health system of organization, comprising the National Ministry of Health, the Provincial Ministry and the County Medical Health Centres, serves the whole country. The County Medical Centres serve as the back-up support for the rural cooperative health services in the 50,000 communes with their barefoot doctors in the brigades and work teams under them. County medical services include preventive and curative medical work. This work is carried out by the Anti-epidemic Stations, Child and Maternal Health Centres, the county hospital and various training classes. The cities have a similar system. This general organization provides the nationwide health delivery care system that now reaches nearly a billion people and is practically free to all.

Medical work is based on a number of basic principles set down in the 1950 National Health Conference. These principles include: having health care serve the common people, placing high priorities on prevention, integrating modern and traditional Chinese medicine and their practitioners and combining health campaigns with other mass campaigns (e.g., agriculture, education and production). In China, being a vast rural country where over 80% of the population are engaged in agriculture, there is a need to focus intensely on the rural areas. This was pointed out by Mao Zedong repeatedly.

Sanitation campaigns are an integral part of preventive work. They revolve around the National Patriotic Health Movement, which is organized and has fixed bodies at all levels. These lead public health education, the elimination of the Four Pests — flies, mosquitoes, rats and bedbugs — and sanitation in the rural areas such as drinking water, sewage disposal, composting, latrines, animal pens and food hygiene. In recent years there has been added the care of the environment, smoke, air, waste water control as part of the mass patriotic health movement. *Curative and preventive services* play a leading role in the national health delivery system, providing free medical and preventive care to nearly a billion people, including maternity and sickness benefits, hospitalization and out-patient care, maternity and sickness benefits, pensions and care of the aged. Preventive vaccinations and medical and surgical needs for family planning are free of charge. Curative work in the city is based on the big hospitals and health stations. They also provide the preventive service just as the cooperative health stations do in the rural areas. The People's Liberation Army, whose precursor Bethune worked with in the 1930s, has its own medical services. It preserves the tradition of close links with the civilian population and its health network. For example, army medical teams go to the countryside or work with the population where they are stationed, to help with treatment and prevention. They also assume part of the training and upgrading of the barefoot doctors. In addition to prevention of acute infectious diseases and endemic diseases, other chronic illnesses and degenerative diseases are being studied. For example, cancer prevention is carried out by massive surveys and field work with follow-up to discover the early cases in such cancers as oesophageal, cervical and nasopharyngeal cancers and primary cancer of the liver. In Linxian County, with a high rate of oesophageal cancer, much work has been done on early diagnosis and treatment. In Guangxi province, more than 4 million women at risk have been checked and followed up for cervical cancer. There are similar projects for lowering the rate of strokes by treatment of hypertension early and regularly on a mass basis.

Research in basic, clinical and epidemiological health work, as well as studies and research on the theory and practice of China's traditional medicine, has been carried out over the years with some success. The Academy of Medical Science, the medical colleges, the big hospitals and special research institutes lead research, while much epidemiological research is carried on in the field. Some of the achievements can be briefly listed: ways and means to eradicate diseases (e.g., smallpox and venereal disease); the elucidation of the theory of acupuncture anaesthesia and its application in surgery; the synthesis of a form of insulin; the successful development of microsurgery in the reimplantation of limbs and fingers (first success in 1963); the treatment of large-area burns (up to 94%); and the integration of traditional and modern treatment of fractures. Although much has been done, there is still much to be done to enable China to catch up with world levels.

Concerning *family planning*, much has been done in population control, education and working out feasible measures. Part of present planning aims at population growth of 1% or less by 1985. Beijin, Shanhai, Tianjin, Hobei Jhejiang, Shansi, Shaanxi, Shandong, Jiangsu and Hubei provinces have already achieved a population increase of 10 per thousand; thus in heavily populated Sichuan province, with nearly 100 million people, there was a 29-per-thousand increase in 1971 but one of 6.1 per thousand in 1978. After 1985 we hope to achieve a rate of less than 10 per thousand, for the whole country.

As far as *education* is concerned, we now have a nationwide network of colleges of higher and middle categories and myriads of training courses and classes. From 1928 to 1947 there were nearly 10,000 graduates from medical university and colleges; after Liberation, from 1949 to 1978, we graduated 370,000 qualified doctors from institutions of higher learning. In the category of middle-level doctors there were only 41,000 trained from 1927 to 1948, while from 1949 to 1978 there were 800,000 trained. Although the school that Bethune helped found and train doctors in had only a few hundred, many of them are now in positions of responsibility in the health services. Many are in the highest positions of leadership.

* * *

If Bethune were alive today, he would recognize much of the basic principles and methods now being used to direct China's medical and health work. He would have been familiar with them in the days he worked in North China and he would recognize his contributions to them and how they emerged from the practice of his day to day work. He would be proud of the many students of his who are now leading figures in the country's medical life; many of his colleagues of those days lead health work at the national level. And many thousands of medical workers have learned from his qualities and spirit of service to the sick and wounded, and have tried to emulate his selflessness, to follow in his footsteps and to keep his spirit alive throughout the length and breadth of the land. Bethune lives on in the heart of the Chinese people.

* * *

REFERENCE

1. Mao Zedong, "In Memory of Dr. Norman Bethune," Yenan, Dec. 21, 1939.

* * *

Abstract

If Bethune were alive today, he would recognize many of the basic principles and methods of medical and health work in China. He would have recognized them from his days in North China; he would note his own contributions to them and their evolution from his day-to-day work. He would be proud of his many students who are leading figures in medicine and of the many medical workers who have learned from his qualities and spirit of service to the sick and wounded. Bethune lives on in the hearts of the Chinese, not only because of his selflessness and internationalism, but also because of his contributions to military medicine at a critical period in China's history. He took to China the latest scientific knowledge and his experience of war surgery; once there he quickly understood the method of war being waged there and the medical organisation needed; and he quickly adapted his knowledge and experience to the needs of the Chinese. He took, too, his competence as a surgeon and his concern for patients. Through travelling and teaching, he improved health care and the morale of the fighting forces in his region. Even today the health of the Chinese, while much improved over that of 40 years ago, owes much to Bethune and the many others who gave their lives to make today possible. Bethune would have approved of the sanitation campaigns, the curative and preventive services, the research and the education that constitute an important part of health care in China today, more than 40 years after his death.

Résumé

Si Bethune vivait aujourd'hui, il reconnaîtrait plusieurs des méthodes et principes de base de la médecine et de l'hygiène pratiquées en Chine. Il les relierait à son séjour en Chine du Nord et il verrait comment ses propres contributions et sa routine quotidienne même contribuèrent à leur évolution. Il serait fier de plusieurs de ses étudiants devenus des sommités médicales et des nombreux travailleurs médicaux qui ont été inspirés par ses qualités et son esprit de dévouement aux malades et aux blessés. Bethune continue à vivre dans le coeur des Chinois, non seulement pour son abnégation et son internationalisme, mais aussi pour ses contributions à la médecine militaire à une période critique de l'histoire de la Chine. Il apporta en Chine les plus récentes connaissances scientifiques et son expérience de chirurgien en temps de guerre. Sur les lieux, il comprit le genre de guerre qu'on y faisait et l'organisation médicale qu'elle nécessitait, et adapta sans tarder ses connaissances et son expérience aux besoins des Chinois. Il apporta aussi sa compétence en tant que chirurgien et sa sollicitude pour les malades. Par ses voyages et son enseignement, il améliora les soins de santé et le moral des troupes dans sa région. Même aujourd'hui, la santé des Chinois, de beaucoup supérieure à ce qu'elle était il y a quarante ans, doit énormément à Bethune et à tous ceux qui donnèrent leur vie pour rendre possible la présente situation. Bethune aurait approuvé les campagnes sanitaires, les services de cure et de prévention, la recherche et l'éducation qui constituent une part importante des soins de santé en Chine aujourd'hui, plus de quarante ans après sa mort.

The Living Bethune
Paul Lin

In the midst of a tremendous transformational period in China, I have around me the visions of a people that are busily working to modernize their country in the best and fastest way possible. It is in this context that I consider the significance of Norman Bethune for China today.

Many things, of course, have been said about Bethune, about his selfless spirit, his dedication and his tremendous militant concern for the oppressed. All of these things are true. But, for me, one other thing perhaps has particular relevancy to China today: what Bethune brought to China's great movement to liberate her people was scientific expertise. He was, after all, first a doctor, and it was this combination of his profession, which was medicine, and his career, which was in fact the emancipation of humanity, this marrying of his skills to his goals in life, his human goals in life, that projected the image of a man whom the Chinese people would like to emulate. It is in this way that I think the Chinese are learning from Bethune.

Perhaps Bethune's message to China today is how important it is to harness the highest and most rigorous scientific skill to the enthusiasm for emancipating the people; and perhaps his message to us Canadians is how to harness the most advanced technology to the goals of improving the welfare of the people and to creating more and more social justice. In any case, the Bethune that is envisaged today as a paradigm of the modern man in the process of the modernization of China perhaps can best be epitomized in the unique and rare combination of passion and compassion that Bethune both as a doctor and as a humanitarian represented. The best expression of that spirit lies in a couplet written by the eminent modern Chinese author Lu Hsun. The first line of that couplet can be roughly translated thus, "With level gaze I stare defiantly at a thousand accusing fingers"; and the second line thus, "With bowed head I humbly serve the children like an ox." It is this compassion plus the passion, this striking contrast between defiance against the oppressor, and tremendous concern and love and faith in the common people that was Bethune's spirit — all of which are very much alive in China today, as China tries to modernize. It is in a sense the best idea, the best concept of how man can modernize himself in the process of modernizing his economy.

* * *

Abstract

One of Bethune's contributions to the liberation of China and to its modernization was his application of scientific expertise. For today's Chinese, the combination of this aspect of Bethune's work with his concern for the emancipation of humanity has especial significance. Bethune's message, for the Chinese and also for other people, is the importance of harnessing scientific and technological skills to a broadly based emancipation of the people.

Résumé

Une des contributions de Bethune à la libération de la Chine et à sa modernisation fut l'application qu'il fit de son savoir scientifique. De nos jours, la combinaison de cet aspect du travail de Bethune avec son intérêt à l'émancipation de l'humanité revêt une signification particulière. Le message de Bethune, pour les Chinois comme pour les autres peuples, souligne l'importance de harnacher les compétences scientifiques et technologiques à la base plus large de l'émancipation du peuple.

Boy-soldier with amputated left arm — follow-up examination by Bethune, China, c. 1938.

Public Archives of Canada, National Film Board Collection. PA 116903

Jeune soldat au bras gauche amputé examiné par Bethune, Chine, v. 1938.

Archives publiques du Canada, Collection de l'Office national du film. PA 116903

Contributions of Norman Bethune to Developing China

Lü Wanru

Norman Bethune was known in China to everybody, both old and young. He enjoys high prestige in the minds of common folk, and is loved and esteemed by them from the bottom of their hearts. The army and people in the Shanxi-Chahar-Hebei border area, where Bethune worked, had flesh-and-blood ties with him in his lifetime. They cordially called him "our doctor" and "our comrade". After his death, Chairman Mao Zedong specially wrote an article "In Memory of Norman Bethune", calling on the people throughout China to learn from him and emulate his spirit of great internationalism and communism[1]. Thus the name of Bethune has become known in all parts of the country, even in remote mountain villages. His meritorious deeds and contributions to the Chinese people are profoundly cherished in the hearts of the people. In order to honour his memory forever, the former medical school under Shanxi-Chahar-Hebei Military Command, which Bethune helped set up and where he once taught, was renamed Bethune Medical School, and the Model Hospital in the rear at the Wutai Mountains, Shanxi Province, which had been personally established by Bethune, was renamed Bethune International Peace Hospital. Now the medical school has grown into a key medical institution — Jilin Bethune Medical College — and the hospital has grown into a full-fledged one giving capable treatment, and doing teaching and scientific research. In the past 40 years, the students and the medical personnel of these institutions were educated in Bethune's selfless revolutionary spirit, his great sense of responsibility and his scientific approach, as shown in his urge to constantly perfect his skill, so that they will better serve the Chinese people. As a result, large numbers of Bethune-type medical workers have been trained and are playing an important role on the medical and health front.

We built a tomb for Bethune in Tangxian County, Hebei Province, where he died. In 1952 his remains were moved to the Cemetery of Revolutionary Martyrs in Shiziazhuang, the capital city of Hebei Province. In the past decades the Chinese people have honoured his memory and have carried out internationalist education at his tomb. Every year, tens of thousands of students, young workers, peasants, army men and office workers come to pay their respects and receive education through listening to the accounts of Bethune's heroic deeds. Since 1952, more than 20 million people have visited Bethune's tomb. Apart from the tomb other relics and sites are associated with Bethune in many places, such as the Wutai Mountains, Yan'an and Xi'an of Shanxi Province, where he once worked or lived; they are protected by the state. Of course the commemoration of Bethune by the Chinese people by no means stops there; the more important aspect is that the spirit of Bethune is deeply rooted in the hearts of the Chinese people. His spirit has become a criterion by which to judge one's loyalty towards the people and his sense of responsibility in work, and he has become a fine example for the Chinese people to learn in giving support to other people's struggles with an internationalist spirit. In the war years in China tens of thousands of soldiers and civilians were inspired by the spirit of Bethune, and, since Liberation, his spirit has continued to encourage people on all fronts to work hard for building a powerful and prosperous socialist China.

* * *

Today, the people's new China for which Bethune fought and died has grown in strength and has entered a new historical period, the period of socialist modernization. Since the downfall of the Gang of Four in 1976, under the leadership of the Central Committee of the Chinese Communist Party headed by Chairman Hua Guofeng, the Chinese people have done tremendous work, cleared the obstacles created by the Gang's sabotage and have made great achievements. Starting from that year the focus of all our work has been shifted to socialist modernization. The people throughout our country are working wholeheartedly for the realization of the four modernizations. To speed up the growth of our national economy, we have begun to readjust, restructure, consolidate and improve our national economy. We are doing well in our industrial production, especially in agricultural production. Our peasants' income has considerably increased, their standard of living has greatly improved, and their enthusiasm in production has risen unprecedentedly; the total output value of industry has gone up remarkably. In the cultural field, a thriving situation of a hundred flowers' blossoming has appeared. Of course we still have work to do, as modernization is not restricted to promoting industry and agriculture and raising the scientifc and educational level. While reforming and perfecting our socialist system, we must also reform and perfect our socialist political system, and institute highly developed socialist democracy and sound socialist legality. While bringing about a highly developed material civilization, we must also achieve a highly developed spiritual civilization by greatly raising the educational, scientific and cultural level and improving the health of the whole nation. We must create a lofty revolutionary ideal and revolutionary habits and morals, and cultivate a noble, rich and colorful cultural life. To fulfil these glorious and arduous historic tasks, all the 900 million people should exert themselves fully and pool their best talents and strength for this great cause. Without the active participation and efficient work of the entire people, it would be impossible to achieve this objective.

At the critical moment when the Chinese people embarked on their new long march, it was of particular significance for us to commemorate the 40th anniversary of Bethune's death. Before taking part in the Montreal conference, we attended the meeting of the people held in Peking. It was a grand meeting, with more than 3,000 people of all walks of life gathered in the Great Hall of the People — the same hall where all the sessions of the National People's Congress were convened. Among those attending were the Canadian delegation invited by the Chinese People's Association for Friendship with Foreign Countries, with

Dr. E.W. Barootes at its head, and Mr. Arthur Menzies, the ambassador of Canada in China as its deputy head, the officials of the Canadian Embassy in China and all the Canadian friends who were then in Peking. The meeting was presided over by Mr. Wang Bingnan, President of the Friendship Association. A speech by Mr. Nieh Rongzhen, Vice-Chairman of the Standing Committee of the National People's Congress and ex-Commander of the Shanxi-Chahar-Hebei Military Area, where Bethune worked, was read by Mr. Wang Bingnan; Qian Xinzhong, Minister of Public Health, gave a speech also, as did the leader of the Canadian delegation.

That mass meeting was an important part of a series of commemorative activities held on this occasion, including an exhibition in Peking on the life of Bethune, and the publication of an album in his memory and other books about him. We also staged modern drama, showed films and issued new commemorative stamps. Meanwhile, the same kind of commemorative meetings and forums were held and performances staged on these days in Tangxian County, Shijiazhuang, Yan'an, Xi'an, Changchun and other places. We held these commemorative activities to express, first, the Chinese people's memory of and profound respect for Bethune and our gratitude and greetings to our foreign friends who gave us assistance for our cause of revolution during the difficult years, and to promote our friendship with the people of Canada and all other countries. Second, through the commemoration of Bethune, we hoped to give our people, particularly the young generation, an internationalist and communist education to encourage the entire Chinese people to continue to learn from Bethune's spirit, to bring this spirit into full play and to devote themselves to the construction of a powerful, modern, socialist country.

These are some inscriptions written by our government leaders specially for the exhibition on the life of Dr. Bethune: "Eternal Glory to Norman Bethune, Great Proletarian Internationalist" by Hua Guofeng, Chairman of the Central Committee of the Chinese Communist Party and Premier of the State Council; "Selfless Help and Brilliant Example" by Ye Jiangying, Chairman of the Standing Committee of the National People's Congress; and "Be a Revolutionary and Scientist of Bethune's Type" by Vice-Premier Deng Xiaoping. These remarks crystallize what the Chinese people should learn from Bethune for the present cause of the four modernizations. In 2 years' work and living in China, Bethune demonstrated that he was a revolutionary with a noble state of mind and a serious scientist. Now on our new Long March toward modernization, it is imperative for us to learn primarily from his revolutionary spirit of daring to pursue the truth and devote ourselves to it, to solve new problems cropping up in the new period in such spirit, and to make efforts to find out the objective laws guiding the speedy realization of the four modernizations as well as the road to socialist modernization suited to the specific conditions in China. We must learn from Bethune's spirit of serving the people heart and soul and his utter devotion to others without any thought of himself. We must restore the fine revolutionary tradition sabotaged by the Gang of Four and fight against such old ideas and habits as ultra-individualism, self-seeking at the expense of public interest and irresponsibility etc, which may hamper modernization. We must learn from his practical spirit of integrating politics with professional work, making strenuous efforts in everything he did and constantly seeking perfection of vocational skill, so that people will vie with one another to become professional experts and make more contributions. We must learn also from Bethune's internationalism as manifest in his selfless aid to other people's cause of liberation, so as to perform better our internationalist duties.

* * *

Bethune made indelible contributions in helping the Chinese people's struggle for Liberation. His spirit is inspiring and will continue to inspire the Chinese people in contributing to the construction of a modern and better China. We must not forget what he did for closer Sino-Canadian friendship. We are pleased to note that Bethune is not only an intimate friend whom the Chinese people felt honoured to have, but also an excellent representative of the Canadian people. He is a hero shared by the Chinese and Canadian people. His name has already become a symbol of the friendship between two peoples. Because of Bethune's heroic deeds, every ordinary Chinese cherishes very friendly and cordial feelings towards the Canadians. Canadian friends will meet smiling faces of welcome and stretching hands of hospitality wherever they go in China; likewise, we Chinese coming to Canada meet with warm welcome everywhere. In recent years, the friendly relations between China and Canada have been further developing. Our trade, cultural, scientific and technological exchanges and other friendly interflows are becoming more and more frequent. We are convinced that the Bethune spirit will live forever in the hearts of our two people and that friendly relations bridged by Bethune between the people of China and Canada will be further consolidated and grow in strength.

Let the Bethune Spirit shine forever!

May friendship between the Chinese and Canadian people remain evergreen!

* * *

REFERENCE
1. Mao Zedong, "In Memory of Norman Bethune," Yanan, Dec. 21, 1939.

* * *

Abstract

The China for which Bethune fought and died has entered a period of socialist modernization. Though Bethune died more than 40 years ago, his contributions form a legacy to modern China. Of great value were his scientific approach, his sense of responsibility and his selfless revolutionary spirit. His scientific approach, as in his urge to perfect his professional skills, is reflected in the training of today's medical workers; educated in the Bethune spirit, they are playing an important role in medical and health care. Bethune's sense of responsibility in work has inspired the Chinese in integrating politics with professional work and in stressing the need to perfect vocational skills. And the selfless revolutionary spirit of Bethune, now rooted in the hearts of the Chinese people continues to serve as a model to be emulated. Of great value are Bethune's pursuit and devotion to the truth and the solving of problems in this spirit, as in the construction of an improved, modernized China; his selfless devotion and loyalty to others; and his sense of internationalism that enables the Chinese to understand international duties. The spirit of Bethune lives on and, among its various benefits, it included the strengthening of ties between Canada, the country of Bethune's birth, and China, where he died a hero.

Résumé

La Chine pour laquelle Bethune lutta et mourut est entrée dans une période de modernisation socialiste. Bien que Bethune soit mort depuis quarante ans, ses contributions constituent un héritage pour la Chine moderne. Son approche scientifique, son sens des responsabilités et son esprit révolutionnaire désintéressé étaient inestimables. Son approche scientifique, manifestée par son insistance à perfectionner ses techniques professionnelles, se réflète aujourd'hui dans l'entraînement des travailleurs médicaux. Formés dans l'esprit de Bethune, ils jouent un rôle important dans les soins médicaux et sanitaires. Le sens des responsabilités dont Bethune fit preuve dans son travail a stimulé les Chinois à intégrer la politique et le travail professionnels et à mettre l'accent sur le besoin de perfectionner leurs techniques professionnelles. Et l'esprit révolutionnaire désinteressé de Bethune, maintenant enraciné dans le coeur du peuple chinois, a servi de modèle à être imité. La poursuite de la vérité et la solution des problèmes dans cet esprit, pour la construction d'une Chine moderne, améliorée par exemple, tel que proposait Bethune, sont d'une grande valeur. Son dévouement désintéressé, sa loyauté, son sens de l'internationalisme qui aida les Chinois à comprendre leurs devoirs internationaux, sont aussi inappréciables. L'esprit de Bethune vit toujours et, parmi ses multiples bienfaits, on doit comprendre la consolidation des liens entre le Canada, pays natal de Bethune, et la Chine où il mourut en héros.

The Legacy/Le message

Perhaps, a miracle as happened once, should come again;
That golden glare were made to stand
And never sink and never leave the land
Desolate and dark,
But stay, suspended overhead
High, serene and clear
Perpetuate.

— Norman Bethune
From an untitled poem

Source: Stewart: The Mind of Norman Bethune, p. 31

The Bethune Legend: Norman Bethune as Hero

Maurice McGregor

What sort of man was Norman Bethune? One who knew him well responded like this when I asked this question: "The man lived a life of drama. His compassion for a patient could be deep and moving. He could sit by a bedside all night holding a patient's hand. But," he continued, "if the spirit moved him — and it often did — he could walk out on a whole ward of postoperative patients without even bothering to hand over to a colleague." If this is true — and I know how history can distort the record — this was no petty foible of an impulsive man but an unpardonable, unprofessional act.

Another respondent was one of the gowned figures who, with Bethune, is seen in a photograph of the main operating room at Montreal's Royal Victoria Hospital assisting Dr. Edward Archibald. He clearly liked and respected Bethune. He could not, however, excuse him for egotistical stunts such as operating too fast simply to break a record — and incidentally to show up Archibald, who was a slow and meticulous operator.

These are small anecdotes, but if we are to understand the "selfless hero" of Spain and China — the legend — we must find room for these pieces of a jigsaw puzzle. And the right way to put puzzles together is to start with the main, the dominant theme. One thing is clear as we sort through the pieces of the Bethune puzzle: he was hero material.

A hero must be not like other men, or he would be no hero; as important, it must be seen that he is not like other men — his individuality must be easily recognized. As for Bethune, his individuality has never been questioned, even if it showed itself in such trivia as his dress and his complete disregard for social convention. More important was his originality of thought and active inventiveness, which characterized his medical and surgical innovations and which was evident in his writing and his painting. His politics reflected this, too, with his early recognition that the Civil War in Spain and the invasion of China were manifestations of a common thought pattern, now called fascist.

But these characteristics alone do not make a hero; many have flouted convention, many surgeons have been innovators. Others shared Bethune's views on the Spanish Civil War and the Japanese invasion of China. In Bethune, however, originality was combined with a thoroughly practical and pragmatic ability. Thus he not only perceived some surgical instruments to be clumsy, he also both designed better ones and had them manufactured and marketed. He not only regretted the inability of the unemployed to afford medical care, he also fashioned, with his friends, a health plan and attempted to have it adopted by society. He not only recognized the fascist menace and volunteered for service in Spain, but did so in such a way with his transfusion service that his contribution would have the greatest impact.

Most of all, Bethune had that critical heroic quality of a sense of drama, a characteristic shared by personalities as diverse as Joan of Arc, Queen Elizabeth I and Winston Churchill. Such people as these see the world as a stage, must perceive their role in it, must dress the part and act it through. When, in times of plodding peace, the plot is not to the audience's liking, the audience may yawn or even vent its displeasure at the over-dramatized performance; but in turbulent times, the audience's needs may coincide with the self-conceived role of the actor. Then the audience may be swept away by the actor's performance, by his larger-than-life role. Thus is the hero legend made.

* * *

It was, of course, in Yanan that this great actor, Bethune, found his greatest role. He found an audience that needed him profoundly, that came to idolize him, that in turn he could idolize. Thus he wrote in his diary for August, 21, 1938 the following:

> It is true I am tired, but I don't think I have been so happy for a long time. I am content. I am doing what I want to do. I am treated like a kingly comrade with every kindness, every courtesy imaginable.
>
> I have the inestimable fortune to be among, and to work among, comrades to whom communism is a way of life, not merely a way of talking or a way of conscious thinking.
>
> Their communism is simple and profound, reflex as a knee jerk, unconscious as the movements of their lungs, automatic as the beating of their hearts. Quiet, steadfast, wise, patient; with unshakable optimism; gentle and cruel; sweet and bitter, unselfish, determined; implacable in their hate; world embracing in their love[1].

So Bethune perceived the people he served.

Other foreigners had, of course, served with the Chinese communists in their hour of need; some, like Ma Haide, still serve with them, with a net sum of service that infinitely outweighs any contribution Bethune could have made. But Bethune brought unique qualities with him; he brought to the beleaguered Chinese communists not only his personal service, but also the illusion that they were not alone. "The eyes of millions of freedom-loving Canadians, Americans and Englishmen," he told them, "are turned to the East and are fixed with admiration on China in their glorious struggle against Japanese imperialism." True, he used the sort of dramatic licence that in normal circumstances would have verged on dishonesty, but here he was speaking to an army fighting in great isolation. He was speaking at a dramatic moment and it was surely what his listeners needed to hear.

By bringing this message, by his service, by his flair and devotion, and of course by dying at this post, Bethune indeed achieved heroism in the eyes of those who knew him in Yenan.

* * *

The extension and the growth of the Bethune legend to its present proportions in China and his exaltation above the millions of Chinese who gave their lives in the same struggle do, however, demand another explanation. The explanation is to be found in the circumstances of the Chinese revolution and in the philosophy of Mao Zedong.

The communism of Mao Zedong has been something more than an economic theory or a form of government, and history will see it also as an ethical and moral movement of major proportions. In time this movement may be subject to the same dilution, corruption and distortion that is the fate of all such teaching, but at least when I visited China, in 1974, its social message was clear and was presented to the Chinese people with conviction. Like all great ethical teachings, its message was simple. One must "serve the people," putting one's fellow men above self; in other words, one must love one's neighbour. The workers and the peasant, the Chinese were told, are the source of wisdom and virtue; that is, the poor and the meek shall inherit the earth. Soldiers must observe the Army's 'five don'ts policy, which stated, in part, "when hit, don't hit back; when cursed, don't curse back" — that is, turn the other cheek. And there is no room for the arrogant bureaucrats and technocrats and higher party cadres (i.e., scribes and pharisees), and there is no way the rich shall enter the Kingdom.

The propagation of such an ethos needs models and parables. For Mao Zedong, Bethune was a local good samaritan who could teach the lessons of self-reliance, internationalism and service to the Chinese people. Mao's essay, "In memory of Norman Bethune", was learned and studied by millions of Chinese; it presents a model quite clearly, of a man "of value to the people:"

> What kind of spirit is this that makes a foreigner selflessly adopt the cause of the Chinese peoples' liberation as his own? It is the spirit of internationalism, the spirit of communism from which every Chinese communist must learn.
> This is our internationalism, the internationalism with which we oppose both narrow nationalism and narrow patriotism . . .
> Comrade Bethune's spirit, his utter devotion to others without any thought of self, was shown in his boundless sense of responsibility in his work and his boundless warm-heartedness towards all comrades and people. Every communist must learn from him. A man's ability may be great or small, but if he has this spirit he is already noble-minded and pure, a man of moral integrity and above vulgar interests, a man who is of value to the people[2].

These are lessons repeatedly drummed into the people in connection with Bethune's name. Thus in the Bethune Museum in Shi Chui Chong, characteristic words of Bethune have been selected for display: "You and we are the internationalists; we recognize no race, colour, no language, no national boundaries to separate and divide us." Bethune indeed thought of himself as one of the Chinese people, and he readily identified with the Chinese wounded. A telegram replying to Mao Zedong's instructions that he should accept a salary is typical of Bethune:

> Beloved Chairman Mao Zedong, replying to your telegram, I refuse to accept offered one hundred dollars a month. I have no need of money for myself as all food, clothing etc. is supplied me. If the money has been sent to me personally from America or Canada, make a special tobacco fund out of it for tobacco and cigarettes for the wounded . . .[3].

* * *

I have tried to respond to the question that was put to me often in 1974, a question asked with pride and pleasure: "How is it we Canadians have a compatriot who is so revered in China?" As justified as our gratification may be, our pride must be restrained, for in fact Bethune is more of a Chinese than a Canadian hero. The Bethune legend, moreover, tells us more of modern China than of Bethune himself. It tells us that China has chosen for two of its principal goals democratic and egalitarian service to its people, together with a spirit of internationalism.

In a tired and blazé world, in a world that is a cynical one, such goals readily may seem too idealistic, even naïve, but in China there is no shadow of a doubt that everyone takes these goals quite seriously.

* * *

REFERENCES AND NOTES

1. Norman Bethune, Entry in diary and letter to a friend, Aug. 21, 1938.
2. Mao Zedong, "In Memory of Norman Bethune," Yenan, Dec. 21, 1939.
3. Bethune, Telegram to Yenan Military Council, Aug. 11, 1938.

* * *

Abstract

A consideration of the puzzle that is Bethune indicates that he was made of hero material. His individuality and his originality of thought and action made him unlike other men, and, together with these qualities, his sense of drama fitted him for the larger-than-life role of a hero. In China, he devoted himself completely to serving the Chinese in their fight against the Japanese — indeed, he died for their cause, and so achieved heroism in their eyes. This was more than 40 years ago, and the present dimensions of the Bethune legend now demand another explanation, as follows: For Mao Zedong, particularly, Bethune was a local good samaritan who taught the Chinese people the lessons of self-reliance, service and internationalism; values exemplified in Bethune that were of especial significance in modern China are responsibility in work and devotion to others without thoughts of self. Bethune, who thought of himself as one of the Chinese, is more of a Chinese than a Canadian hero; and the Bethune legend tells us more of modern China than of Bethune himself. The Bethune legend tells us that modern China has chosen for two of its principal goals democratic and Egalitarian service to its people and a spirit of internationalism.

Résumé

La légende autour de Bethune s'explique si on le perçoit comme un héros. Chez le héros, la personnalité compte tout autant que l'originalité de la pensée et de l'action et que le pragmatisme apporté dans l'exécution de la tâche. Le héros doit aussi être pénétré d'un sens dramatique; il doit voir le monde comme une scène et se plaire à s'y produire dans un rôle plus grand que nature. C'est au Yanan, en Chine du Nord, que Bethune a joué son plus grand rôle. Il y a trouvé un auditoire qui avait besoin de lui et qui l'idolâtrait. De son côté, il s'est identifié à son auditoire. Il s'est dévoué au service des Chinois et, en partie parce que son destin était d'y mourir, il est devenu pour eux un héros d'abnégation. La légende qui s'est créée autour de lui, héros étranger, trouve aussi son explication dans la révolution chinoise et dans la philosophie de Mao Zedong. Le leader chinois s'est servi de l'exemple de ce bon samaritain pour enseigner à son peuple l'autonomie, l'idéal internationaliste et le dévouement à la nation chinoise. Bethune s'est sûrement défini comme membre du peuple chinois. Il s'est identifié aux blessés chinois et s'est lui-même reconnu comme internationaliste lorsqu'il a affirmé de lui et des ses camarades: "Nous ne reconnaissons aucune race, aucune couleur, aucune langue, aucune frontière nationale qui puissent nous séparer et nous diviser". La légende de Bethune nous renseigne davantage sur la Chine moderne que sur les relations de Bethune avec le Canada puisqu'il demeure bien plus un héros chinois que canadien.

First monument to Bethune in Chu Ch'eng (Juncheng), southwest of Peking, China, 1940. Thousands of Chinese stream to honour their "Baiquen" (Pai Chiu-en) at original tomb for dedication May Day, 1940.

Public Archives of Canada, National Film Board Collection. PA 116906

Le premier monument à Bethune en Chu Ch'eng (Juncheng), au sud-ouest de Pékin, Chine, 1940. Des milliers de Chinois défilent devant la tombe de "Baiquen" (Pai Chiu-en) lors de son inauguration le 1er mai, 1940.

Archives publiques du Canada, Collection de l'Office national du film. PA 116906

Après Bethune:
l'expérience des soins médicaux au Québec

Table ronde: Rob Robson, Pierre Delva, Suzanne Dubreuil, Claire Dutrisac, Marc Lavallée, Marc Renaud, Denis Lazure

Rob Robson

Je désirerais présenter brièvement les propositions formulées par le *Montreal Group for the Security of the People's Health*. Ce groupe de personnes progressistes, des médecins, des infirmières, des gens travaillant dans le domaine des statistiques, des professionnels de la santé, des travailleurs de la santé se réunissaient dans le but d'étudier, d'analyser les liens entre la médecine, la santé et le peuple, ainsi que la situation dans différents pays, en vue de formuler des solutions pratiques à des problèmes pratiques.

Ils avaient la nette impression que la médecine, telle que pratiquée, ne répondait aux besoins ni du patient, ni des professionnels de la santé. Du point de vue des patients, on remarque que le niveau de santé des gens était très bas. Plusieurs raisons expliquent cet état de chose: tout d'abord la vaste majorité de la population à cette époque était incapable de payer pour les services. Deuxièmement, les services étaient souvent rendus dans des buts charitables et souvent très inadéquats. On peut aussi constater un manque total de services préventifs.

Du point de vue des médecins et des autres professionnels de la santé tout n'allait pas très bien non plus. Tout d'abord, on relevait le problème de la pratique individuelle, les difficultés des médecins à rendre un bon service en travaillant seuls. On remarquait aussi un manque total de services préventifs donnés par les médecins pour la simple raison que ça ne payait pas. Il n'y avait aucune motivation de leur part à avoir une approche préventive envers les problèmes de santé. Et enfin, la situation économique de beaucoup de médecins à cette époque était chancelante. Les membres du groupe identifiaient deux problèmes: le maintien inadéquat de la santé du peuple et l'insécurité économique des médecins et autres professionnels de la santé.

De là, ils ont perçu un principe fondamental, soit l'obligation du gouvernement de maintenir la santé de la population. Cette obligation, il me semble, est tout simplement le complément du droit fondamental du peuple, son droit à la santé, à des services de santé convenables. Les membres du groupe ont donc formulé plusieurs propositions concrètes. Vu le grand nombre de chômeurs à Montréal à ce moment-là, le groupe cherchait la meilleure façon de répondre à leurs besoins de santé. Ils ont aussi avancé différents modèles, proposé toutes sortes d'expériences différentes pour résoudre le problème: assurance-maladie, assurance-volontaire Croix-Bleue ou autres formes d'assurance. Ils ont aussi demandé une meilleure considération des services de santé, problème qui était alors flagrant, et ils ont beaucoup misé sur une approche multidisciplinaire. Qu'est-il arrivé de toutes ces réformes proposées pour améliorer le système de santé?

Nous pouvons constater tout de suite que le second problème, celui de l'insécurité économique des médecins, est pas mal résolu. Cela ne veut pas dire, par exemple, qu'ils sont plus incités à pratiquer la médecine préventive. Il n'y a pas encore beaucoup d'encouragements pour les médecins à mettre l'accent sur les soins préventifs. Il reste aussi les problèmes de pratique individuelle.

Pour les patients, il y a eu des changements assez frappants. Il n'y a plus de barrière financière à la disponibilité des soins de santé. Des barrières géographiques sont toujours là pour les personnes habitant les régions rurales. Il y a encore de grandes faiblesses concernant les soins préventifs.

Un peu plus tard, après le rapport du groupe, Bethune a acquis une vision plus fondamentale des problèmes de la santé. En tant que révolutionnaire il a vu que vraiment le problème principal était un problème de fonctionnement du système socio-économique. La plupart des problèmes de santé découlaient de ce système. Cela laissait supposer que pour une amélioration importante de la situation il fallait aussi un changement profond dans le fonctionnement de la société.

* * *

Pierre Delva

Depuis Norman Bethune, le Canada a développé un système d'assurance hospitalisation et assurance-maladie; le docteur Wendell MacLeod était doyen à l'Université de Saskatchewan lors de l'introduction de l'assurance-maladie dans cette province, et dès le début a encouragé sa réalisation; c'était une première pour l'Amérique du Nord. Maintenant, au Québec, l'hospitalisation est "gratuite", c'est-à-dire, payée par nos taxes. Il y a de plus un double système public de soins de première ligne: premièrement un réseau de CLSC (Centres locaux de services communautaires), encore très incomplet, assure certains services médicaux et sociaux. Tout le personnel est salarié. Les services rendus sont encore marginaux et les médecins qui y travaillent se sentent marginaux, mais ce système s'étend lentement. Deuxièmement, il y a la *carte soleil*. Avec cette carte, n'importe quel citoyen peut se rendre chez n'importe quel médecin qui veut le recevoir, pour demander un service. C'est donc en fait une carte *Chargex* ou *Master-Charge* payée par nos taxes. Un tel système n'encourage pas la prise en charge par l'individu de sa santé. Nous verrons par exemple, que le nombre d'actes médicaux posés est en relation directe avec les heures de disponibilité des médecins, et a peu de relation avec le niveau de santé de cette population.

Dans une étude dont la publication a été bloquée, dans une province du Canada il y avait, en 1967, 110 000 habitants et entre 80 et 90 médecins. Dix ans plus tard en 1977, il y avait 120 000 habitants, et entre 130 et 140 médecins. Cette augmentation de médecins n'était pas accompagnée par une amélioration du niveau de santé: les statistiques usuelles sont certes les plus mauvaises du pays, mais les coûts ont fort augmenté. Donc, une *carte soleil* n'est pas un instrument économique, elle encourage la surconsommation de services médicaux et n'augmente pas tellement le niveau de santé d'une population.

Comme professeur, je puis affirmer que le cours de médecine en Amérique du Nord ne prépare pas le jeune médecin à fonctionner dans la communauté. Le cours est contrôlé le plus souvent par des médecins ultraspécialisés dans un domaine relativement étroit: il y a entre 35 et 40 de ces spécialités au Canada. De plus, au-delà de 95% de l'enseignement médical se donne dans les hôpitaux, alors que les problèmes de santé courants sont à l'extérieur des hôpitaux. Il y a une résistance farouche et pratiquement inébranlable à changer ce système. Il faut que nous arrivions à former nos étudiants à l'extérieur des hôpitaux du moins pour 30% de leur temps, et cet enseignement doit se faire par des médecins qui peuvent comprendre les problèmes globaux des individus et des populations.

Mais le problème est encore plus difficile car même si l'on forme un médecin idéal, il est pratiquement incapable de s'intégrer: il est considéré à présent comme marginal s'il va travailler dans un CLSC, et il a de la difficulté à gagner sa vie avec la *carte soleil* s'il prend du temps avec ses patients. De fait, ses dépenses sont d'au moins $500 par semaine. Et il est pratiquement forcé de voir beaucoup de patients avant de couvrir ses frais et pouvoir commencer à gagner sa vie. S'il prend le temps pour aller au fond des problèmes de ses clients, il a de la difficulté à boucler son budget. Comme professeur en médecine de première ligne, je suis tiraillé dans tous les sens: l'université nous donne des ressources insuffisantes et, si je travaille efficacement, j'aide à former un médecin excellent qui a des difficultés à fonctionner dans le système actuel.

* * *

Suzanne Dubreuil

Je voudrais partager avec vous les observations que mon travail quotidien m'amène à faire et quelques considérations qui s'en dégagent. J'ajouterais même que j'ai une certaine confiance en ces observations parce que ce ne sont pas des chiffres mais des cris et des réalités de femmes et d'enfants de mon milieu. Ce milieu où je travaille c'est le quartier St-René-Goupil à Montréal, au nord de la ville de Montréal-Nord, à l'est de la ville de St-Léonard. C'est un quartier complètement situé aux limites est et nord de la ville de Montréal. Il est isolé et souffre de ce fait d'absence de services pouvant améliorer la qualité de vie, de plans d'habitation à loyer modique, d'habitations à loyers multiples gérées par la centrale d'hypothèque et de logement de Montréal, etc... C'est une population de 16 000 personnes, 4 000 familles environ, population ouvrière dans sa totalité, composée de jeunes foyers. Le quartier compte toutefois 30% d'assistés sociaux déclarés et près de 40% de familles monoparentales déclarées. Ce milieu est exclusivement populaire vivant dans un environnement déplorable. Un seul parc est aménagé, le parc Caron, pour desservir cette population. Seul le centre éducatif communautaire René-Goupil, où je travaille, et un centre de loisirs exercent un travail dans le milieu. Les autres ressources possibles et nécessaires sont inexistantes, CLSC ou autres. L'aménagement du quartier pose de sérieuses questions; l'absence d'espaces verts, de terrains sportifs, de pistes de randonnée oblige la population à se déplacer à la recherche d'équipement ou de terrains favorables à l'exercice physique et à la vie de plein air. Or, un grand nombre de familles de ce quartier ne peuvent s'offrir ces déplacements et ne possèdent pas d'équipement personnel. Pour ce faire, le centre éducatif communautaire René-

Goupil intervient dans le but d'offrir à cette population des chances égales au niveau de l'accès à la santé physique et psychologique en percevant d'abord les besoins de ce quartier, leurs attentes, et en tentant avec eux de mettre sur pied divers projets pour améliorer les conditions de vie.

Quelle est l'expérience que j'ai des femmes que je côtoie dans ce milieu? Dans un contexte psycho-socio-économique instable la dépression, les ulcères d'estomac, les actes de violence contre soi et/ou contre autrui sont monnaie courante. L'angoisse et l'anxiété poussent bien au-delà de la réalité les symptômes de tel ou tel malaise, et conduit à des diagnostics hâtifs qui soulagent pour un instant. "J'ai été voir mon médecin. Il me dit que je souffre de telle ou telle maladie. Il m'a prescrit tel médicament." Mais où est la cause? Dans mon milieu, le mariage fait souvent échec et l'enfant est un fardeau dans plusieurs de ces foyers.

Un grand nombre de personnes ayant vécu des échecs ou des rejets à quelque niveau que ce soit, courent d'un hôpital à l'autre et vont ainsi continuer la ronde jusqu'à ce qu'ils soient enfin compris. Mais le seront-ils? Impossible d'aller au psychologue d'un bureau à gages privé. Le psychiatre reçoit le client une fois le mois parce que la clientèle est trop nombreuse. La tentation normale est le recours à la médecine et la réponse facile est souvent le médicament, mais après ou pendant, y a-t-il investigation, concertation et/ou suivi? Dans les cas de tentative de suicide, par exemple, les gens n'ont souvent aucune protection contre la récidive. Que pense-t-on de la médication prescrite à la sortie d'un hôpital à la suite de telle tentative sans un suivi psychologique ou psychiatrique? J'ai eu souvent, par exemple, à garder chez moi des bouteilles de médicaments parce que la femme ou l'homme disait: "J'ai peur de prendre toute la bouteille. Donne-m'en donc une fois par jour". Mais est-ce que les hôpitaux savent ça? Probablement. Un jeune homme dans la vingtaine après une tentative de suicide sort d'un hôpital avec un rendez-vous dans un autre hôpital pour un suivi psychologique. Il s'y rend pour une évaluation, environ une heure d'attente et une heure de bureau pour se faire dire qu'il n'est pas dans le bon district. Aura-t-il le courage et la force physique de poursuivre? Une jeune adolescente subit un avortement il y a deux mois. Elle est retournée chez elle, après qu'on lui ait installé un stérilet, sans aucun suivi psychologique et sans aide, dans un foyer pertubé qui la rejette. Elle me disait il y a environ deux semaines: "Tu sais, le soir je me couche toujours après mes parents ou j'attends que le monde dorme, ou je rentre, en tout cas, de façon à ce que le monde puisse dormir quand je rentre". Elle dit: "J'entens un bébé pleurer". Elle a 14 ans et demi.

Problèmes financiers

Les femmes sur le bien-être social ne peuvent pas arriver avec leurs prestations à subvenir aux besoins alimentaires et primaires de leurs enfants. Pour boucler ou pour accéder à un loisir nécessaire, plusieurs personnes font du travail payé sous la table ce qui cause des craintes et des peurs qui minent la santé et rendent muet devant les justes revendications. On a de la misère à mobiliser une telle population. Les déplacements sont coûteux, les enfants sont jeunes, les femmes sont seules et les garderies sont inexistantes ou coûteuses. Avec ce tableau, il est facilement déductible que la maladie devienne l'échapatoire à ces situations angoissantes.

Les hommes de mon milieu

Ils sont des journaliers, camionneurs, vendeurs. Ils constatent et/ou portent souvent la marque de nombreux accidents de travail. Il y a beaucoup de chômage, peu de débouchés, d'où insécurité, aggressivité et alcool. Les lieux de vacances en plein air sont coûteux et inaccessibles. Il faudrait encourager les regroupements des familles par la formule des camps familiaux à prix modique; les infirmières présentes dans ces champs en savent quelque chose.

Les enfants de mon milieu

Ce que les parents vivent, les enfants le ressentent bien jeunes. Il somatisent déjà, ils s'envolent et se durcissent. J'ai connu une fillette de sept ans qui s'en allait dans l'escalier geler plutôt que d'entendre sa mère parler de maladie. Le régime de vie des enfants est peu en harmonie aussi avec les conditions d'une bonne santé: les heures irrégulières, le manque de repos, les repas incomplets, pas de déjeuner, beaucoup de grignotage. Les enfants sont fatigués, nerveux, impatients, violents et incapables d'attention à l'école. Les problèmes de drogue et de consommation d'alcool au secondaire sont nombreux et pour les jeunes les lieux éducatifs dans un quartier, en dehors des heures de classe, sont très très rares, — chez moi ils sont presque inexistants, excepté le centre, — et l'exiguïté des logis force l'enfant à rester tranquille.

Permettez-moi de vous laisser sur une image: un logement 4½, petit, quatrième étage, un balcon, une femme monoparentale dans la trentaine, quatre enfants de neuf ans à huit mois, intelligents et débrouillards, — parce que l'on pense toujours que les gens ne sont pas intelligents et débrouillards dans les populaces, ce qui est faux. Septembre: diagnostic de son médecin de famille: phlébite, médicaments, deux semaines de repos. Octobre: Télémédic appelé par elle un soir d'angoisse; pas de phlébite, angoisse, calmant. Novembre: maux de tête, maux de cou; diagnostic provisoire: torticolis. Examen de la colonne vertébrale, analyse du sang et de l'urine. Elle court pour faire garder la petite et recherche un moyen de transport à cause de la grève. A deux reprises, elle vient au centre et nous la visitons à domicile: "J'aime les enfants et j'ai besoin de vivre, je voudrais refaire ma vie, mais quel homme va m'accepter avec quatre enfants?" Pas de réponses au foyer modique, la laveuse qui coule, les tuiles qui se décollent. Evidemment, peur de mourir, d'avoir des maladies dangereuses, mal dans le cou, mal de tête. Vous devinez un peu de quoi il s'agit. Elle oublie tout çà, quand on parle avec elle. Mais, le soir, celle qui a été la visiter dit ceci: "J'ai vu l'enfant de huit mois se réveiller à plusieurs reprises, s'asseoir dans son lit, se raidir, reprendre sa sucette et se calmer sous l'effet de la mère chaleureuse qui l'accueillait". L'enfant de huit mois ressentait profondément l'angoisse de sa mère. Et, le médecin dans tout cela avec ses examens, le sait-il ou passe-t-il à côté du problème?

Si, en 1935-36, Bethune et son groupe pouvait dire que la vaste majorité de la population ne pouvait pas se payer une aide médicale adéquate, en 1979-80, dans mon quartier, l'observation me permet de constater que dans bien des situations des soins nombreux gratuits sont présents. De nombreux médicaments sont prescrits et ingurgités. Des sommes coûteuses y sont investies. Mais, elles sont souvent inefficaces, parce que décollées du contexte psycho-socio-économique qui engendre des problèmes de santé, parce que l'argent qui est investi devrait l'être dans la prévention, dans le travail en quartier, dans les visites de familles, dans des garderies, dans des suppléments de revenus, dans des logements. Il serait important que le médecin soit autant un promoteur de vie dans son quartier qu'un traitant. Cela dépend d'une nouvelle conscience médicale ouverte sur les problèmes sociaux plutôt que sur la médication, une médecine encourageante et proche des intervenants du quartier, une médecine engagée dans le quartier.

* * *

Claire Dutrisac

Je veux simplement me faire l'écho des plaintes que je reçois de différents groupes de la population, dans mon métier de journaliste. Je dois vous dire tout de suite que la qualité qu'on demande aux malades, c'est la patience: la patience pour attendre un rendez-vous au bureau du médecin, parfois dans les cliniques des hôpitaux, au centre de prélèvements; trois semaines pour avoir un rendez-vous dans un centre de prélèvements d'un grand hôpital de Montréal. Une fois rendu, l'attente se fait souvent dans les salles d'urgence. On demande d'abord au patient de déclarer son nom, son adresse, une personne à avertir au cas où, le nom de son père, sa grand-mère, ses antécédents, mais on ne lui demande pas ce qu'il a. Après, on le lui demande; je crois que cette situation est bien connue, ça s'est corrigé dans certains hôpitaux, mais pas partout. On lui demande aussi de la patience pour essayer d'obtenir des explications de son médecin sur son propre cas et beaucoup trop de médecins ne se donnent pas la peine d'expliquer au patient ce qu'il a. C'est un mépris inconscient d'ailleurs que le patient ressent, et peut-être se demande-t-on aussi si le médecin ne veut pas rester un peu le grand sorcier du village qui ne livre pas ses secrets. Il y a aussi difficulté pour la famille d'obtenir des nouvelles après une intervention chirurgicale sur un des membres de la famille, que ce soit le père, la mère, le mari, la femme, l'épouse.

On se plaint du temps très court alloué à chaque visite par le médecin. Le patient n'arrive pas à expliquer, se sent poussé dans le dos. Il revient en disant: "Je voulais parler de çi, je voulais parler de çà". Il a oublié. Il est d'ailleurs toujours un peu impressionné devant son médecin et l'aspect psychologique du patient n'est pas assez pris en considération. On fait une médecine de tests et d'examens de laboratoire et on ne se fie plus à l'examen clinique. La médecine devient de plus en plus science et de moins en moins art, elle est de plus en plus déshumanisée.

Les CLSC sont une trouvaille merveilleuse et la plupart des gens qui fréquentent les CLSC en sont vraiment très satisfaits, même s'ils sont en nombre insuffisant. Ils sont bien chanceux les gens qui ont un CLSC dans leur quartier et qui savent surtout quoi en attendre, parce qu'on ne connait pas trop les services très variés que dispensent les CLSC. C'est une souplesse qui, peut-être, leur a permis de s'approcher beaucoup des besoins du milieu mais, d'autre part, qui nous laisse un peu perdus. Il y a les cliniques privées qui leur ont fait la guerre et qui sont allées jusqu'à les boycotter. Ceci a été nié fortement, mais je pense qu'il y a très peu de gens qui sont convaincus que cette idée qui est venue aux médecins de créer des cliniques privées pour répondre aux besoins de santé n'avait aucun rapport avec les CLSC, sauf que c'est lorsqu'on a créé les CLSC qu'ils y ont pensé tout d'un coup. Mais il y avait longtemps qu'on n'avait plus de visites à domicile de la part des médecins. Ces visites à domicile manquent particulièrement, surtout pour les personnes âgées, pour les personnes à revenus modestes, pour les gagne-petit. Il n'y a presque plus de médecins qui vont à domicile et la personne âgée se sent dans la plus grande insécurité. On a assisté avec Télémédic et autres systèmes de ce genre à un effort pour répondre à ce besoin. L'expérience est trop nouvelle pour qu'on en fasse une analyse valable. Elle a un petit aspect commercial aussi, qui nous laisse un peu perplexe. Il y a des gens qui en sont satisfaits, mais, j'ai ouï dire par exemple que Télémédic ait été voir cinq fois la même personne dans une journée. Bon, on vous dira que la gratuité des soins était une invitation à la surconsommation, mais si on met un ticket modérateur, moi je sais très bien que ça ne vas pas modérer les gens comme moi, ça ne modérera pas les syndiqués ou les travailleurs qui ont des assurances collectives, ça va modérer les gagne-petit, tous ceux qui ont peu de moyens de payer, et c'est encore la partie à l'aise de la population qui, elle, pourra surconsommer sans qu'on lui dise que vraiment, elle vient voir son médecin trop souvent. Il y a peut-être aussi une trop grande complaisance de la part des médecins à revoir leurs patients sous prétexte de très bonne médecine. Cela peut se justifier, on est mal placé pour dire aux médecins: vous voyez votre patient trop souvent mais, quand on analyse l'ensemble d'une population, je pense qu'on est en droit de se poser des questions. Il y a aussi la nécessité d'être référé par un médecin généraliste pour voir un spécialiste.

Je désirerais, pour terminer, traiter des médecins qui vont dans des foyers clandestins et qui deviennent complices des tenanciers/tenancières. J'aimerais que la corporation des médecins se penche sur ce problème: il est certain que les personnes étant dans ces foyers ont besoin d'être soignées. On nous force cependant à dénoncer les personnes qui maltraitent les animaux et les enfants, mais on n'en est pas encore rendu à protéger les personnes âgées dans ces foyers. Je crois que les médecins qui vont les soigner dans ces foyers, qui ne s'inquiètent pas de savoir pourquoi ces personnes sont malades et qui parfois d'ailleurs sont des complices actifs — à part ceux qui sont des complices passifs et qui se contentent de ne rien dire — je crois que ces médecins ont une grave responsabilité.

* * *

Marc Lavallée

Ce n'est pas d'aujourd'hui que les gens critiquent la médecine et les médecins. Le premier volume qui ait jamais été écrit, ce n'était pas un volume d'ailleurs, mais des tablettes d'argile, il y a 5 000 ans, c'est le chant de Gilgamesh et il relate justement la critique, c'est-à-dire la manifestation d'impuissance devant la maladie et la mort et la critique d'une personne qui va mourir et qui se plaint qu'on la laisse ainsi subir ce sort. Maintenant, Bethune n'a fait que tracer un tableau des gens de son époque. Aujourd'hui on peut se demander si la médecine actuelle colle à ce qu'on appelle les "normes contemporaines". J'en prendrai trois exemples: les causes de mortalité, les inégalités sociales devant la maladie et la mort, puis, la notion de santé et la vie, c'est-à-dire en dehors, au-delà de l'être biologique, l'être psycho-social qui forme ce qu'on appelle un être humain.

Cinq mille ans après le premier livre qui traçait un portrait de l'homme devant la mort, un autre livre, écrit cette fois par ordinateur, *The Facts of Life at Death,* démontre la compilation des statistiques vitales de l'homme en Amérique du Nord. On y apprend notamment que la population vieillit et que les maladies dégénératives et chroniques sont la plus grande cause de mort, qu'il ne reste comme maladie infectieuse à l'état épidémique que la gonorrhée qui ne fait qu'augmenter d'incidence. Les causes de mort sont les maladies cardiaques, le cancer, les maladies cérébro-vasculaires, les accidents, les morts violentes et le suicide.

Pour ce qui est des inégalités sociales, je reviens à un contexte plus particulier qui nous intéresse et je vous cite une étude québécoise: *La mortalité dans les aires sociales de la région métropolitaine de Montréal* par Luc Cellier, direction générale de la planification du Ministère des Affaires sociales. On y apprend, pour ce qui concerne le territoire de notre CLCS, Pointe-aux-Trembles, Montréal-Est, que le taux de mortalité néonatale est de deux fois plus élevé que dans le West Island. On y apprend également qu'à Pointe-aux-Trembles le taux de mortalité pour bronchite, emphysème et asthme est quatre fois plus élevé que dans la moyenne du territoire métropolitain; conséquence évidemment de la pollution atmosphérique d'origine industrielle et conséquence aussi de la pollution industrielle à l'intérieur des usines. Je vous souligne un troisième exemple pour tracer un tableau très bref de ce qu'on appelle la condition humaine contemporaine: le processus de vieillissement. La personne âgée bénéficie maintenant de services gratuits, services d'ambulance, services de médicaments, d'hospitalisation, de médecins et de centres d'accueils, mais est sujette à des douzaines de ruptures humaines. On appelle ça des petites morts et, quand on est à domicile, on a des soins à domicile et on est coupé de son entourage. Lorsqu'on est en centre d'accueil, placé par le CSS dans un ordinateur, on peut venir de Pointe-aux-Trembles, et se retrouver à Saint-Henri et vice versa, on est à Saint-Henri et on se retrouve à Montréal-Nord. Coupure, rupture, c'est le lot des personnes âgées qui sont de plus en plus dépossédées dans un système qui veut lui fournir beaucoup mais qui ne lui fournit pas l'essentiel, c'est-à-dire une espèce de continuité, ou une capacité de vivre dans l'environnement psycho-social que ces personnes ont connu, car les personnes âgées sont moins aptes à subir ces ruptures. Par rapport à ce tableau, notre médecine est à mon avis le reflet des valeurs sociales et économiques de la société. Je ne suis pas prêt à blâmer la médecine, pas plus que le Ministère des Affaires sociales, parce que c'est collectivement que nous exerçons cette responsabilité.

Je me suis amusé par contre à regarder le curriculum des facultés de médecine et à tracer un portrait de l'homme contemporain à partir du curriculum. On y remarque par exemple, 85% de biologique, 10% de psychologique et 5% de social. Ce tableau correspond à la psychologie primitive et à l'existence grégaire de notre ancêtre préhistorique d'il y a 1 000 000 d'années qui était surtout biologique, un peu psychologique et pas très social. Nous, si l'on trace aussi un portrait de l'homme contemporain par le système de rémunération, c'est-à-dire ce qu'on soigne, on y trouve un portrait qui est aussi fidèle à ce que je viens de décrire. On n'apprend pas aux étudiants en médecine quoi faire devant la mort, sinon la fuite ou l'abandon du patient: il est fini, on ferme la valise et on s'en va. L'homme contemporain souffre et meurt de maladies qu'on ne peut pas guérir mais qu'on peut prévenir. Mais je me demande où on en est actuellement dans notre réseau de prévention et ce qui en est de la réorganisation des soins en fonction du concept de santé tel qu'on le conçoit maintenant, c'est-à-dire étendu au psychologique et au social. L'industrie des soins bio-médicaux prolifère actuellement grâce à un système de taxation privilégié, qui fait qu'elle échappe aux contraintes des enveloppes gouvernementales.

Le système, pour des centaines de nouveaux gradués qui débouchent chaque année en médecine, s'appelle "la castonguette": c'est un mot proprement québécois, un système par lequel ils ont la voie facilitée, aisément praticable, immédiatement accessible, parée de richesses assurées et de liberté garantie. La castonguette est une espèce d'idole moderne, syncrétique qui réunit toute sorte de cultes: le culte original d'un ministre bourgeois qui a été l'auteur de la réforme de santé de l'époque, le culte des cartes de crédit qui donne l'illusion d'une fausse gratuité et aussi, le culte de la vache sacrée qu'est la libre entreprise. Il est toutefois une poignée de médecins qui pratiquent à salaire, ce qu'on appelle honoraires fixes, pour protéger la susceptibilité de la fédération des omnipraticiens, mais qui sont des salaires à toutes fins pratiques et, ce sont à peu près les seuls médecins étant capables d'intervention sociale puisque leur rémunération leur permet aussi de faire une telle chose et ils sont capables d'intervention dans le domaine psychologique puisqu'ils peuvent se permettre aussi de prendre le temps de le faire.

Les seuls véhicules, en dehors des départements de santé communautaire destinés à ce qu'on appelle la prévention ou la santé publique, sont les CLSC. Il y en a 80 sur un potentiel de 200. On peut dire, comme la théorie du verre de vin à demi plein ou à demi vide, que c'est déjà pas mal. Ce qui est plus inquiétant, c'est qu'il n'y a pas eu de nouveaux CLSC mis en chantier depuis trois ans et que les CLSC actuels, même à l'état embryonnaire, se sont vus plafonnés. Ce qui est encore plus inquiétant, c'est qu'on n'ait pas mis sur la table une alternative pour la création d'un réseau de prévention qui puisse être compréhensif, c'est-à-dire qui comprenne tout l'ensemble du territoire et qui couvre toute la population. Comme l'affirme Pierre Delva, il n'y a pas d'enseignement dans les CLSC. Les étudiants ne sont pas exposés à ce genre de pratique, ce sont des étudiants qui ne sont pas de jeunes médecins aventureux. N'ayant pas l'expérience des CLSC, ils sont exposés surtout à la médecine d'hôpital, c'est-à-dire qu'ils se trouvent à répéter les modèles auxquels ils ont été exposés au cours de leur enseignement.

La difficulté d'inscrire les nouveaux médecins dans les CLSC provient également du fait que lorsqu'un médecin commence à pratiquer à l'acte, il reçoit à l'intérieur de sa rémunération tous les frais liés à sa pratique. Il peut donc se payer une téléphoniste, une infirmière, payer son loyer, etc... Lorsqu'on inscrit un médecin à la Régie, à salaire, le médecin reçoit son salaire, l'établissement ne reçoit rien du tout et doit assumer, à partir d'un budget qui est plafonné depuis des années, les frais de fourniture médicale et les frais du personnel nécessaire à la pratique de ce médecin, avec le résultat que les postes sont extrêmement restreints pour les médecins qui veulent pratiquer, et par ailleurs la voie de facilité est celle de la soi-disant libre entreprise. Le déséquilibre, loin de se corriger, s'aggrave et on voit que, alors que plusieurs centaines de médecins ont toute la liberté de s'inscrire en polyclinique, les règles du jeu font qu'il est très difficile d'avoir une certaine croissance dans ce qu'on appelle le réseau public.

Pour ce qui est des inégalités sociales, certes beaucoup de travail a été fait, même par le présent gouvernement. On avait eu l'assurance maladie, l'assurance hospitalisation; depuis on a obtenu les médicaments gratuits, l'ambulance, les soins à domicile, les soins dentaires jusqu'à 14 ans, les prothèses gratuites. Cependant, il reste encore beaucoup d'inégalités des chances en matière de qualité de vie, d'espérance de vie. Je souligne particulièrement les conditions de santé au travail où il reste beaucoup à faire pour le travailleur d'usine, en tout cas pour ce qui est de notre territoire à Pointe-aux-Trembles. Les chances ne sont pas égales non plus pour la population générale de notre territoire. Lorsqu'on considère l'homme contemporain et sa condition, il reste encore un grand décalage pour que la médecine s'adapte et je reviens à mon premier livre écrit en sumérien où l'homme qui se meurt fait le reproche suivant à celui qui survit: "Je te criais, sauve-moi, mais tu ne m'as pas sauvé, tu avais peur et tu ne bougeais pas"; je pense qu'on mérite encore les mêmes reproches.

* * *

Marc Renaud

Je suis contre les héros. Je suis contre le fait que notre société donne très souvent une importance démesurée, quasi mystique, à certains individus. Je m'oppose à ce qu'on crée des demi-dieux avec certains individus. Je m'oppose à ceci par tempérament, par raison de ma formation sociologique, mais aussi à cause de ma vision propre de l'histoire. Quand on lit l'histoire de Norman Bethune, ce qui frappe, à part des nombreuses animosités qu'il a suscitées dans certains milieux, c'est le fait que ce sont les peuples de Montréal, d'Espagne et de Chine qui ont en réalité forgé sa conscience sociale et politique. C'est le peuple de

Montréal qui, au moment de la grande crise, marchait dans les rues pour revendiquer de meilleures conditions de vie. C'est le peuple d'Espagne qui luttait contre le fascisme, c'est le peuple de Chine qui luttait pour se libérer d'un joug séculaire. Ce sont ces peuples-là qui ont forgé la pensée sociale et politique de Bethune et qui ont fait d'un chirurgien compétent et remarquable, un homme qui était profondément engagé socialement, un ardent défenseur de l'assurance maladie, un avocat d'une réorientation plus sociale de la médecine et, un peu plus tard dans sa vie, un ardent communiste. Ce sont les peuples qui sont les véritables héros de cette histoire. Plutôt que de s'intituler le colloque Norman Bethune, ce colloque aurait peut-être dû s'intituler "colloque à la gloire du peuple montréalais des années 30", avec sous-titre, "pour tous ces hommes et ces femmes qui au cours des dernières décennies ont lutté pour l'amélioration de leur condition de vie et de santé".

Il faut bien sûr reconnaitre que Bethune était doté d'une imagination, d'une humanité, d'un courage, d'une réceptivité qui étaient remarquables. Ces qualités étaient exceptionnelles puisqu'il a réussi à incarner un certain nombre des aspirations de ces peuples et à lutter côte à côte avec ces peuples.

Pour identifier, d'un point de vue sociologique, quels étaient les problèmes les plus importants dans le domaine de la santé, je me suis demandé: "Qu'est-ce que Bethune lui-même penserait s'il était actuellement vivant et s'il habitait Montréal? Quels problèmes pour lui seraient les plus importants?" Je vous avoue que j'ai eu beaucoup de plaisir à trouver une réponse parce que Bethune était un de ces très rares personnages dans l'histoire de la médecine qui, premièrement avait un taux de non-conformisme assez élevé et, deuxièmement, s'opposait farouchement à la capacité de certains médecins, en général au corporatisme professionnel et qui, à la fin de sa vie, a décidé d'abandonner une pratique lucrative et prestigieuse pour faire cause commune avec un mouvement qu'il croyait capable d'améliorer le sort de l'humanité, capable d'améliorer la santé des gens. Il me semble qu'il serait intéressant de réfléchir à ce qu'il aurait dit, lui, aujourd'hui sur trois questions dont je me propose de traiter: l'assurance maladie, deuxièmement, les réformes Castonguay et troisièmement, les mouvements sociaux qui existent à l'heure actuelle dans le secteur de la santé.

Bethune était fort préoccupé par la nécessité de redistribuer les revenus des plus riches vers les plus pauvres dans notre société de façon à ce que la pauvreté cesse d'être la principale cause de mortalité et plusieurs de ses revendications étaient axées vers la création d'un programme d'assurance maladie. Bethune vivait au Québec au moment de la grande crise, c'est-à-dire avant que les états modernes aient développé des politiques économiques d'inspiration keynesienne, avant que ces états aient développé des programmes de sécurité sociale tels l'assurance-chômage, l'assurance-maladie, le bien-être social. Ces programmes agissent aujourd'hui comme des espèces de coussins qui empêchent la société d'éclater au moment d'une chute de l'économie et qui font en sorte que les problèmes tels le chômage, la pauvreté ou la maladie ne prennent plus des formes aussi apparemment catastrophiques qu'à l'époque de Bethune. Par exemple, nous vivons aujourd'hui dans une situation où les de taux chômage varient de 8 à 15% d'après les régions. A l'époque de Bethune, cela aurait conduit à des manifestations violentes. Aujourd'hui ce n'est pas le cas. Depuis les années trente, les gouvernements ont réussi à gérer la pauvreté, les inégalités et l'ensemble des problèmes de santé et autres qui sont associés à la pauvreté ou aux inégalités, de manière à ce que ces problèmes ne soient pas trop insupportables pour les individus impliqués, pour qu'ils ne soient pas trop explosifs, de façon à ce qu'ils ne provoquent pas une crise sociale.

Comment Bethune verrait-il cette situation? D'abord, il se préoccuperait certainement du programme d'assurance-maladie, pour lequel il s'était considérablement battu. Il verrait, et un ensemble d'études l'a démontré, que ce programme d'assurance-maladie est effectivement un programme très redistributif, c'est-à-dire qu'il améliore vraiment le sort qui est fait aux plus démunis de notre société. C'est une affirmation qui devrait être nuancée mais qui est globalement vraie: l'assurance-maladie est un programme considérablement redistributif dans ses effets. Mais, il verrait aussi des menaces sérieuses: qu'on regarde par exemple ce qui est en train de se préparer dans les provinces anglophones, en Ontario en particulier. Quand on constate qu'en Ontario, autour de 20% des médecins se désaffilient du régime d'assurance-maladie de telle manière à pouvoir charger aux patients des tarifs excédentaires à ce que l'état peut payer, on peut se poser de sérieuses questions pour l'avenir du système d'assurance-maladie. Au Québec, notre législation nous protège contre la désaffiliation des médecins. Mais, quand on regarde les discours qui se tiennent sur le ticket modérateur, quand on constate le soutien qu'obtiennent les médecins ontariens du monopole américain, on peut se demander très sérieusement si le système d'assurance-maladie québécois ne sera pas un jour menacé lui aussi. Bethune regarderait non seulement le programme d'assurance-maladie, mais il regarderait l'ensemble des politiques de sécurité sociale et essayerait de voir dans quelle mesure les politiques de sécurité sociale ont eu un impact redistributif.

Si l'on examine l'ensemble des politiques de sécurité sociale, on doit examiner à la fois le système coché bien-être pour les riches, les paiements de transferts pour les pauvres de même que les programmes de bien-être social. Il en ressort une image qui n'est vraiment pas très rose. Malgré l'ensemble des programmes de sécurité sociale qui ont été développés depuis vingt ans, le niveau relatif de pauvreté a augmenté au Canada au cours de la dernière décennie et l'écart des revenus entre les plus riches et les plus pauvres à l'intérieur de notre population est deux fois et demi plus élevé qu'en 1951. Donc, malgré les programmes de sécurité sociale il n'y a pas eu amélioration de la condition des gens mais, véritablement, la situation de la pauvreté s'est empirée. En d'autres mots, malgré toute la rhétorique qu'ont faite nos politiciens autour de la création d'une société juste, il semble que nos sociétés ne soient pas vraiment plus égalitaires qu'elles l'étaient au moment où vivait Bethune, en particulier en ce qui concerne les plus démunis de notre société.

Bethune se préoccuperait également des réformes qu'on a connues au Québec au cours des années soixante-dix. Dans certains de ses textes, Bethune a traité les politiciens de "charlatans qui ne savent que proposer des palliatifs". Il a aussi écrit à propos de la médecine et je cite: "pourriture à la médecine, la notion de projet, pourriture dans notre profession de la capacité individualiste; faisons en sorte qu'il soit mal vu de s'enrichir aux dépens de la misère humaine". Constamment Bethune s'est opposé à toute forme de demi-mesure, comme incidemment d'ailleurs notre actuel Ministre des Affaires sociales lorsqu'il signait le rapport Bédard en 1962. Pour toutes ces raisons, Bethune se serait profondément intéressé aux réformes Castonguay. Il y a dix ans, à la fin des années soixante et au début des années soixante-dix, au moment où M. Castonguay déposait un rapport et devenait ministre, un monde de possibilités nouvelles semblait pouvoir s'ouvrir. Il semblait que les problèmes de santé de la population seraient mieux pris en charge et qu'en conséquence l'état général de la santé de la population s'améliorerait. C'est ainsi par exemple que l'idée des comités de citoyens des années soixante, et plus généralement de l'ensemble du mouvement communautaire des années soixante suivant lequel les usagers seraient capables de prendre en charge les institutions sanitaires au Québec, prenait force de loi. On créait de plus de nouvelles organisations de soins de première ligne, les CLSC où, par la multidisciplinarité, la participation des citoyens devrait être en mesure de provoquer un espèce de renouvellement de la pensée médicale et de l'approche des problèmes de santé et de maladie. Pour essayer de résoudre les multiples tiraillements qui s'étaient développés à l'intérieur de la division du travail médical dans différents groupes professionnels au cours des années soixante et pour tenir compte également de l'explosion des connaissances des spécialités qui s'étaient développées, on avait essayé, au Québec, de développer une nouvelle législation, le code des professions, qui devait conduire à une certaine forme d'égalisation des statuts des différents professionnels impliqués dans le travail médical. Bref, ce qu'on avait proposé, ce qu'on avait essayé d'implanter comme législation, c'était, sinon une révolution dans le secteur de la santé, au moins une réforme en profondeur, une réforme qui allait assez loin dans ses implications.

Or, quand on regarde la situation actuelle, on ne peut être que déprimé. A l'enthousiasme des débuts a succédé la dure réalité des conflits d'intérêts des groupes extrêmement privilégiés dans notre société. Il ne fait aucun doute que le système de santé a été modernisé au Québec, en tout cas dans sa gérance. Mais le contrôle qu'on voulait donner aux citoyens, aux travailleurs, n'est peut-être pas plus significatif que le contrôle qu'ils avaient avant que les réformes soient introduites.

La course au statut professionnel et aux privilèges s'est accélérée plutôt qu'elle n'a diminué. De nouveaux centres de pouvoir sont apparus et on se demande dans quelle mesure ces nouveaux centres de pouvoir se sont établis pour véritablement aider le public ou s'ils n'ont pas simplement suscité de nouveaux conflits d'intérêts entre groupes. Peut-être est-ce là un jugement prématuré. La professionnalisation et la bureaucratisation semblent avoir été des phénomènes qui se reproduisent à outrance et, dans une certaine mesure également la syndicalisation. L'ensemble de ces trois phénomènes semble avoir provoqué une certaine fixation du système qui fait que la population bénéficie relativement peu des réformes qui ont été introduites. A cela s'ajoute la crise économique et les pressions, en particulier des milieux gouvernementaux, pour l'augmentation de la productivité des services. Ces pressions pour l'augmentation de la productivité des services ont tendance à démoraliser les travailleurs, à empêcher les initiatives créatrices et, à plus ou moins long terme, à déshumaniser les soins, à dégrader la qualité du travail et, à long terme, à dégrader la qualité de santé de ceux qui oeuvrent dans les institutions sanitaires.

Troisièmement, Bethune serait préoccupé par les mouvements sociaux qui existent à l'heure actuelle dans le secteur de la santé. Bethune, vous le savez, était un artiste, un artiste, non pas seulement par les toiles qu'il peignait, mais également par le genre de sensibilité, de réceptivité qu'il manifestait. Nul doute qu'en raison de ses qualités, il aurait été éminemment sensible aux revendications qu'expriment de nombreux groupes dans notre société. Le secteur de la santé est aujourd'hui dans une situation de remue-ménage et de remue-méninge certainement des plus incroyables, probablement la plus grande situation de remue-ménage qu'on ait vu depuis la création de la médecine scientifique moderne au milieu du siècle dernier. Quand on pense, par exemple, aux demandes soulevées par le mouvement féministe, aux demandes de professionnalisation, d'autonomie de développement d'un nouveau rapport au corps; qu'on songe au symbole que ce mouvement féministe met de l'avant la main levée avec le spéculum; qu'on songe également à tous ces groupes de personnes handicapées, de personnes âgées, qui essaient de se regrouper en coopérative ou autrement pour donner un sens à leur vie; qu'on songe au projet d'un espèce de changement radical des habitudes pathogènes de vie suggéré par les spécialistes de la santé communautaire, aux différentes demandes qui s'articulent à notre époque.

On est probablement la première génération de l'histoire humaine qui connaît, de façon vague, mais qui connaît néanmoins les causes des maladies dont les gens meurent. C'est pourquoi un ensemble de mouvements sociaux se mobilisent afin d'agir par rapport à ces causes. Il est cependant frappant qu'il y ait relativement peu de choses qui soient faites pour agir sur ces causes. Les blocages viennent de la nature même de notre vie économique, de la facon dont notre vie économiqe est organisée, où coexistent une logique industrielle orientée vers le progrès et une logique des besoins humains, une prise en charge par un système de sécurité sociale qui joue le rôle d'ambulance en situation de catastrophe personnelle, sans qu'on enraye les causes véritables des problèmes. C'est un ensemble d'autres enjeux par rapport auquel Bethune aurait été très sensible s'il avait vécu aujourd'hui. Il aurait certainement insisté profondément, par exemple, pour que les différents groupes professionnels se reprofessionnalisent, dans le sens du mot profession, quand le mot "profession" a été créé au début du 19e siècle, c'est-à-dire ce sens très digne, très noble de rendre service à la population. Il est certain que Bethune aurait insisté pour que les médecins, les infirmières cessent leurs chicanes corporatives et se mettent véritablement au service de la population.

Pour conclure si l'on croit que les enjeux pour lesquels se battait Bethune pendant les années trente au Québec sont des enjeux qui sont dépassés, je pense qu'on se trompe largement. Bien sûr, les enjeux fondamentaux dans le secteur de la santé à l'heure actuelle ont pris une forme nouvelle, au point, dans certains cas, qu'ils deviennent méconnaissables. Ainsi l'état a vu son rôle se modifier d'un rôle supplétif et de gestion des crises vers un rôle de leader, vers un nouvel ordre social. Mais au fond, les questions fondamentales que vivait Bethune n'ont pas été résolues. La santé de la population s'est améliorée, si on regarde un certain nombre d'indicateurs: espérance de vie, taux de mortalité. Des efforts réels ont été faits pour rendre notre société plus égalitaire. Mais, par ailleurs, la pratique médicale ne s'est pas ou s'est peu transformée dans une direction plus sociale. Au niveau de la division du travail, les écarts de revenus, de pouvoirs et de prestiges persistent de façon démesurée. La pauvreté, bien que plus cachée, persiste aussi. L'aliénation, la perte d'autonomie de l'ensemble des personnes humaines, a crû plutôt que diminué. Il est évident que nous ne vivons pas encore dans un monde très semblable à celui que Bethune souhaitait, semblable à celui que souhaitait *The Montreal Group for the Security of the People's Health.*

* * *

Denis Lazure

Il y a exactement trente ans cette année, c'est-à-dire en 1949, étudiant en médecine, j'avais l'occasion d'entrer en contact avec l'oeuvre et le personnage de Bethune et c'était précisément ici à l'Université McGill, dans certaines réunions étudiantes où nous étudions à l'époque les plans d'assurance hospitalisation qui étaient en train d'être installés à Saskatchewan. Nous étions un groupe d'étudiants en médecine qui nous préoccupions des aspects anti-sociaux de la médecine à l'époque. Si on s'en remet aux collègues qui nous ont parlé jusqu'ici, plusieurs de ces aspects anti-sociaux de la médecine continuent d'exister. Moi aussi je me suis posé la question, si Bethune était ici en 1979, qu'est-ce qu'il verrait comme action prioritaire de la part d'un gouvernement? Sans parler au nom du gouvernement, je vais quand même vous faire part de certaines réflexions. Le segment de la population qui inquiétait Bethune au plus haut point dans les années trente à Montréal, c'était évidemment la population en chômage dont le taux s'élevait à 30-35%, population très pauvre. On n'a plus une pauvreté aussi évidente de nos jours, mais on a quand même, au sein de la population, certaines clientèles, certains groupes qui sont méprisés, je pèse bien mes mots, méprisés et évidemment ignorés par un grand nombre de professionnels de la santé. Je parle de façon plus spécifique des personnes âgées, des personnes handicapées, des malades chroniques. Ce sont les trois clientèles, ce sont les trois groupes de population qui, depuis notre arrivée au pouvoir en 1976, retiennent notre attention prioritaire. Je pense qu'au-delà de l'accessibilité économique qui est maintenant garantie depuis plusieurs années il y a, il ne faut pas l'oublier, une non-accessibilité qui est due à des facteurs psycho-sociaux, sans parler évidemment de la non-accessibilité due à des facteurs géographiques. En ce qui concerne la non-accessibilité due à des facteurs géographiques, nous faisons des efforts considérables pour l'améliorer, y compris, par exemple, à travers la loi 103 pour la première fois un gouvernement a osé contingenter la répartition des médecins dans les hôpitaux des grands centres urbains. La cinquantaine d'hôpitaux qui ont des liens universitaires, à partir du 1er juillet prochain, ne pourra pas admettre des médecins sans avoir, dans leur hôpital, l'autorisation du conseil régional des services de santé et des services sociaux. Ça veut dire que dans un hôpital de Montréal, hôpital universitaire où on retrouve par exemple 35 internistes ou 32 pédiatres, il y aura en gel imposé pour que notre population sur la Côte Nord, en Gaspésie, en Abitibi puisse aussi avoir accès aux internistes, aux pédiatres et aux autres spécialités, même à des omnipraticiens.

L'autre inaccessibilité est encore plus importante, inaccessibilité due à des facteurs sociaux et à des mentalités de la part des professionnels de la santé. Pour ces trois groupes de population, les personnes âgées, les malades chroniques et les malades qui ont besoin de soins prolongés, plus les personnes handicapées et j'ajouterais comme quatrième groupe, les travailleurs qui subissent des agressions constantes à leur santé dans leur milieu de travail; pour ces quatre groupes de citoyens et de citoyennes, il est grandement temps que les facultés de médecine et leur corporation de médecins, se donnent comme mission, une fois pour toute, de former des médecins qui vont s'intéresser à ces populations. Je n'ai aucune hésitation à dire que la plupart des médecins qui graduent de nos quatre écoles de médecine au Québec ont un bagage tout-à-fait insuffisant de connaissances et théoriques et pratiques, en ce qui concerne la santé et la sécurité au travail, la réadaptation des handicapés, la réorientation des malades âgés et des malades qui ont besoin de soins prolongés. Je pense que Bethune serait un allié vigoureux dans cette entreprise qui vise à changer la mentalité des enseignants dans nos facultés de médecine. Ceci s'applique aussi, en faisant les transformations nécessaires, à la formation des autres professionnels de la santé, les travailleurs sociaux plus particulièrement. Je pense qu'il est grandement temps que notre corporation des médecins ainsi que les facultés de médecine, donc les universités, s'arrêtent et décident d'améliorer la conscience sociale des futurs médecins et des autres professionnels de la santé, décident d'améliorer la formation et de stimuler l'intérêt du futur médecin pour les soins auprès des personnes âgées, des malades chroniques, des malades handicapés et des travailleurs. Je pense que c'est l'essentiel de mon message.

Il y aurait bien des choses à dire sur les CLSC, idée généreuse qui continue d'être extrêmement valable; idée généreuse qui a été rabotée au départ par une grande confusion de la part du Ministère des Affaires sociales de l'ancien gouvernement, une grande confusion dans les règles du jeu pour la création et le fonctionnement des CLSC, confusion qui allait jusqu'à ne pas tenir compte des services de santé et des services sociaux qui existaient ou qui n'existaient pas dans la région ou le quartier. J'ai pu constater dès le début de 1977, à mon grand désarroi, que les soixante-dix CLSC qui existaient alors dans le Québec ont été créés au hasard, sans que les fonctionnaires du ministère et encore moins le ministre, tiennent compte des services qui existaient dans les quartiers et les régions. C'est la première fois que j'ai l'occasion de rendre publique une telle constatation et, le jour où l'on fera une étude en profondeur du fonctionnement des CLSC, je pense qu'il faudra attribuer une bonne partie du blâme à cette espèce d'insouciance de la part du Ministère des Affaires sociales à l'époque.

Le deuxième facteur qui nous empêche d'avoir une attitude totalement positive vis-à-vis les CLSC, c'est la bureaucratisation et la professionnalisation des employés dans beaucoup trop de CLSC. Illustration: dans un très grand nombre de CLSC les heures d'ouverture sont de neuf à cinq, cinq jours par semaine. Si c'est ça des soins de première ligne, à ce moment-là je me vois obligé, comme ministre responsable, de mettre en doute la compréhension de ce personnel des CLSC. Des soins de première ligne, une action communautaire qui doit rejoindre les trois objectifs fondamentaux du CLSC à l'origine: action sanitaire, action sociale, action communautaire, ces trois actions ne doivent pas être limitées de façon bureaucratique à du neuf à cinq. Je suis encore désolé d'avoir à inciter périodiquement les CLSC et la fédération des CLSC à ouvrir leur porte sept jours par semaine et tous les soirs de la semaine. Je n'arrive pas à comprendre pourquoi le même personnel des CLSC qui parfois reproche au gouvernement actuel de ne pas faire confiance suffisamment aux CLSC, avec les moyens qui existent n'a pas encore vraiment rendu plus sociale leur action, en se mettant disponibles justement non seulement le jour mais le soir aussi. Ceci étant dit, nous avons créé onze nouveaux CLSC il y a deux ans. Nous en créérons probablement d'autres l'an prochain. Nous avons préféré nous abstenir d'une création massive pour pouvoir mieux consolider. Finalement, cette année, pour la première fois, nous avons ajouté des fonds aux CLSC qui existaient, mais nous avons surtout mieux consolidé l'action sociale des CLSC. A venir jusqu'au changement de gouvernement, je peux vous affirmer que les trois clientèles déjà mentionnées étaient largement négligées par les CLSC: les personnes âgées, les malades chroniques, les personnes handicapées et un quatrième groupe, les travailleurs. A notre demande, les CLSC ont finalement initié une action majeure auprès des personnes âgées, surtout en ce qui touche l'aide à domicile. Et le jour où l'ensemble des CLSC en viendra à un esprit Bethune, plus qu'à un esprit fédération de médecins omnipraticiens ou fédération de médecins spécialistes, le jour où l'ensemble du personnel dans les CLSC manifestera une attitude beaucoup plus ouverte aux besoins souvent marginaux de la clientèle, ce jour-là je serai le premier à m'en réjouir et, à ce moment-là, on pourra assister à un déblocage plus important.

Une autre remarque concernant les CLSC. Le ministère et la fédération des CLSC ont récemment complété une étude, une évaluation, sur un grand nombre de CLSC, échantillonnage significatif, milieux urbain, rural, semi-rural. Il ressort nettement que le degré de satisfaction de la population vis-à-vis les CLSC est beaucoup supérieur en milieu rural et semi-rural. Il ressort aussi que le degré de production, si on me pardonne le mot, le degré de services rendus, est infiniment plus grand en milieu rural et semi-rural qu'en milieu urbain. Je pense, comme dernière remarque sur les CLSC, qu'un troisième facteur a fait ralentir le développement du réseau des CLSC: le manque de préoccupation du personnel des CLSC pour le service et une préoccupation excessive, d'autre part, pour une planification et une programmation professionnelle et bureaucratique. Sans vouloir revenir sur l'histoire ancienne, il faut se souvenir que, dans les premières années des CLSC, plusieurs CLSC ont mis deux ans avant de distribuer des services concrets à la population. C'est-à-dire que pendant deux ans, les CLSC pouvaient avoir, par exemple, six à neuf employés payés par les fonds publics sans fournir un seul service. Ça allait strictement à l'encontre de l'esprit Bethune. Je pense que Bethune, s'il revenait aujourd'hui ici, constatant l'abondance des moyens financiers dont disposent les CLSC, même si c'est peu comparé aux hôpitaux, serait sévère vis-à-vis la "production" de beaucoup de CLSC. Ceci étant dit, les CLSC, dans la grande majorité des cas, ont procédé depuis quelques années à une révision non seulement des programmes mais aussi de leurs attitudes. Je suis le premier à rendre hommage à la plus grande souplesse qu'on voit actuellement par les dirigeants de la plupart des CLSC.

Un dernier mot sur les modes de rémunération médicale. On connaît mes préjugés en faveur du salariat. J'ai la conviction que le mode de pratique médicale à l'acte, à la castonguette, est au départ un mode qui défavorise la prévention. C'est un mode de rémunération qui favorise, qui incite à la multiplication des actes nécessaires ou non, la nature humaine étant ce qu'elle est. Quand le revenu du médecin à la fin de l'année est strictement proportionnel au nombre d'actes qu'il a posés, il y aura certainement une tentation presque irrésistible de poser des actes nécessaires et d'autres qui ne le sont pas. Nous sommes devant une situation qu'il faut corriger, au moins en partie. Nous allons bientôt entrer en négociation intensive avec les fédérations des médecins.

Ce qu'ont dit des dirigeants syndicaux au Québec depuis quelques temps, peut s'appliquer jusqu'à un certain point aux dirigeants des syndicats professionnels: il y a abus de pouvoir quand un syndicat professionnel, un syndicat de médecins, obtient d'un gouvernement, comme il l'a fait avant l'élection en 1976 avec le gouvernement Bourassa, dans la convention collective, un droit de véto pour le président d'un syndicat de médecins, un droit de véto sur la décision qu'un médecin individuel peut prendre de pratiquer à salaire dans un établissement ou non. J'ai réagi avec beaucoup de désarroi et d'indignation en apprenant que le gouvernement antérieur a accepté que les présidents des syndicats de médecins puissent empêcher un des membres de leur syndicat d'aller pratiquer à salaire dans un établissement. Il y a souvent des médecins qui demandent d'aller pratiquer à salaire ou à la vacation dans un centre d'accueil pour personnes agées, par exemple, et leurs dirigeants syndicaux leur disent: "Non, n'y allez pas. Nous, nous favorisons les médecins à l'acte." Je pense que ces vérités doivent être dites et je demande aux dirigeants des syndicats de médecins de faire preuve d'un peu plus de sens démocratique vis-a-vis les désirs de leurs membres.

* * *

Pendant que se déroulait le colloque sur Norman Bethune, le gouvernement du Québec proposait une modification à la loi 17 sur la santé et la sécurité au travail pour l'appliquer à tous les travailleurs et non seulement aux travailleurs syndiqués. En guise de protestation, certains travailleurs syndiqués qui craignaient que le gouvernement ne se substitue aux syndicats, avaient déclaré la grève et le ministre Lazure était en négociation. Le colloque n'en avait que plus d'actualité. Plusieurs questions de la part de l'auditoire portaient sur ce sujet. D'autre participants poursuivirent le débat dans le même sens que les panelistes. Nous présentons ici quelques unes de leurs interventions. (Eds.)

Augustin Roy

Certains CLSC n'ont pas répondu à des besoins lorsqu'ils ont été organisés, mais dans les milieux ruraux comme Farnham, Lac Etchemin et d'autres ils ont très bien fonctionné et rendu les services dont la population avait besoin. Un des problèmes mentionnés à plusieurs reprises est de développer la conscience sociale des médecins, d'améliorer le cours de médecine dans ce sens, et de favoriser la distribution des médecins. Il faudrait que le gouvernement prenne le courage de s'occuper de la distribution des médecins. Actuellement il y a assez de jeunes qui veulent étudier la médecine. C'est devenu un privilège d'être admis en médecine où il y a de 3 000 à 3 300 étudiants par année. Je voudrais, comme condition d'admission, que le gouvernement oblige les étudiants en médecine, après leur cours, à passer un certain nombre d'années dans ce qu'on pourrait appeler un service civil, un service social dans les régions désignées par le gouvernement lui-même où il y aurait manque des médecins et de spécialistes.

Question: Si j'étais Bethune, je me demanderais: est-ce qu'on est capable de faire des changements sociaux aussi profonds dans notre système sans une révolution?

Suzanne Dubreuil

Je pense qu'un jour il faudra qu'on se décide à mettre l'économique au service de notre conscience québécoise; on a la conscience sociale, mais il faut que l'économique suive. Il faudrait y mettre l'argent. Une fois arrivé à ça, la seule révolution qu'il faudrait serait de changer le porte-monnaie de place, le mettre là où sont les problèmes. On a tout ce qu'il faut. On n'a pas besoin de "singer" les autre pays en terme de révolution: c'est ça la nôtre, il s'agit juste qu'on prenne nos mains et qu'on mette les bonnes affaires aux bonnes places.

Marc Renaud

C'est vraiment une bonne question, une question qui peut alimenter une discussion pendant des heures. Il me semble évident qu'il n'y a pas moyen d'avoir des changements importants dans le secteur de la santé sans qu'il n'y ait une révolution générale de l'ensemble de la société. Ceci étant dit, il reste le problème que la révolution ne se produira pas du jour au lendemain. On ne peut pas s'attendre à ce que quelque chose se produise à un moment donné, qui va entraîner un bouleversement complet de l'ordre social. Je travaille avec des gens qui ont été militants dans le temps, des vieux militants du parti communiste français, du parti communiste de l'Union Soviétique et qui, aujourd'hui, affichent une mine un peu désabusée, se disant: "on s'est battu à mort quand on était jeune et ce que l'on constate maintenant est extrêmement désespérant par rapport aux choix, aux idéaux qu'on avait au moment où on se battait à l'intérieur de ces partis". Il me semble néanmoins que, comme on ne peut espérer une révolution à court terme, il faut réfléchir sur une autre piste. L'auteur français André Gorze dit que ce qu'il fallait faire, c'était des réformes révolutionnaires, c'est-à-dire, pas des réformes qui sont les "réformettes" ne faisant que déplacer des dés sur une table, mais faire des réformes qui ont vraiment une signification pour le futur. Il y a des changements qu'on peut introduire maintenant, qui sont significatifs parce qu'ils améliorent la qualité de la vie des gens. Je pense que ce sont là les critères de base.

Dans la mesure où un changement améliore véritablement la qualité de la vie des gens, et non pas seulement celle de quelques groupes privilégiés à l'intérieur de la société, à ce moment là, ce sont des réformes acceptables. Et, c'est à ce moment là qu'on peut parler de réformes révolutionnaires, qui vont plus loin que changer les pions de place sur un échiquier.

M. Michel

Je suis médecin à salaire et je suis convaincu que c'est une bonne formule. La seule chose qui me fait peur maintenant, c'est qu'on essaie de la voir comme *la* solution et que dès qu'on aura atteint ce point-là, disons inévitable, tout va être rentré dans l'ordre. Je pense que ce qu'on attend, c'est un changement quel qu'il soit. Cela pourrait être de l'acte à l'horaire fixe, de l'honoraire fixe à l'acte. On essaie de voir par un changement que cela donne en effet un résultat. Ce n'est peut-être pas le salariat ou le travail à l'acte qui va donner ce résultat, mais le fait qu'on va changer quelque chose. Je me réfère un peu aux premiers médecins qui sont allés travailler à salaire, par exemple dans les CLSC. C'était une provocation que d'accepter d'être à salaire, mais ce n'était pas le fait d'être salarié, c'était le fait d'accepter d'être à salaire qui était important, qui faisait progresser l'affaire. Par la suite, je trouve que le fait d'aller travailler à salaire est devenu moins menaçant que c'est presque devenu une mode et, pour quelqu'un qui ne veut pas se casser la tête avec un bureau, c'est quasiment plus facile d'être à salaire. Donc, l'acte de défi, d'affirmation de quelque chose était moins fort. On le constate en regardant un peu la diminution du niveau du débat avec des gens qui sont entrés à salaire parce que c'est une formule qui était moins dangereuse qu'avant. Et je me dis que peut-être, si on constate qu'il y a une bureaucratisation, qu'on devient fonctionnaire à salaire, le danger est toujours là et que, si on commençait avec des gens qui allaient à salaire par décision, on est rendu avec des gens qui vont à salaire parce que c'est aussi bon et qu'à un moment donné on est rendu avec des gens à salaire par obligation, je me demande si on ne va pas simplement perpétuer le problème.

Claire Dutrisac

Je pense que dans les deux systèmes le médecin n'a pas de conscience sociale. S'il travaille à l'acte, il va passer ses patients très vite pour avoir plus d'argent. S'il travaille à salaire il va en passer le moins possible pour ne pas se fatiguer et on revient d'abord et avant tout à une question de conscience. Et, j'ose croire que nos médecins en ont et que nos jeunes médecins en auront encore davantage.

Maurice McGregor

I ask myself what would Bethune think about this panel, sitting down here today and I must honestly say I can't believe he would have been sitting down. I believe that, as I perceive things, he had a way of looking at the vital, important elements of what he was doing, some of them quite small and some of them big. And I think that he would cherish the reality of a health system which he was talking about in the 1930s: this revolution is ours. We have got a health system. We have been discussing doctors' salaries, cutbacks on beds, and these are very important details. I do not belittle them but I do believe that there is a reasonable sort of a health system in existence, probably better than in any other country in the world. And, I do not think he would be worrying any more about the health system. I think he would be tuning in on some of the massive social injustices in our society. If there was one thing in the health system which might rile him I suspect it would be our system of arranging the appropriate salaries or incomes, for doctors, for nurses, residents, interns and other health workers, of closing hospitals, of shutting sick people out of beds and using them as pawns and hostages. He was an ingenuous man and I would love to know what he would have suggested. But I cannot believe he would have stood by and seen his patients kicked out, shut out in the street because of some financial reason.

Marc Renaud

Je ne suis pas d'accord avec votre affirmation initiale suivant laquelle on vit maintenant dans un système extraordinaire, un système à l'intérieur duquel les problèmes sont relativement mineurs finalement, par rapport aux problèmes qui se présentaient du temps de Bethune. Je pense que c'est une illusion que de réfléchir en ces terme là. Effectivement on a un programme d'assurance-maladie; effectivement c'est redistributif, il ne faut pas se le cacher. C'est important de le dire, c'est un pas en avant; c'est une réforme révolutionnaire. C'est une réforme qui a effectivement amélioré la qualité de la vie pour les gens. Il reste néanmoins que si Bethune était présent ici aujourd'hui, il ne serait pas sensibilisé exactement aux mêmes problèmes: il a vécu il y a quarante ans à Montréal. Il serait sensibilisé aux problèmes de la sécurité. Les mécanismes de sécurité sociale qui nous sont présentés sont, dans l'ensemble, des mécanismes qui ne sont pas redistributifs. Il serait sensible au fait que la division du travail à l'intérieur des hôpitaux est une division qui est souvent très aliénante pour les travailleurs non-médicaux, par les médecins, les infirmières et les autres. Il serait sensible au fait que le mouvement féministe revendique une nouvelle façon d'approcher le corps, revendique, de la part des médecins, de la société en général, que notre société cesse d'être une oppression des corps et cesse d'être constamment en train de contrôler les individus par le biais de la médecine. Bethune s'opposerait également probablement au fait qu'on fasse toujours dévier le débat des revenus des médecins, de leur niveau de revenus par rapport au revenu général de la population, qu'on fasse constamment dévier ces débats sur des questions de salaire versus des paiements à l'acte. Il me semble qu'il y ait un ensemble d'enjeux actuels aussi importants que ceux par rapport auxquels Bethune s'est confronté. S'il vivait maintenant, c'est à ces enjeux là qu'il se confronterait.

Milla Ryerson

I think one of the first things he might think of is to think of one of his main concerns and that is peace and to try to do what he would, and convince others because it is our problem. To work for peace and to stop holding up for war, the preparations for war because if we just took one bomber and transferred it into medical care we would have lots of money. We have to make democracy work and we have to seek priorities and work for them. I am also concerned with what has taken the place of TB as number one social disease that is the psychiatric problems. They have not come up today and I am rather surprised because I feel we have to develop an alternative to the hospital for people with psychiatric problems. I started an experiment as an alternative to the hospital and we had a very good experience with a psychiatrist from a CLSC who liked what we were doing and is going to come to us once a week. I thought that would be a great thing for a doctor to go to a place of work of people with their problems instead of them going though the traumatic experience of going to her office. I think that by working together this way we can come up with all kinds of good solutions but we have to make democracy work. We can't elect a government and wait for them to do the whole job.

* * *

Abstract

Forty years after Norman Bethune's insistent demand for reform of the arrangements for health care in Depression Montreal there appear still to be grave inequalities in the availability and accessibility of medical services. The Montreal Group for the Security of the People's Health organized by Bethune, urged an experimental health care plan with four different arrangements for hospital and medical care insurance and the remuneration of physicians (see Libbie Park, this book pp. 138-144). Nevertheless the group recognized that only fundamental socioeconomic change would alleviate the discrepancies in the health status of the depressed sector of the population.

Since then, governments have assumed responsibility for hospital and medical care insurance and recently have set up local centres for community services or Centres locaux de services communautaires (CLSC). *Some eighty CLSC were established by the Quebec Government since 1971. They vary greatly in the scope and accessibility of services, in their relevance to local needs and in the avoidance of duplication of other local services and bureaucratic excess. The CLSC performance in general, has been better in rural areas.*

One of the most effective CLSC however, serves a depressed, polluted, industrial residential area where the respiratory disease mortality may be four times that of metropolitan Montreal. Close cooperation with its trade unions and the presence of medical students at work in the CLSC are features. Everywhere, however, the aged, the handicapped and the long-term ill are still underserved or neglected.

Young physicians in CLSCs are scorned by the profession for working on salary. Most are poorly prepared for community roles, especially in health promotion and responsibility sharing. Consequently, narrow patterns of medical practice are perpetuated. Better undergraduate exposure to community medicine would help.

Justice in comprehensive health care, the panelists asserted, requires basic socioeconomic change, reform in the fee-for-service remuneration system and training for all health personnel based on broader social goals and community experience. The professional corporations (guilds) should quibble less over issues of pay and prestige, and heed more the growing social conscience in society. That would be the mood of Bethune today. It was the plight and the strength of the peoples of Montreal, Spain and China, says Marc Renaud, who really forged the social and political conscience of Norman Bethune.

Résumé

Quarante ans après la présence de Norman Bethune à Montréal, un bilan des réalisation et des lacunes dans la distribution et la consommation des soins de santé révèle la persistance d'inégalités profondes. Le Montreal Group for the Security of the People's Health, *auquel appartenait Bethune, avait proposé des réformes pour relever le niveau de santé de la population en insistant sur la prévention, la diffusion des soins et le rôle accru de l'état. Le groupe reconnaissait que seuls des changements socio-économiques fondamentaux permettraient l'application des ces réformes.*

Depuis cette époque les gouvernements ont davantage assumé leur responsabilité. L'assurance maladie, l'assurance hospitalisation, la création de Centre locaux de services communautaires (CLSC) assurent une plus grande accessibilité aux soins médicaux. Ces innovations n'ont cependant pas apporté une amélioration générale du niveau de santé. Les principales causes de mortalité — maladies cardiaques, cancer, maladies cérébro-vasculaires, accidents et morts violentes — sont maintenant établies sans pouvoir être prévenues; l'espérance de vie et la qualité de la vie sont inférieures dans les milieux populaires urbains; les inégalités économiques sont responsables de problèmes non seulement physiques mais aussi psychologiques et sociaux; des secteurs de la population, personnes agées, handicappées, malades chroniques, travailleurs industriels, sont toujours négligés. La rémunération des médecins à l'acte médical conduit souvent à des abus individuels sans pour autant améliorer la qualité des traitements pour l'ensemble des gens. Par contre, le médecin qui opte pour le salariat se marginalise et l'enseignement qu'il a reçu dans les écoles de médecine ne le prépare d'ailleurs pas au service communautaire. Seules des transformations dans la mentalité des professionnels de la santé assureront un accès égal aux soins médicaux, une réorientation vers la prévention et la qualité du milieu.

A la question: "Comment Bethune aurait-il réagi à la situation actuelle?" il faut répondre qu'ayant constaté que malgré les réformes accomplies les problèmes de santé persistent, il aurait continué à mettre son esprit créateur à la recherche de solutions innovatrices non seulement pour soulager les malades, mais surtout pour éliminer les inégalités socio-économiques et l'individualisme. Si, comme il l'a déjà dit, "il est mal vu de s'enrichir aux dépens de la misère humaine", il ferait tout pour que cette misère soit pour toujours extirpée.

* * *

Reflections — Réflexions

Wendell MacLeod

Like Bethune, the planners of the conference were not content to look at the past — his times and what he did — nor at medical problems alone. I can imagine Bethune's scathing retort if we were to talk about health needs and services without thinking also how they tie in with the urgent social and economic issues of the day. He would ask, of course, for a report on our accomplishments in the past 40 years; then dare us to list our objectives for the next stage and explain our mode of planning.

The achievement of universal hospital and medical care insurance would have pleased him, particularly as it came about in Saskatchewan and Quebec. In both, planning in the health sector was the expression of relatively progressive social values and goals for action. Elsewhere in Canada, for the most part, these were neither as well defined nor as progressive. Often there was an element of expediency: to take advantage of the Federal sharing of the cost of provincial programs; also to avoid adverse public opinion at the polls.

I believe Bethune would have been excited by Quebec's decision to provide, on a large, even grandiose scale, both health and social services in cooperation with local communities, the CLSCs. He would note that some of them were highly successful and others much less so. What an opportunity for some important comparative research! What is the relative weight of different factors that determine outcome?

Bethune's respect for systematic planning was evident in 1936 in his Montreal Group for the Security of the People's Health. Earlier, his style was to harangue passionately for a mammoth state-medicine scheme that could be accomplished only by radical restructuring of society. His political advisors soon induced him, however, to concentrate on a more limited objective, one that would meet quite soon the most pressing and visible need in medical services. This was the need for access by all to decent care, both curative and preventive, without financial or other barriers. As Libbie Park has described succinctly elsewhere in this book (pages 138-144), the method was one of controlled experimentation: to try out, concurrently if possible, four types of service organization, not different in essence from others under way at that time or projected elsewhere in Canada. Expert evaluation of the outcome would shape further health policies. It was to be research for action that would benefit *all* people. Meanwhile it was necessary to persuade the health professions and the politicians; the public, with its own awareness of need, would follow. You know the rest of the story: Duplessis was elected in August and Bethune went in October to the Spanish Civil War.

Looking back on those months of high-pitched zeal and effort, from January through August 1936, I marvel at our considerable innocence in what we may call the art and science of communication. To send out several hundred letters to argue for immediate, innovative action, no matter how urgent and logical, in the very conservative field of largely private hospitals and ancient professions, hoping for acceptance or even lively debate, was naïve. It was a far cry from today's sophisticated techniques in "social marketing", which may have some success in planting an idea or changing an attitude, even if only to buy a new soap. In some other respects, however, our communication skills are still far from well developed. I am thinking of the trouble we still have in "coping with difference" — between institutions, nations, cultural entities and, particularly, ideologies. Some decades from now, unless we have another world war, perhaps today's efforts to communicate effectively will appear as primitive as we now regard the sanitary arrangements of a century ago.

Suzanne Dubreuil and Claire Dutrisac have pointed out how important it is for us as professionals and health workers to have better communication with the people who receive our care. We must explore various approaches that we haven't used very much. For example, it is often difficult for a solo practitioner to get to know his patient's background. When people work together as a team, with different skills and aptitudes, it is possible to make more progress in understanding the total milieu, not only the technological things (being handled so well at Pointe-aux-Trembles by Marc Lavallée and his colleagues), but also the very private things that make health problems difficult to tolerate. Perhaps doctors' offices should have meetings from time to time with the people who receive the care and who could say out loud how it all looks to them; but this should be easier in a group practice or in a CLSC.

For nearly 20 years I have not been a doctor in the ordinary sense. I have lived in Ottawa without being licensed to serve there, but I hear what our medical system looks like in the eyes of many people who come to it for help. It's not only a problem of accessibility in the ordinary sense but often the cultural distance between the doctor or nurse, in many private offices, and many of those who come for care is so wide that it is almost impossible to do the best job. It is vital, of course, to learn to listen patiently to the person, to encourage an unfolding of the whole story, perhaps to meet the family in the home. This is where the street clinic, the CLSC and other types of multi-resource centre can make a unique contribution. It includes experimentation in sharing responsibility for various components of care among professionals, other health workers and volunteers trained on the spot. Basic to the whole effort is becoming skilled in cooperation in a continuing partnership with the people being served. Guidelines emerging from such experience would be immensely useful.

The Montreal Group did not use today's term "interdisciplinary". Group medical practice was the obvious pattern and we took for granted that the planning process would involve *all* who provided care, as we did the judgment of those who would receive it. The first job was to study the experience of other countries in trying to provide basic services for all its citizens — and some had been at it for a century or more. So each member took a country (mine was Denmark), read up on it and reported to the group. Out of the study came proposals that seemed to be feasible but, as it turned out, the time was not yet ripe.

This kind of historical, comparative study is only the first step in scientific method but it helps us to recognize trends and the reasons for them. What I am suggesting is that much of the angry, shouting argument about some of today's problems will subside when more of us determine to collect the facts objectively and analyse them rationally. More than one hypothesis may need testing and some solutions can only be tentative. But in the long run we will make better progress that way.

Bethune would notice, no doubt, great gaps in our accomplishments. We have yet to learn how to distribute health personnel geographically and by social class in order to serve all groups fairly. Part of our population still has the dismal health and social record of a considerably less developed country. We have made only a slight dent in the problem of faulty lifestyles that cause misery, inefficiency and premature disability and death. Even more sad is our still widespread apathy in these matters.

Perhaps we, today, need an angry, energetic Bethune committed foremost to serving his patients and sensitive to others in need. Certainly he would not hesitate to criticize our attitudes to work and money. What would he make, for example, of our squabbles over hours of duty, incomes and matters of status? For in China, he rejected the extra $100 a month offered him, asking that it be used to bring small comforts to his sick and wounded soldiers and peasants.

Looking at our society as a whole, beyond the health care system, Bethune would have a crisp reaction. I think he would explode! He would recognize too much of what had revolted him before: our selfish preoccupation; our general indifference to gross disparities and indignities, at home and abroad; and our narrow nationalism and failure in so many ways to profit from the experience of two world wars and other conflicts. He would point the finger at an economic and social structure that leads inevitably towards self-destruction. I doubt that he would spend much time on conferences unless they led to action.

Bethune has left us a legacy. The challenge is in our court.

Résumé

Le bilan social et médical des quarante années qui se sont écoulées depuis la mort de Bethune trace la voie aux réformes qu'il reste toujours à opérer. Si nous avons aujourd'hui l'assurance maladie l'assurance hospitalisation, les CLSC, néanmoins plusieurs problèmes demeurent non résolus. Nous n'avons pas résolu la question de l'acceptance des différences sociales; nous n'avons pas éliminé la distance culturelle qui sépare le médecin, l'infirmière et le/la patient(e); et nous n'avons pas réussi à rejoindre tous les groupes sociaux, quelle que soit leur région ou leur classe sociale, de façon égalitaire. Il faut admettre que Bethune, aujourd'hui, reconnaîtrait trop de problèmes, d'attitudes, de situations qu'il nous reste à changer en s'inspirant de son message.

* * *

REFERENCE AND NOTES

1. Malcolm G. Taylor, *Health Insurance and Canadian Public Policy. The Seven Decisions that Created the Canadian Health Insurance System,* McGill-Queen's University Press, Montreal, 1978. (Quebec Medicare, pp. 379-413).
2. Ministère des Affaires sociales, direction des services communautaires, *Compilation régionale et provinciale de données factuelles portant sur la situation respective des CLSC au 31 décembre 1979, Québec, avril 1980.* Ministère des Affaires sociales, Hôtel du Governement, Québec, (Province Québec).
3. Le CLSC, acteur d'une meilleure politique de santé au Québec, document support au congrès annuel de la Fédération des CLSC du Québec, septembre 1980, Fédération des CLSC, 284, Carré St-Louis, Montréal, (Québec) H2X 1A4.

Appendix — Annexe A

BETHUNE

His Times and His Legacy / Son époque et son message

Programme

November 16-18, 1979
McGill University,
Montreal, Quebec

Du 16 au 18 novembre, 1979
Université McGill
Montréal, Québec

The Bethune Foundation is sponsoring a conference to mark the 40th anniversary of Dr. Norman Bethune's death in China, on November 12, 1939. The conference will focus on the significant interests and experiences of Bethune in their historical context and their implications for today. The conference is not an exercise in Bethune idolatry, but presents an interdisciplinary approach to his times, and to issues that were important to him.

La Fondation Bethune organise une conférence pour marquer le quarantième anniversaire de la mort du docteur Norman Bethune survenue en Chine le 12 novembre 1939. Cette conférence place les intérêts et les expériences de Bethune dans leur contexte historique et examine tout ce que cet homme nous a laissé. Loin d'être la manifestation d'un culte rendu à Bethune, elle donne un aperçu interdisciplinaire de son époque et des causes qu'il prenait à coeur.

Friday, November 16, 1979 / Le vendredi 16 novembre 1979

Welcome and Introduction / Discours de bienvenue et présentation
Mary Rosamond Weil
The Bethune Foundation / de la Fondation Bethune
S.O. Freedman
Dean, Faculty of Medicine, McGill University / doyen de la Faculté de Médecine de l'Université McGill

1st Session: Early years — A son of the manse and labourer-teacher / 1ère séance: Les années de jeunesse: né d'un père pasteur et éducateur d'ouvriers
Moderator / Présidente: Hilary Russell

The Presbyterian and evangelical setting / Le milieu évangélique et presbytérien
Richard Allen

Frontier College: worker education and illiteracy, 1899-1979 / Frontier College: l'instruction des travailleurs et l'analphabétisme 1899-1979

Historical / Perspective historique
Marjorie Zavitz Robinson

Contemporary / Points de vue contemporains
Jack Pearpoint

2nd Session: Crises — World War I and tuberculosis / 2e séance: Les crises: la Première Guerre mondiale et la tuberculose
Moderator / Président: William C. Gibson

Battlefield medicine and the stretcher bearer's experience / La médecine des champs de bataille et le brancardier
Charles G. Roland

Fighting the "White Plague": The anti-tuberculosis campaign
Katherine McCuaig

Personal reflections
G.J. Wherrett

3rd Session: Professional life — Montreal between the wars
Moderator: Augustin Roy

Dr. Edward Archibald and the new medical science
H. Rocke Robertson

Life and death at two Montreal hospitals:

   The Royal Victoria Hospital
   Jessie Boyd Scriver

   l'Hôpital du Sacré-Coeur
   Pierre Delva

The creative impulse — medical instruments
David A.E. Shephard

4th Session: Artistic life — poetry and painting
Moderator: Leo Kennedy

"Bethune and his brethren": depression poetry in English Montreal
Lee Thompson

Painting in the thirties and the children's art school
Panelists: Charles Hill, Louis Mulhstock, Marian Scott

Saturday, November 17, 1979

1st Session: The health of the people in depression Montreal
Moderator: Wendell MacLeod

The health of the working class
Terry Copp

The Bethune health group
Libbie Park

La lutte contre la tuberculose
Katherine McCuaig

Réflexions personnelles
G.J. Wherrett

3e séance: La vie professionnelle — Montréal entre les deux guerres
Président: Augustin Roy

Le docteur Edward Archibald et la nouvelle science médicale
H. Rocke Robertson

La vie et la mort dans deux hôpitaux montréalais:

   L'hôpital Royal Victoria
   Jessie Boyd Scriver

   L'hôpital du Sacré-Coeur
   Pierre Delva

L'impulsion créatrice — les instruments médicaux
David A.E. Shephard

4e séance: La vie artistique — poésie et peinture
Président: Leo Kennedy

"Bethune et ses confrères": la poésie anglaise pendant la Crise à Montréal
Lee Thompson

La peinture dans les années trente et les classes d'art pour enfants
Participants: Charles Hill, Louis Mulhstock, Marian Scott

Le samedi 17 novembre 1979

1ère séance: L'état de santé des Montréalais pendant la Crise
Président: Wendell MacLeod

L'état de santé de la classe ouvrière
Terry Copp

Le groupe d'étude de Bethune
Libbie Park

2nd Session: Political commitment — views from the inside
Moderator: Andrée Lévesque

The left and the working-class movement

In the thirties
Stanley B. Ryerson

After the thirties
Madeleine Parent

3rd Session: Bethune's Spain
Moderator: Graham Spry

Reminiscences of the War
Henning Sorensen (letter)

By a foreign correspondent and Bethune's friend and colleague
Ted Allan

By a veteran of the Mackenzie-Papineau Batallion
Ross Russell

Moving blood in war time
Paul G. Weil

4th Session: Bethune's China and China's Pai Chiu-en
Moderator: Robert Garry

With Bethune in Yenan
Ma Haide (George Hatem)

The living Bethune
Paul T.K. Lin

Developing China
Lü Wanru

Banquet Address: The Bethune Legend
Maurice McGregor

Sunday, November 18, 1979

Beyond Bethune: Controversy in today's health care — the Quebec experience
Moderator: Pierre Delva

Claire Dutrisac
Marc Lavallée
Denis Lazure
Marc Renaud
Robert Robson

2e séance: L'engagement politique — vue de l'intérieur
Présidente: Andrée Lévesque

La gauche et le mouvement ouvrier dans les années trente
Stanley B. Ryerson

L'organisation syndicale après les années trente
Madeleine Parent

3e séance: L'Espagne de Bethune
Président: Graham Spry

Souvenirs de guerre
Henning Sorensen (lettre)

Par un correspondant étranger, ami et collègue de Bethune
Ted Allan

Par un ancien combattant du bataillon Mackenzie-Papineau
Ross Russell

Le transport du sang en temps de guerre
Paul G. Weil

4e séance: La Chine de Bethune et le Pai Chiu-en des Chinois
Président: Robert Garry

Avec Bethune à Yenan
Ma Haide (George Hatem)

Bethune toujours vivant
Paul T.K. Lin

Le développement de la Chine
Lü Wanru

Causerie: Bethune, sa légende
Maurice McGregor

Le dimanche 18 novembre 1979

Après Bethune: controverse actuelle concernant les soins médicaux — l'expérience québécoise
Président: Pierre Delva

Claire Dutrisac
Marc Lavallée
Denis Lazure
Marc Renaud
Robert Robson

Appendix — Annexe B

BIBLIOGRAPHY OF SOURCES RELATING TO NORMAN BETHUNE/ BIBLIOGRAPHIE D'ÉCRITS DE BETHUNE ET D'OUVRAGES SUR BETHUNE

I: References to Articles on Medical Topics by Bethune/ Articles par Bethune sur des sujets médicaux

"Some New Instruments for the Injection of Lipiodol, — Oil-guns and a Combined Cannula and Mirror," *Canadian Medical Association Journal*, 20 (1929), pp. 286-287.

"Note on Bacteriological Diagnosis of Spirochaetosis of the Lung," *Canadian Medical Association Journal*, 20 (1929), pp. 365-368.

"A New Combined Aspirator and Artificial Pneumothorax Apparatus," Ibid., 20 (1929), 662.

"The Technique of Bronchography for the General Practitioner,"*Canadian Medical Association Journal*, 21 (1929), pp. 662-667.

With David T. Smith and J.L. Wilson, "Etiology of Spontaneous Pulmonary Disease in the Albino Rat," *Journal of Bacteriology*, 20 (1930), pp. 361-370.

"A Plea for Early Compression in Pulmonary Tuberculosis," *Canadian Medical Association Journal*, 27 (1932), pp. 36-42.

"A Phrenicectomy Necklace," *American Review of Tuberculosis*, 26 (1932), pp. 319-321.

"Cotton-seed Oil in Progressively Obliterative Artificial Pneumothorax," *American Review of Tuberculosis*, 26 (1932), pp. 763-770.

"The Silver Clip Method of Preventing Hemorrhage While Severing Interpleural Adhesions. —With With a Note on Transillumination", *Journal of Thoracic Surgery*, 2(1933), pp. 302-306.

"With William Moffatt, Experimental Aspergillosis with Aspergillus Niger; Superimposition of this Fungus on Primary Pulmonary Tuberculosis," *Journal of Thoracic Surgery*, 3 (1933), pp. 86-98.

"Pleural Poudrage. — A New Technique for the Deliberate Production of Pleural Adhesions as a Preliminary to Lobectomy," *Journal of Thoracic Surgery*, 4 (1935), pp. 251-261.

"A Case of Chronic Thoracic Empyema Treated with Maggots," *Canadian Medical Association Journal*, 32 (1935), pp. 301-302.

"Maggot and Allantoin Therapy in Tuberculosis and Non-tuberculosis Suppurative Lesions of the Lung and Pleura," *Journal of Thoracic Surgery*, 5 (1936), pp. 322-328.

"Reflections on Return from 'Through the Looking Glass'," *Bulletin of the Montreal Medico-Chirurgical Society* (March-April, 1936), pp. 31-33.

"Some New Thoracic Surgical Instruments," *Canadian Medical Association Journal*, 35 (1936), pp. 656-662.

"Take Private Profit Out of Medicine," *Canadian Doctor*, 3 (January, 1937), pp. 11-16.

II: Some General References about Bethune/ Quelques références générales sur Bethune

Ted Allan, "The Making of a Martyr," *Canadian Magazine*, 12 July 1975, pp. 20-3.

―――――, "The Sinner who Became a Saint," *Canadian Magazine*, 5 July 1975, pp. 2-8.

Ted Allan and Sydney Gordon, *The Scalpel, the Sword: the Story of Dr. Norman Bethune* (Rev. ed.), McClelland and Stewart, Toronto, 1971, c. 1952.

Martin Avery, "Chinese Gold," In *80 Best Canadian Stories,* Clarke Blaise and John Metcalfe (eds.), Oberon, Ottawa, 1980.

E.W. Barootes, "Dr. Norman Bethune: Inspiration for a Modern China," *Canadian Medical Association Journal*, 122 (1980), pp. 1176-84.

Bethune: His Story in Pictures/ Son Histoire illustrée, (Trans. J. Endicott et al; Intro. Barry Lord), NC Press, Toronto, 1975.

Harry Bloch, "Norman Bethune M.D. (1890-1939): Medical Humanist," *New York State Journal of Medicine*, 74 (1974), p. 1856.

Harvey Botting, "Dr. Norman Bethune the Unknown Legend," *Canada and the World*, 37 (February, 1972), p. 22.

Chih Cheng Chung, (adapted by), *Norman Bethune in China,* Foreign Languages Press, Peking, 1975.

Ioan Davies, "Fairy Tale IV," *Canadian Forum*, October 1975, pp. 30-1.

"Dr. Henry Norman Bethune," *Canadian Medical Association Journal,* 42 (1940), p. 95.

"Dr. Norman Bethune: Red China's Canadian Hero. He is a Legend to Millions — But at Home Few Even Know His Name," *Weekend Magazine,* No. 46, 1964, pp. 42-6.

Sylvia Du Vernet. *Poems of Pride for Norman Bethune,* Herald-Gazette Press, Bracebridge, Ont., 1976.

_____, *Pai Chiu-en, Poems the Chinese People Told Me About Norman Bethune,* Herald-Gazette Press 1978.

Leo Eloesser, "In Memoriam: Norman Bethune 1980-1939," *Journal of Thoracic Surgery,* 9 (1940), pp. 460-1.

Jean Ewen, *China Nurse: 1932-1939: A Young Canadian Witnesses History,* McClelland and Stewart, Toronto, 1981.

F.H. Fish, "Norman Bethune 1889-1939," *Calgary Associate Clinic Historical Bulletin,* 10 (February, 1946), pp. 151-9.

Lincoln Fisher, "Obituary, Norman Bethune 1890-1939," *American Review of Tuberculosis,* 41 (1940), pp. 819-21.

David Frank, "N. Bethune: National Hero," *Canadian Dimension,* 9 (March, 1973), pp. 7-8.

William C. Gibson, "Bethune's China — 40 Years On," *Journal of the American Medical Association,* 242 (1979), p. 2091.

Sydney Gordon and Ted Allan, *Docteur Bethune* (Trad. Jean Paré), Editions de l'Etincelle, Montréal, 1973.

Harold Horwood, "Norman Bethune: the Rebel China Reverses," *Readers' Digest,* January 1975, pp. 36-41.

Paul Jackson, *Norman Bethune, 1890-1939: Médecin du Peuple,* Editions Drapeau Rouge, Montréal, 1979.

_____, *Norman Bethune, 1890-1939: People's Doctor,* Red Flag Publications, Montreal, 1979.

Rod Langley, *Bethune: A Play,* Talonbooks, Vancouver, 1975.

Anne MacDermot, "Norman Bethune, Médecin canadien, L'un des cinq héros de la Chine," *Le Magazine MacLean,* août 1962, pp. 20, 48-50.

_____, "The only Canadian the Chinese Ever Heard Of," *MacLean's,* 19 May 1962, pp. 18-9, 62-4.

Wendell MacLeod, Libbie Park and Stanley Ryerson, *Bethune: the Montreal Years. An Informal Portrait,* Lorimer, Toronto, 1978.

Mao Zedong, "In Memory of Norman Bethune," *Chinese Medical Journal,* 84 (1965), pp. 699-700.

_____, "In Memory of Norman Bethune," *China's Medicine,* 5 (1967), pp. 325-33.

Gabriel Nadeau, "A TB's Progress. The Story of Dr. Norman Bethune," *Bulletin of the History of Medicine,* 8 (1940), pp. 1135-71.

"Norman Bethune in Muskoka," *Monthly Review,* 28 (June, 1976), pp. 56-8.

"Norman Bethune — Internationalist Fighter Imbued with Mao Tse-tung's Thought," *China's Medicine,* 7 (1968), pp. 371-85.

"Norman Bethune, the Great Champion of Internationalism," *Chinese Medical Journal,* 84 (1964), pp. 701-2.

Obituary, "The Path of Genius," *Saturday Night,* 55, (9 December, 1939), p. 1.

Jean Paré, "Le Docteur rouge," *Le Magazine MacLean,* mars 1973, pp. 26-7, 43-6.

T. Redekop, "Dr. Norman Bethune, 1890-1939," *University of Manitoba Medical Journal,* 37 (1965), pp. 18-22.

C.G. Ross, "Thoughts upon Norman Bethune — the Great Nightfall Looms," *Canada Month,* 12 (1972), pp. 8-10.

Mary Larratt Smith, *Prologue to Norman: the Canadian Bethunes,* Mosaic Press, Valley Editions, Oakville, 1976.

Ellen Stafford (ed.), *Flamboyant Canadians,* Baxter Publishing, Toronto, 1964.

Peter Stevens, *And the Dying Sky Like Blood: a Bethune Collage for Several Voices,* Borealis Press, Ottawa, 1974.

Roderick Stewart, *Bethune,* New Press, Toronto, 1973.

_____, *Bethune* (Trad. Jacques Gouin), Editions du Jour, Montréal, 1976.

_____, *The Mind of Norman Bethune,* Fitzhenry and Whiteside, Toronto, 1977.

_____, *Norman Bethune,* Fitzhenry and Whiteside, Toronto, 1974.

_____, *Norman Bethune* (Trad. Albert Ledoux), Editions Julienne, Longueil, 1976.

George Woodcock, "Norman Bethune: the Man and the Myth," *Quill & Quire,* 43 (13 October 1977), p. 5.

Appendix — Annexe C

An open letter to all political candidates seeking election in Montreal

Dear Sir:

The enclosed are the proposals made by the Montreal Group for the Security of the People's Health to the various political parties in the coming election. We earnestly urge you to give them you deepest consideration for inclusion as a health plank on your platform. These proposals have been drawn up after considerable study by a large group of Montreal doctors, dentists, nurses, statisticians and Social Service Workers. Would you be good enough to send us a written reply in regard to these proposals.

We ask you to bring up the question of state responsibility for the maintenance of the People's Health in all your public meetings and addresses to the electorate, so that the medical, dental and nursing professions may know your stand in this tremendously important matter.

Very sincerely yours,

Norman Bethune,
Secretary,
Montreal Group for the Security of the
 People's Health,
1154 Beaver Hall Square,
Montreal, P.Q.

NB/MW
August 10th, 1936

The Montreal Group for the Security of the People's Health is a non-political organization of Physicians, surgeons, dentists, nurses, social service workers and statisticians formed in the winter of 1935-1936 to study the relationship of present day medicine to the people and to the state, in all the civilized countries of the world, with particular attention to the Dominion of Canada and the Province of Quebec.

The reasons for the urgent necessity of such a study were drawn up by the group in its fundamental platform.

1. There is an underlying feeling that medicine, as now practiced in this country, does not serve adequately either the patient or the physician.

2. Our civilization in recent years has undergone and is undergoing profound socio-economic changes which have altered both individual and group relationships. Although medical science has made tremendous progress, yet the application of these advances have not been fully utilized either to the benefit of the people or the profession.

3. The cause of this incomplete utilization lies in the uneven distribution of the products of scientific knowledge and research, with a lack of purchasing power of the people.

The doctor is a producer. The doctor is a commodity producer; the commodity he produces is the application of his knowledge of health and the means and measures he takes to combat disease. He, like the rest of society into which he is closely interwoven, is suffering today because he can find but few consumers able to pay for his product. In short, "production relationships", in terms of political economics, between producer and consumer are maladjusted and distorted. Medicine as a part of modern society presents the same contradictions in miniature as effects the whole. These contradictions may be characterized as poverty of purchasing power in the midst of plenty.

4. There is a growing realization that the adequate prevention and cure of disease has gone beyond the capacity of individual practitioners or charitable institutions, and that it demands the recognition by the state of the following principle — the maintenance of the health of the population is one of the fundamental functions and duties of the state and should be undertaken by the state under the same necessities as it has taken over public education, the police, the army and fire protection.

5. What's wrong with our practice of Medicine at present?

A. *Patient's View*

1. The vast majority of the population (based on sociological division of three groups) cannot pay for adequate medical aid.

2. Even such medical aid as supplied by charity is inadequate, unless in cases of extreme illness requiring hospitalization.

3. There is an appalling lack of provision for preventive and hygienic measures in the community.

B. *Doctor's View*

1. Individualistic general practice of medicine cannot supply the full benefits of modern science owing to the high degree of specialization demanded by advancing knowledge.

2. Preventive medicine in the real sense of the term is not practiced being non-remunerative.

3. Since the vast majority of people cannot even pay for inefficient service which the doctor is willing to render, the demands made on the physician's charity are beyond those of any other social group. This produces an accentuation of the economic crisis of medicine which leads to a lowering of altruistic principles and high morale of the profession; the doctor is enslaved by drudgers work, his relative poverty prevents post-graduate work and vacation, his economic security is precarious, and the incidence of early death is well known.

4. The state has already recognized in part its obligations to its citizens by taking over certain medical functions, e.g. the care of contagious diseases, inspection of school children, food inspection, pre-natal care, etc. Should it not extend these activities to cover the entire field of prevention and cure of disease for all classes of society.

In view of the coming Provincial Elections in this Province, it would appear to be a most opportune time to put forward some definite plan or plans to the political parties seeking election, expressing the collective demands of the allied medical, dental and nursing professions.

The recently instituted Unemployment Medical Relief Commission in Montreal is a step in the right direction. At the same time, other plans should be presented by the organized professions (the English and French doctors, dentists and nurses) to embrace the entire province.

The following suggestions are made:

1. It is the grave duty of the combined professions to point out to our politicians the present deplorable, yet remediable, condition of the health of our citizens. Our knowledge of health and disease places this moral responsibility firmly on our shoulders.

2. From each political party, demands should be made that, as a prominent plank on their respective platforms, State responsibility for the health of its citizens — whether employed or otherwise — is a primary principle. A man should not lose his rights as a citizen because he loses his job. The Honourable Norman Rogers in the House of Commons, March 30th, 1936 said "The Welfare of its citizens is the prime duty of the State".

3. That on no account an attempt be made after the election, on the false ground of economy, to abolish the present medical relief for the unemployed in Montreal.

4. That, if alterations in the present set-up of the Commission be contemplated in the future, they should tend towards increasing the amount set aside for the Commission's functioning. This is 25¢ a month per person on relief. An increase to 50¢ per month (as the Ontario Government has found advisable in certain districts) should be demanded.

5. That, in view of the possibility of a reduction in the monthly accounts of doctors under the Commission, such reductions should be strenuously opposed unless a proportionate reduction be made in the accounts of the other recipients, i.e. the druggists. Here the principle that the doctor (precisely as the druggist) is selling a commodity, should be rigidly maintained. This should be the end of the exploitation of the medical profession. It has been carrying the burden of the unemployed and low income groups for years.

6. If the proposed proportionate distribution of funds to doctors (80%) and to druggists (20%), dentists nil, nurses nil, on the basis of 25¢ a month allocated for each unemployed, be found to be, in practice, out of all proportion to this, that the municipalities should set up three or more city drug dispensaries to take the excessive profits out of filling prescriptions, and furnish drugs to its unemployed citizens at cost price.

That such an event of uneven distribution is not beyond possibility, the experience of the Municipality of Lachine, in 1935, may be quoted: —

To drug stores	—	$9,224	equals	60%
To doctors	—	4,918	"	32%
To dentists	—	1,263	"	8%
TOTAL		$15,405	"	100%

Under the present Montreal Commission, the distribution proposed would have been as follows:

To drug stores	—	$3,081	equals	20%
To doctors	—	12,324	"	80%
To dentists	—	Nil	"	Nil
TOTAL		$15,405	"	100%

7. That in the event of a marked reduction of doctors' monthly accounts for service to the unemployed being made (for example, 25% to 50% of their total) on the plea of the Commission's inability to pay, that the following plan be substituted. The factual basis of the following plan is founded on the figures of the Montreal Relief Commission for March:

Heads of families (men or women) unemployed	—	65,785
Dependents of the above	—	102,122
Unemployable	—	2,269
TOTAL ON RELIEF	—	170,176

At 25¢ per month, the yearly income of the Commission for medical relief for distribution to doctors and druggists is 170,176 x .25 x 12 equals $510,528.00. Of this amount, the doctors' share will be 80% equals $408,420.00. Of the 1200 doctors in Montreal, 800 have registered on the Commission's list. This would permit an average of $500.00 odd per year for each registered doctor. If the 170,176 persons on relief would be evenly divided, each of the registered doctors would have 212 patients. The proposed plan, in the event of the probability of the breakdown of the present scheme, is as follows: —

8. A City Medical Planning Board be formed by representatives of the English and French doctors, dentists and nurses. Any registered doctor in good standing in his medical society (this would be necessary for proper disciplinary control) may register with the Board and practice under this scheme. He might be allowed to accept a maximum of 500 patients on his list. The patients should have the right of choice of doctor and also right of change at certain fixed intervals. For these doctors accepting relief patients, abolish entirely the antiquated system of fee-for-service and substitute a per capita payment for an all-in service. It would cost no more than the present system ($3.00 a year for each patient). It would do an end with padding accounts, dishonest calls, dishonest prescriptions. It would reduce the overhead of the commission. An Appeal Board should be set up to deal with patients and doctors complaints.

Additional Medical Relief

Not only must the present medical relief be maintained, but it must be expanded and increased to include surgical dental treatment, home nursing and proportionate payments to the hospitals for the use of the outdoor departments.

9. The outdoor departments of our Hospitals would be utilized as consultant departments. A staff fund to be distributed equitably among doctors, internes, and nurses should be allocated to each Hospital treating the unemployed, both in indoor and outdoor department. Doctors treating relief patients urgently require the service of the outdoors for special investigation and advice and the hospitals should be paid for this service. An additional $3.00 per capita per year would cover this essential service.

10. The present hospitalization plan under the Q.P.C.A. to continue, but amended to eliminate the property-owning clause.

11. Thus, an additional 25¢ per month bringing medical expenditure per capita for those on relief to 50¢ per month, instead of the present 25¢ would cost approximately $1,021,056.00 a year, or $6.00

per capita on relief a year (based on the March 1936 figures of 170,000). The suggestion is made that the additional 25¢ per month be paid by the Provincial Government.

12. Resistance should be made to the appointment of "Relief Doctors" on salary. The English experience of this system is unsatisfactory.

13. A City Nursing Planning Board should be set up to unify the activities of the County Health Unit Nurses, Welfare Nurses, School Nurses and Victorian Order of Nurses, and work in close conjunction with the City Medical Planning Board. There is much wasteful re-duplication of administration and there should be a marked extension of all the above mentioned groups, each autonomous in their individual field but under central control. The Home Nursing Service for the Unemployed should be paid for out of the additional 25¢ per month.

14. That the Central City and Provincial Medical Planning Boards set up a Medical Commission to study the effect of the depression and continued unemployment with the low subsistance food allowance under relief. Malnutrition predisposition to deficiency diseases, tuberculosis, etc. should be studied. This group of nearly 200,000 people should be thoroughly investigated from the physical, psychiatric, racial, sociological, occupational points of view. The present situation presents a unique opportunity to collect a mass of invaluable data and must be seized. Routine inspection of school children in 1935 found that over 50% were suffering from various defects. Half of the defective had dental caries (due to lack of minerals and Vitamins) and 8626 (14%) were suffering from malnutrition. The effects of undernourishment may not show themselves for years as Dr. G.C.M. McGonigle, medical officer of Health for Stockton-on-Tees, England, in his recent book "Poverty and Public Health" has shown. It is true those on relief are not starving to death — they are merely starving.

15. To educate the wives and daughters of men on relief in the purchase and preparation of a more evenly balanced diet than they are at present obtaining, it is suggested that the Relief Commission set up a number of model kitchens in each ward, (vacant stores can be utilized) where expert dietitians will give practical demonstrations of the preparation of balanced meals, even on the present low relief allowance for food. The church and press should be urged to give these demonstrations wide publicity. The Montreal Light, Heat and Power Commission should be enlisted to furnish gas stoves, and other commercial firms, utensils etc. The cooked food so prepared could be sold at cost price to those on relief, so that eventually a communal centre with communal kitchens (especially for the single) would be set up with cooperative pooled resources. This might be extended to include "Infant Parking" for exhausted mothers, free movies and occupational therapy shops such as a co-operative shoe-repair, carpentry, dress-making. The result of unemployment is gradual deterioration of physical and mental morale. We must actively combat this deterioration.

16. A physical examination of every unemployed man or woman, put to work with the proposed Bouchard Plan, should be demanded. Continued under-nourishment under the present relief food allowance combined with inadequate clothing (a single man now has $1.80 a week to feed himself and 15¢ a week for clothing) will most certainly predispose many such men and women to serious illness if forced to work under unfavorable climatic conditions.

17. That, following the resolution passed by the Ontario Medical Association at their last meeting, favoring experimental programmes under the auspices of the local medical societies, the following plans be tried in carefully selected localities in the Province of Quebec. These four plans are typical of the large number now under discussion all over the world and could be used as controls to each other in a proper scientific manner.

18. *FIRST PLAN — MUNICIPAL MEDICINE.*

This would be an amplification and extension of the present full-time health unit system of the Public Health Service of the Province. A full-time team of doctors, dentists, nurses, including all specialties such as surgery, gynecology, obstetrics, paediatrics, etc., should be selected (*not* politically appointed) by a Provincial Medical Planning Board (to be set up by the Medical, dental and nursing societies) and placed in a given municipality, provided with a small modern hospital (a new one to be built or an older one to be modernized). They would take over and control the health prevention and cure of disease for the entire population, irrespective of economic or social grouping. All such members of this combined medico-surgical, dental, nursing group should be placed on salary. Such a team of active, keen and highly trained men and women could be easily recruited from among the younger and more energetic members of these professions. A high sense of social responsibility would be essential for appointment. The total cost of such a plan to be borne by municipal taxes and assisted by provincial grant. The Life Officers Association should be approached to offer their services (as they offered them in British Columbia) to work out the cost of such a scheme and place the whole on a firm actuarial basis. This is also necessary for the second plan.

19. *SECOND PLAN — COMPULSORY HEALTH INSURANCE.*

Select a municipality which presents a fairly homogeneous economic pattern of income-level groups, and where relief recipients are at an irreducible minimum. No exclusion must be made, but all wage-earners and these gainfully employed must be included, irrespective of income. Only in such a way can true mutualization of insurance be possible. The actuarial figures will determine the premiums to be paid.

20. *THIRD PLAN.*

Voluntary Hospitalization of Health Insurance in a selected urban municipality of from five to ten thousand people.

21. *FOURTH PLAN.*

Care of the unemployed on a fee-for-service basis covering the entire province based on Essex (Ontario) County Model, with consideration of province-wide plans to include the low-income groups.

22. The necessity of a province-wide plan is made evident by the Speech of the Honourable Norman Rogers, On the National Employment Commission (official report of the House of Commons Debates) March, 1936.

The relief situation in Quebec: —		% of Dominion Total
Employable	104,220	31.37%
Dependents	146,410	29.4%
Unemployable	23,510	48.71%
Farmers' Families	72,350	22.15%
TOTAL	346,490	12% of population

Percentage in relation to Dominion-wide relief (1,233,390)

$$\frac{346,490 \times 100}{1,233,390} = 28\% \text{ of Canada's unemployed.}$$

The % of unemployable on relief in Quebec is the highest in Canada and comprises 48.71% of the total unemployable in Canada. Such an appalling figure demands immediate investigation.

23. *CONCLUSION.*

That in view of the emergency of the situation and the necessity for planning for permanent poverty, a Congress of French, English doctors, dentists, nurses, social service workers, Public Health officials, representatives of the Trades and Labor Council, the Unemployed, The Federated Charities, The Relief Commission and the Church should be called, sponsored by the French and English medical, dental and nursing societies to formulate plans for action. Only through the demands made by such a United Professional Front will the politicians be made to realize the potential force which the 10,000 members of the allied professions in Quebec represent.

Unless we, as the combined profession, formulate and implement some plan or plans to give adequate medical service to the unemployed and the low-income groups, we may have to accept what may be forced on us. An additional plan should be prepared for consideration of Public Medicine on the same basis as Public Education, Fire Protection, the Army, and the Police Forces. Medicine must be controlled by medicine. Action should be immediate, united and decisive.

24. *DOCTOR, DENTIST, NURSE AND SOCIAL SERVICE WORKER!*

Join your local society, urge unification of French, English doctors, dentists, nurses and social service workers. Fight racial and professional isolation. We must unite in a common cause — health security for our people, and economic security for ourselves.

Appendix — Annexe D

Canada in Spain

*A Radio Dramatization of the Work of the
Canadian-Spanish Blood Transfusion Unit
During the Spanish Civil War*

by Graham Spry

The scene is the office of the Canadian-Spanish Blood Transfusion Unit in Madrid, early in 1937. The action comprises, first, a telephone conversation between Norman Bethune, who formed the Unit, and Ben Spence, of the Committee to Aid Spanish Democracy, in Toronto, and, second, a conversation in the office between Bethune and Hazen Sise, a young architect who worked with Bethune in Spain. The other voices represented are those of a radio announcer and a telephone operator. Dramatic personnel, therefore, number four only; to support them, sound effects are required of a telephone, gunfire, a window being opened and closed, and an automobile engine.

The sound of warfare must be realistic. The action takes place at a time when the nation of Spain was divided by bloody fighting, when even families were divided, brother fighting brother. To many outside Spain, the Spanish Civil War seemed far away, yet a few recognized the threat of fascism that arose when German and Italian forces entered the conflict to support General Franco. Among Canadians who recognized this threat were the 1200 men who served in the MacKenzie-Papineau Battalion of the International Brigades — and Norman Bethune and Hazen Sise, whose voices must convey the sense of urgency and conflict that underly the action.

Programme Announcer:	"Canada in Spain" — this is the first of a series of Sunday broadcasts presented as dramatized discussions in the headquarters of the Canadian Blood Transfusion Unit, serving the wounded of the loyalist forces on the battlefronts of democracy in Spain. This Blood Transfusion Unit is an independent and distinctively Canadian service given to the Spanish people through the Committee to Aid Spanish Democracy, 414 Manning Chambers, Toronto.
(Theme music.)	
Announcer:	The scene is laid in the office of the Canadian-Spanish Blood Transfusion Unit, Madrid. We present "Canada in Spain".
(Telephone rings.)	
Long Distance Operator:	Madrid, Spain is calling Toronto, Canada, Ben H. Spence is wanted by Dr. Norman Bethune.
(Long distance effects.)	
Man:	Just a moment. Here is Mr. Spence.
(Click of telephone, in changeover.)	
Spence:	Hello, Spence speaking.
Long Distance Operator:	Hold the line. We will connect you with Madrid.
(Long distance effects; sounds of Spanish voices.)	
Bethune:	Hello, Ben? Norman Bethune speaking from the headquarters of the Canadian Institute of Blood Transfusion in Madrid. How are you? How are things going?
Spence:	Hello. Glad to hear from you. Our campaign here is going well. We have passed the $25,000 mark. Money is coming in from all parts of Canada. Did you get the last $3,000 in Paris?
Bethune:	Yes, the money came o.k. We will need lots more. It takes the $500 a

	week you are sending us regularly to maintain our service. Could you raise a few thousand more for food?

(Dull roar of gunfire in distance.)

Spence:	What's that you say about food?
Bethune:	We need condensed milk. Milk for the wounded and children.
Spence:	Hello. Repeat — I did not get what you said.
Bethune:	Milk — just a minute till I close the windows.

(Sound of windows being closed; end of gunfire.)

Bethune:	There we are . . .
Spence:	What was the noise?
Bethune:	Gunfire. You know there's a war on here — a real war.
Spence:	Sounds like it. What were you saying before history interrupted us?
Bethune:	We need milk, condensed milk. I could use a carload of condensed milk right now. We need the milk for both our own patients and for the blood donors, and for the children. There is a great shortage of milk and food of that kind.
Spence:	We can arrange that . . . How many blood donors have you now?
Bethune:	We broadcast an appeal for Spaniards to give blood. This broadcast goes out daily. We have 1200 donors. They report to the headquarters here, are classified, the blood is drawn, treated and kept in refrigerators. We operate a fleet of cars with refrigerators and rush the blood to a hundred hospitals on the various battlefronts.
Spence:	All fronts?
Bethune:	All fronts, but in the Basque country. The Spanish Government asked the Canadian unit to set up a similar unit for blood donors in Barcelona as well as Madrid. I consulted with Spanish doctors and they have adopted the entirely new technique worked out here by the Canadian unit. All units are co-ordinated. The Canadian service serves all fronts and all hospitals.
Spence:	We will back you up to the limit. We have met every request you have made yet 100%. Milk will be shipped immediately.
Bethune:	Good. We know the Canadian people won't let us down. The name of Canada — the name of Canadian medicine, Canadian humanitarian aid — is known throughout Spain. Our cars are seen everywhere. Our broadcasts are heard daily. It would be letting down the name of Canada if the Committee to Aid Spanish Democracy did not stay with it for "the duration".
Spence:	We have an efficient organization here. There are committees at work in practically every Canadian city. Money is coming from all types and classes of Canadians, hundreds of them, particularly from the working people and the farmers. It is flowing in every day, and we cable it straight to you.

(Roar of car in distance.)

Bethune:	Here comes one of our cars now. I guess it is Hazen Sise; just a moment while I look out the window.

(Sound of his moving to window; roar of car louder as window opened.)

Bethune:	It is Sise. You had better hang up. But just a word. Did I tell you about our new headquarters? It is a 40-room palace in the centre of Madrid. We have six cars, and a staff of 25 doctors, nurses, biologists and assistants. Scotland, England, Sweden, United States, France and other countries, have medical units here. Canada has her own medical unit. This Canadian Blood Transfusion Institute is making a name for Canada. You may tell the people of Canada that the democracy of Spain will never be conquered. Madrid will never fall. The Fascists are on the run on every front. The people of Spain are winning. They have command of the land,

	the sea and the air, and wherever the battle of democracy is being fought medical unit is there serving them. We have saved hundreds of lives. Every Canadian dollar means that the lives of Spanish heroes are saved. Salud! Salud!
Spence:	Goodbye. We will back you up. You are doing a great job for Spain and for Canada. My best to all the Canadian lads there. Say hello to Hazen Sise. Goodbye and good luck!

(Sound of door opening and closing.)

Bethune:	Hello, Hazen. Where are you from?
Sise:	I am just in from the field hospital in front of Guadalajara. It is being moved a few miles further northeast. The Fascist forces are still retreating.
Bethune:	What of the wounded?
Sise:	The field hospital will need an immediate supply of blood; I left 50 bottles, but more will be needed.
Bethune:	It will go at once. Let me see, car five is on the Cordoba front. Car four is on its way back to Valencia. Car six is touring the ten hospitals in northwest Madrid. Car two is being repaired — the radiator had to be replaced after that machine gun ripped into us on the Valencia road. Car three could go. Fernandez will take it.

(Roar of guns.)

Sise:	Hello! air raid.

(Sound of opening window, roar of guns louder.)

Bethune:	Can you see anything?

(Roar of guns continues.)

Sise:	Not yet. They're over southeast by the sound.

(Monotonous roar of engine against gunfire.)

Bethune:	German, by the sound of the engines.
Sise:	They are flying over the working class quarter. Fascits terror tactics.
Bethune:	You can't frighten madrilenos. Yesterday, I saw women and children in Gran Via picking up splintered wood from a building that had been hit by shellfire a few seconds before. And the shelling was still going on!

(Battle of machine gun — not too close.)

Bethune:	There goes the machine gun on the square. The Fascists must be flying low.
Sise:	It is not that gun. Aeroplanes. The government machines are going into combat. Hospital 24 will be calling. The bombs seemed to have been dropped somewhere in their area.
Bethune:	More women and children. Check the emergency car.

(Sound of telephone.)

Sise:	Hello, Miss Allen. Check the emergency car ... It's ready? Twenty-four is calling ... Yes (while listening). Right. (Hangs up.)
Bethune:	What's the word?
Sise:	May says Hospital 24 just called. Wants blood. Emergency car is leaving.

(Roar of car departing.)

Sise:	Seven bombs were dropped before the Junkers were driven away. One of them was shot down and fell in *Parca del Retiro*. A German machine. May says the hospital does not know the total casualties, several killed at least, all women and children.
Bethune:	Well, I must get back to work. Just called Canada before you came in. The Committee to Aid Spanish Democracy says the total amount of

	money raised for our medical unit has passed $25,000. I asked for condensed milk for our blood donors and wounded women and children — 48,000 cans — 16 oz. cans — all on the way. Money is coming in from all over Canada.
Sise:	That's fine. Well, I must get some rest. I am on another driving shift in four hours. So long.
Bethune:	The gang sent greetings to you. Sleep well.

(Sound of Sise leaving.)
(Buzz of phone.)

Bethune:	Hello? Hello? Yes, nurse. Tell Professeur Haldane that I am coming up to the laboratory. Ask the orderly to prepare the blood donors. I want to make several transfusions. Get Sorensen to write a strong appeal for more donors over tomorrow's broadcast. These new offensives will make additional demands for blood. I will be right up. Don't let Professor Haldane leave until I have a word with him.

(Sound of distant guns.)

That sounds like University City.
Another raid, I suppose.

(Sound of a door slowly closing; outside noises gradually diminish.)
(Few seconds' silence.)

Programme Announcer:	You have just been listening to a dramatized long-distance telephone conversation between the Committee to Aid Spanish Democracy in Toronto and the Canadian-Spanish Blood Transfusion Unit in Madrid, Spain. This distinctively Canadian medical unit has served the Spanish people since last autumn. It has been maintained and financed by money collected from the people of Canada. It takes at least $500 a week to finance the unit. Money for this humanitarian service is urgently needed. Money is also needed to ship Canadian condensed milk for those who give their blood to the Canadian Transfusion service in Madrid, for the wounded, for the children of the beleaguered city.
Programme Announcer:	Contributions, large or small, may be sent to the Committee to Aid Spanish Democracy, 414 Manning Chambers, corner Bay and Queen, Toronto. This is the organization that finances the medical unit in Spain. We repeat the address, 414 Manning Chambers, corner Bay and Queen, Toronto, where you may obtain more information and especially where we will welcome your donations.

(In background, music of "No Pasaran", low and soft.)

Biographies

Ted Allan
Playwright, co-author of *The Scalpel, The Sword: The Story of Doctor Norman Bethune;* author of *Lies My Father Told Me* and *Willie the Squowse;* foreign correspondent in the Spanish Civil War and Bethune's friend and colleague.

Richard Allen
Department of History, McMaster University; author of *The Social Passion: Religion and Social Reform in Canada, 1914-1928.*

J. Terry Copp
Department of History, Sir Wilfrid Laurier University, author of *The Anatomy of Poverty: The Condition of the Working Class in Montreal, 1897-1929.*

Dr. Valentin de la Loma
Deputy Director, Biological and Serum Therapy Institute, Madrid; Bethune's closest medical colleague in the Spanish-Canadian blood transfusion unit in 1936-7.
(Deceased, in Spain, November 16, 1979)

Dr. Pierre Delva
President of the Bethune Foundation; Professor of Social and Preventive Medicine and Assistant Dean, Université de Montréal.

Suzanne Dubreuil
Community worker, Centre éducatif René Goupil, St.-Michel, Montreal.

Claire Dutrisac
Journalist, *La Presse.*

Robert Garry
Lecturer on civilizations of the Far East, Université de Montréal.

Ted Allan
Dramaturge, co-auteur du *Docteur Norman Bethune;* auteur de *Lies My Father Told Me* et de *Willie the Squowse;* correspondant étranger pendant la guerre civile d'Espagne et ami et collègue de Bethune.

Richard Allen
Département d'histoire, Université McMaster; auteur de *The Social Passion: Religion and Social Reform in Canada, 1914-1928.*

J. Terry Copp
Département d'histoire, Université Sir Wilfrid Laurier; auteur de *Classe ouvrière et pauvreté.*

Dr. Valentin de la Loma
Sous-directeur, Institut de thérapeutique biologique et sérique, Madrid; collègue intime de Bethune au service canadien-espagnol de transfusion sanguine en 1936-37.
(Décédé en Espagne, le 16 novembre, 1979)

Dr. Pierre Delva
Président de la Fondation Bethune; Département de médecine sociale et préventive, Doyen adjoint, Université de Montréal; directeur du service des soins familiaux de l'hôpital du Sacré-Coeur.

Suzanne Dubreuil
Travailleuse communautaire, Centre éducatif René Goupil, St-Michel, Montréal.

Claire Dutrisac
Journaliste à *La Presse.*

Robert Garry
Chargé de cours sur les civilisations de l'Extrême-Orient, Université de Montréal.

Dr. William C. Gibson
The Bethune Foundation; Chairman, Universities Council of British Columbia; formerly Professor of History of Science and Medicine, University of British Columbia.

Charles Hill
Curator of Canadian Art, National Gallery of Canada, and organizer of the exhibition *Canadian Painting in the Thirties*.

Leo Kennedy
Poet, an editor of *New Frontier* and friend of Bethune, author of *The Shrouding*.

Dr. Marc Lavallée
Director, Local Community Services Centre, Pointe-aux-Trembles; former Vice-Dean, Faculty of Medicine, Université de Sherbrooke.

Dr. Denis Lazure
Minister of Social Affairs, Government of Quebec.

Andrée Lévesque
Department of History, University of Ottawa.

Paul T.K. Lin
Director, Centre for East Asian Studies, McGill University.

Lü Wanru
Representative of the Chinese People's Association for Friendship with Foreign Countries.

Ma Haide (George Hatem)
Consultant, Ministry of Health, People's Republic of China. An associate of Bethune, and a leader in the battle against epidemic disease.

Katherine McCuaig
MA thesis, McGill University, "*The campaign against tuberculosis in Canada, 1900-1950*".

Dr. William C. Gibson
Fondation Bethune; président du Conseil des universités de la Colombie-Britannique; ancien professeur d'histoire des sciences et de la médecine, Université de Colombie-Britannique.

Charles Hill
Conservateur adjoint de l'art canadien, Galerie nationale du Canada, et organisateur de l'exposition *Peinture canadienne des années trente*.

Leo Kennedy
Poète, rédacteur du *New Frontier* et ami de Bethune, auteur de *The Shrouding*.

Dr Marc Lavallée
Directeur, Centre local des services communautaires, Pointe-aux-Trembles; ancien vice-doyen, faculté de médecine, Université de Sherbrooke.

Dr Denis Lazure
Ministre des Affaires sociales, Gouvernement du Québec.

Andrée Lévesque
Département d'histoire, Université d'Ottawa.

Paul T.K. Lin
Directeur, centre des études extrêmes-orientales, Université McGill.

Lü Wanru
Représentante de l'Association du peuple chinois pour l'amitié avec l'étranger

Ma Haide (George Hatem)
Collaborateur de Bethune et l'un des principaux combattants contre les épidémies en République Populaire de le Chine.

Katherine McCuaig
Mémoire de maîtrise, Université McGill, "*The Campaign against tuberculosis in Canada, 1900-1950*".

Dr. Maurice McGregor
Senior physician, Royal Victoria Hospital; Professor of Medicine, McGill University; former Bethune Exchange Professor in Peking.

Dr. J. Wendell MacLeod
The Bethune Foundation; junior colleague of Bethune at the Royal Victoria Hospital and member of the Bethune health group; former Dean, College of Medicine, University of Saskatchewan; co-author of *Bethune: The Montreal Years*.

Louis Muhlstock
Montreal artist, honorary LLD., Concordia University and, to date "owner of the largest extant collection of original Muhlstocks"

Madeleine Parent
A founder of the Confederation of Canadian Unions, and textile workers' organizer since 1942.

Libbie Park
Member of the Bethune health group; co-author of *Bethune: The Montreal Years* and *Anatomy of Big Business*.

Jack Pearpoint
President, Frontier College, Toronto.

Marc Renaud
Department of Sociology, Université de Montréal.

Dr. H. Rocke Robertson
Former Professor of Surgery and former Principal and Vice Chancellor, McGill University; Member of the Board of Curators, Osler Library; Honorary Librarian and Archivist, Royal College of Physicians and Surgeons of Canada.

Marjorie Zavitz Robinson
Former staff member of Frontier College, co-author of a forthcoming history of the College, with George Cook.

Dr Maurice McGregor
Médecin à l'hôpital Royal Victoria; professeur de médecine, Université McGill; autrefois professeur dans le cadre du programme d'échanges Bethune à Pékin.

Dr J. Wendell MacLeod
Fondation Bethune; jeune collègue de Bethune à l'hôpital Royal Victoria et membre du groupe d'étude de Bethune; ancien doyen, collège de médecine, Université de Saskatchewan; co-auteur de *Bethune: The Montreal Years*.

Louis Muhlstock
Artiste montréalais, LLD. honoris causa, Université Concordia, et jusqu'à aujourd'hui "propriétaire de la plus importante collection d'originaux Muhlstock!"

Madeleine Parent
Un des fondateurs de la Confédération des syndicats canadiens; permanente syndicale auprès des travailleurs du textile depuis 1942.

Libbie Park
Membre du groupe d'étude de Bethune; co-auteur de *Bethune: The Montreal Years* et de *Anatomy of Big Business*.

Jack Pearpoint
Président, Frontier College, Toronto.

Marc Renaud
Département de sociologie, Université de Montréal.

Dr. H. Rocke Robertson
Ancien professeur de chirurgie et ancien principal et vice-chancelier de l'Université McGill; membre du comité des conservateurs de la bibliothèque Osler; archiviste et bibliothécaire honoraire, Collège royal des médecins et chirurgiens du Canada.

Marjorie Zavitz Robinson
Ancien membre du personnel de Frontier College, co-auteur d'une histoire du Collège qui paraîtra prochainement.

Dr. Robert Robson
Past-president, Canada-China Society Montreal; Montreal General Hospital; co-founder of a Bethune health group at McGill in the 70s; associated for a decade with the Pointe St-Charles Community Clinic.

Dr. Charles G. Roland
Hannah Professor of the History of Medicine, McMaster University.

Hilary Russell
Historian, Parks Canada; researcher on the Bethune Memorial House in Gravenhurst.

Ross Russell
Chairman of The Veterans of the International Brigade, Mackenzie-Papineau Batallion of Canada, and group leader of the veterans who recently revisited their battlefields in Spain.

Dr. Augustin Roy
The Bethune Foundation; President, Corporation Professionnelle des Médecins du Québec.

Stanley B. Ryerson
Professor of History, Université du Québec à Montréal, co-author of *Bethune: The Montreal Years;* author of *The Founding of Canada* and other books on Canadian history.

Marian Scott
Montreal artist; former colleague of Bethune in children's art classes.

Dr. Jessie Boyd Scriver
First woman intern at the Royal Victoria Hospital, later head of Paediatrics; author of *The Montreal Children's Hospital.*

Dr. David A.E. Shephard
Former scientific editor of the *Canadian Medical Association Journal;* clinical assistant professor, department of anaesthesia, University of Saskatchewan.

Dr. Robert Robson
Président sortant, société Canada-Chine, Montréal; Hôpital Général de Montréal; co-fondateur d'un groupe Bethune dans les années 70 à McGill; associé pendant une décennie à la clinique Communautaire de Pointe-St-Charles.

Dr Charles G. Roland
Titulaire de la chaire Hannah d'histoire de la médecine, Université McMaster.

Hilary Russell
Historienne, Parcs Canada; recherchiste sur La Maison Bethune à Gravenhurst.

Ross Russell
Président des anciens combattants de la Brigade internationale, bataillon canadien Mackenzie-Papineau et chef du groupe d'anciens combattants qui sont récemment retournés en Espagne voir leurs champs de bataille.

Dr Augustin Roy
Fondation Bethune; président, Corporation professionnelle des médecins du Québec.

Stanley B. Ryerson
Professeur d'histoire, Université du Québec à Montréal; co-auteur de *Bethune: The Montreal Years* auteur de *The Founding of Canada* d'autres ouvrages sur l'histoire canadienne.

Marian Scott
Artiste montréalaise; ancienne collègue de Bethune dans le cadre des classes d'art pour enfants.

Dr Jessie Boyd Scriver
Première femme interne à l'hôpital Royal Victoria; ultérieurement directrice des soins pédiatriques; auteur de *The Montreal Children's Hospital.*

Dr David A.E. Shephard
Ancien rédacteur scientifique du *Journal de l'association médicale canadienne;* professeur adjoint clinique, Département d'anesthésie, Université de Saskatchewan.

Hazen Sise

Well known Montreal and Ottawa architect, erudite in the history and literature of the 30s and subsequent decades, was a member of Bethune's blood transfusion team in Spain. As founder and president of the Bethune Memorial Committee (later The Bethune Foundation) he led its delegation on a China tour in September 1973 as guests of the Friendship Association in Peking. He died suddenly in mid-February, 1974.

Graham Spry

Former Chairman of the Ontario C.C.F. and editor of *The New Commonwealth* whose appeal for medical aid to Spain was answered by Bethune.

Lee Thompson

Department of English and Canadian Studies, University of Vermont; specialist in the poetry of the depression.

Mary Rosamond Weil

Past-president, The Bethune Foundation; consultant in Health Public Relations; former Director of Public Relations, Royal Victoria Hospital.

Dr. Paul G. Weil

The Bethune Foundation; medical consultant, Ste Anne de Bellevue Hospital; former Director of the Transfusion Service, Royal Victoria Hospital.
(Deceased — October 13, 1980)

Dr. G.J. Wherrett

Former Executive Secretary of the Canadian Anti-tuberculosis Association; author of *The Miracle of the Empty Beds: A History of Tuberculosis in Canada*.
(Deceased — February 27, 1981)

Hazen Sise

Architecte bien connu de Montréal et d'Ottawa, érudit en histoire et en littérature, était membre de l'équipe de transfusion sanguine de Bethune en Espagne. En tant que fondateur et président du Comité commémoratif de Bethune (plus tard la Fondation Bethune), en septembre 1973 il conduisit en Chine un groupe d'invités de l'Association d'amitié à Pékin. Il mourut subitement à la mi-février 1974.

Graham Spry

Ancien directeur du C.C.F. ontarien et rédacteur *The New Commonwealth* à l'appel duquel Bethune répondit en organisant une aide médicale en Espagne.

Lee Thompson

Département d'anglais et d'études canadiennes, University of Vermont; spécialiste de la poésie pendant la Crise.

Mary Rosamond Weil

Présidente sortante de la Fondation Bethune; consultante, relations publiques dans le domaine de la santé, ancienne directrice des relations publiques, hôpital Royal Victoria.

Dr Paul G. Weil

La Fondation Bethune; consultant à l'hôpital de Ste-Anne-de-Bellevue; anciennement directeur de service de transfusion de l'hôpital Royal Victoria.
(Décédé le 13 octobre, 1980)

Dr G.J. Wherrett

Ancien secrétaire administratif de la Ligue canadienne contre la tuberculose, auteur de *The Miracle of the Empty Beds: A History of Tuberculosis*.
(Décédé le 27 février, 1981)

Conference Committee

Dr. Pierre Delva, Chairman
Dr. J. Wendell MacLeod and Hilary Russell, co-directors

Dr. Margaret Becklake
Joan Delva
Dr. K.A.C. Elliott
Marilyn Fransiszyn
Dr. Francis McNaughton
Dr. Robert Robson
Dr. Gérard Rolland
Jolanta Sise
Mary Rosamond Weil
Dr. Paul Weil

The collaboration of Dean S.O. Freedman of the Faculty of Medicine, McGill University, and the cooperation of Dr. P. Teigen of the Osler Library, and the Conferences and Special Events Office of McGill University is gratefully acknowledged.

Support for the conference was provided by the following:

Bethune Foundation
Canadian International Development Agency, Non-governmental Organizations Program
City of Montreal — Mayor's Reception
Health and Welfare Canada
Ministry of Social Affairs, Quebec — Banquet l'Hôpital Sacré-Coeur
National Film Archives, Public Archives of Canada
Secretary of State Canada
Social Sciences and Humanities Research Council of Canada

Aluminium Company of Canada
The Birks Family Foundation
CP Air
CP Ltd.
Canada Steamship Lines
Ciba-Geigy Ltd.
De Havilland Aircraft of Canada, Ltd.
Eldee Foundation
Extendicare Ltd.

Comité organisateur de la conférence

Pierre Delva, président
J. Wendell MacLeod et Hilary Russell, co-directeurs

Margaret Becklake
Joan Delva
K.A.C. Elliott
Marilyn Fransiszyn
Francis McNaughton
Robert Robson
Gérard Rolland
Jolanta Sise
Mary Rosamond Weil
Paul Weil

Le comité d'organisation remercie le doyen S.O. Freedman de la Faculté de médecine, le service des conférences et le docteur P. Teigen de la bibliothèque Osler, tous trois de l'université McGill, de leur aide indispensable.

Les organisations, entreprises et personnes suivantes ont contribué au financement de la conférence:

La Fondation Bethune
Agence canadienne de développement international, organisation non gouvernementale
Ville de Montréal
Santé et Bien-être social Canada
Ministère des Affaires sociales du Québec
Les archives nationales du film, Archives publiques du Canada
Le secrétariat d'État
Conseil de recherches en sciences sociales et humaines du Canada

La compagnie d'aluminium du Canada
The Birks Family Foundation
C.P. Air
C.P. Ltée.
Canada Steamship Lines
CIBA-Geigy Canada Ltée.
De Havilland Aircraft of Canada, Ltd.
Eldee Foundation
Extendicare Ltd.

Mrs. H. Barnwell Brown in memory of her brother, Dr. John Barnwell David Burt J.C. Flanagan A.L. Hepworth Arnold Issenman	Mme H. Barnwell Brown, en souvenir de son frère, le docteur John Barnwell David Burt J.C. Flanagan A.L. Hepworth Arnold Issenman
Merck Sharp & Dohme Ltd. Ortho Pharmaceuticals Ltd. Pfizer Canada Inc. A.H. Robins Ltd. Sandoz Ltd. Schering Corp. Ltd. Smith Kline & French Ltd. Star Ken. Investments Travel Unlimited	Merck Sharp & Dohme Ltd. Ortho Pharmaceuticals Ltd. Pfizer Canada Inc. A.H. Robbins Ltd. Sandoz Ltée. Schering Canada Ltée. Smith Kline & French Ltd. Star Ken. Investments Travel Unlimited
Walter Koerner Maurice McGregor Dr. and Mrs. Max Miller Helen Mussallem Libbie Park Marian Scott	Walter Koerner Maurice McGregor Dr. et Mme Max Miller Helen Mussallem Libbie Park Marian Scott
And other friends of Bethune	ainsi que les nombreux amis de Bethune